I0592379

Jean Froissart

The Boy's Froissart

Being Sir John Froissart's Chronicles of adventure, battle, and custom in England,

France, Spain, etc.

Jean Froissart

The Boy's Froissart
Being Sir John Froissart's Chronicles of adventure, battle, and custom in England, France, Spain, etc.

ISBN/EAN: 9783337239718

Printed in Europe, USA, Canada, Australia, Japan

Cover: Foto ©ninafisch / pixelio.de

More available books at **www.hansebooks.com**

THE

BOY'S FROISSART

BEING

SIR JOHN FROISSART'S CHRONICLES

OF

*Adventure Battle and Custom in
England France Spain etc.*

EDITED FOR BOYS WITH AN INTRODUCTION

BY

SIDNEY LANIER

Illustrated by Alfred Kappes

NEW-YORK
CHARLES SCRIBNER'S SONS
743 & 745 BROADWAY
1879

COPYRIGHT, 1879,

By CHARLES SCRIBNER'S SONS

INTRODUCTION.

PERHAPS no boy will deny that to find the world still
reading a book which was written five hundred years
a ro is a very wonderful business. For the world grows, —
f ster than a boy; and when you remember how it is only
. out ten years since you were reading Jack the Giant-
iler, and how you are *infinitely* beyond all that *now*, —you
.ow, —you readily see that it must be a very manful man
.deed who can make a book so strong and so all-time like
. to go on giving delight through the ages, spite of prodi-
.ous revolutions in customs, in governments, and in ideas.

Now, Froissart sets the boy's mind upon manhood and
the man's mind upon boyhood. In reading him the young
soul sifts out for itself the splendor, the hardihood, the daring, the valor, the generosity, the boundless conflict and
unhindered action, which make up the boy's early ideal of
the man; while a more mature reader goes at once to his
simplicity, his gayety, his passion for deeds of arms, his
freedom from consciousness and from all internal debate—
in short, his boyishness. Thus Froissart helps youth forward and age backward.

With this enchanting quality, by which he not only
defies, but even reverses, the passage of time, our fine Sir
John has always had and will long have readers, both old
and young; and if it were not for some peculiarities of

his manner, growing mainly out of the habits of his time, there would be no need of any special edition of him for boys. But the latter sort find many halting-places and many skipping-places in him, by reason of his long dialogues, his tranquil way of telling *all* the particulars, and his gay habit of often relating events in chapter fifty which happened before those in chapter forty. The first two of these faults were virtues in Froissart's day, when the longer a story the better it helped to pass the time between battles; and the last one probably arose from the manner in which he collected many of his facts, — which was as follows.

You must know that in the year 1357 this lively young Hainaulter, being at that time but about twenty years old, was asked by the Count Robert de Namur to write a history of the wars of those times. The idea tickled his fancy, and he went straightway to work.

If any of *you* should set about writing a history, you would most likely go up into the library, take down a great many books, pamphlets, and manuscripts, and pore and peer and scribble, until after a while when your back was aching and your eyes burning you would look at your watch and say, "Bless me! it's two o'clock in the morning," and so to bed; and such would be your day's work until the history was finished. But not so with our young Froissart. Instead of painfully burrowing among dusty books, he saddled his horse, strapped on his portmanteau behind, and cantered off along the road through the bright French air, with his faithful greyhound following.*

---

* Froissart's own cunning little poem of *Le Débat dou Cheval et dou Levrier*, recently printed for the first time by M. Buchon, gives such a picture of himself: —

> "Froissars d'Escoce revenoit
> Sus un cheval qui gris estoit;
> Un blanc levrier menoit en lasse."

Presently he was pretty sure to overtake or be overtaken by some knight or esquire : whereupon Froissart
would salute him, politely inquire his name, and ply him
with artful questions as to the battles he had fought, the
lords he had served, the negotiations he had conducted or
assisted in, the events he had witnessed or heard of ; and
thus the two would converse by the way, the horses mean-
time embracing the opportunity to slacken pace, and the
greyhound taking his chance to nose about here and there
on each side the road. When the inn or friendly castle
would be reached where lodgment was to be had in the
evening, Froissart would jot down notes of all that he had
learned from fellow-travellers during the day. Sometimes
such a journey would terminate in a long visit at the castle
of a great man, — as when he went to see the Count of
Foix, referred to in the Third Book of these Chronicles ;
and then in the long evenings he would learn, either from
the actors themselves or from knights or attendants about
their persons, the deeds and events with which they had
been connected.

Although from Hainault, he was much in England. He
loved the society of the great, and was often in it. He
was at different times attached to the households of King
Edward III. of England, and of King John of France ;
and became an especial favorite of his countrywoman
Queen Philippa, wife to Edward III., who made him the
Clerk of her Chamber. He had various offices and pre-
ferments, but is most commonly associated with the
Church of Chimay in France, of which he was canon.
He knew how to please his powerful friends : when he
visited the Count of Foix, — who loved dogs, and had sixteen hundred of them about him, — he carried four grey-
hounds as a present to that nobleman ; he bore a beautiful

copy of his love-poem "Meliador" to Richard II. of England; he presented the earlier portions of his Chronicles
to Queen Philippa, who was fond of letters.

He was romantic and poetical. It would seem that he
began his travels early, in order to escape the torments of
an unfortunate love for a certain lady which had attacked
him when a mere boy, and which endured with more or
less strength for some time. He was engaged in writing
his Chronicles from the year 1357 certainly to the year
1400, for they include events up to the latter date. Without burdening my young readers' minds, there are three
names of great Englishmen which I cannot forbear begging them to associate with this period. These are, the
names of Geoffrey Chaucer, who wrote the "Canterbury
Tales" and many other works; of William Langland, or
Langley, who probably wrote the wonderful "Book concerning Piers the Plowman;" and of John Wyclif, who did
the greatest service both for our religion and our language
by giving forth the first complete translation of the Bible
into English. Three large and beautiful souls; so large
and beautiful, that one could scarcely frame a finer wish
for any boy than that he should make friends with them,
and live with them when he becomes a man.

Froissart did not confine himself to history: he wrote
many poems, — rondeaus, virelays, pastorals, romances.
He lived a bright, genial, active, fruitful, and happy life;
and died after the year 1400.

As you read of the fair knights and the foul knights, —
for Froissart tells of both, — it cannot but occur to you
that somehow it seems harder to be a good knight nowa-
days than it was then. This is because we have so many
more ways of fighting now than in King Edward the
Third's time. A good deal of what is really combat now-

adays is not *called* combat. Many struggles, instead of
taking the form of sword and armor, will present themselves to you after a few years in the following shapes :
the strict payment of debts ; the utmost delicacy of na-
tional honor ; the greatest openness of party discussion,
and the most respectful courtesy towards political opponents ; the purity of the ballot-box ; the sacred and liberal
guaranty of all rights to all citizens ; the holiness of marriage ; the lofty contempt for what is small, knowing,
and gossipy ; and the like. Nevertheless the same qualities which made a manful fighter then make one now.
To speak the very truth ; to perform a promise to the
uttermost ; to reverence all women ; to maintain right and
honesty ; to help the weak ; to treat high and low with
courtesy ; to be constant to one love ; to be fair to a bitter foe ; to despise luxury ; to preserve simplicity, modesty, and gentleness in heart and bearing : this was in
the oath of the young knight who took the stroke upon
him in the fourteenth century, and this is still the way to
win love and glory in the nineteenth.

You will find all these elements of knighthood which I
have just named particularly puzzling in many affairs connected with money. This was always so : indeed, I cannot help somewhat sadly reminding you that as you read
along in these Chronicles of Froissart's you will here and
there perceive how money is already creeping into the
beautiful institution of knighthood in the fourteenth century and corrupting it. After each battle related in this
book, Froissart is pretty apt to say something about the
great wealth acquired by this or that fighter through the
ransom paid him by or for such prisoners as he took. In
other words, war is becoming a trade ; and in succeeding
centuries of European history the young student will

quickly notice that the great organized armies were no whit less thieves and rascals than the rogues who composed the Free Companies about whom Froissart will presently speak. The fair ideal of the knight-errant, as he who goes forth in the world to help every one that may need him, and who despises wealth and personal ease whenever they interfere with this great object — an ideal which is presented to us in Sir Lancelot, and, less finely, in other knights of the Round Table — grows dim.

And here I could do no better service to the American boy of the present day than by calling his attention to a certain curious and interesting connection between these present Chronicles of Froissart and Sir Thomas Malory's History of King Arthur and the knights of the Round Table, which was written in the following century and which must some day come to be known more widely than now as one of the sweetest and strongest books in our language.

The connection I mean is this: that Froissart's Chronicle is, in a grave and important sense, a sort of continuation of Malory's novel. For Malory's book is, at bottom, a picture of knighthood in the twelfth and thirteenth centuries; while Froissart's is a picture of knighthood in the fourteenth century. It is true that Malory's King Arthur is a personage, if not fabulous, at least unhistorical, while Froissart's Edward III. is actual flesh and blood, and is almost in sight; it is true that Froissart gives us real events occurring in definite localities during the last three-quarters of the fourteenth century, while Malory drags Joseph of Arimathea alongside of Merlin the Magician, and sets Briton, Saxon, Roman, Frenchman, Scotchman, Irishman, Welshman, and Saracen face to face in scenes which often defy place and time: yet it is no less true that Froissart's work is a continuation of Malory's, since what Malory gives us is substantially a view of life in the twelfth and thirteenth centuries, which Froissart follows with a view of life in the fourteenth century. A boy who reflects that Sir Thomas Malory wrote a hundred years later than Froissart will be puzzled to know how he comes to give a picture of chivalry a hundred years earlier, until certain facts appear which show in what manner Sir Thomas Malory's book was made, and what were the habits of the writers whom he followed.

About the year 1147 all England was delighted with a narration which was published by Geoffrey of Monmouth, concerning the deeds of a glorious man whom Geoffrey declared to have been an old king of that country, and whose name he gave as Arthur. Geoffrey, who was a Welsh priest living in England at that time, declared that he had found this account of King Arthur in a Welsh book, and gave it as true history. Whether history or fable, — upon this modern opinion is divided, — his story of the great knight Arthur so charmed the people that the poets and prose-writers, not only of England, but of France, straightway took hold of it, turned it into verse, amplified it, added to it, retold it in long prose tales, and in various ways spread it abroad, until there came to be what is called a cycle — that is, a connected ring — of Arthurian romances. In this cycle all the prominent characters of the modern story made their appearance : besides King Arthur, the fascinated world read of Sir Lancelot du Lake, of Queen Guenever, of Sir Tristram, of Queen Isolde, of Merlin, of Sir Gawaine, of the Lady of the Lake, of Sir Galahad, and of the wonderful search for the Holy Cup called the "Saint Graal," which was said to have received the blood that flowed from the wounds of our Saviour when he hung on the cross.

I hope that every boy will hereafter become acquainted
with the names of many of these old writers who contrib-
uted to the collection of romances that make up the
Arthurian cycle; but for the present, without perplexing
young minds with a long list, I wish to impress four of
these names upon your memories. They are *Wace, Layamon, De Borron*, and *Walter Map*. I should wish particularly that my young readers would remember the name of
Layamon, because he wrote his account of King Arthur
in English, and is therefore to be reverenced as the sturdy
poet who made a great stand for our native tongue after
William the Conqueror had imposed his French dialect
upon us.

But now to come to Sir Thomas Malory. These stories
of King Arthur, and Sir Lancelot, and Sir Tristram, and
Merlin, written by Wace, and Layamon, and Map, and
others, were, as I said, carried about and read with great
delight through England and France during the thirteenth
and fourteenth centuries; and the important point to
remember here is that the writers who developed them
from the original stock furnished by Geoffrey of Monmouth, although professing to tell of things which happened in the early centuries of our era, really did nothing
more than present a picture of their own times — that is,
of the twelfth and thirteenth centuries — in which nothing
was ancient but the names of the figures. This was a
notable custom of all the middle-age artists, not only of
the artists in words — the poets and prose tale-tellers —
but even of the later artists who drew and painted actual
pictures. Just as an old picture-maker would represent
King Solomon in a costume of the ninth century; or as
the old writer of Arthurian romances speaks of the Bib-
lical Joshua as *Duke* Joshua, thus bringing the old Jew

before us with a title some thousands of years younger than his name : so these twelfth and thirteenth century writers merely took the characters of Geoffrey of Monmouth's story and clothed them as mediæval knights and ladies, while they re-arranged the events similarly into such relations as accorded with their own times. Now, in the fifteenth century, Sir Thomas Malory re-arranged this series of stories about King Arthur, Sir Lancelot, Sir Tristram, the Round Table, and the Holy Cup, which had been written in the twelfth and thirteenth centuries, and which were really pictures of life in those centuries, though grouped about legendary figures ; while Sir John Froissart wrote chronicles which present us pictures of life grouped about the historic characters of his own fourteenth century.

But though, as I said, the ideal of knighthood begins to be lowered in Froissart by the temptations of ransom-money, there are still many beautiful features of it which come out with perfect colors in these following chronicles. The kingliness of Edward III. ; the stern lessons of hardihood, of self-help, and of perseverance unto the end, which he teaches his son Edward in refusing to send him re-enforcements when he is so dreadfully bested before Crecy ; the beautiful courtesy and modesty with which this same young Edward attends upon King John of France at supper in his own tent on the night after he had taken the king prisoner and routed his army at Poictiers ; the pious reverence with which Sir Walter Manny seeks out the grave of his father ; the energy with which the stout abbot of Hennecourt hews, whacks, and pulls the blooded knights about ; the frequent expostulations of generous gentlemen against the harsh treatment of prisoners ; the prayer of the queen in favor of the citizens

of Calais, and King Edward's knightly concession to her
ladyhood; the splendor and liberality of the Count de
Foix; the unconquerable loyalty of Sir Robert Salle, who
prefers a brave death at the hands of Wat Tyler's rebels,
to the leadership of their army; the dash and gallantry of
the young Saracen Agadinquor Oliferne, who flies about
like a meteor before the besieging crusaders round about
the town of Africa: these, and many fine things of like
sort, will not fail to strike the most inexperienced eyes.

My main task in editing this book for you has been to
choose connected stories which would show you as many
of the historic figures in Froissart as possible; though
I have tried to preserve at the same time the charm which
lies in his very rambling manner. I have not altered his
language at all. Every word in this book is Froissart's;
except of course that he wrote in French, and his words
are here translated into English. A very noble translation
was made in the time of King Henry the Eighth, by Lord
Berners, whose name I hope you will remember. I should
have greatly preferred to give you his Froissart for the
present edition: it is beautiful English, and infinitely
stronger, brighter, and more picturesque, than the translation here used; but it would have been difficult for you to
read. Yet, in order that you might see what the English
of King Henry the Eighth's time looks like, I have given a
chapter of Lord Berners', on the battle of Crecy, without
alteration; and, believing that many of my young readers
who may be studying French might be curious to read a
little of that language in one of its earlier stages, I have
added the same chapter in French from the manuscripts
printed by Buchon. For similar reasons, at the chapter
describing the battle of Neville's Cross, I have added an
old English ballad upon the same fight, giving it unaltered

from Messrs. Hales and Furnivall's edition of Bishop Percy's Manuscript.

Again, when the Chronicle reaches King Richard II., I have embraced the opportunity to show you the kind of English which was spoken in Froissart's time, by adding to one of the chapters the robust "Ballad sent to King Richard" by Geoffrey Chaucer, — begging you to believe that our time cries out to every young American man, as Chaucer to his prince, to

> "Do law, love truth and worthiness,
> And wed thy folk again to steadfastness."

Finally, do not think that to read this book is to exhaust Froissart. Only about one-ninth of his Chronicle could be got into the space here assigned ; and you have the comfort of knowing that there is a great deal more.

To him, then ; and I envy every one of you !

"For herein," — as old William Caxton, the first English printer, says in his Prologue to Sir Thomas Malory's history of King Arthur, — "for herein may be seen chyvalryc, curtosye, humanyte, frendlynesse, hardynesse, love, frendshyp, cowardyse, murdre, hate, vertue, synne. Doo after the good, and leve the evil, and it shall bring you to good fame and renommee."

SIDNEY LANIER.

BALTIMORE, MD., 1879.

CONTENTS.

BOOK I.

CHAPTER I.

PAGE.

THE OCCASION OF THE WARS BETWEEN THE KINGS OF FRANCE
AND ENGLAND I

CHAPTER II.

HOW EARL THOMAS OF LANCASTER, AND TWENTY-TWO OF THE
GREATEST NOBLES IN ENGLAND, WERE BEHEADED . . . 2

CHAPTER III.

THE QUEEN OF ENGLAND GOES TO COMPLAIN OF SIR HUGH SPENCER
TO HER BROTHER, THE KING OF FRANCE 4

CHAPTER IV.

SIR HUGH SPENCER CAUSES THE QUEEN ISABELLA TO BE SENT OUT
OF FRANCE 5

CHAPTER V.

THE QUEEN ISABELLA LEAVES FRANCE, AND GOES TO GERMANY . 6

CHAPTER VI.

QUEEN ISABELLA ARRIVES IN ENGLAND WITH SIR JOHN DE HAI-
NAULT 10

CHAPTER VII.

THE QUEEN OF ENGLAND BESIEGES HER HUSBAND IN THE CITY OF
BRISTOL 11

CHAPTER VIII.

THE KING OF ENGLAND AND SIR HUGH SPENCER ARE TAKEN AT
SEA AS THEY ARE ENDEAVORING TO ESCAPE FROM THE CASTLE
OF BRISTOL 13

CHAPTER IX.

PAGE.

THE CORONATION OF KING EDWARD THE THIRD 16

CHAPTER X.

ROBERT BRUCE, KING OF SCOTLAND, DEFIES KING EDWARD . . 18

CHAPTER XI.

A DISSENSION BETWEEN THE ARCHERS OF ENGLAND AND THE
HAINAULTERS 20

CHAPTER XII.

HOW THE FIGHT BETWEEN THE ARCHERS AND THE HAINAULTERS
ENDED 22

CHAPTER XIII.

HOW THE KING AND HIS ARMY MARCHED TO DURHAM . . . 24

CHAPTER XIV.

OF THE MANNERS OF THE SCOTS, AND HOW THEY CARRY ON WAR 25

CHAPTER XV.

KING EDWARD'S FIRST EXPEDITION AGAINST THE SCOTS . . . 26

CHAPTER XVI.

KING EDWARD MARRIES THE LADY PHILIPPA OF HAINAULT . 40

CHAPTER XVII.

DOUGLAS IS KILLED FIGHTING FOR THE HEART OF KING ROBERT . 42

CHAPTER XVIII.

PHILIP OF VALOIS CROWNED KING OF FRANCE 46

CHAPTER XIX.

KING EDWARD IS ADVISED BY HIS COUNCIL TO MAKE WAR AGAINST
KING PHILIP OF FRANCE. HE EFFECTS GREAT ALLIANCES IN
GERMANY, AND IS MADE VICAR OF THE EMPIRE . . . 47

CHAPTER XX.

KING EDWARD AND HIS ALLIES SEND CHALLENGES TO THE KING
OF FRANCE 49

CHAPTER XXI.

PAGE.

KING EDWARD CREATES SIR HENRY OF FLANDERS A KNIGHT, AND AFTERWARDS MARCHES INTO PICARDY 50

CHAPTER XXII.

THE TWO KINGS RETIRE FROM VIRONFOSSE WITHOUT GIVING BATTLE 56

CHAPTER XXIII.

THE SEA-FIGHT BETWEEN THE KING OF ENGLAND AND THE FRENCH, BEFORE SLUYS 58

CHAPTER XXIV.

THE KING OF ENGLAND BESIEGES THE CITY OF TOURNAY WITH A POWERFUL ARMY 62

CHAPTER XXV.

THE SCOTS RECOVER GREAT PART OF THEIR COUNTRY DURING THE SIEGE OF TOURNAY 64

CHAPTER XXVI.

SIR WILLIAM DE BAILLEUL AND SIR VAUFLART DE LA CROIX MAKE AN EXCURSION TO PONT-À-TRESSIN 68

CHAPTER XXVII.

THE EARL OF HAINAULT ATTACKS THE FORTRESS OF MORTAGNE IN VARIOUS MANNERS 71

CHAPTER XXVIII.

THE EARL OF HAINAULT TAKES THE TOWN OF ST. AMAND DURING THE SIEGE OF TOURNAY 73

CHAPTER XXIX.

SIR CHARLES DE MONTMORENCY, AND MANY OTHERS OF THE FRENCH, CAPTURED AT PONT-À-TRESSIN 77

CHAPTER XXX.

THE SIEGE OF TOURNAY RAISED BY MEANS OF A TRUCE . . 80

CHAPTER XXXI.

KING EDWARD INSTITUTES THE ORDER OF ST. GEORGE, AT WINDSOR 82

CHAPTER XXXII.

PAGE.

THE KING OF ENGLAND SETS AT LIBERTY SIR HERVÉ DE LÉON . 83

CHAPTER XXXIII.

THE KING OF ENGLAND SENDS THE EARL OF DERBY TO MAKE
WAR IN GASCONY 85

CHAPTER XXXIV.

THE EARL OF DERBY CONQUERS BERGERAC 88

CHAPTER XXXV.

THE COUNT DE LISLE, LIEUTENANT FOR THE KING OF FRANCE, IN
GASCONY, LAYS SIEGE TO THE CASTLE OF AUBEROCHE . . 93

CHAPTER XXXVI.

THE EARL OF DERBY MAKES THE COUNT OF LISLE AND NINE MORE
COUNTS AND VISCOUNTS PRISONERS BEFORE AUBEROCHE . . 96

CHAPTER XXXVII.

THE EARL OF DERBY TAKES DIFFERENT TOWNS IN GASCONY, IN
HIS ROAD TOWARD LA RÉOLE 99

CHAPTER XXXVIII.

THE EARL OF DERBY LAYS SIEGE TO LA RÉOLE, WHICH SURRENDERS
TO HIM 103

CHAPTER XXXIX.

SIR WALTER MANNY FINDS IN LA RÉOLE THE SEPULCHRE OF HIS
FATHER 106

CHAPTER XL.

THE EARL OF DERBY CONQUERS THE CASTLE OF LA RÉOLE . . 108

CHAPTER XLI.

THE EARL OF DERBY TAKES CASTEL MORON, AND AFTERWARDS
VILLEFRANCHE, IN PERIGORD. 110

CHAPTER XLII.

JACOB VON ARTAVELD IS MURDERED AT GHENT 113

CHAPTER XLIII.

PAGE.

SIR JOHN OF HAINAULT QUITS THE ALLIANCE OF ENGLAND FOR THAT OF FRANCE 117

CHAPTER XLIV.

THE DUKE OF NORMANDY MARCHES WITH A GREAT ARMY INTO GASCONY, AGAINST THE EARL OF DERBY 117

CHAPTER XLV.

SIR JOHN NORWICH ESCAPES FROM ANGOULÊME, WHEN THAT TOWN SURRENDERS TO THE FRENCH 119

CHAPTER XLVI.

THE DUKE OF NORMANDY LAYS SIEGE TO AIGUILLON WITH A HUNDRED THOUSAND MEN 122

CHAPTER XLVII.

THE KING OF ENGLAND MARCHES INTO NORMANDY WITH HIS ARMY IN THREE BATTALIONS 129

CHAPTER XLVIII.

THE KING OF FRANCE COLLECTS A LARGE FORCE TO OPPOSE THE KING OF ENGLAND 131

CHAPTER XLIX.

THE BATTLE OF CAEN. — THE ENGLISH TAKE THE TOWN . . 134

CHAPTER L.

THE ENGLISH COMMIT GREAT DEPREDATIONS IN NORMANDY. — SIR GODFREY DE HARCOURT ENCOUNTERS THE MEN AT ARMS OF AMIENS, ON THEIR WAY TO PARIS, AND KING EDWARD MARCHES INTO PICARDY 137

CHAPTER LI.

THE KING OF FRANCE PURSUES THE KING OF ENGLAND, IN THE COUNTRY OF BEAUVAIS 141

CHAPTER LII.

THE BATTLE OF BLANCHETAQUE, BETWEEN THE KING OF ENGLAND AND SIR GODÉMAR DU FAY 144

CHAPTER LIII.

PAGE.

THE ORDER OF BATTLE OF THE ENGLISH AT CRECY, WHO WERE
DRAWN UP IN THREE BATTALIONS ON FOOT 148

CHAPTER LIV.

THE ORDER OF THE FRENCH ARMY AT CRECY 150

CHAPTER LV.

THE BATTLE OF CRECY, BETWEEN THE KINGS OF FRANCE AND OF
ENGLAND 152

CHAPTER LVI.

THE ENGLISH ON THE MORROW AGAIN DEFEAT THE FRENCH . . 166

CHAPTER LVII.

THE ENGLISH NUMBER THE DEAD SLAIN AT THE BATTLE OF CRECY 167

CHAPTER LVIII.

THE KING OF ENGLAND LAYS SIEGE TO CALAIS. — THE POORER
SORT OF THE INHABITANTS ARE SENT OUT OF IT . . . 169

CHAPTER LIX.

THE DUKE OF NORMANDY RAISES THE SIEGE OF AIGUILLON . . 170

CHAPTER LX.

SIR WALTER MANNY, BY MEANS OF A PASSPORT, RIDES THROUGH
FRANCE FROM AIGUILLON TO CALAIS 172

CHAPTER LXI.

THE KING OF SCOTLAND, DURING THE SIEGE OF CALAIS, INVADES
ENGLAND 174

CHAPTER LXII.

THE BATTLE OF NEVILLE'S CROSS 176

CHAPTER LXIII.

JOHN COPELAND TAKES THE KING OF SCOTLAND PRISONER, AND
RECEIVES GREAT ADVANTAGES FROM IT 183

CHAPTER LXIV.

PAGE.

THE YOUNG EARL OF FLANDERS IS BETROTHED, THROUGH THE CON-
STRAINT OF THE FLEMINGS, TO THE DAUGHTER OF THE KING
OF ENGLAND. — HE ESCAPES TO FRANCE IN A SUBTLE MANNER   186

CHAPTER LXV.

THE KING OF ENGLAND PREVENTS THE APPROACH OF THE FRENCH
ARMY TO RAISE THE SIEGE OF CALAIS, AND THE TOWN SUR-
RENDERS   190

CHAPTER LXVI.

THE KING OF ENGLAND RE-PEOPLES CALAIS   198

CHAPTER LXVII.

A ROBBER OF THE NAME OF BACON DOES MUCH MISCHIEF IN
LANGUEDOC, AND A PAGE OF THE NAME OF CROQUART TURNS
ROBBER   200

CHAPTER LXVIII.

SIR AYMERY DE PAVIE PLOTS WITH SIR GEOFFRY DE CHARGNY TO
SELL THE TOWN OF CALAIS   203

CHAPTER LXIX.

THE BATTLE OF CALAIS, BETWEEN THE KING OF ENGLAND, UNDER
THE BANNER OF SIR WALTER MANNY, WITH SIR GEOFFRY DE
CHARGNY AND THE FRENCH   204

CHAPTER LXX.

THE KING OF ENGLAND PRESENTS A CHAPLET OF PEARLS TO SIR
EUSTACE DE RIBEAUMONT   209

CHAPTER LXXI.

THE SEA-FIGHT OFF SLUYS. (FROM THE MANUSCRIPT IN THE
HAFOD LIBRARY)   210

CHAPTER LXXII.

THE DEATH OF KING PHILIP, AND CORONATION OF HIS SON KING
JOHN   217

CHAPTER LXXIII.

THE KING OF FRANCE ISSUES OUT A SUMMONS FOR ASSEMBLING AN
ARMY TO COMBAT THE PRINCE OF WALES, WHO WAS OVER-
RUNNING THE PROVINCE OF DERBY   218

CHAPTER LXXIV.

PAGE.

THE PRINCE OF WALES TAKES THE CASTLE OF ROMORANTIN. . 221

CHAPTER LXXV.

THE KING OF FRANCE LEADS A GREAT ARMY TO THE BATTLE OF
POITIERS 223

CHAPTER LXXVI.

THE DISPOSITION OF THE FRENCH BEFORE THE BATTLE OF POITIERS 226

CHAPTER LXXVII.

THE CARDINAL DE PERIGORD ENDEAVORS TO MAKE PEACE BETWEEN
THE KING OF FRANCE AND THE PRINCE OF WALES, PREVIOUS
TO THE BATTLE OF POITIERS 230

CHAPTER LXXVIII.

THE BATTLE OF POITIERS, BETWEEN THE PRINCE OF WALES AND
THE KING OF FRANCE 233

CHAPTER LXXIX.

TWO FRENCHMEN, RUNNING AWAY FROM THE BATTLE OF POITIERS,
ARE PURSUED BY TWO ENGLISHMEN, WHO ARE THEMSELVES
MADE PRISONERS 242

CHAPTER LXXX.

THE MANNER IN WHICH KING JOHN WAS TAKEN PRISONER AT
THE BATTLE OF POITIERS 244

CHAPTER LXXXI.

THE PRINCE OF WALES MAKES A HANDSOME PRESENT TO THE
LORD JAMES AUDLEY, AFTER THE BATTLE OF POITIERS . . 248

CHAPTER LXXXII.

THE PRINCE OF WALES ENTERTAINS THE KING OF FRANCE AT
SUPPER, THE EVENING AFTER THE BATTLE 250

CHAPTER LXXXIII.

THE PRINCE OF WALES RETURNS TO BORDEAUX, AFTER THE BATTLE
OF POITIERS 252

CHAPTER LXXXIV.

THE PRINCE OF WALES CONDUCTS THE KING OF FRANCE FROM
BORDEAUX TO ENGLAND 256

CHAPTER LXXXV.

PAGE.

THE ARCHPRIEST ASSEMBLES A COMPANY OF MEN AT ARMS. — HE
IS MUCH HONORED AT AVIGNON 258

CHAPTER LXXXVI.

A WELSHMAN, OF THE NAME OF RUFFIN, COMMANDS A TROOP OF
THE FREE COMPANIES 259

CHAPTER LXXXVII.

THE PROVOST OF THE MERCHANTS OF PARIS KILLS THREE KNIGHTS
IN THE APARTMENT OF THE PRINCE 260

CHAPTER LXXXVIII.

THE COMMENCEMENT OF THE INFAMOUS JACQUERIE OF BEAUVOISIS 262

CHAPTER LXXXIX.

THE BATTLE OF MEAUX IN BRIE, WHERE THE VILLAINS ARE DIS-
COMFITED BY THE EARL OF FOIX AND THE CAPTAL OF BUCH . 264

BOOK II.

CHAPTER I.

CORONATION OF KING CHARLES OF FRANCE 266

CHAPTER II.

A COMBAT BETWEEN AN ENGLISH AND A FRENCH SQUIRE . . 268

CHAPTER III.

THE POPULACE OF ENGLAND REBEL AGAINST THE NOBILITY . . 274

CHAPTER IV.

THE POPULACE OF ENGLAND COMMIT MANY CRUELTIES ON THOSE
IN OFFICIAL SITUATIONS. — THEY SEND A KNIGHT AS AMBAS-
SADOR TO THE KING 278

CHAPTER V.

THE NOBLES OF ENGLAND ARE IN GREAT DANGER OF BEING
DESTROYED. — THREE OF THE PRINCIPAL LEADERS OF THE
REBELS ARE PUNISHED, AND THE REST SENT BACK TO THEIR
HOMES 284

CHAPTER VI.

PAGE.

THE EARL OF FLANDERS AGAIN LAYS SIEGE TO GHENT   .   . 296

CHAPTER VII.

THE EARL OF FLANDERS SENDS A HARSH ANSWER TO THOSE WHO
WISHED TO MEDIATE A PEACE BETWEEN HIM AND GHENT   . 298

CHAPTER VIII.

THE CITIZENS OF GHENT, AFTER HAVING HEARD FROM PHILIP VON
ARTAVELD THE TERMS OF PEACE WHICH HE HAD BROUGHT
FROM THE CONFERENCES AT TOURNAY, MARCH OUT, TO THE
NUMBER OF FIVE THOUSAND, TO ATTACK THE EARL OF FLAN-
DERS IN BRUGES   300

CHAPTER IX.

THE ORDER OF BATTLE OF THE GHENT MEN. — THEY DEFEAT THE
EARL OF FLANDERS AND THE MEN OF BRUGES. — THE MEANS
BY WHICH THIS WAS BROUGHT ABOUT   303

CHAPTER X.

BRUGES IS TAKEN BY THE GHENT ARMY. — THE EARL OF FLANDERS
SAVES HIMSELF IN THE HOUSE OF A POOR WOMAN   .   . 309

CHAPTER XI.

THE EARL OF FLANDERS QUITS BRUGES, AND RETURNS TO LILLE,
WHITHER SOME OF HIS PEOPLE HAD ALREADY RETREATED   . 314

CHAPTER XII.

THE DUKE OF BURGUNDY INSTIGATES HIS NEPHEW KING CHARLES
TO MAKE WAR ON GHENT AND ITS ALLIES, AS WELL IN REVENGE
FOR THE BURNT VILLAGES AS TO ASSIST IN THE RECOVERY OF
FLANDERS FOR THE EARL, WHO WAS HIS VASSAL   .   .   . 315

CHAPTER XIII.

CHARLES THE SIXTH, KING OF FRANCE, FROM A DREAM, CHOOSES
A FLYING HART FOR HIS DEVICE   317

CHAPTER XIV.

KING CHARLES, AT THE INSTIGATION OF THE EARL OF FLANDERS,
WHO WAS PRESENT, ASSEMBLES HIS ARMY IN ARTOIS AGAINST
THE FLEMINGS. — PHILIP VON ARTAVELD GUARDS THE PASSES
INTO FLANDERS   319

CHAPTER XV.

SEVERAL KNIGHTS OF THE PARTY OF THE EARL OF FLANDERS, HAVING PASSED PONT-AMENIN, ARE DEFEATED AND KILLED ON THEIR ATTEMPT TO REPASS IT, THE FLEMINGS HAVING BROKEN DOWN THE BRIDGE. — PHILIP, HEARING THIS NEWS WHEN AT YPRES, MAKES USE OF IT TO ENCOURAGE THE INHABITANTS . . 321

CHAPTER XVI.

THE ORDER OF THE FRENCH ARMY IN ITS MARCH TO FLANDERS, AFTER THEY HAD HEARD THE BRIDGES WERE BROKEN AND GUARDED 325

CHAPTER XVII.

SOME FEW OF THE FRENCH, NOT BEING ABLE TO CROSS THE LIS AT THE BRIDGE OF COMMINES, FIND MEANS OF DOING SO BY BOATS AND OTHER CRAFT, UNKNOWN TO THE FLEMINGS . . 330

CHAPTER XVIII.

A SMALL BODY OF FRENCH, HAVING CROSSED THE LIS, DRAW UP IN BATTLE-ARRAY BEFORE THE FLEMINGS 335

CHAPTER XIX.

THE FRENCH WHO HAD CROSSED THE LIS DEFEAT, WITH GREAT SLAUGHTER, PETER DU BOIS AND THE FLEMINGS. — THE VANGUARD OF THE FRENCH ARMY REPAIR AND PASS OVER THE BRIDGE OF COMMINES 339

CHAPTER XX.

THE KING OF FRANCE CROSSES THE LIS AT THE BRIDGE OF COMMINES. — THE TOWN OF YPRES SURRENDERS TO HIM. — THE KING OF FRANCE LODGES IN YPRES. — PETER DU BOIS PREVENTS BRUGES FROM SURRENDERING TO THE KING. — PHILIP VON ARTAVELD ASSEMBLES HIS FORCES TO COMBAT THE FRENCH 344

CHAPTER XXI.

PHILIP VON ARTAVELD, HAVING ENTERTAINED HIS CAPTAINS AT SUPPER, GIVES THEM INSTRUCTIONS HOW THEY ARE TO ACT ON THE MORROW AT THE BATTLE OF ROSEBECQUE 347

CHAPTER XXII.

PAGE.

PHILIP VON ARTAVELD AND HIS FLEMINGS QUIT THE STRONG
POSITION THEY HAD TAKEN IN THE MORNING, TO ENCAMP ON
MONT D'OR, NEAR TO YPRES. — THE CONSTABLE AND ADMIRAL
OF FRANCE, WITH SIR WILLIAM OF POITIERS, SET OUT TO RE-
CONNOITRE THEIR SITUATION. 351

CHAPTER XXIII.

THE BATTLE OF ROSEBECQUE, BETWEEN THE FRENCH AND FLEM-
INGS. — PHILIP VON ARTAVELD IS SLAIN, AND HIS WHOLE ARMY
DEFEATED 354

CHAPTER XXIV.

THE NUMBER OF SLAIN AT THE BATTLE OF ROSEBECQUE, AND
PURSUIT AFTERWARDS. — PHILIP VON ARTAVELD IS HANGED
AFTER HE WAS DEAD 359

BOOK III.

CHAPTER I.

FROISSART SETS OUT ON JOURNEY TO BÉARN TO SEEK ADMISSION
TO THE HOUSEHOLD OF THE COUNT DE FOIX 361

CHAPTER II.

SIR JOHN FROISSART, IN HIS JOURNEY TOWARD BÉARN, IS ACCOM-
PANIED BY A KNIGHT ATTACHED TO THE COUNT DE FOIX, WHO
RELATES TO HIM HOW THE GARRISON OF LOURDE TOOK ORTINGAS
AND LE PALLIER, ON THE RENEWAL OF THE WAR IN GUYENNE,
AFTER THE RUPTURE OF THE PEACE OF BRETIGNY . . . 363

CHAPTER III.

FROISSART CONTINUES HIS JOURNEY. — IN TRAVELLING FROM TOUR-
NAY TO TARBES, THE KNIGHT RELATES TO HIM HOW THE GAR-
RISON OF LOURDE HAD A SHARP RENCOUNTER WITH THE
FRENCH FROM THE ADJACENT GARRISONS 367

CHAPTER IV.

SIR JOHN FROISSART ARRIVES AT ORTHÈS. — AN OLD SQUIRE RE-
LATES TO HIM THE CRUEL DEATH OF THE ONLY SON OF THE
COUNT DE FOIX 372

BOOK IV.

CHAPTER I.

PAGE.

THE DUKE OF BOURBON IS APPOINTED CHIEF OF AN EXPEDITION
TO AFRICA, THAT IS UNDERTAKEN BY SEVERAL KNIGHTS OF
FRANCE AND ENGLAND AT THE SOLICITATION OF THE GENOESE . 382

CHAPTER II.

THE CHRISTIAN LORDS WEIGH ANCHOR, AND LEAVE THE ISLAND OF
COMINO, IN ORDER TO LAY SIEGE TO THE TOWN OF AFRICA.—
THE MANNER IN WHICH THEY CONDUCT THEMSELVES .   . 387

CHAPTER III.

THE CONDUCT OF THE SARACENS DURING THE SIEGE OF THE TOWN
OF AFRICA.—THEY SEND TO DEMAND FROM THE FRENCH THE
CAUSE OF THEIR MAKING WAR AGAINST THEM 398

CHAPTER IV.

SOME MIRACLES ARE SHOWN TO THE SARACENS AS THEY ATTEMPT
TO ATTACK THE CAMP OF THE CHRISTIANS.—SEVERAL SKIR-
MISHES DURING THE SIEGE.—THE CLIMATE BECOMES UNWHOLE-
SOME, AND OTHER ACCIDENTS BEFALL THE BESIEGERS .   .   . 403

CHAPTER V.

A CHALLENGE IS SENT BY THE SARACENS TO OFFER COMBAT OF TEN
AGAINST TEN CHRISTIANS.—THE SARACENS FAIL IN THEIR EN-
GAGEMENT.—THE TOWN OF AFRICA IS STORMED, BUT UNSUC-
CESSFULLY, AND WITH THE LOSS OF MANY WORTHY MEN .   . 407

CHAPTER VI.

THE SIEGE OF AFRICA IS RAISED.—THE CAUSE OF IT.—THE
KNIGHTS AND SQUIRES RETURN TO THEIR OWN COUNTRIES   . 414

CHAPTER VII.

DEATH AND BURIAL OF KING RICHARD II.   421

LIST OF ILLUSTRATIONS.

PAGE.

' THE MONK SIR FROISSART IN THE BREACH OF THE MONAS-
TERY WALL . . . . *Frontispiece.*
LORD JAMES DOUGLAS THROWING THE HEART OF BRUCE
AMONG THE SARACENS 45
HOW SIR WILLIAM DOUGLAS AND HIS COMPANIONS CAP-
TURED THE CASTLE OF EDINBURGH BY STRATAGEM . 67
HOW THE FRENCH FLUNG A SERVANT OVER THE WALLS
INTO AUBEROCHE. 95
THE DEATH OF JACOB VON ARTAVELD 115
KING EDWARD III. PRAYING IN HIS TENT THE NIGHT BE-
FORE THE BATTLE OF CRECY 149
THE BLIND KING OF BOHEMIA DEAD ON THE BATTLE-FIELD
OF CRECY 155
HOW THE SIX CITIZENS OF CALAIS DELIVERED THEMSELVES
UP TO THE ENGLISH KING. 197
THE SURRENDER OF KING JOHN OF FRANCE. . . . 245
THE THREE KNIGHTS RECONNOITRING THE FLEMINGS IN THE
MIST 353
HOW THE BOURG D'ESPAIGN FED THE FIRE IN THE GREAT
FIRE-PLACE OF THE COUNT OF FOIX 371
HOW A WONDERFUL APPARITION TERRIFIED THE SARA-
CENS 403

THE CHRONICLES OF ENGLAND, FRANCE, SPAIN, &c.

BOOK I.*

CHAPTER I.

The Occasion of the Wars between the Kings of France and England.

HISTORY tells us that Philip, King of France, surnamed the Fair, had three sons, besides his beautiful daughter Isabella married to the King of England.
These three sons were very handsome. The eldest, Lewis,
King of Navarre during the lifetime of his father, was
called Lewis Hutin ; the second was named Philip the
Great, or the Long ; and the third, Charles. All these

---

* Froissart's Chronicles were written in four volumes, or books. The
parts I have taken from the first book cover a period of about thirty years,
counting from the coronation of the young King Edward the Third of England in the year 1326 to the battle of Poitiers in the year 1356. The times
covered by the other three books will be given as we come to them.

I have thought that the young readers of Froissart would care to know
exactly how it was that such a wonderful amount of fighting had to be done
during the fourteenth century, in England, France, and Flanders, as is described in this book ; and I have therefore devoted the first forty or fifty
pages to such extracts as would inform them upon the causes of these terrible and long-continued wars. — ED.

1

were kings of France after their father Philip by legiti-
mate succession, one after the other, without having any
male heirs: yet on the death of the last king, Charles,
the twelve peers and barons of France did not give the
kingdom to Isabella the sister, who was Queen of England, because they maintained, and do still insist, that
the kingdom of France is too noble to go to a woman,
consequently either to Isabella, or to her son the King of
England; for they hold that the son of a woman cannot
claim any right of succession where that woman has none
herself. For these reasons the twelve peers and barons of
France unanimously gave the kingdom of France to the
Lord Philip of Valois, nephew to King Philip; and so put
aside the Queen of England, who was sister to Charles,
the late King of France, and her son. Thus, as it seemed
to many people, the succession went out of the right line,
which has been the occasion of the most destructive wars
and devastations of countries in France and elsewhere, as
you will learn hereafter: the real object of this history
being to relate the grand enterprises and deeds of arms
achieved in these great wars; for, from the time of good
Charlemagne, King of France, never were such feats performed.

CHAPTER II.

How Earl Thomas of Lancaster, and Twenty-two of the greatest
Nobles in England, were beheaded.

KING EDWARD THE SECOND, father to the noble
King Edward the Third of whom our history speaks,
governed his kingdom very indifferently by the advice of

Sir Hugh Spencer, who had been brought up with him from his youth.

This Sir Hugh had managed matters so that his father and himself were the great masters of the realm, and were ambitious to surpass all the other great barons in England; for which reason, after the great defeat at Stirling, the barons and nobles, and even the council of the king, murmured much, particularly against Sir Hugh Spencer, to whom they imputed their defeat on account of his partiality for the King of Scotland. The barons had many meetings on this matter to consult what was to be done. The chief of them was Thomas, Earl of Lancaster, uncle to the king. Sir Hugh soon found it would be necessary for him to check them; and he was so well beloved by the king, and so continually in his presence, that he was sure of gaining belief, whatever he said. He soon took an opportunity of informing the king that these lords had entered into an alliance against him, and that, if he did not take proper measures, they would drive him out of the kingdom; and thus operated so powerfully on the king's mind, that his malicious intentions had their full effect. The king caused all these lords to be arrested on a certain day when they were met together, and without delay ordered the heads of twenty-two of the greatest barons to be struck off, without assigning any cause or reason. Thomas, Earl of Lancaster, suffered the first. The hatred against Sir Hugh Spencer was increased by this deed, particularly that of the queen, and of the Earl of Kent, brother to the king; which when he perceived, he fomented such a discord between the king and the queen, that the king would not see the queen, or come to any place where she was. This quarrel lasted some time: when the queen and the Earl of Kent were secretly informed, that, if they did not speedily quit the court, they would repent it; for Sir Hugh was endeavoring to stir up much mischief against them. Then the queen, having made preparations for passing secretly to France, set out as if to go on a pilgrimage to St. Thomas of Canterbury; whence she went to Winchelsea, and that night embarked on board a vessel prepared for her reception, accompanied by her young son Edward, the Earl of Kent, and Sir Roger Mortimer. Another vessel was loaded with luggage, &c.; and, having a fair wind, they landed the next morning at Boulogne.

CHAPTER III.

The Queen of England goes to complain of Sir Hugh Spencer to her Brother, the King of France.

WHEN the Queen Isabella landed at Boulogne with her son and her brother-in-law the Earl of Kent, the governor of the town and the abbot waited on her, and conducted her to the abbey, where she and her suite were joyfully received, and remained two days. On the third she continued her route toward Paris.

King Charles, her brother, being informed of her coming, sent some of the greatest lords at that time near his person to meet her; among whom were Sir Robert d'Artois, the Lord of Crucy, the Lord of Sully, and the Lord of Roy, and many others, who honorably received and conducted her to Paris to the king, her brother. When the king perceived his sister (whom he had not seen for a long time) entering his apartment, he rose to meet her, and, taking her in his arms, kissed her, and said, "You are welcome, my fair sister, with my fine nephew, your son:"

then, taking one in each hand, he led them in. The queen, who had no great joy in her heart except for being near her brother, would have knelt at his feet two or three times; but the king would not suffer it, and, holding her by the right hand, inquired very affectionately into her business and affairs. Her answers were prudent and wise; and she related to him all the injuries done to her by Sir Hugh Spencer, and asked of him advice and assistance.

When the noble King Charles had heard the lamentations of his sister, who with many tears had stated her distress, he said, "Fair sister, be appeased; for, by the faith I owe to God and to St. Denis, I will provide a remedy." The queen then kneeled down in spite of the king, and said to him, "My dear lord and brother, I pray God may second your intentions." The king then, taking her by the hand, conducted her to another apartment, which was richly furnished for her and her young son Edward: he then left her, and ordered that every thing should be provided, becoming the state of her and her son, from his treasury.

CHAPTER IV.

SIR HUGH SPENCER CAUSES THE QUEEN ISABELLA TO BE SENT OUT OF FRANCE.

THE queen [had] made all her preparations for her expedition very secretly, but not so much so as to prevent its coming to the knowledge of Sir Hugh Spencer, who thought that his most prudent plan would be to win over to his interest the King of France. For this purpose he sent over trusty and secret messengers laden with gold, silver, and rich jewels. These were distributed among the king and his ministers with such effect, that the king and his council were in a short time as cold toward the cause of Isabella as they had before been warm.

Sir Hugh also endeavored to get the queen into his and the king's power, and to this end made the king write an affectionate letter to the pope, entreating him to order the King of France to send back his wife. There were similar letters written at the same time to the cardinals. The nearest relations of the pope, and those most in his counsels, managed the pope in such a manner, that he wrote to the King of France to send back Isabella, Queen of England, to her husband, under pain of excommunication. These letters were carried to the King of France by the Bishop of Xaintes, whom the pope sent thither as his legate.

The king, on receipt of them, caused his sister to be acquainted with their contents (for he had held no conversation with her for a long time), and commanded her to leave the kingdom immediately, or he would make her leave it with shame.

CHAPTER V.

The Queen Isabella leaves France, and goes to Germany.

WHEN the queen heard this account, she knew not what to say, or what measures to adopt: for the barons had already withdrawn themselves by the king's command, and she had no resource or adviser left but in her dear cousin, Robert of Artois; and he could only advise and assist her in secret, as the king had forbidden it. He well knew that the queen had been driven from

England through malice and ill-will: but he durst not speak of it to the king; for he had heard the king say and swear that whoever should speak to him in her behalf should forfeit his land, and be banished the kingdom. He was also informed that the king was not averse to the seizure of the persons of the queen, her son Edward, the Earl of Kent, and Sir Roger Mortimer, and to their being delivered into the hands of the King of England and Sir Hugh Spencer. He therefore came in the middle of the night to inform the queen of the peril she was in. She was thunder-struck at the information; to which he added, "I recommend you to set out for the empire, where there are many noble lords who will greatly assist you, particularly William, Earl of Hainault, and his brother, who are both great lords, and wise and loyal men, and much dreaded by their enemies."

The queen ordered her baggage to be made ready as secretly as she could; and, having paid for every thing, she quitted Paris, accompanied by her son, the Earl of Kent, and all her company, and took the road to Hainault. After some days she came into the country of Cambray. When she found she was in the territories of the empire, she was more at her ease; passed through Cambresis; entered L'Ostrevant in Hainault, and lodged at the house of a poor knight called Eustace d'Ambreticourt, who received her with great pleasure, and entertained her in the best manner he could; insomuch that afterwards the Queen of England and her son invited the knight, his wife, and all his children, to England, and advanced their fortunes in different ways.

The arrival of the queen in Hainault was soon known in the house of the good Earl of Hainault, who was then at Valenciennes. Sir John, his brother, was also informed of the hour when she alighted at the house of the Lord of Ambreticourt. This Sir John, being at that time very young, and panting for glory like a knight-errant, mounted his horse, and, accompanied by a few persons, set out from Valenciennes for Ambreticourt, where he arrived in the evening, and paid the queen every respect and honor.

The queen was at that time very dejected, and made a very lamentable complaint to him of all her griefs; which affected Sir John so much, that he mixed his own tears with hers, and said, "Lady, see here your knight, who will not fail to die for you, though every one else should desert you: therefore will I do every thing in my power to conduct you and your son, and to restore you to your rank in England, by the grace of God, and the assistance of your friends in those parts. And I, and all those whom I can influence, will risk our lives on the adventure, for your sake; and we will have a sufficient armed force, if it please God, without fearing any danger from the King of France." The queen, who was sitting down, and Sir John standing before her, rose, and would have cast herself at his feet out of gratitude for the great favor he had just offered her; but the gallant Sir John, rising up quickly, caught her in his arms, and said, "God forbid that the Queen of England should ever do such a thing! Madam, be of good comfort to yourself and company; for I will keep my promise: and you shall come and see my brother, and the countess his wife, and all their fine children, who will be rejoiced to see you; for I have heard them say so." The queen answered, "Sir, I find in you more kindness and comfort than in all the world besides; and I give you five hundred thousand thanks for what you have said and offered me. If you will keep what you have promised me with so much courtesy, I and my son shall be forever bound unto you; and we will put the kingdom of England under your management, as in justice it ought to be."

The queen set off, accómpanied by Sir John, Lord of Beaumont, who with joy and respect conducted her to Valenciennes. Many of the citizens of the town came out to meet her, and received her with great humility. She was thus introduced to William, Earl of Hainault, who, as well as the countess, received her very graciously. Many great feasts were given on this occasion, as no one knew better than the countess how to do the honors of her house. This Earl William had at that time four daughters, — Margaret, Philippa, Joan, and Isabella. The young King Edward paid more court and attention to Philippa than to any of the others; the young lady also conversed more frequently with him, and sought his company oftener, than any of her sisters. The queen remained at Valenciennes during eight days with the good earl and countess Joan of Valois. In the mean time the queen made every preparation for her departure; and Sir John wrote very affectionate letters unto certain knights, and those companions in whom he put the most confidence, in Hainault, in Brabant, and Bohemia, beseeching them, from all the friendship that was between them, that they would accompany him in his expedition to England.

There were great numbers in these countries who were willing to go with him from the love they bore him, and many who refused, notwithstanding his request: and even Sir John himself was much reproved by the earl his brother, and by some of his council, because it seemed to them that this enterprise was of much hazard, on account of the great divisions and enmities which at that time subsisted among the great barons and commons in England; and

also because the English are always very jealous of strangers, which made them doubt whether Sir John de Hainault and his companions would ever return. But, notwithstanding all their blame and all their advice bestowed
upon him, the gallant knight would not change his purpose; saying that he could die but once; that the time
was in the will of God; and that all true knights were
bound to aid, to the utmost of their power, all ladies and
damsels driven from their kingdoms comfortless and for-
lorn.

CHAPTER VI.

Queen Isabella arrives in England with Sir John de Hainault.

THE Queen of England took leave of the earl and
countess, thanking them much for the honor they
had shown her, and kissed them at her departure. The
queen, her son, and suite set off, accompanied by Sir John,
who with great difficulty had obtained his brother's permission.

They travelled in such a manner as to arrive at Dordrecht by the time limited for their friends to meet them.
At that place they provided themselves with vessels of
different sizes; and having embarked their cavalry, baggage, &c., they set sail, first recommending themselves to
the care of the Lord. When they left the harbor of Dordrecht, the fleet, considering the force, made a beautiful
appearance from its good order, and from the weather
being clear and temperate. They came opposite to the
dikes of Holland the first tide after their departure. The
next day they cast anchor, and furled their sails, intending
to follow the coast of Zealand, and to land at a port which

they had descried ; but they were prevented by a violent tempest, which drove them so far out of their course, that for two days they knew not where they were. In this God was very merciful to them ; for, had they landed at the port they intended, they would have fallen into the hands of their enemies, who, apprised of their coming, waited for them at that place to put them to death. At the end of two days the storm abated ; and the sailors, descrying England, made for it with great joy, and landed upon the sands, having neither harbor nor safe port. They remained there three days at a short allowance of provisions, while they disembarked their cavalry, and landed their baggage. They were ignorant in what part of England they were, whether that part of the country was friendly to them or not. The fourth day they began their march, putting themselves under the protection of God and St. George ; having suffered much from cold and hunger in addition to their late fears, of which they had not yet divested themselves. They marched over hill and dale until they came to some villages. Soon afterwards they saw a large monastery of black friars, called St. Hamons, where they refreshed themselves during three days.

CHAPTER VII.

THE QUEEN OF ENGLAND BESIEGES HER HUSBAND IN THE CITY OF BRISTOL.

THE news of her arrival, being spread abroad, soon came to the knowledge of those lords by whose advice she had returned. They got themselves ready as soon as possible to join her son, whom they wished to have for their sovereign. The first who came was Henry, Earl of Lancaster, surnamed Wryneck, brother to the Earl Thomas who had been beheaded, and father of the Duke of Lancaster who makes so conspicuous a figure in the following history. This Earl Henry was attended by a great number of men at arms. After him came, from different parts, earls, barons, knights, and esquires, with such an armed force, that they no longer thought they had any thing to apprehend. As they advanced, their forces were still increased; so that a council was called to consider if they should not march directly to Bristol, where the king and the two Spencers then were.

Bristol was at that time a large town, well enclosed, and situated on a good port. Its castle was very strong, and surrounded by the sea. The queen, with all her company, the lords of Hainault, and their suite, took the shortest road for that place. Their forces were augmenting daily until they arrived at Bristol, which they besieged in form. The king and the younger Spencer shut themselves up in the castle: old Sir Hugh and the Earl of Arundel remained in the town.

When the citizens saw the queen's force, and the affections of almost all England on her side, alarmed at their own perilous situation, they determined to surrender the town on condition that their lives and property should be spared. They sent to treat with the queen on this subject; but neither she nor her council would consent to it unless Sir Hugh Spencer and the Earl of Arundel were delivered up to her discretion, for she had come purposely to destroy them.

The citizens, seeing they had no other means of saving the town, their lives, and their fortunes, acceded to the queen's terms, and opened their gates to her. She entered the town accompanied by Sir John de Hainault, with all her barons, knights, and esquires, who took their lodging therein: the others, for want of accommodation, remained without. Sir Hugh Spencer and the Earl of Arundel were delivered to the queen, to do with them as it should please her. Her children were also brought to her, — John and her two daughters, — found there in the keeping of Sir Hugh Spencer. As she had not seen them in a long time, this gave her great joy as well as all her party.

The king and the younger Spencer, shut up in the castle, were much grieved at what had passed, seeing the whole country turned to the queen's party and to Edward, the eldest son.

CHAPTER VIII.

The King of England and Sir Hugh Spencer are taken at Sea as they are endeavoring to escape from the Castle of Bristol.

THE king and Sir Hugh Spencer, seeing themselves so closely pressed, and being ignorant whether any succor was coming to them, embarked one morning with a few followers in a small boat behind the castle, intending, if possible, to reach the principality of Wales. They were eleven or twelve days in this small boat; and, notwithstanding every effort to get forward, the winds proved so contrary by the will of God, that once or twice a day they were driven back within a quarter of a league of the castle whence they set out. At length Sir Henry Beaumont, espying the vessel, embarked with some of his companions in a barge, and rowed so vigorously after it, that the king's boatmen, unable to escape, were overtaken. The king and Sir Hugh Spencer were brought back to Bristol, and delivered to the queen and her son as prisoners. Thus ended this bold and gallant enterprise of Sir John de Hainault and his companions, who, when they embarked at Dordrecht, amounted to no more than three hundred men at arms. By their means Queen Isabella recovered her kingdom, and destroyed her enemies ; at which the whole nation, except some few who were attached to the Spencers, was greatly rejoiced.

When the king and Sir Hugh Spencer were brought to Bristol by Sir Henry Beaumont, the king was sent to Berkeley Castle under a strong guard. Many attentions were paid to him, and proper people were placed near his person to take every care of him, but on no account to suffer him to pass the bounds of the castle. Sir Hugh Spencer was delivered up to Sir Thomas Wager, marshal of the army.

The queen and all the army set out for London, which is the principal city in England. Sir Thomas Wager caused Sir Hugh Spencer to be fastened on the poorest and smallest horse he could find, clothed with a tabard such as he was accustomed to wear. He led him thus in derision, in the suite of the queen, through all the towns they passed, where he was announced by trumpets and cymbals by way of greater mockery, till they reached Hereford, where she and her suite were respectfully and joyfully received. The feast of All Saints was there celebrated with the greatest solemnity and magnificence, out of affection to her son, and respect to the noble foreigners that attended him.

When the feast was over, Sir Hugh was brought before the queen and knights assembled. The charges were read to him; to which he made no reply. The barons and knights then passed sentence on him,—that he should be drawn on a hurdle, attended by trumpets and clarions, through all the streets in the city of Hereford, and then conducted to the market-place, where all the people were assembled : at that place he was to be bound upon a high scaffold, in order that he might be more easily seen by the people.

Afterwards his heart was thrown into the fire, because it had been false and traitorous; since he, by his treasonable counsels, so advised the king as to bring shame and mischief on the land, and had caused some of the greatest lords to be beheaded by whom the kingdom ought to have been supported and defended. His head was cut off, and sent to London.

After the execution, the queen and all the lords, with a great number of common people, set out for London. As they approached it great crowds came out to meet them, and received both her and her son, as well as those who accompanied her, with great reverence.

The citizens presented handsome gifts to the queen, as well as to those of her suite where they thought them best bestowed. After fifteen days passed in feasts and rejoicings, the companions of Sir John de Hainault were impatient to return home. When the queen and her companions saw this, they addressed themselves to Sir John de Hainault, and requested him to remain only until after Christmas, and that he would detain as many of his followers as possible. He detained as many of his companions as he could; but small was the number, the greater part refusing to stay on any account.

The queen ordered a large sum of money to be given them for their expenses, besides jewels of high price,

which she presented to each according to his rank; so
that all were perfectly satisfied. She also paid to each, in
ready money, the value of their horses that they chose to
leave behind, according to their own estimation, without
any demur.

CHAPTER IX.

The Coronation of King Edward the Third.

MOST of the followers of Sir John de Hainault having
returned home, the queen gave leave to many of
her household to return to their country-seats, — except
a few of the nobles, whom she kept with her as her council, — expressly ordering them to come back at Christmas to a great court which at that time she intended to
hold. When Christmas came, she held the court above
mentioned; and it was very fully attended by all the nobles
and prelates of the realm, as well as by the principal
officers of the chief cities and towns. In this assembly it
was determined that the kingdom could no longer remain
without a sovereign; and when all the acts done by the
king, or having his consent, had been read, the chiefs of
the assembly consulted together, and agreeing that such
a man was not worthy to be a king, neither to bear a
crown nor the title of king, they unanimously resolved
that his elder son and true heir, then present, should be
crowned instead of the father. They ordered that his
father should be kept a prisoner, having every attention
paid to his rank, as long as he should live.

The young King Edward, since so fortunate in arms,
was crowned with a royal diadem in the Palace of West-

minster on Christmas Day, 1326. He completed his six-teenth year on the feast of the Conversion of St. Paul following.

At this coronation Sir John de Hainault and all his companions, noble or otherwise, were much feasted, and many rich jewels were given to him and those that staid with him. He and his friends remained during these grand feasts, to the great satisfaction of the lords and ladies that were there, until Twelfth Day; when he re-ceived information that the King of Bohemia, the Earl of Hainault his brother, and many great lords of France, had ordered a tournament to be proclaimed at Condé. Sir John, therefore, would no longer stay, notwithstanding their entreaties, from the great desire he had to attend this tournament to see his brother and the other princes, especially that gallant and generous prince, Charles, King of Bohemia.

When the young King Edward, his mother, and the barons, saw that it was not possible to detain him any longer, they gave him permission to depart, very much against their will. The king, by the advice of the queen, granted him an annuity of four hundred marks sterling, hereditable rent, to be held of him in fee, payable in the city of Bruges. He gave also to Philip de Chateaux, his principal esquire and chief counsellor, a hundred marks sterling of rent, to be paid at the same time and place. He ordered many knights to accompany him to Dover, and that his passage should be free of all cost. He pre-sented the Countess de Garennes, sister to the Count de Bar, and some other ladies who had accompanied the queen to England, with many rich jewels, on their taking leave.

Sir John and his company immediately embarked on

board the vessels prepared for them, to be in time for the tournament. The king sent with him fifteen young and hardy knights to attend him at this tournament, there to try their skill, and to get acquainted with the lords and knights that were to be there. Sir John and his company paid them all the attention in their power, and on this occasion tourneyed at Condé.

CHAPTER X.

ROBERT BRUCE, KING OF SCOTLAND, DEFIES KING EDWARD.

AFTER the departure of Sir John de Hainault, King Edward and his mother governed the kingdom by the counsels of the good Earl of Kent and of Sir Roger Mortimer. Both of them had been banished with the queen. They also took the advice of Sir Thomas Wager, and of others who were esteemed the wisest in the land. This, however, created much envy, which never dies in England, but reigns there as well as in other places. Thus passed the winter and Lent in perfect peace until Easter; when it happened that Robert, King of Scotland, who, though brave, had suffered much in his wars with England, having often been defeated by King Edward, grandfather of the young king, being at this time very old and afflicted with leprosy, hearing that the king had been taken prisoner and deposed, and his counsellors put to death, thought it a favorable opportunity to send a defiance to the present king, as yet a youth, whose barons were not on good terms with each other, and to attempt the conquest of some part of England. About Easter,

1327, he sent a defiance to King Edward and all the country, informing them that he would enter the kingdom, and burn it as far as he had done before after the defeat of Stirling, in which the English suffered so much.

When the young king and his council received this challenge, they published it throughout the kingdom, and ordered that all the nobles and others should come properly accoutred and accompanied, according to their different ranks, to York, the Day of Ascension following. He also sent a considerable body of men at arms to guard the frontiers of Scotland, and messengers to Sir John de Hainault, begging him very affectionately to assist and accompany him in this expedition, and to meet him at York on Ascension Day with as many companions in arms as he could bring with him.

Sir John and his company reached York by the appointed time, and were welcomed and magnificently entertained by the king, queen, and all the barons. The handsomest suburbs of the city were assigned them for their quarters, and a monastery of white friars was allotted for him and his household. In company with the knight came from Hainault the Lord of Anghien (called Sir Walter), Sir Henry, Lord of Antoing, the Lord of Seignoles, and the following knights, — Sir Fastres de Reu, Sir Robert de Bailleul, Sir William de Bailleul his brother, the Lord of Havereth (castellan of Mons), Sir Alart de Briseil, Sir Michael de Ligne, Sir John de Montigny the younger, and his brother Sir Sause de Boussac, Sir Percival de Severies, the Lords of Gommegines, De Biaurien, and De Folion. There came also from Flanders, first, Sir Hector de Vilains, Sir John de Rhodes, Sir Vaufflat de Guistelle, Sir James de Guistelle his brother, Sir Gossuin de la Muelle, and the Lord of Tarces. Many came from Brabant; as

the Lord of Dusle, Sir Thierry de Vaucourt, Sir Rasses
de Gres, Sir John de Cassebegne, Sir John Pilestre, Sir
William de Courterelles, the three brothers De Harle-
beque, Sir Walter de Hauteberguc, and several others.
Of the Bohemians were, Sir John de Libeaux, Henry his
brother, Sir Henry de la Chappelle, Sir Hugh de Hay, Sir
John de Limies, Sir Lambert des Prez, Sir Gilbert de
Hers.   There came also other volunteer knights out of ·
Cambresis and Artois, in hopes of advancement ; so that
Sir John had five hundred good men in his company, well
apparelled and richly mounted.

CHAPTER XI.

A DISSENSION BETWEEN THE ARCHERS OF ENGLAND AND THE HAI-
NAULTERS.

THE King of England, in order to entertain and feast
the strangers and their company, held a great court
on Trinity Sunday, at the house of the black friars, where
he and the queen were lodged, and where each kept their
household separate ; the king with his knights, and the
queen with her ladies, whose numbers were considerable.
At this court the king had five hundred knights, and created fifteen new ones.   The queen gave her entertainment
in the dormitory, where at least sixty ladies, whom she had
invited to entertain Sir John de Hainault and his suite,
sat down at her table.   There might be seen a numerous
nobility well served with plenty of strange dishes, so dis-
guised that it could not be known what they were.   There
were also ladies most superbly dressed, who were expecting with impatience the hour of the ball, or a longer con-

tinuance of the feast: but it fell out otherwise; for, soon after dinner, a violent affray happened between some of the grooms of the Hainaulters and the English archers, who were lodged with them in the suburbs. This increased so much that the archers collected together with their bows strung, and shot at them so as to force them to retreat to their lodgings. The greater part of the knights and their masters, who were still at court, hearing of the affray, hastened to their quarters. Those that could not enter them were exposed to great danger; for the archers, to the number of three thousand, aimed both at masters and servants. It was supposed that this affray was occasioned by the friends of the Spencers and the Earl of Arundel, in revenge for their having been put to death through the advice of Sir John de Hainault. The English also, at whose houses the Hainaulters lodged, barricaded their doors and windows, and would not suffer them to enter: nevertheless some of them got admittance at the back doors, and quickly armed themselves, but durst not advance into the street, for fear of the arrows. The strangers immediately sallied from behind their lodgings, breaking down the hedges and enclosures, until they came to a square, where they halted, waiting for their companions, till they amounted to a hundred under arms, and as many without, who could not gain admittance to their lodgings. United thus, they hastened to assist their friends, who were defending their quarters in the great street in the best manner they could: they passed through the hotel of the Lord of Anghien, which had great gates before and behind open into the street, where the archers were dealing about their arrows in a furious manner. Many Hainaulters were wounded with them.

CHAPTER XII.

HERE we found the good knights, Sir Fastres de Rue, Sir Percival de Severies, and Sir Sause de Boussac, who, not getting admittance into their lodgings, performed deeds equal to those that were armed. They had in their hands great oaken staves, taken from the house of a carter: they dealt their blows so successfully that none durst approach them, and, being strong and valiant knights, beat down, that evening, upward of sixty men. At last the archers were discomfited and put to flight. There remained on the ground dead three hundred men, or thereabouts, who were all from the bishopric of Lincoln. I believe that God never showed greater grace or favor to any one than he did in that day to Sir John de Hainault and his company; for these archers certainly meant nothing less than to murder and rob them, notwithstanding they were come upon the king's business. These strangers were never in such great peril as during the time they remained at York; nor were they in perfect safety until their return to Wissan; for, during their stay, the hatred of the archers was so greatly increased against them, that some of the barons and principal knights informed the lords of Hainault that the archers and others of the commonalty of England, to the number of six thousand, had entered into an agreement to massacre and burn them and their followers in their lodgings either by night or day, and there was no one on the part of the king, or of the barons, that could venture to assist them. The Hainaulters, therefore, had no other resource left than to stand by each other, and to sell their lives as dearly as possible. They made many prudent regulations for their conduct, were frequently obliged to lie on their arms, to confine themselves to their quarters, and to have their armor ready, and their horses always saddled. They were also obliged to keep detachments continually on the watch in the fields and roads round the city, and to send scouts to the distance of half a league, to see if those people, of whom they had received information, were coming; with orders, that, if they perceived any bodies in motion advancing toward the town, they were immediately to return to the detachments in the fields, in order that they might be quickly mounted, and collected together under their own banner, at an appointed alarm-post. They continued in the suburbs four weeks in this distressing situation; and none except a few of the great lords, who went to court to see the king and his council, or to the entertainments to hear the news, ventured to quit their quarters or their arms. If this unfortunate quarrel had not happened, they would have passed their time very pleasantly; for there was such plenty in the city and surrounding country, that during more than six weeks, while the king and the lords of England, with upward of forty thousand men at arms, remained there, the provisions were not dearer; for as much was to be bought for a penny as before their arrival. Good wines from Gascony, Alsace, and the Rhine were in abundance, and reasonable; poultry and other such provisions at a low price. Hay, oats, and straw, of a good quality, and cheap, were delivered at their quarters.

CHAPTER XIII.

How the King and his Army marched to Durham.

AFTER remaining three weeks from the time of this affray, the king issued a proclamation by his marshals, that every one in the course of the ensuing week should be provided with carts, tents, and every thing necessary for their march toward Scotland. When every one was properly equipped, the king and all his barons marched out of the city, and encamped six leagues from it. Sir John de Hainault and his company were encamped near the king, as a mark of distinction, and to prevent the archers from taking any advantage of him. The king and this first division remained there two days and two nights, waiting the arrival of money for his expenses, as well as to examine whether any thing were wanting. On the third day the army dislodged, and before daybreak marched till they came to the city of Durham, a long day's journey, at the entrance of a country called Northumberland, which is wild, full of deserts and mountains, and poor in every thing except cattle. The river Tyne runs through it, full of flints and large stones. Upon this river is situated the town called Newcastle-upon-Tyne. The lord marshal of England was there, with a numerous army to guard the country against the Scots. At Carlisle was a considerable body of Welsh, under the command of Lord Hereford and Lord Mowbray, to defend the passage of the Eden; for the Scots could not enter England without passing one of these rivers. The English could get no certain information of the Scots until they arrived at this place: they had passed the river so privately, that neither those of Carlisle nor those of Newcastle had the smallest knowledge of it. These towns are said to be distant from each other four and twenty English miles.

CHAPTER XIV.

OF THE MANNERS OF THE SCOTS, AND HOW THEY CARRY ON WAR.

THE Scots are bold, hardy, and much inured to war. When they make their invasions into England, they march from twenty to four and twenty miles without halting, as well by night as day; for they are all on horseback, except the camp-followers, who are on foot. The knights and esquires are well mounted on large bay horses, the common people on little galloways. They bring no carriages with them, on account of the mountains they have to pass in Northumberland; neither do they carry with them any provisions of bread or wine; for their habits of sobriety are such, in time of war, that they will live for a long time on flesh half sodden, without bread, and drink the river-water without wine. They have, therefore, no occasion for pots or pans: for they dress the flesh of their cattle in the skins, after they have taken them off; and, being sure to find plenty of them in the country which they invade, they carry none with them. Under the flaps of his saddle, each man carries a broad plate of metal; behind the saddle, a little bag of oatmeal: when they have eaten too much of the sodden flesh, and their stomach appears weak and empty, they place this plate over the fire, mix with water their oatmeal, and, when the plate is heated, they put a little of the paste upon it, and make a thin cake, like a cracknel or biscuit, which they eat to warm their stomachs: it is therefore no wonder that they perform a longer day's march than other soldiers. In this manner the Scots entered England, destroying and burning every thing as they passed. They seized more cattle than they knew what to do with. Their army consisted of four thousand men at arms, knights and esquires, well mounted; besides twenty thousand men, bold and hardy, armed after the manner of their country, and mounted upon little hackneys, that are never tied up or dressed, but turned, immediately after the day's march, to pasture on the heath or in the fields. This army was commanded by two valiant captains. The King of Scotland himself, who had been very brave, yet being old, and laboring under a leprosy, appointed for one that gallant prince, so renowned in arms, the Earl of Moray, who bore upon his banner argent three pillows gules; the other was Sir James Douglas, esteemed the bravest and most enterprising knight in the two kingdoms: he bore for arms azure on a chef argent. These two lords were the greatest barons, and most renowned for their prowess and other feats of arms.

CHAPTER XV.

King Edward's First Expedition against the Scots.

WHEN the English king and all his host had seen the smoke of the fires which the Scots had made, the alarm was immediately sounded, and every one ordered to dislodge and to follow his banners: they all, therefore, withdrew to the fields, armed for immediate combat. Three battalions of infantry were formed; each battalion having two wings, composed of five hundred men at arms, who were to remain on horseback.

It was said that there were eight thousand men at arms, knights and esquires, and thirty thousand men armed and equipped, half of whom were mounted on small hackneys : the other half were countrymen on foot, sent by the towns and paid by them. There were also twenty-four thousand archers on foot, besides all the crew of followers of the army. Thus being drawn up, they marched in battle array after the Scots, towards the place whence the smoke came, until it was night. The army halted in a wood, by the side of a small river, to rest themselves, and to wait for their baggage and provisions.

And all that day the Scots had burnt and wasted and pillaged the country about within five miles of the English host, but the Englishmen could not overtake them. They could not approach near to the Scots, who went wasting the country before them.

At daybreak the next morning every one was armed, and with banners displayed marched in good order over mountains and through valleys, but could never approach the Scots; for there were so many marshes and dangerous places, that it was ordered, under pain of death, that no one should quit his banner except the marshals. When it drew toward night, the cavalry, and those who attended the baggage, more especially the infantry, were so fatigued that they could march no farther.

The king then ordered the marshals to encamp the army there for the night, in order that they might consider what was to be done the next day. The army lay in a wood upon the banks of a small river, and the king was lodged in a poor monastery hard by. When each had chosen a spot of ground to encamp himself on, the lords retired apart, to consider what would be the best method to force the Scots, considering the situation of the country in which they were. It appeared to them that the Scots were sheering off to their own country, burning and pillaging as they went, and that it would be impossible to fight with them in these mountains without a manifest disadvantage, supposing they should overtake them, which they could not; but, as they must repass the Tyne, it was determined in full council, that, if they were to get themselves ready about midnight, and hasten their march next day, they might cut off the passage of the river, and force them to fight at a disadvantage, or remain shut up prisoners in England.

After this resolution had been entered into, each retired to his quarters, to eat and drink what he could find there; and they desired their companions to be silent, in order that the trumpets might be heard: at the first sounding of which, the horses were to be saddled and made ready; at the second, every one was to arm himself without delay; and, at the third, to mount their horses immediately, and join their banners. Each was to take only one loaf of bread with him, slung behind him, after the manner of hunters. All unnecessary arms, harness, and baggage were ordered to be left behind, as they thought they should, for a certainty, give battle the next day, whatever might be the consequences. As it had been ordered, so was it executed; and all were mounted and ready about midnight. Some had but little rest, notwithstanding they had labored hard the day before. Day began to appear, as the battalions were assembled at their different posts. The banner-bearers then hastened on, over heaths, moun-

tains, valleys, rocks, and many dangerous places, without
meeting any level country. On the summits of the mountains, and in the valleys, were large marshes and bogs,
and of such extent that it is a miracle many were not lost
in them; for each galloped forward without waiting for
either commander or companion. Those who fell into
them found difficulty in getting any one to help them.
Many banners remained there; and several baggage and
sumpter horses never came out again.

In the course of the day there were frequent cries of
alarm, as if the foremost ranks were engaged with the
enemy; which those behind believing to be true, they
hurried forward as fast as possible, over rocks and mountains, sword in hand, with their helmets and shields prepared for fighting, without waiting for father, brother, or
friend. When they had hastened about half a league
toward the place from which the noise came, they found
themselves disappointed, as the cries proceeded from some
herds of deer or other wild beasts, which abounded in
these heaths and desert places, and which fled before the
banners, pursued by the shouts of the army, which made
them imagine it was something else.

In this manner the young King of England, agreeably
to the advice of his council, rode all that day over mountains and deserts, without keeping to any fixed road, or
finding any town. About vespers, and sorely fatigued,
they reached the Tyne, which the Scots had already
crossed, though the English supposed they had it still to
repass. Accordingly they went over the ford, but with
great difficulty, owing to the large stones that were in the
river.

When they had passed over, each took up his lodging
on its banks, as he could; and at this time the sun was

set. There were few among them that had any hatchets, wedges, or other instruments, to cut down trees to make themselves huts ; many of them had lost their companions, and even the foot had remained behind, not knowing what road to ask for. They were forced to lie this night on the banks of the river in their armor, and at the same time hold their horses by their bridles, for there was not any place where they could tie them. Thus the horses had nothing to eat, neither oats nor any forage ; and the men had only their loaf that was tied behind them, which was wetted by the sweat of the horses. They had no other beverage but the water of the river, except some great lords who had bottles among their baggage ; nor had they any fire or light, not having any thing to make them of, except some few lords who had some torches which they had brought on sumpter-horses. In such a melancholy manner did they pass the night, without taking the saddles from off the horses, or disarming themselves. And when the long-expected day appeared, when they hoped to find some comfort for themselves and horses, or to fight the Scots, which they very much wished for, to get out of their disagreeable situation, it began to rain, and continued all the day, insomuch that the river was so increased by noon that no one could pass over, nor could any one be sent to know where they were, or to get forage and litter for their horses, or bread and wine for their own sustenance : they were therefore obliged to fast another night. The horses had nothing to subsist on but the leaves of the trees, and grass. They cut down with their swords young trees, and tied their horses to them. They also cut down brushwood to make huts for themselves.

Having continued a whole week without hearing any tidings of the Scots, who they imagined must pass that way, or very near it, on their return home, great murmurs arose in the army; and many laid the fault on those who had given such advice, adding that it was done in order to betray the king and his host. Upon which, the lords of council ordered the army to make ready to march, and cross the river seven leagues higher up, where the ford was better; and it was proclaimed, that every one was to be in readiness to march the next day, and to follow his banners. There was another proclamation made, that whoever chose to take pains and find out where the Scots were, and should bring certain intelligence of it to the king, the messenger of such news should have one hundred pounds a year in land, and be made a knight by the king himself. When this was made known among the host, many knights and esquires, to the number of fifteen or sixteen, eager to gain such rewards, passed the river with much danger, ascended the mountains, and then separated, each taking different routes.

The next day the army dislodged; marched tolerably well, considering that they were but ill clothed; and exerted themselves so much, that they repassed the river, though with much danger from its being swollen by the rains. Many were well washed, and many drowned. When they had crossed over, they remained there for that night, finding plenty of forage in the fields near to a small village, which the Scots had burnt as they passed. The next day they marched over hill and dale till about noon, when they came to some burnt villages, and some fields where there were corn and hay, so that the host remained there for that night. The third day they marched in the same manner; but many were ignorant where they were going, nor had they any intelligence of the enemy.

They continued their route the fourth day in this order;

when, about three o'clock, an esquire, galloping up hastily
to the king, said, "Sire, I bring you news of the Scots:
they are three leagues from this place, lodged on a mountain, where they have been this week, waiting for you.
They knew no more where you were than you did of
them: and you may depend on this as true; for I approached so near to them, that I was taken, and led a
prisoner to their army, before their chiefs. I informed
them where you were, and that you were seeking them to
give them battle. The lords gave me up my ransom, and
my liberty, when I informed them that you had promised
a hundred pounds a year to whoever should first bring intelligence of them, upon condition that he rested not until
he brought you this information; and I now tell you that
you will find them in the place I have mentioned, as eager
to meet you in battle as yourself can be." As soon as the
king heard this news he ordered his army to be prepared,
and turned his horses to feed in the fields, near to a monastery of white monks, which had been burnt, and which
was called in King Arthur's time Blanche Land. Then
the king confessed himself, and each made his preparations according to his abilities. The king ordered plenty
of masses to be said, to housel such as were devoutly
inclined. He assigned a hundred pounds' value of land,
yearly, to the esquire, according to his promise, and made
him a knight with his own hands, in the presence of the
whole army. When they had taken some repose, and
breakfasted, the trumpets sounded; and, all being mounted,
the banners advanced as the young knight led them on;
but each battalion marched by itself in regular array, over
hill and dale, keeping their ranks according to order.
Thus they continued marching, when about twelve o'clock
they came within sight of the Scots army.

As soon as the Scots perceived them, they issued forth from their huts on foot, and formed three good battalions upon the descent of the mountain on which they lodged. A strong, rapid river ran at the foot of this mountain, which was so full of large rocks and stones, that it was dangerous to pass it in haste. If the English had passed this river, there was not room between it and the mountain for them to draw up their line of battle. The Scots had formed their two first battalions on the two sides of the mountain, and on the declivity of the rock, which was not easy to climb to attack them: but they themselves were posted so as to annoy them with stones, if they crossed the river; which, if the English effected, they would not be able to return.

When the English lords perceived the disposition of the Scots, they ordered their men to dismount, take off their spurs, and form three battalions as before. Many new knights were made; and, when the battalions were formed, some of the chief lords brought the young king on horseback along the lines, to encourage the men. The king spoke most graciously to all, and besought them to take every pains to do him honor and preserve their own. He ordered, under pain of death, that no one should advance before the banners of the marshals, or move without orders. Shortly afterwards the battalions were commanded to advance toward the enemy in slow time, keeping their ranks. This was done; and each battalion moved on a considerable space, and came to the ascent of the mountain where the Scots were posted. This manœuvre was intended in order to see whether the enemy would retire, or make any movement; but neither one nor other was to be perceived, and the armies were so near each other that they could see the arms on their shields. The army was ordered to halt to consider what was to be done; and some companions were mounted to skirmish with the enemy, and to examine the passage of the river and their appearance more clearly. They sent heralds to make an offer of retiring on the morrow, if they would pass the river, and fight upon the plain; or, if the Scots would not consent to this, that they would do the same.

When the Scots received this proposal, the chiefs retired to counsel, and returned for answer by the heralds, that they would do neither the one nor the other; that the king and his barons saw that they were in his kingdom, and had burnt and pillaged wherever they had passed; and that, if it displeased the king, he might come and amend it, for they would tarry there as long as it pleased them. When the council of the King of England heard the answer, he ordered it to be proclaimed, that each should take up his quarters where he was, without quitting the ground or his arms: they therefore lay that night very uncomfortably upon the hard ground, among rocks and stones, with their armor on; nor could they get any stakes for the purpose of tying their horses, or procure either litter, or forage, or any bushes to make fires.

The Scots, seeing the English thus take up their quarters, ordered part of the army to remain where the battalions had been drawn up; and the remainder retired to their huts, where they made marvellously great fires, and about midnight such a blasting and noise with their horns, that it seemed as if all the great devils from hell had been come there. Thus were they lodged this night, which was the night of the feast of St. Peter, the beginning of August, 1327, until the next day, when the lords heard mass; afterwards every one armed himself, and the battalions were formed as on the preceding day. When the

Scots saw this, they came and lodged themselves on the same ground they had done before; and the two armies remained thus drawn up until noon, when the Scots made no movement to come toward the English, nor did these on their part make any advances, for they dared not to attempt it with so great disadvantage. Several companions passed the river on horseback, as did some of the foot, to skirmish with the Scots, who also quitted their battalions to meet them; and many on each side were killed, wounded, and taken prisoners. In the afternoon the lords ordered every one to retire to their quarters, as it seemed to them that they were drawn up to no purpose. In this manner they remained for three days. The Scots, on their side, never quitted the mountain; but there were continued skirmishes on both sides, and many killed and taken prisoners. In the evenings they made large fires, and great noises with their horns and with shouting. The intention of the English lords was to keep the Scots besieged there; for, as they could not well fight with them, they hoped to starve them. They knew from the prisoners that they had neither bread, wine, salt, nor other provision, except cattle, of which they had plenty, that they had seized in the country: of these they might eat, indeed, without bread, which would not be very palatable. But they had some little flour to make such cakes as have been before mentioned, and which some of the English use on their inroads beyond the borders.

The fourth day, in the morning, the English looked for the Scots on the mountain, but saw none of them, for they found they had decamped secretly at midnight. Scouts of horse and of foot were immediately despatched through the mountains to know what was become of them. They found them, about four o'clock, posted upon another

mountain, much stronger than that they had left, upon the
same river, near a large wood, to be more concealed, and
in order more privately to advance or retreat at pleasure.

As soon as this was known, the English had orders to
dislodge, and to march in battle array toward the place
where the enemy was posted; and they encamped on a
mountain opposite. They formed their battalions, and
seemed as if they meant to advance to them. The Scots
no sooner perceived this, than they sallied out of their
quarters, and came and posted themselves by the side of
the river, directly in front; but they were unwilling to
advance or come nearer. The English could not attack
them in such a situation without great disadvantage and
loss. They remained full eighteen days in this situation
upon this mountain, whence the lords sent frequent heralds
to the Scots, to offer to give them full place of plain
ground to draw up their battalions, or else they would
accept the same from them; but they would not agree to
either of these proposals.

The two armies had little comfort during the time they
remained in this position. The first night that the English were posted on this second mountain, the Lord James
Douglas took with him about two hundred men at arms,
and at midnight crossed the river, at such a distance from
the camp that he was not noticed, and fell upon the English army most valiantly, shouting, "Douglas forever!
Ye shall die, ye thieves of England!" He and his companions killed more than three hundred; and he galloped
up to the king's tent, and cut two or three of its cords,
crying, at the same time, "Douglas! Douglas forever!"
when he set off; and in his retreat he lost some of his
followers, but not many: he returned to his friends on the
mountain. Nothing more of the sort was attempted from

that time; but the English in future kept a strong and
attentive guard, for they were fearful of another attack
from the Scots, and had placed sentinels and scouts to
give notice of the smallest movement of the enemy; the
chief lords also slept in their armor. There were frequent
skirmishes, and many lives lost on both sides. The
twenty-fourth day from the time they had received intelligence of the enemy, a Scots knight was taken prisoner,
who, sore against his will, gave an account to the lords of
the state of the enemy. He was so closely examined, that
he owned his lords had given orders that morning for
every one to be armed by vespers, and follow the banner
of Lord James Douglas; that it was to be kept secret;
but he was not for a certainty acquainted with their intentions further. Upon this the English lords held a council;
and they judged, from the information of the Scots knight,
that the enemy might perhaps come in full force at night
to attack them on both sides at once, and from their
sufferings by famine, which they could endure no longer,
make it a very bloody and doubtful combat. The English
formed into three battalions, and posted themselves before
their quarters, on three separate spots of ground. They
made large fires, in order to see better, and left their pages
in their quarters to take care of their horses. They remained under arms all the night, and each was placed
under his own standard or banner.

Toward daybreak two Scots trumpeters fell in with one
of the patrols, who took them, and brought them before
the lords of the council, to whom they said, " My lords,
why do you watch here? You are losing your time; for
we swear, by our heads, that the Scots are on their march
home since midnight, and are now four or five leagues off,
and they left us behind, that we might give you the infor-

mation." The English said that it would be in vain to follow them, as they could never overtake them; but, fearing deceit, the lords ordered the trumpeters to close confinement, and did not alter the position of the battalions until four o'clock. When they saw that the Scots were really gone, they gave permission for each to retire to his quarters, and the lords held a council to consider what was to be done. Some of the English, however, mounted their horses, passed the river, and went to the mountain which the Scots had quitted, and found more than five hundred large cattle, which the enemy had killed, as they were too heavy to carry with them, and too slow to follow them, and they wished not to let them fall into the hands of the English alive. They found there, also, more than three hundred caldrons, made of leather with the hair on the outside, which were hung on the fires full of water and meat, ready for boiling. There were also upward of a thousand spits with meat on them, prepared for roasting; and more than ten thousand pairs of old worn-out shoes, made of undressed leather, which the Scots had left there. There were found five poor English prisoners, whom the Scots had bound naked to the trees, and some of them had their legs broken. They untied them, and sent them away, and then returned to the army, just as they were setting out on their march to England, by orders from the king and council.

They followed all that day the banners of the marshals, and halted at an early hour in a beautiful meadow, where there was plenty of forage for their horses; and much need was there of it, for they were so weakened by famine, that they could scarce move. The next day they decamped betimes, and took up their quarters still earlier, at a large monastery within two leagues of Durham. The

king lay there that night, and the army in the fields around
it, where they found plenty of grass, pulse, and corn.
They remained there quiet the next day ; but the king and
lords went to see the church of Durham.   The king paid
his homage to the church and the bishopric, which he had
not before done, and gave largesses to the citizens.

They found there all their carriages and baggage, which
they had left in a wood thirty-two days before at midnight,
as has been related.   The inhabitants of Durham, finding
them there, had brought them away at their own cost, and
placed them in empty barns.   Each carriage had a little
flag attached to it, that it might be known.   The lords
were much pleased at finding them again.

The king and nobles reposed two days at Durham, and
the army in its environs, for there would not have been
sufficient room to lodge them in that city.   They had all
their horses well shod, and set out on their march toward
York.   They made such haste, that in three days they arrived there, and found the queen mother, who received the
king and nobles with great joy, as did all the ladies of the
court and city.   The king disbanded the army, and gave
permission for every one to return to his home, and made
many acknowledgments to the earls, barons, and knights,
for the services they had rendered him by their advice and
prowess.   The knights made out their accounts for horses
which had been ruined or lost, or had died, and gave them
in to the council ; and also a statement of their own expenses, which Sir John de Hainault took upon him as his
own debt toward his followers, for the king and his ministers could not immediately collect such a sum as their
horses amounted to ; but he gave them sufficient for
their own expenses, and to carry them back to their own
country.

When the Hainaulters had received their demand for horses, they purchased small hackneys to ride more at their ease, and sent their carriages, sumpter-horses, trunks, and servants on board of two ships, which the king had provided for them, and which landed them at Sluys, in Flanders.   They took leave of the king, queen, the earls of Kent and Lancaster, and of all the barons, who paid them many honors ; and the king had them escorted by twelve knights and two hundred men at arms, for fear of the archers, of whom they were not well assured, as they must pass through the bishopric of Lincoln.   Sir John and all his company set out, escorted as above, and by easy journeys came to Dover, where they embarked on board vessels ready provided for them.   The Hainaulters arrived at Wissan, where they tarried two days in order to deck out their horses and the remains of their armor ; during which time Sir John de Hainault and some other knights went on a pilgrimage to Our Lady of Boulogne. They returned together to Hainault, when they separated, and each went to his own house : but Sir John went to his brother, who was at that time at Valenciennes ; he was received by him with great joy, as he was much beloved by him.   The Lord of Beaumont then related to him all the above-mentioned history.

CHAPTER XVI.

KING EDWARD MARRIES THE LADY PHILIPPA OF HAINAULT.

SHORTLY afterwards, the king, queen, the Earl of Kent, his uncle, Earl Henry of Lancaster, the Earl of Mortimer, and all the barons who were of the council, sent a bishop, two knights bannerets, and two able clerks, to Sir John de Hainault, to beg of him to be the means that the young king, their lord, should marry; and that the Count of Hainault and Holland would send over one of his daughters, for he would love her more dearly, on his account, than any other lady. The count said he gave many thanks to the king, queen, and the lords by whose counsel they were sent thither to do him so much honor; and that he most willingly complied with their request, if the pope and the holy Church of Rome would agree.

They immediately despatched two of the knights and the clerks to the pope at Avignon, to entreat his consent; for without the pope's dispensation it could not be done, on account of their near relationship; being in the third degree connected, for their two mothers were cousins-german, being the children of two brothers. As soon as they came to Avignon their business was done, for the pope and the college gave their consent most benignantly.

When these gentlemen were returned to Valenciennes from Avignon, with all their bulls, this marriage was directly settled and consented to on each side; and immediate preparations were made for the dress and equipage of such a lady, who was to be Queen of England.

She was then married, by virtue of a procuration which the King of England had sent thither, and went on board a ship at Wissan, and landed at Dover with all her suite. Her uncle, Sir John de Hainault, conducted her to London, where she was crowned; and there were great crowds of the nobility, and feastings, tournaments, and sumptuous entertainments every day, which lasted for three weeks.

CHAPTER XVII.

Douglas is killed fighting for the Heart of King Robert.

AFTER the Scots had in the night quitted the mountain where the young King Edward and the nobles of England had held them besieged, as you have before heard, they marched twenty-two miles without halting, and crossed the Tyne pretty near to Carlisle, where by the orders of the chiefs all disbanded and went to their own homes. Shortly afterwards some of the lords and barons so earnestly solicited the King of England, that a truce was agreed on between the two kings for three years.

During this truce it happened that King Robert of Scotland, who had been a very valiant knight, waxed old, and was attacked with so severe an illness that he saw his end was approaching: he therefore summoned together all the chiefs and barons in whom he most confided, and, after having told them that he should never get the better of this sickness, he commanded them upon their honor and loyalty to keep faithfully the kingdom for his son David, to crown him king when he was of a proper age, and to marry him with a lady suitable to his station.

He after that called to him the gallant Lord James Douglas, and said to him, in presence of the others,—

"My dear friend Lord James Douglas, you know that I have had much to do, and have suffered many troubles, to support the rights of my crown. At the time that I was most occupied I made a vow, the non-accomplishment of which gives me much uneasiness: I vowed, that, if I could finish my wars in such a manner that I might have quiet to govern peaceably, I would go and make war against the enemies of our Lord Jesus Christ. To this point my heart has always leaned ; but our Lord gave me so much to do in my lifetime, and this last expedition has delayed me so long, followed by this heavy sickness, that, since my body cannot accomplish what my heart wishes, I will send my heart in the stead of my body to accomplish my vow.

"I will that as soon as I shall be dead you take my heart from my body, and have it well embalmed ; you will also take as much money from my treasury as will appear to you sufficient to perform your journey, as well as for all those whom you may choose to take with you in your train : you will then deposit your charge at the Holy Sepulchre of our Lord, where he was buried, since my body cannot go there. You will not be sparing of expense ; and, wherever you pass, you will let it be known that you bear the heart of King Robert of Scotland, which you are carrying beyond seas by his command, since his body cannot go thither."

All those present began bewailing bitterly ; and, when the Lord James could speak, he said, " Gallant and noble king, I return you a hundred thousand thanks for the high honor you do me, and for the valuable and dear treasure with which you intrust me ; and I will most willingly do all that you command me, with the utmost loyalty in my power. Never doubt it, however I may feel unworthy of such a high distinction."

The king replied, " Gallant knight, I thank you. You promise it me, then ? "

"Certainly, sir ; most willingly," answered the knight. He then gave his promise upon his knighthood.

The king said, " Thanks be to God ! For I shall now die in peace, since I know that the most valiant and accomplished knight of my kingdom will perform that for me which I am unable to do for myself."

Soon afterwards the valiant Robert Bruce, King of Scotland, departed this life. His heart was embalmed, and his body buried in the monastery of Dunfermline.

Early in the spring the Lord James Douglas, having made provision of every thing that was proper for his expedition, embarked at the port of Montrose, and sailed directly for Sluys in Flanders, in order to learn if any one were going beyond the sea to Jerusalem, that he might join companies. He remained there twelve days, and would not set his foot on shore, but staid the whole time on board, where he kept a magnificent table, with music of trumpets and drums, as if he had been the King of Scotland. His company consisted of one knight banneret, and seven others, of the most valiant knights of Scotland, without counting the rest of his household. His plate was of gold and silver, consisting of pots, basins, porringers, cups, bottles, barrels, and other such things. He had likewise twenty-six young and gallant esquires of the best families in Scotland to wait on him; and all those who came to visit him were handsomely served with two sorts of wine, and two sorts of spices, — I mean those of a certain rank. At last, after staying at Sluys twelve days, he heard that Alphonso, King of Spain, was waging war against the Saracen King of Grenada. He considered that, if he should go thither, he should employ his time and journey according to the late king's wishes; and, when he should have finished there, he would proceed farther, to complete that with which he was charged. He made sail therefore toward Spain, and landed first at Valencia; thence he went straight to the King of Spain, who was with his army on the frontiers, very near the Saracen King of Grenada.

Lord James Douglas throwing the Heart of Bruce among the Saracens.

It happened, soon after the arrival of the Lord James Douglas, that the King of Spain issued forth into the fields, to make his approaches nearer the enemy: the King of Grenada did the same, and each king could easily distinguish the other's banners; and they both began to set their armies in array. The Lord James placed himself and his company on one side, to make better work and a more powerful effort. When he perceived that the battalions on each side were fully arranged, and that of the King of Spain in motion, he imagined they were about to begin the onset; and, as he always wished to be among the first rather than last on such occasions, he and all his company struck their spurs into their horses, until they were in the midst of the King of Grenada's battalion, and made a furious attack on the Saracens. He thought that he should be supported by the Spaniards; but in this he was mistaken, for not one that day followed his example. The gallant knight and all his companions were surrounded by the enemy: they performed prodigies of valor, but these were of no avail, as they were all killed.* It was a

---

* The young readers of Froissart will be interested in some particulars of this exploit not given by our author. When Douglas made his first impetuous onset, it seemed as if he would be successful, even alone. The Saracens retreated in confusion, and Douglas and his party were tempted into a hot pursuit. "Taking the casket from his neck" (says Hailes, in the Annals of Scotland), "which contained the heart of Bruce," Douglas "threw it before him, and cried, 'Now pass thou onward, as thou wast wont; and Douglas will follow thee, or die.'" Presently the Saracens rallied, and surrounded the Scotch with overwhelming numbers. "Douglas fell while attempting to rescue Sir William Clare of Roslin, who shared his fate. Robert and Walter Logan, both of them knights, were slain with Douglas. . . . His few surviving companions found his body in the field, together with the casket, and reverently conveyed them to Scotland. The remains of Douglas were interred in the sepulchre of his fathers, in the church of Douglas; and the heart of Bruce was deposited at Melrose."

great misfortune that they were not assisted by the Spaniards.

About this time many of the nobles and others, desirous
of a settled peace between the Scots and English, proposed a marriage between the young King of Scotland
and the sister of the King of England. This marriage
was concluded and solemnized at Berwick, with great
feasts and rejoicings on both sides.

CHAPTER XVIII.

PHILIP OF VALOIS CROWNED KING OF FRANCE.

CHARLES, King of France, died without heirs male.
The twelve peers and barons of France assembled at
Paris without delay, and gave the kingdom with one consent to Philip of Valois. They passed by the Queen of
England, and the king her son, although she was cousin-
german to the king last deceased; for they said that the
kingdom of France was of such great nobleness that it
ought not to fall by succession to a female. They crowned
the Lord Philip King of France, at Rheims, the Trinity
Sunday following.

CHAPTER XIX.

KING EDWARD IS ADVISED BY HIS COUNCIL TO MAKE WAR AGAINST KING PHILIP OF FRANCE. HE EFFECTS GREAT ALLIANCES IN GERMANY, AND IS MADE VICAR OF THE EMPIRE.

THE Lord Robert d'Artois * was in England very near the king's person, whom he was continually advising to make war upon the King of France, for wrongfully withholding his inheritance. The king saw clearly that it was impossible for him, and all the force he could bring from his own country, to subdue such a great kingdom as that of France, if he did not obtain powerful friends and assistance in the empire, and in other parts, by means of his money.

The King of England, when the winter was over, embarked, accompanied by many earls, barons, and knights, and came to the city of Antwerp, which at that time was held for the Duke of Brabant. He sent to the Duke of Brabant, his cousin, his brother-in-law the Duke of Gueldres, to the Marquis of Juliers, the Lord John of Hainault, and to all those from whom he expected support and assistance, that he should be happy to have some conversation with them.

When all the lords of the empire were assembled in the city of Halle, they had long deliberations together, and said to the King of England, "Dear sir, there is an ordinance of a very old date, sealed, that no king of France

* Who, although he had been the chief supporter of Philip for the crown, had afterwards become the object of Philip's violent hatred, and had been banished the kingdom.

should take and keep possession of any thing that belongs to the empire. Now, King Philip has gotten possession of the castles of Crevecœur in Cambresis, and of Arleux in Artois, as well as the city of Cambray; for which the emperor has good grounds to challenge him through us, — if you will have the goodness to obtain his consent, in order to save our honor." The King of England replied that he would cheerfully conform himself to their advice.

It was then determined that the Marquis of Juliers should go to the emperor, and with him knights and counsellors from the king, and some from the Duke of Gueldres; but the Duke of Brabant would not send any : he lent, however, his castle of Louvain to the king for his residence.

The Marquis of Juliers and his company returned from the emperor about All Saints' Day ; and, when he sent to inform the king of this, he congratulated him on the good success of his mission. The king wrote him for answer that he should come to him on the feast of St. Martin, and demanded of the Duke of Brabant to name the place where he wished this conference to be holden ; who replied, at Arques, near to his own country. Upon this the king gave notice of it, that all his allies might be there.

The town-hall of Arques was hung with rich and fine cloths, like to the presence-chamber of the king. His Majesty was seated five feet higher than the rest of the company, and had on his head a rich crown of gold. The letters from the emperor to the king were publicly read, by which the King of England was constituted and established his vicar and lieutenant, and full powers granted to him to do all the acts of law and justice to every one, in his name, and also to coin money in gold and silver.

On this occasion an ancient statute was renewed and

confirmed, which had been made in former times at the court of the emperor. It directed that any one meaning to hurt or annoy another should send him a sufficient defiance three days before he committed any hostile act; and that whoever should act otherwise should be degraded as an evil-doer. When all this was completed, the lords took their leave, and gave each other their mutual promises to be fully equipped, without delay, three weeks after the feast of St. John, to sit down before the city of Cambray; which of right belonged to the emperor, but had turned to the French.

CHAPTER XX.

King Edward and his Allies send Challenges to the King of France.

WINTER was now over, and the summer come, when, the feast of St. John the Baptist approaching, the lords of England and Germany made preparations for undertaking their intended expedition. The King of France also made his preparations to meet them; for he was well acquainted with part of what they intended, though he had not yet received any challenge. King Edward collected his stores in England, where he made his armaments ready; and, as soon as St. John's Day was passed, transported them across the sea to Vilvorde, whither he went himself. He made all his people, on their arrival, take houses in the town; and, when this was full, he lodged them in tents and pavilions in the fine meadows along the side of the river. He remained thus from Magdalen Day until the feast of Our Lady in September, expecting week after week the arrival of the lords of the empire, especially the Duke of Brabant, for whom all the others were waiting. When the King of England saw that they came not, he caused them to be summoned to be at the city of Mechlin on St. Giles's Day, according to their promises, and give reasons for their delays.

The lords of Germany, in obedience to the summons, came to Mechlin, where, after many debates, they agreed that the king should be enabled to march in a fortnight, when they would be quite ready; and, that their cause might have a better appearance, they determined to send challenges to King Philip. These challenges were written and sealed by all except the Duke John of Brabant, who said he would do his part at the proper time and place. They were given in charge to the Bishop of Lincoln, who carried them to Paris, and performed his errand so justly and well that he was blamed by no one. He had a passport granted him to return to his lord, who, as said before, was at Mechlin.

CHAPTER XXI.

KING EDWARD CREATES SIR HENRY OF FLANDERS A KNIGHT, AND
AFTERWARDS MARCHES INTO PICARDY.

AS soon as the King of England had passed the Scheld, and had entered the kingdom of France, he called to him the Lord Henry of Flanders, who was but a young esquire, and knighted him; at the same time giving him two hundred pounds sterling a year, properly secured in England. The king was lodged in the abbey of Mont St. Martin, where he remained two days. His troops were scattered round about in the country. The Duke of

Brabant was quartered at the monastery of Vaucelles. When the King of France, who was at Compiègne, heard this news, he increased his forces everywhere, and sent the Earl of Eu and Guines, his constable, with a large body of men at arms, to St. Quentin, to guard that town and the frontiers against his enemies. He sent the Lords of Coucy and of Ham to their castles, and a great number of men at arms to Guise, Ribemont, Bouchain, and the neighboring fortresses on the borders of his kingdom; and came himself to Peronne, in the Vermandois. During the time the King of England was at the abbey of Mont St. Martin, his people overran the country as far as Bapaume, and very near to Peronne and St. Quentin : they found it rich and plentiful, for there had not been any wars in those parts.

Sir Henry of Flanders, to do credit to his newly acquired knighthood, and to obtain honor, made one of a party of knights, who were conducted by Sir John de Hainault. There were among them the Lords of Fauquemont, Bergues, Vaudresen, Lens, and many others, to the number of five hundred combatants. They had a design upon a town in the neighborhood, called Hennecourt, whither the greater number of the inhabitants of the country had retired, who, confiding in the strength of this fortress, had carried with them all their movables. Sir Arnold of Bacqueghen and Sir William du Dunor had already been there, but had done nothing; upon which all these lords had collected together, and were desirous of going thither to do their utmost to conquer it. There was an abbot at that time in Hennecourt, of great courage and understanding, who ordered barriers to be made of woodwork around the town, and likewise to be placed across the street, so that there was not more than half a foot from one post to another: he then collected armed men, provided stones, quicklime, and such like instruments of annoyance, to guard them. As soon as the lords above mentioned came there, the abbot posted his people between the barriers and the gate, and flung the gate open. The lords dismounted, and approached the barriers, which were very strong, sword in hand; and great strokes were given to those within, who defended themselves very valiantly. Sir Abbot did not spare himself; but, having a good leathern jerkin on, dealt about his blows manfully, and received as good in his turn. Many a gallant action was performed; and those within the barriers flung upon the assailants stones, logs, and pots full of lime, to annoy them.

It chanced that Sir Henry of Flanders, who was one of the foremost, with his sword attached to his wrist, laid about him at a great rate: he came too near the abbot, who caught hold of his sword, and drew him to the barriers with so much force, that his arm was dragged through the grating, for he could not quit his sword with honor. The abbot continued pulling; and, had the grating been wide enough, he would have had him through, for his shoulder had passed, and he kept his hold, to the knight's great discomfort. On the other side, his brother knights were endeavoring to draw him out of his hands; and this lasted so long, that Sir Henry was sorely hurt: he was, however, at last rescued, but his sword remained with the abbot. And at the time I was writing this book, as I passed through that town, the monks showed me this sword, which was kept there, much ornamented. It was there that I learnt all the truth of this assault. Hennecourt was very vigorously attacked that day; and it lasted until vespers. Many of the assailants were killed or wounded.

Sir John of Hainault lost a knight from Holland, called Sir Herman, who bore for arms a fess componé gules, and in chief, three buckles azure. When the Flemings, Hainaulters, English, and Germans, who were there, saw the courage of those within the town, and that, instead of gaining any advantage, they were beaten down and wounded, they retreated in the evening, carrying with them to their quarters the wounded and bruised.

On the next morning the king departed from Mont St. Martin, and ordered, under pain of death, that no damage should be done to the abbey, which was observed. They then entered the Vermandois, and at an early hour took up their lodgings on Mont St. Quentin. They were in a regular order of battle, and those of St. Quentin might have encountered them had they chosen it; but they had no desire to issue out of the town. The scouts of the army went up to the barriers, and skirmished with those who were there. The Constable of France and Sir Charles le Blois drew up their people in order of battle before the barriers; and when the Englishmen, among whom were the Earl of Suffolk, the Earl of Northampton, Sir Reginald Cobham, and many others, saw the manner in which it was done, they retreated to the main army of the king, which remained encamped on the hill until four o'clock the next morning. A council was then held, to consider whether they should march straight into France, or draw toward Tierache, keeping near the borders of Hainault. By the advice of the Duke of Brabant, the latter plan was followed, as from that country they drew all their provision; and they resolved, that if King Philip should follow them with his army, as they supposed he would, they would wait for him in the plains, and give him battle without fail. They then set out from Mont St. Quentin, ranged in a regular order, in three battalions. The marshals and the Germans led the van, the King of England the centre, and the Duke of Brabant the rear. They advanced not more than three or four leagues a day, halting early, but burning and pillaging all the country they passed through.

We must now speak of the expedition of Sir John of Hainault, who had with him full five hundred fighting men. He came first to Guise, which he burnt, and destroyed the mills. In the fortress was the Lady Jane, his daughter, wife of Lewis, Earl of Blois. She begged of her father to spare the lands and heritage of his son-in-law; but in vain, for Sir John would not depart until he had completed the purpose of his expedition. He then returned to the king, who was lodged in the abbey of Sarnaques, while his people overran the country. The Lord of Fauquemont led sixscore German lances to Lonnion, in Tierache, a large level town; the inhabitants of which had almost all retired with what they could carry off into the woods, and there had fortified their position by cutting down large trees. The Germans followed them, and, being joined by Sir Arnold Bacqueghen and his company, they attacked the people of Lonnion in the wood, who defended themselves as well as they could; but they were overpowered and obliged to flee. There were about forty killed and wounded, and all they brought there plundered. Thus was this country ruined without any hinderance; and the English acted as they thought proper.

When the King of England had halted in the champaign country of Tierache, he was informed that the King of France was within two leagues of him, and eager to give him battle. He therefore summoned the chiefs of his army, and demanded of them the best method of preserving his honor, as his intention was to accept the combat. The lords looked at each other, and requested the Duke of Brabant to give his opinion. The duke replied, that he was for fighting, as they could not depart honorably without it ; and he advised that a herald should be sent to the King of France, to offer him battle, and to fix the day. A herald who belonged to the Duke of Gueldres, and spoke French well, had this commission. After being informed what he was to say, he rode to the French army, and, coming to the king and his counsellors, told them that the King of England, having halted in the plains, demanded and required the combat of one army against the other. To this King Philip answered willingly, and appointed the Friday following for the day, this being Wednesday. The herald returned back, well clothed with handsome furred mantles, which the king and lords of France had given him for the sake of the news he had brought, and related the good cheer he had received. The day being thus fixed, information of it was given to the captains of either army, and every one made his preparations accordingly.

On the Thursday morning, two knights belonging to the Earl of Hainault, the Lords of Faguinelles and Tupegny, mounted their steeds ; and these two, leaving their own army, set out to view that of the English. They rode on for some time boldly along the line of the English army ; when it chanced that the horse of the Lord of Faguinelles took fright, ran off in spite of all the efforts of his master, and carried him, whether he would or no, to the quarters of the enemy. He fell into the hands of the Germans, who, soon perceiving he did not belong to their party, surrounded him and his horse, and took him prisoner. He remained prisoner to five or six German gentlemen, who immediately ransomed him. When they found out that he was a Hainaulter, they asked him whether he knew Sir John of Hainault; he replied, *Yes*, and begged of them, for the love of God, to carry him to him, because he was sure he would be security for his ransom. The Germans were delighted at this, and carried him to Sir John, who pledged himself for his ransom. The Lord of Faguinelles thereupon returned to the army of Hainault, to his earl and other lords. His steed was returned to him through the entreaties of the Lord of Beaumont. Thus passed that day without any other thing occurring worthy of being recorded.

CHAPTER XXII.

The Two Kings retire from Vironfosse without giving Battle.

IT was a matter of much wonder, how two such fine armies could separate without fighting. But the French were of contrary opinions among themselves. Some said it would be a great shame, and very blamable, if the king did not give battle when he saw his enemies so near him, and drawn up in his own kingdom in battle array: others said it would exhibit a singular instance of madness to fight, as they were not certain that some treachery was not intended; besides, if fortune should be unfavorable, the king would run a great risk of losing his kingdom, and, if he should conquer his enemies, he would not be the nearer to gain possession of England or of the land of the allies. Thus the day passed until near twelve o'clock in disputes and debates. About noon a hare was started in the plain, and ran among the French army, who began to make a great shouting and noise, which caused those in rear to imagine the combat was begun in front; and many put on their helmets, and made ready their swords. Several new knights were made, especially by the Earl of Hainault, who knighted fourteen; and they were after called *knights of the hare.*

In this situation the two armies remained all Friday. In the midst of the debates of the council of the King of France, letters were brought from Robert, King of Sicily, addressed to him and his council. This King Robert was, as they said, a very great astrologer, and full of deep science; he had often cast the nativities of the kings of France and England, and had found by his astrology and the influence of the stars, that, if the King of France fought with the King of England in person, he would surely be defeated; in consequence of which he, as a wise king, and much fearing the danger and peril of his cousin the King of France, had sent, long before, letters most earnestly to request King Philip and his council never to give battle to the English when King Edward should be there in person. These doubts, and this letter from the King of Sicily, made many of the lords of France sore disheartened, of which the king was informed, who nevertheless was very eager for the combat; but he was so strongly dissuaded from it, that the day passed quietly, and each man retired to his quarters.

When the Earl of Hainault saw that there was no likelihood of a battle, he departed with all his people, and returned to Quesnoy. The next day the Germans and Brabanters took their leave, and returned to their homes. The King of England went to Brabant with the duke, his cousin. Thus ended this great expedition, and every man returned to his own house.

When the king's vessel was ready, he embarked with a numerous attendance at Antwerp, and sailed for London, where he arrivéd about St. Andrew's Day, and was joyfully received by his subjects, who were anxious for his return. Great complaints were made to him of the ravages which the Normans, Picards, and Spaniards had committed at Southampton ; upon which he answered, that, whenever it came to his turn, he would make them pay dearly for it — and he kept his word before the end of that year.

CHAPTER XXIII.

THE SEA-FIGHT BETWEEN THE KING OF ENGLAND AND THE FRENCH, BEFORE SLUYS.

THE King of England embarked for Flanders, in order to go to Hainault to assist his brother-in-law in his war against France. He and his whole navy sailed from the Thames, the day before the eve of St. John the Baptist, 1340, and made straight for Sluys. Sir Hugh Quiriel, Sir Peter Bahucet, and Barbenoire, were at that time lying between Blanckenburgh and Sluys with upward of one hundred and twenty large vessels, without counting others : these were manned with about forty thousand men, Genoese and Picards, including mariners. By the orders of the King of France, they were there at anchor, waiting the return of the King of England, to dispute his passage.

When the king's fleet was almost got to Sluys, they saw so many masts standing before it, that they looked like a wood. The king asked the commander of his ship what they could be ; who answered, that he imagined they must

be that armament of Normans, which the King of France
kept at sea, and which had so frequently done him much
damage, had burnt his good town of Southampton, and
taken his large ship the " Christopher." The king replied, "I have for a long time wished to meet with them,
and now, please God and St. George, we will fight them ;
for, in truth, they have done me so much mischief, that I
will be revenged on them if it be possible." The king
drew up all his vessels, placing the strongest in the front,
and on the wings his archers. Between every two vessels
with archers there was one of men at arms. He stationed
some detached vessels as a reserve, full of archers, to
assist and help such as might be damaged. There were
in this fleet a great many ladies from England, countesses,
baronesses, and knights' and gentlemen's wives, who were
going to attend on the queen at Ghent : these the king
had guarded most carefully by three hundred men at arms
and five hundred archers. When the King of England
and his marshals had properly divided the fleet, they
hoisted their sails to have the wind on their quarter, as
the sun shone full in their faces, which they considered
might be of disadvantage to them, and stretched out a
little, so that at last they got the wind as they wished.
The Normans, who saw them tack, could not help wonder-
ing why they did so, and said they took good care to turn
about, for they were afraid of meddling with them. They
perceived, however, by his banner, that the king was on
board, which gave them great joy, as they were eager to
fight with him : so they put their vessels in proper order,
for they were expert and gallant men on the seas. They
filled the " Christopher," the large ship which they had
taken the year before from the English, with trumpets
and other warlike instruments, and ordered her to fall

upon the English.   The battle then began very fiercely;
archers and crossbow-men shot with all their might at
each other, and the men at arms engaged hand to hand.
In order to be more successful, they had large grapnels,
and iron hooks with chains, which they flung from ship to
ship, to moor them to each other.   There were many
valiant deeds performed, many prisoners made, and many
rescues.   The "Christopher," which led the van, was re-
captured by the English, and all in her taken or killed.
There were then great shouts and cries, and the English
manned her again with archers, and sent her to fight
against the Genoese.

This battle was very murderous and horrible.   Combats
at sea are more destructive and obstinate than upon the
land, for it is not possible to retreat or flee: every one
must abide his fortune, and exert his prowess and valor.
Sir Hugh Quiriel and his companions were bold and determined men, had done much mischief to the English at
sea, and destroyed many of their ships.   This combat,
therefore, lasted from early in the morning until noon;
and the English were hard pressed, for their enemies were
four to one, and the greater part men who had been used
to the sea.   The king, who was in the flower of his youth,
showed himself on that day a gallant knight, as did the
Earls of Derby, Pembroke, Hereford, Huntingdon, Northampton, and Gloucester; the Lord Reginald Cobham, Lord
Felton, Lord Bradestan, Sir Richard Stafford, the Lord
Percy, Sir Walter Manny, Sir Henry de Flanders, Sir
John Beauchamp, Sir John Chandos, the Lord Delaware,
Lucie Lord Malton, and the Lord Robert d'Artois, now
called Earl of Richmond.   I cannot remember all the
names of those who behaved so valiantly in the combat;
but they did so well, that, with some assistance from

Bruges and those parts of the country, the French were completely defeated, and all the Normans and the others killed or drowned, so that not one of them escaped. This was soon known all over Flanders; and, when it came to the two armies before Thin-l'Evêque, the Hainaulters were as much rejoiced as their enemies were dismayed.

After the king had gained this victory, which was on the eve of St. John's Day, he remained all that night on board of his ship before Sluys; and there were great noises with trumpets, and all kinds of other instruments. The Flemings came to wait on him, having heard of his arrival, and what deeds he had performed. The king inquired of the citizens of Bruges after Jacob von Artaveld; and they told him he was gone to the aid of the Earl of Hainault with upward of sixty thousand men, against the Duke of Normandy. On the morrow, which was Midsummer Day, the king and his fleet entered the port. As soon as they were landed, the king, attended by crowds of knights, set out on foot on a pilgrimage to Our Lady of Ardembourg, where he heard mass, and dined. He then mounted his horse, and went that day to Ghent, where the queen was, who received him with great joy and kindness. The army and baggage, with the attendants of the king, followed him by degrees to the same place.

The king had sent notice of his arrival to the lords that were before Thin-l'Evêque, opposing the French; who, as soon as they heard of it, and of his victory over the Normans, broke up their camp. The Earl of Hainault disbanded all his troops, except the principal lords, whom he carried with him to Valenciennes, and treated most nobly, especially the Duke of Brabant, and Jacob von Artaveld. Jacob von Artaveld, in the full market-place, explained the right King Edward had to the crown of France, to all

those lords that chose to hear him, and of what importance
it was to the three countries, — that is to say, Flanders,
Brabant, and Hainault, — when closely united. He spoke
so clearly, and with so much eloquence, that he was praised
by all, who agreed that he was worthy to exercise the dig-
nity of Earl of Flanders. These lords then took their
leave, and agreed to meet in eight days' time at Ghent, to
see the king. A day of conference was then appointed to
be held at Vilvorde.

It was then determined that the King of England
should move about Magdalen-tide, and lay siege to the city
of Tournay; and all the lords present promised to be
there, as well as all the forces from the principal towns.
They then set off for their homes, to get ready, and prepare themselves properly for the business.

CHAPTER XXIV.

THE KING OF ENGLAND BESIEGES THE CITY OF TOURNAY WITH A POWERFUL ARMY.

KING PHILIP, soon after the departure of these lords,
was informed of all that had passed, and how King
Edward was to come to Tournay: he therefore determined
to provide it so well with ammunition, &c., and with so
many good knights, that the city should be well served
and well advised. He sent directly to the city of Tournay
the flower of his chivalry, — the Earl Raoul of Eu, Constable of France; the young Earl of Guines, his son; the
Earl of Foix, and his brothers, the Earl of Aymery and
Narbonne; the Lord Aymery of Poitiers; the Lord Geoffry of Chargny; the Lord Gerard of Montfaucon; his two

marshals, the Lord Robert Bertrand, and Lord Matthew de Trie; the Lord of Caieux, seneschal of Poitou; the Lord of Chatillon; and Sir John of Landas, — who had with them many knights and esquires renowned in arms. The king entreated of them earnestly that they would pay so much care and attention to Tournay, that nothing unfortunate might happen; which they all promised him. They took leave of the King of France, left Arras, and arrived at Tournay, where they found Sir Godémar du Fay, who had been sent thither before them. He received them joyfully, as did those of the town; and, after having well examined the purveyances which were there, as well of artillery as of provision, they ordered great quantities of corn, oats, and other articles of food, to be brought into it from the country round about, so that the city was in a good state to hold out for a long time.

The King of England, when the time for being before Tournay approached, and the corn was nearly ripe, set out from Ghent, accompanied by seven earls from his own country, two prelates, twenty-eight bannerets, two hundred knights, four thousand men at arms, and nine thousand archers, without counting the foot-soldiers. He passed through the town of Oudenarde, crossed the Scheld, and encamped before Tournay, near St. Martin's Gate, on the road to Lisle and Douay. Soon after came his cousin, the Duke of Brabant, with upward of twenty thousand men, knights and esquires, and the companies from the different towns. The Brabanters were encamped at Pontaries upon the Scheld, as you return from the fields by the gate Valentinois. The Earl of Hainault came with the fine cavalry of his country, with many Dutchmen and Zealanders, who attended upon his person as their lord. The earl was encamped between the King of England and the

Duke of Brabant. Jacob. von Artaveld came next with
more than forty thousand Flemings, not reckoning those
from Ypres, Poperingue, Cassel, and Bruges, who were
ordered to another part, as you will hear presently. He
was quartered near the gate St. Fontaine, on both sides of
the Scheld, over which they had thrown a bridge of boats,
that they might have free intercourse. The Duke of
Gueldres, the Earl of Juliers, the Marquis of Blanckenberg, the Marquis of Nuys, the Earl of Mons, the Earl of
Savines, the Lord of Fauquemont, Sir Arnold de Bacqueghen, and all the Germans, were stationed on the side
toward Hainault, so that the city of Tournay was very
completely surrounded. Each division of the army had
open communication with each other ; and no one could
enter or come out of the city without permission, or without being seen.

CHAPTER XXV.

THE SCOTS RECOVER GREAT PART OF THEIR COUNTRY DURING THE SIEGE OF TOURNAY.

FOR the present we must return to Scotland, and see
what is going on there during this siege of Tournay.
    The reader should be informed that Sir William Douglas, son of the brother of Sir James Douglas, who was
killed in Spain, the Earl of Moray, the Earl Patrick of
Dunbar, the Earl of Sutherland, Sir Robert Keith, Sir
Simon Fraser, and Alexander Ramsay, had remained as
governors of the remnant of Scotland that was not in the
possession of the English. During the space of seven
years they had secreted themselves in the forest of Jedworth, in winter as well as summer, and thence had car-

ried on a war against all the towns and fortresses wherein
King Edward had placed any garrisons; in which many
perilous and gallant adventures befell them, and from
which they acquired much honor and renown. While
King Edward was beyond sea, before Tournay, the King
of France sent over some forces to Scotland, which arrived
safe in the town of Perth; and he entreated the noblemen
above mentioned to carry on so bitter a war in England
that King Edward should be obliged to desist from his
present enterprise before Tournay, promising them every
aid and assistance: in consequence of which these lords
collected their forces, and made themselves ready. They
quitted the forest of Jedworth, traversed Scotland, retook
as many fortresses as they were able, passed by Berwick,
and, crossing the river Tyne, entered Northumberland,
which was formerly a kingdom of itself, where they found
plenty of fat cattle. Having wasted and burnt the whole
country as far as Durham, and even beyond it, they re-
entered Scotland, and gained all the fortresses which the
King of England held, except the good town of Berwick,
and three other castles which annoyed them much, and
which are so strong that you will scarcely find their equals
for strength in any country: one is called Stirling, the
other Roxburgh, and the third, which may be styled the
sovereign of Scotland, Edinburgh. This last is situate
upon a high rock, commanding a view of the country
round about; and the mountain has so steep an ascent,
that few can go up it without stopping twice or thrice.
The governor of it at that time was a gallant English
knight, called Sir Walter Limousin.

A bold thought came into Sir William Douglas's mind,
which he mentioned to his companions, the Earl of Dunbar, Sir Robert Fraser, who had been tutor to King David

of Scotland, and Alexander Ramsay, who all agreed to
try to execute it. They collected upward of two hundred
lances of Highlanders, went to sea, and purchased oats,
oatmeal, coal, and straw, and landed peaceably at a port
about three miles from the castle of Edinburgh, which
had made a stronger resistance than all the other castles.
When they had armed themselves, they issued forth in
the night-time; and having chosen ten or twelve from
among them, in whom they had the greatest confidence,
they dressed them in old, threadbare clothes, with torn
hats, like poor tradesmen, and loaded twelve small·horses,
with a sack to each, filled with oats, meal, or coal; they
then placed the rest in ambuscade in an old abbey, that
was ruined and uninhabited, close to the foot of the mountain on which the castle was situate. At daybreak these
merchants, who were privily armed, took the road with
their horses, the very best way they could, toward the
castle. When they had got about half-way up the hill,
Sir William Douglas and Sir Simon Fraser advanced before the others, whom they ordered to follow in silence,
and came to the porter's lodge. They informed him that
they had brought, with many risks and fears, coal, oats,
and meal; and, if there were any want of such articles, they
should be glad to dispose of them, and at a cheap rate.
The porter replied, that the garrison would thankfully
have them, but it was so early that he dared not awake
either the governor or his steward. At the same time he
told them to come forward, and he would open the other
gate. They all then passed quietly through, and entered
with their loads to the gate of the barriers, which he
opened for them.

Sir William Douglas had remarked that the porter had
all the great keys of the castle-gates; and had, in an

How Sir William Douglas and his Companions captured the Castle of Edinburgh by Stratagem.

apparently indifferent manner, inquired which opened the great gate, and which the wicket. When the first gate was opened, they turned in their nags, and flung off the loads of two, which consisted of coal, directly upon the sill of the gate, so that it could not be shut; and then seized the porter, whom they slew so suddenly that he did not utter a word. They then took the keys, and opened all the gates, and Sir William Douglas gave a blast upon his horn as a signal for his companions; they then flung off their torn clothes, and placed all the remainder of the coal between the gates, so that they could not be shut. When those in the ambuscade heard the horn, they sallied forth, and hastened forward to the castle. The noise of the horn awakened the watch of the castle, at that time asleep, who, seeing these armed men running up the castle hill, blew lustily on his horn, and bawled out, "Treason! treason! Arm yourselves, my masters, as fast as you can; for here are men at arms advancing to our fortress." They all roused themselves as quickly as they could, and when armed came to the gate; but Sir William and his twelve companions defended the gate, so that it could not be shut. The combat then grew hotter; but those from without maintained their ground with great valor, until their ambuscade arrived. The garrison made a very gallant defence, killing and wounding many of their enemies; but Sir William and his party exerted themselves so much, that the fortress was taken, and all the English killed, except the governor and six esquires, to whom they showed mercy. The Scots remained in the castle all that day, and appointed for governor a squire of that country, called Sir Simon de Vesci, and left with him many of his countrymen. This news was brought to the King of England while he lay before Tournay.

CHAPTER XXVI.

THE King of France published a special summons
throughout his kingdom, and also in many parts of
the empire, for levying of forces. It had so good an
effect, that Charles, King of Bohemia, the Duke of Lorrain, the Earl of Bar, the Bishop of Metz, the Bishop of
Verdun, the Earl of Montbeliard, the Lord John of Cha-
lons, the Earl of Geneva, the Earl of Savoy, and the Lord
Lewis, his brother, came to serve under the King of
France, with as many men as they could collect together.
There came to him also, the Dukes of Brittany, Burgundy,
and Bourbon, the Earls of Alençon, Flanders, Foretz,
Armagnac, Blois, Harcourt, and Dammartin, the Lord
Charles of Blois, the Lord of Coucy, and many other
knights and barons. The King of Navarre afterwards
came with a number of men at arms, to serve for the lands
he held in France, and for which he was a homager to the
king. The King of Scotland was also there, under the
appointment of the King of France, and had a handsome
body of men given him.

Soon after the King of France had taken up his quarters, with his army, near the bridge of Bouvines, a company of Hainaulters put themselves in motion by the
exhortations of Sir Vauflart de la Croix, who told them he
knew all the country well, and he could lead them to a
part of the French army which they would be sure of
conquering. About one hundred and twenty of them,

knights and esquires, set out one day through love to each other, to do some deeds of arms, and advanced toward Pont-à-Tressin. They made the Lord of Bailleul their captain, and it was under his banner that they were to enlist.

That same morning, some of the Liegeois made also an excursion, under the command of Sir Robert de Bailleul, brother-german to the above-mentioned Sir William de Bailleul; for he had made a promise to do this, to the Bishop of Liege, and was bound to execute it with his whole company. The Liegeois had passed Pont-à-Tressin, were foraging for their horses, and looking out to see if they could find any chance to profit by. The Hainaulters had rode on, and passed the bridge, without meeting with any one; for there was such a fog that they could not distinguish any thing at the distance of a lance's-length. When all had passed the bridge, they ordered Sir William de Bailleul and his banner to remain there, and Sir Vau-flart de la Croix, Sir Raflet de Monceaux, and Sir John de Verchin, to advance as far as the quarters of the King of Bohemia, and Bishop of Liege, which were near the bridge, and to attack them. The Lord of Rodemach had had the guard that night of the army of the King of Bohemia, and was on the point of retiring, when the light-horse of the Hainaulters appeared. They attacked them, as they came up, very valiantly; and they were repulsed also by the Liegeois. The conflict was sharp, and the Hainaulters behaved themselves well. To secure a retreat, however, to their banner, the Hainaulters drew toward the bridge, where they were followed by those of Liege and Luxembourg, and the engagement was renewed. Sir William de Bailleul was advised to recross the bridge with his banner, for many of his people remained there;

and many a gallant deed was performed, many a capture made, and many a rescue. Sir Vauflart, unluckily, was not able to gain the passage of the bridge : so he got out of the crowd, and saved himself the best way he could, by taking a road he was acquainted with, and hiding himself among thorns and quagmires, where he remained a considerable time. The rest still continued the combat ; but the Liegeois, and those from Luxembourg, had overthrown Sir William de Bailleul.

While this was passing, Sir Robert's company, who had been out foraging, returned, and, hearing the noise, came to the bridge. Sir Robert ordered his banner to advance, which was carried by a squire called James de Forsines, crying out, "Moriennes." The Hainaulters, who were much heated, perceiving the banner of Moriennes, which is quite straight, thought it was their own, which they had been ordered to rally under, for there is but very little difference between the two; the Morienne arms having bars counterbarred with two chevrons, gules, and the chevron of Sir Robert had on it a small cross or. The Hainaulters made a sad mistake, and ran into the midst of Sir Robert's troop, who received them most fiercely, repulsed and discomfited them. They lost, on their side, Sir John de Vargny, Sir Walter de Pont-à-l'Arche, Sir William de Pipempoix, Sir John de Soire, Sir Daniel de Bleze, Sir Race de Monceaux, Sir Lewis Dampelu, and many other knights and squires. Sir William de Bailleul saved himself in the best manner he could, but he lost a great many of his men. Sir Vauflart de la Croix, who hid himself among the reeds in the marshes, hoped to have remained there until the night, but he was perceived by some troopers who were riding through these marshes : they made such a shouting and noise, that Sir Vauflart

came out, and surrendered himself to them, who led him
to the army, and gave him up to their commander. He
detained him a whole day in his quarters, and would willingly, through pity, have saved him, as he knew his head
would probably suffer. But the King of France, having
heard of it, wished to take cognizance of it himself: so Sir
Vauflart was given up to him, and the king sent him to
Lisle, where, as he had done much harm to the inhabitants, they would not accept of any ransom, but put him
to death.

CHAPTER XXVII.

The Earl of Hainault attacks the Fortress of Mortagne in Various Manners.

THE King of France was much rejoiced at the arrival
of Sir Robert de Bailleul, and his defeat of the Hainaulters. Shortly afterwards, the Earl of Hainault, Sir
John his uncle the seneschal of Hainault, with full six
hundred lances, Hainaulters and Germans, set out from
the siege before Tournay. The earl had sent orders for
those of Valenciennes to take another route, and place
themselves between the Scarpe and the Scheld, to attack
the town of Mortagne. They came there in a large body,
and brought with them many engines, to throw things
into the place. I have before told how the Lord of Beaujeu had been sent thither as governor. He had expected
an attack, from the situation of Mortagne upon the Scheld,
and bordering upon Hainault, and had driven upward of
twelve hundred piles in the bed of the river to prevent its
navigation. It was not long before the earl and his Hainaulters arrived on one side of the town, and the Valen-

ciennois on the other. They made preparations for an immediate attack. The Valenciennois ordered their cross-bow-men to shoot, and to advance to the barriers; but they were unable to do so, on account of the wide and deep trenches which had been made before them. They then bethought themselves to cross the Scarpe at any rate below Château l'Abbaie, and, passing near St. Amand, to make an assault upon the gate which opens toward Mande. This they executed, and full four hundred troops crossed the river, and Mortagne's three gates were besieged. The weakest was certainly that leading to Mande: however, that was tolerably strong.

At that post the Lord of Beaujeu placed himself; for he knew that all the rest were safe. He had armed himself with a very stout lance, having the head of tempered steel, and on the under side a sharp hook, so that, when he made his stroke, he could fix the hook into the jackets or armor of those who attacked, draw them to him, and make them fall into the river. By this means, in the course of the day, he caught and destroyed more than twelve of the assailants. At this gate the conflict was much more severe than anywhere else, and the Earl of Hainault was ignorant of it: he was hard by toward Brisnal, drawn out in order of battle, upon the bank of the Scheld. The lords took counsel how they might draw out the piles, either by force or ingenuity, from the bed of the river, so that they might advance upon it up to the walls of the town. They ordered an engine to be made in a large vessel, for the purpose of drawing them out one after another, and all the carpenters were directly set upon this business. This same day the Valenciennois, on their part, erected a handsome engine, which cast stones into the town and castle, and much annoyed the inhabitants of

Mortagne. In this manner passed the first day and the following night. On the morrow they returned to the attack on all sides. The third day the vessel and engine were ready to draw out the piles, and those ordered to that duty were set to work; but they had so much trouble and labor in drawing out one, that the lords thought they should never accomplish it, and therefore made them desist. There was at that time a very able engineer at Mortagne, who, having considered the machine of the Valenciennois, and how much it annoyed the town, — for it was perpetually in action, — made another in the castle, which was not very large, but well made and tempered, and so well pointed that it was used only three times. The first stone fell within twelve paces of the engine of the Valenciennois; the second was nearer to the box; and the third was so well aimed that it struck the machine upon the shaft, and split it in two. The soldiers of Mortagne made a great shouting at this event. The Hainaulters were thus two days and two nights before Mortagne without conquering any part of it. The earl and his uncle thought it advisable to return toward Tournay, which they did; and the Valenciennois went back to their town whence they had come.

CHAPTER XXVIII.

THE EARL OF HAINAULT TAKES THE TOWN OF ST. AMAND DURING THE SIEGE OF TOURNAY.

THREE days after the Earl of Hainault had returned from before Mortagne, he made a request to his companions that they would come with him to St. Amand; for he had received many complaints of the soldiers of

St. Amand having burnt the monastery of Hanon, and of their attempt to do the same at Vicoigne, as well as of many other troubles which they had wrought upon the borders of Hainault. The earl set out from the siege of Tournay with three thousand combatants, and came before St. Amand by the way of Mortagne, which town was only enclosed with a palisade. A knight from Languedoc, and seneschal of Carcassonne, was governor of it; and he had told the monks of the abbey, as well as the inhabitants, that it was not tenable against any body of men, not that he meant to give it up, but on the contrary to defend it as long as he could, and mentioned it merely as a piece of information. These words were not much attended to, or believed: however, he had some time before sent to Mortagne all the jewels of the monastery, and thither went also the abbot and his monks, who were not very well calculated to defend themselves.

The Valenciennois, who had been ordered by the earl their lord to be before St. Amand on a certain day, came with twelve thousand combatants, and, posting themselves before the town, armed all the crossbow-men, and made them advance toward the bridge over the Scarpe. The conflict was here very sharp: it lasted all that day, without the Valenciennois being able to make any impression; but they had a great many of their men killed and wounded, and the besieged, mocking them, called out, "Go your ways, and drink your good ale." Towards the evening they retired from before the town, much wearied, and surprised that they had not heard any tidings of their lord. They called a council, and resolved to return back to their own town. On the morrow after their departure, the Earl of Hainault arrived, as has been said, by the way of Mortagne, and he immediately began the attack: it was so violent that the barriers were instantly won, and they advanced to the gate which opens toward Mortagne. The earl and his uncle headed this attack: they fought most valiantly, and spared none. Each of them at this place received two such blows from stones thrown down upon them, that their helmets were split through, and themselves stunned. One present then said to the earl, "Sir, we shall never do any thing effectual in this place, for the gate is very strong, the passage narrow, and it will cost you too many of your people to gain it; but if you will order some large beams of wood to be brought, and shod with iron in the manner of piles, and strike with them against the walls of the monastery, I will promise you that you will make breaches in many places. If once we get into the monastery, the town is ours, for there is nothing to stop us between it and the town." The earl ordered this advice to be followed; for he perceived it was reasonable, and the shortest method of getting possession of the town. Great beams of oak were brought, formed, and sharpened like piles; and to each were ordered twenty or thirty men, who, bearing it in their hands, retreated some paces, and then ran with it with great force against the wall, which they battered down in many places, so that they entered valiantly, and crossed a small rivulet.

The seneschal of Carcassonne was there, with his banner displayed before him, which was gules, with a chef argent, three chevrons in chief, and an indented border, argent; and near him were collected many companions from his own country, who received the Hainaulters very gallantly, and fought as well as they were able; but it was in vain, as they were overpowered by numbers. It may be worth remembering, that, on their entering the monastery, there remained a monk called Sir Froissart, who did wonders, killing and wounding, at one of the breaches where he had posted himself, upward of eighteen, so that no one durst venture to pass through. At last he was forced to fly, for he perceived that the Hainaulters were entering the monastery by various other breaches: the monk therefore made off as fast as he could, and saved himself in Mortagne. As soon as the earl, Sir John, and the knights of Hainault had entered the monastery, the earl ordered no quarter to be given, so much was he enraged at the violences they had committed in his territories. The town was soon filled with soldiers, who pursued all they met from street to street, and from house to house: very few escaped being put to death. The seneschal was slain under his banner, and upward of two hundred men with him. The earl returned that evening to Tournay.

On the morrow the men at arms of Valenciennes and the commonalty came to St. Amand, burnt the town, the monastery, and the great minster; breaking and destroying all the bells, of which there were numbers of very good and melodious ones. The Earl of Hainault made another excursion from the siege of Tournay, with about six hundred men at arms, in order to burn Orchies, Landas, and Le Celle. He afterwards crossed, with his army, the river Scarpe above Hanon, and, entering France, came before a large and rich monastery at Marchiennes, of which Sir Aymé de Vervaulx was governor, who had with him a detachment of crossbow-men from Douay. The attack was violent; for the knight had strongly fortified the first gate, which was surrounded by wide and deep ditches, and the French and monks withinside defer'd themselves valiantly. The Hainaulters exerted themselves much; and, having procured boats, they by this means gained entrance into the monastery : but a German knight, attached to the Lord of Fauquemont, was drowned ; his name was Sir Bacho de la Wiere. At the attack of the gate, the earl, his uncle the seneschal of Hainault, and many others, proved themselves such good knights, that the gate was gained, Sir Aymé slain, and the greater part of the others. Many monks who were there were captured, the monastery pillaged and burnt, as well as the village. The earl after this returned with his army to Tournay.

CHAPTER XXIX.

Sir Charles de Montmorency, and many others of the French, captured at Pont-à-Tressin.

THE siege of Tournay lasted a long time, and the town held out well; but the King of England thought he must gain it, for he knew that there were within it great numbers of men at arms, and a scarcity of provision, which would oblige them to yield through hunger. But others said that they would find supplies through the country of the Brabanters, who permitted frequent and large quantities of provisions to pass through their army, and even to enter the town. Those from Brussels and Louvain were quite weary of remaining there so long, and petitioned the marshal of their army for leave to return to Brabant. The marshal replied that he was very willing to consent to their departure, but they must leave their arms and accoutrements behind them. This made them so ashamed, that they never again repeated their request. During this siege, the Germans made an excursion toward Pont-à-Tressin, where Sir

Robert de Bailleul had defeated the Hainaulters. The Lord of Rauderondenc, Sir John of Rauderondenc his son (at that time a squire), Sir John de Randebourgh (a squire also, and tutor to the Lord of Rauderondenc's son), Sir Arnold de Bacqueghen, Sir Reginald d'Escouvenort, Sir Courrat d'Astra, Sir Bastien de Basties, Candrelier his brother, the Lord Strauren de Leurne, with many others, from the duchies of Juliers and Gueldres, held a conference together, and resolved to make an excursion on the morrow, by break of day ; for which purpose they armed and prepared themselves well that night.

Some knights bachelors from Hainault joined them ; among whom were Sir Florent de Beaurieu, Sir Latas de la Haye (marshal of the army), the Lord John of Hainault, Sir Oulphart de Guistelles, Sir Robert Glewes from the county of Los (at that time only a squire), and many more ; amounting altogether to upward of three hundred good men at arms. They came to Pont-à-Tressin, which they crossed without loss. They then held a council, on what would be the most advantageous plan for them to beat up and skirmish with the army of the French. It was determined that the Lord of Rauderondenc, and his son, Sir Henry de Kalkren, a mercenary knight, Sir Thilman de Saussy, Sir Oulphart de Guistelles, Sir l'Alleman of Hainault, Sir Robert Glewes, and Jacquelot de Thiaulx, should act as light-horse, and skirmish up to the tents of the French ; that the rest of the knights and squires, who might amount to three hundred, should remain at the bridge to keep and defend that pass in case of any attack. This advanced body then set out : they were forty persons altogether, well mounted upon handsome and strong chargers. They rode on till they came to the French camp, when they immediately dashed in, and began to cut down tents and pavilions, and do every possible damage by skirmishing with all that opposed them. That night two great barons, the Lord of Montmorency and the Lord of Saulieu, had the watch, and were with their guard when the Germans fell upon them. As soon as they heard the noise, they and their banners moved toward it.

When the Lord of Rauderondenc saw them approach, he turned his horse about, and ordered his pennon and his party to push for the bridge, the French following him closely. In this chase the French captured Sir Oulphart de Guistelles; for he could not follow their track, his sight being indifferent. He was surrounded by the enemy, and made prisoner, as were two esquires of the names of Mondrop and Jacquelot de Thiaulx. The French galloped after them, but the Germans escaped; and, being scarcely more than half an acre separated from them, they could plainly hear them crying out, "Ha, gentlemen! you shall not return as easy as you came." Then one of his party rode up to the Lord of Rauderondenc, and said, "Sir, consider what you are about, or the French will cut us off from the bridge." The Lord of Rauderondenc replied, "If they know one road to it, I know another;" and, turning to his right, led his party along a road tolerably well beaten, which brought them straight to the river before mentioned, which is very deep, and surrounded by marshes. On their coming thither they found they could not ford it, so that they must return, and pass over the bridge. The French, thinking to cut off and take the Germans, went on full gallop toward the bridge. When they were come near to it, and saw the large body of men waiting for them, they said to one another, "We are making a foolish pursuit, and may

easily lose more than we can gain;" upon which many
turned back, particularly the banner-bearer of the Lord
of Saulieu, as well as that lord himself. But the Lord
of Montmorency would not retire, but pushed forward
courageously, and with his party attacked the Germans.
This attack was very fierce on both sides, and each
party had many unhorsed. While they were engaged,
the light troops made a circuit, and fell upon their flank:
notwithstanding this, and the hard blows given, the French
stood their ground. But Sir Reginald d'Escouvenort,
knowing the banner of Montmorency, under which the
knight was, with sword in hand, dealing his blows about
him, came up on his right hand, and, with his left hand
seizing the reins of his horse, stuck spurs into his own,
and drew him out of the combat. The Lord of Montmorency gave many blows with his sword upon the
helmet and back of Sir Reginald, which at once broke
and received them. However, the Lord of Montmorency
remained his prisoner; and the Germans fought so well,
that they maintained their ground, and made fourscore
gentlemen prisoners. They then repassed the bridge
without hindrance, and returned to Tournay, where each
retired to his own quarters.

CHAPTER XXX.

THE SIEGE OF TOURNAY RAISED BY MEANS OF A TRUCE.

THE siege of Tournay had lasted a long time (eleven
weeks, all but three days), when the lady of John
de Valois — sister to the King of France, and mother to
the Earl of Hainault — took great pains with both parties

to make up a peace, so that they might separate without a battle. The good lady had frequently, on her knees, besought it of the King of France. She at last so far prevailed, by the help and assistance of the Lord Lewis d'Augimont, who was well beloved by both parties, that a day was fixed for a negotiation, when each of the parties was to send five well-qualified persons to treat upon the best means of bringing about a reconciliation. These commissioners were to meet at a chapel situated in the fields, called Esplotin. On the day appointed, having heard mass, they assembled after dinner, and took the lady with them. When they had all entered this chapel, they saluted each other most politely, with every mark of respect : they then began on the business. This first day, however, passed away without any thing being decided. The next day they came to their appointment, began on the treaty as before, and fell upon some arrangement that seemed likely to end to their mutual satisfaction. The third day these lords returned, and agreed upon a truce, to last for one year, between the kings and all the allies that were present.

The truce was immediately proclaimed in each army, to the great joy of the Brabanters, who were heartily tired of the siege. The day after, at daybreak, tents and pavilions were struck, wagons loaded, and every one in motion to depart.

Thus the good city of Tournay remained unhurt ; but it had a narrow escape, for there were no more provisions in it than would have been sufficient for three or four days.

CHAPTER XXXI.

KING EDWARD INSTITUTES THE ORDER OF ST. GEORGE, AT WINDSOR.

ABOUT this time the King of England resolved to rebuild and embellish the great castle of Windsor, which King Arthur had first founded in time past, and where he had erected and established that noble Round Table from which so many gallant knights had issued forth, and displayed the valiant prowess of their deeds at arms over the world. King Edward therefore determined to establish an order of knighthood, consisting of himself, his children, and the most gallant knights in Christendom, to the number of forty. He ordered it to be denominated "knights of the blue garter," and that the feast should be celebrated every year at Windsor, upon St. George's Day. He summoned, therefore, all the earls, barons, and knights of his realm, to inform them of his intentions. They heard it with great pleasure; for it appeared to them highly honorable, and capable of increasing love and friendship. Forty knights were then elected, according to report and estimation the bravest in Christendom, who sealed and swore to maintain and keep the feast and the statutes which had been made. The king founded a chapel at Windsor, in honor of St. George, and established canons there to serve God, with a handsome endowment. He then issued his proclamation for this feast by his heralds, whom he sent to France, Scotland, Burgundy, Hainault, Flanders, Brabant, and the empire of Germany; and offered to all knights and squires that might come to this ceremony passports to last for fifteen days after it was over. The celebration of this order was fixed for St. George's Day next ensuing, to be held at Windsor, 1344; and the queen was to be present, accompanied by three hundred ladies and damsels, all of high birth, and richly dressed in similar robes.

CHAPTER XXXII.

THE KING OF ENGLAND SETS AT LIBERTY SIR HERVÉ DE LÉON.

WHILE the King of England was employed in making preparations for the reception of the lords and ladies whom he expected at this feast, news was brought him of the death of the Lord of Clisson and the other knights. He was so much enraged at it, that he had determined to retaliate upon the body of Sir Hervé de Léon, who was his prisoner; and would surely have executed it, if the Earl of Derby, his cousin, had not remonstrated, and showed in council such good reasons, as, for the sake of his own personal honor, induced him to refrain from this revenge. He added, "My lord, if that King Philip has, through rashness, had the villany to put to death such valiant knights as these were, do not suffer your courage to be tainted by it; for in truth, if you will but consider a little, your prisoner has nothing to do with this outrage: have a goodness, therefore, to give him his liberty at a reasonable ransom." The king ordered the captive knight to be brought before him, and said, "Ha, Sir Hervé, Sir Hervé! my adversary Philip de Valois has shown his treachery in too cruel a manner, when he put to death so many knights. It has given me much displeasure, and it appears as it were done in despite of us. If I were to take his conduct for my example, I ought to do the like to you, for you have done me more harm in Brittany than any other; but I shall endure it, and let him act according to his own will. I will preserve my own honor unspotted, and shall allow you your liberty at a trifling ransom, out of my love for the Earl of Derby, who has requested it; but upon condition that you perform what I am going to ask of you." The knight replied, "Dear sir, I will do, to the best of my power, whatever you shall command." The king said, "I know, Sir Hervé, that you are one of the richest knights in Brittany; and, if I were to press you, you would pay me thirty or forty thousand crowns for your ransom. But you will go to King Philip de Valois, my adversary, and tell him from me, that, by putting so many knights to death in so dishonorable a manner, he has sore displeased me; and I say and maintain, that he has by this means broken and infringed the truce which we had agreed to, and that from this moment I consider it as broken, and send him by you my defiance. In consideration of your carrying this message, I will let you off for ten thousand crowns, which you will pay, or send to Bruges, in five days after you shall have crossed the sea. You will also inform all such knights and squires as wish to attend my feast (for we shall be right glad to see them) not to desist on this account, for they shall have passports for their safe return, to last for fifteen days after it be over." — "Sir," answered the knight, "I will perform your message to the best of my abilities; and God reward you and my Lord of Derby for your kindness to me!"

Sir Hervé de Léon did not after this remain long in prison, but, having taken leave of the king, went to Southampton, and embarked on board a vessel, with the intention of landing at Harfleur. A violent storm, however, which lasted fifteen days, prevented it. He lost his horses, as well as those of his servants, which were thrown overboard; and he himself was so ill by it, that he never after enjoyed good health. At last the mariners, with much danger, landed at Crotoy, from whence Sir Hervé and his suite went on foot to Abbeville, where they procured horses; but Sir Hervé was so ill, he could not bear the motion of the horse. He was therefore put in a litter, and came to Paris, to King Philip, to whom he delivered his message word for word. But he did not live long. He died in returning to his own country, in the city of Angers. God have mercy on his soul!

CHAPTER XXXIII.

THE KING OF ENGLAND SENDS THE EARL OF DERBY TO MAKE WAR IN GASCONY.

ST. GEORGE'S DAY drew near, when the grand feast was to be celebrated at the castle of Windsor. The king had made great preparations for it; and there were earls, barons, ladies, and damsels most nobly entertained. The festivities and tilts lasted a fortnight. Many knights came to them from beyond sea, from Flanders, Hainault, and Brabant, but not one from France. During the holding of these feasts the king received intelligence from different countries, particularly from Gascony. The Lord de l'Esparre, the Lord de Chaumont, the Lord de Mucident, were sent thence by the other barons and knights who at that time were dependent on the King of England; such as the Lord d'Albret, the Lord de Pumiers, the Lord de Montferrant, the Lord of Duras, the Lord of Craton, the Lord of Grailley, and many others; and some were likewise sent by the cities of Bordeaux and Bayonne. These ambassadors were most courteously entertained and received by the king and his council; to whom they explained the weakness of the country of Gascony, and that his good friends in that country and the loyal city of Bordeaux wanted aid: they therefore entreated that he would send thither such a captain and force of men at arms as he might think able to make head against the French, who kept the field in opposition to all that were sent to meet them. The king soon afterwards appointed his cousin the Earl of Derby leader of this expedition, and nominated those knights that he had fixed upon to be under him: first the Earl of Pembroke, the Earl of Oxford, the Lord Stafford, Sir Walter Manny, Sir Frank van Halle, Sir Henry Eam of Brabant, Sir Richard Fitzsimon, Sir Hugh Hastings, Sir Stephen Tombey, Sir Richard Haydon, Sir John Norwich, Sir Richard Radcliffe, Sir Robert Oxendon, and several more. They were fully three hundred knights and squires, six hundred men at arms, and two thousand archers. The king advised the earl his cousin to take plenty of gold and silver with him, and to bestow it liberally among the knights and squires, in order to acquire their good opinion and affection.

The king also, during the time of these festivals, sent Sir Thomas Dagworth into Brittany to re-enforce the Countess of Montfort, and assist her in preserving that country; for, notwithstanding the truce, he doubted not but that King Philip would begin the war on account of the message he had sent to him by Sir Hervé de Léon. He therefore despatched thither one hundred men at arms, and two hundred archers under the command of Sir Thomas. He likewise ordered the Earl of Salisbury into

the county of D'ulnestre ; for the Scots had rebelled
against him, had burnt much in Cornwall, and had advanced as far as Bristol, and besieged the town of D'ulnestre. However, the Earl of Salisbury marched thither,
with three hundred men at arms and six hundred archers
well appointed. Thus the king sent forth his people, and
directed his treasurers to deliver out to the commanding
officers a sufficiency of money for their own expenses, and
to pay their fellow-soldiers ; and each set out according to
the orders he had received.

We will speak first of the Earl of Derby, as he had
the greatest charge, which he conducted to Southampton,
and, embarking on board the fleet stationed there for him,
made sail for Bayonne. It was a handsome city, and had
always held out for the English. He arrived there, without accident, on the sixth day of June, 1344, when he disembarked, and landed his stores. They were joyfully received by the inhabitants, and he remained there seven
days to refresh himself and his horses. The Earl of
Derby and his army left Bayonne the eighth day after his
arrival, and set out for Bordeaux, where a grand procession
came out to receive him. The earl was lodged in the Abbey of St. Andrew, and his people within the city. When
the Count de Lisle was informed of the arrival of the
English, he sent for the Count de Comminges, the Count
de Perigord, the Count de Carmain, the Viscount de Villemur, the Count Duras, the Count de Valentinois, the
Count de Mirande, the Lord of Mirade, the Lord de la
Barde, the Lord of Pincornet, the Viscount de Châtillon,
the Lord of Chateauneuf, the Lord de Lescun, the Abbot
of St. Savin, and for all the other lords who were attached
to the King of France. As soon as they were all assembled, he demanded their counsel on the arrival of the Earl

•of Derby. The lords in reply said they were sufficiently strong to defend the passage of the river Dordogne, at Bergerac, against the English. This answer mightily pleased the Count de Lisle, who was at that time like a king in Gascony, and had been so since the commencement of the wars between the two kings. He had taken the field, captured towns and castles, and waged war upon all who were of the English army. These lords sent immediately to assemble their dependants on all sides, and advanced to Bergerac, where they entered the suburbs, which are large, strong, and partly surrounded by the Dordogne. They had all their purveyances brought to them there in safety.

CHAPTER XXXIV.

The Earl of Derby conquers Bergerac.

WHEN the Earl of Derby had remained at Bordeaux for about fifteen days, he was informed that the barons and knights of Gascony were in Bergerac: he therefore one morning marched that way with his army, and ordered his marshals, Sir Walter Manny and Sir Frank van Halle, to push forward. The English marched that morning no more than three leagues, to a castle called Montcroullier, which belonged to them, and was situated a short league from Bergerac. At this castle of Montcroullier they tarried that day and night. The day following, their scouts were sent as far as the barriers of Bergerac; and on their return they related to Sir Walter Manny that they had reconnoitred the position of the French, which did not appear to them any thing very for-

midable. This day the English dined early ; and during
the repast Sir Walter Manny, addressing himself to the
Earl of Derby, said, " My lord, if we were good knights,
and well armed, we might this evening partake of the
wines of these French lords who are garrisoned in Bergerac." The earl answered that it should not be his fault
if they did not. When their companions heard this they
said, " Let us hasten to arm ourselves ; for we will ride
toward Bergerac." It was no sooner said than done : they
were all armed and mounted in an instant. When the
Earl of Derby perceived such willingness in his men, he
was exceedingly joyful, and cried out, "In the name of
God and of St. George, let us march to our enemies ! "
They then rode on, with banners displayed, during the
greatest heat of the day, until they came to the barriers
of Bergerac ; which was not a place easily to be taken, for
a part of the river Dordogne surrounded it. The French
lords who were in the town, seeing the English coming to
attack them, said they should be well received, and sallied
forth in battle-array : they had with them a multitude of
foot-soldiers, and country-people badly armed. The English made their approaches in close order, so that they
were plainly to be distinguished by the townsmen, and the
archers began to shoot thickly. When the foot-soldiers
felt the points of the arrows, and saw the banners and
pennons glittering in the air, which they had not been
accustomed to see, they fell back upon their men at arms.
The archers continued to shoot with great quickness,
doing much mischief to them. The lords of England then
advanced, mounted on their excellent coursers, with lances
in rests, and, dashing into the midst of their infantry,
drove them down at pleasure, and killed and wounded the
French men at arms in abundance ; for they could not in

any way exert themselves, as these runaways had blocked up the road.

Thus were those of Bergerac driven back again to the suburbs ; but with so much loss that the first bridge and bars were taken by storm, and the English entered with them. Upon the pavement were many knights and squires slain and wounded, and many prisoners made of those who came forward to defend the passage. The Lord of Mirepoix was slain under the banner of Sir Walter Manny, who was the first that entered the suburbs. When the Count de Lisle saw that the English had got possession of the suburbs, and were knocking down and killing his people without mercy, he and the other lords of Gascony made a handsome retreat towards the town, and passed the bridge with great difficulty. At this place the engagement was very severe, and lasted a considerable time : the noblemen of France and of England, named in the preceding chapters, combated most valiantly, hand to hand. Neither knight nor bachelor could there conceal himself. Sir Walter Manny had advanced so far among his enemies, that he was in great danger. The English made prisoners of the Viscount de Bousquetin, the Lords of Châtillon, of Chateauneuf, and of Lescun. The French retreated into the fort, let down the portcullis, and, getting upon the battlements, began to throw stones and other things to drive their enemies away. This assault and skirmish lasted until vespers, when the English retreated, quite weary, into the suburbs which they had won ; where they found such quantities of provision and wine as might on occasion have lasted them most plentifully for four months.

When the morrow dawned, the Earl of Derby had his trumpets sounded, and his forces drawn out in battle-array, to approach the town, and make a mighty assault, which lasted till noon. They had not much success; for they found that there were within it men who defended themselves valiantly. At noontide the English retreated, perceiving that they only lost their time. The lords then assembled in council, and determined to attack the town on the side next the river, for it was there fortified only by palisades. The Earl of Derby sent, therefore, to the fleet at Bordeaux for vessels, which he ordered to come to him up the Dordogne: there were upward of sixty barks and other vessels lying at Bordeaux, that came to Bergerac. In the evening of the following day the English made their arrangements; and at sunrise all those who were ordered to attack the town, as well as the fleet, were quite ready, under the command- of the Lord Stafford. There were many knights and squires who had requested to be on this expedition, in hopes of preferment, as well as a body of archers. They advanced in haste, and came to some large round piles placed before the palisades, which they flung down. The townsmen, seeing this, went to the Count de Lisle, the lords, knights, and squires who were present, and said to them, "Gentlemen, we pray you to take heed what you are about; for we run a great risk of being ruined. If the town be taken, we shall lose all we have, as well as our lives. It will therefore be much better that we surrender it to the Earl of Derby, before we suffer more damage." The count replied, "We will go to that quarter where the danger is; for we will not consent to surrender it so easily." The Gascon knights and squires came, therefore, to defend the palisades; but the archers who were in the barks kept up so vigorous an attack with their arrows, that none dared to show themselves, unless they chose to run the risk of

being either killed or wounded. In the town there were
with the Gascons two or three hundred Genoese crossbow-men, whose armor shielded them from the arrows.
They kept the archers well employed all the day, and
many on each side were wounded. At last the English
who were in the vessels exerted themselves so much that
they broke down a large piece of the palisade : those of
Bergerac then retreated, and requested time to consider
if they should not surrender the place.

The remainder of that day and night was granted them,
upon condition that they should not attempt to repair the
breaches ; and every one retired to his quarters. The
lords of Gascony held that night a long council ; and
about midnight, having packed up all their baggage, they
set out from Bergerac, and followed the road to La Réole,
which is not far distant, whose gates were opened to
them ; and there they took up their quarters.

The English, on the morrow morning, re-embarked on
board their fleet, and came to the part where the palisades
had been broken down. They found in that place great
numbers of the townsmen, who entreated the knights that
they would beseech the Earl of Derby to have mercy on
them, and allow them their lives and fortunes, and thence-
forward they would yield obedience to the King of England. The Earl of Pembroke and the Earl of Oxford
replied that they would cheerfully comply with their
request ; and went to the Earl of Derby, who was not
present, and related to him what the inhabitants of Bergerac had desired of them. The Earl of Derby answered,
"He who begs for mercy should have mercy shown him :
tell them to open their gates, and let us enter, and we
will assure them of safety from us and from our people."
The two lords returned, and reported what the earl had

said. Upon which the townsmen went to the market-
place, where every one, men and women, being assembled,
they rang the bells, threw open the gates, went out in
procession to meet the Earl of Derby, and with all humility conducted him to the church, where they swore
homage and fealty to him, acknowledging him as their
lord, for the King of England, by virtue of a procuration which he had with him.

CHAPTER XXXV.

The Count de Lisle, Lieutenant for the King of France, in Gascony, lays Siege to the Castle of Auberoche.

WE will now return to the Count de Lisle, whom we
left in La Réole. As soon as he was informed that
the Earl of Derby had returned to Bordeaux, and had
taken up his residence there, he did not think it probable
he would undertake any more expeditions this season.
He sent letters therefore to the Earls of Perigord, of Carmain, of Comminges, of Bruniguel, and to all the barons
of Gascony that were in the French interest, to desire
that they would collect as many people as they could, and
come with them properly armed, by an appointed time, to
meet him at Auberoche, as he intended to besiege it.
They all obeyed his summons; for he was as a king in
these parts of Gascony. The knights who were in Auberoche were not aware of this until they found themselves
so closely besieged on all sides that no one could go out
of the garrison without being seen. The French brought
from Toulouse four large machines, which cast stones into
the fortress night and day; and they made no other

assault: so that in six days' time they had demolished all
the roofs of the towers, and none within the castle dared
to venture out of the vaulted rooms on the ground-floor.
It was the intention of the army to kill all within the castle,
if they would not surrender themselves unconditionally.

News was brought to the Earl of Derby, that Auberoche
was besieged; but he did not imagine his friends were so
hard pushed. When Sir Frank van Halle, Sir Alain de
Finefroide, and Sir John Lendal, who were thus besieged,
saw how desperate their situation was, they asked their
servants if there were not one among them who would,
for a reward, undertake to deliver the letters they had
written to the Earl of Derby at Bordeaux. One from
among them stepped forward, and said he would be the
man who would cheerfully undertake the commission, not
through lust of gain, but from his desire to deliver them
from the peril they were in. The following night the
servant took the letters, sealed with their seals, and sewed
them up in his clothes. He was let down into the
ditches: when he was at the bottom, he climbed up the
opposite side, and took his road through the army, for he
could not avoid passing through it. He was met by the
first guard, but was not stopped, for he understood the
Gascon language well, and named one of the lords of
the army, as if belonging to him; so he was suffered to
pass on: but he was afterwards arrested, and detained
under the tents of some other lords, who brought him to
the main watch. He was interrogated, searched, and the
letters found upon him, and guarded until morning, when
the principals of the army assembled in the tent of the
Count de Lisle, where the letters were read. They were
rejoiced to find that the garrison were so much straitened
that they could not hold out longer; and, seizing the

How the French flung a Servant over the Walls into Auberoche.

servant, they hung the letters round his neck, thrust him into one of the machines, and flung him into Auberoche. The valet fell quite dead amid the other valets of the castle, who were much terrified at it.

About this time the Earl of Perigord, his uncle Sir Charles de Poitiers, the Earl of Carmain, and the Lord of Duras, mounting their horses, rode as near to the walls of the castle as they could, and, calling out to those within by way of derision, said, "Gentlemen, inquire of your messenger where he found the Earl of Derby, and whether he is prepared to assist you, since your man was so eager to quit your fortress, and has returned as quickly." Sir Frank van Halle replied, "By my faith, gentlemen, if we be so closely confined in this place, we will sally forth whenever it shall please God and the Earl of Derby. I wish to heaven he were acquainted with our situation, for, if he were, the proudest of you all would be afraid of standing your ground ; and, if you will send any one to give him this information, one of us will surrender himself to you, to be ransomed as becomes a gentleman." The French answered, "Nay, nay, matters must not turn out so. The Earl of Derby, in proper time, shall be made acquainted with it ; but not until our engines have battered your walls level with the ground, and you shall have surrendered yourselves to save your lives." — "That, for certain, will never happen," said Sir Frank van Halle ; "for we will not surrender ourselves, should we all die upon the walls." The French lords then rode on, and returned to their army. The three English knights remained in Auberoche, quite confounded by the force of these engines, which flung such quantities of stones that in truth it seemed as if the thunder from heaven were battering the walls of the castle.

CHAPTER XXXVI.

THE EARL OF DERBY MAKES THE COUNT OF LISLE AND NINE MORE
COUNTS AND VISCOUNTS PRISONERS BEFORE AUBEROCHE.

ALL these speeches, the treatment of the messenger,
the contents of the letters, and the perilous situation
of Auberoche, were known to the Earl of Derby by means
of a spy he had in the French army. The earl therefore
sent orders to the Earl of Pembroke in Bergerac to meet
him at an appointed place and hour; and also to the Lord
Stafford and Sir Stephen Tombey, who were at Libourne.
The Earl of Derby then, accompanied by Sir Walter
Manny and the forces he had with him, took the road to
Auberoche as secretly as possible; for he had guides who
were acquainted with all the by-roads. They came to
Libourne, where they waited a whole day for the Earl of
Pembroke; but hearing no tidings of him, and being im-
patient to succor their friends who were so distressed, the
Earl of Derby, the Earl of Oxford, Sir Walter Manny, Sir
Richard Hastings, Sir Stephen Tombey, the Lord Ferrers,
and other knights, set out from Libourne: riding all night,
they came on the morrow within two leagues of Auberoche.
They entered a wood; when, alighting from their horses,
they tied them to the trees, and allowed them to pasture,
in expectation of the arrival of the Earl of Pembroke.
They waited all that morning, and until noon, in vain, not
knowing what to do; for they were but three hundred
lances and six hundred archers, and the French were from
ten to twelve thousand men. They thought it would be
cowardice to suffer their friends to be lost, when they

were so near them. At last Sir Walter Manny said, "Gentlemen, let us who are now here mount our horses, skirt this wood, and advance until we come to their camp : when we shall be close to it, we will stick spurs into our horses, and, with loud shouts, fall upon them. It will be about their hour for supper; and we shall see them so much discomfited, that they can never rally again." The knights present replied that they would all do as he had proposed. Each went to his horse, re-girthed him, and tightened his armor : they ordered their pages, servants, and baggage to remain where they were.

They advanced in silence by the side of the wood until they came to the other end, where the French army was encamped in a wide valley, near a small river : they then displayed their banners and pennons, and, sticking spurs into their horses, dashed into the midst of the French and Gascon forces, who were quite confounded and unprepared for this attack, as they were busy about their suppers, many having set down to table. The English were well prepared to act; and crying, "Derby, Derby forever!" they cut down tents and pavilions, and slew and wounded all that came in their way. The French did not know where to turn, so much were they surprised ; and when they got into the plains, if there were any large body of them, the archers and crossbow-men made such good use of their weapons that they were slain or dispersed. The Count de Lisle was taken in his tent, badly wounded ; the Earl of Perigord in his pavilion, and also Sir Charles his uncle ; the Lord of Duras was killed, and so was Sir Aymery de Poitiers, but his brother the Earl of Valentinois was made prisoner. Every one took to his heels as fast as he could ; but the Earl of Comminges, the Earls of Carmain, Villemur, and Bruniguel, the Lords de la

Barde and de la Taride, with others, who were quartered on the opposite side of the castle, displayed their banners, and, having drawn up their men, marched for the plain: the English, however, who had already defeated the largest body of the army, fell upon them most vigorously. In this engagement many gallant deeds of arms were performed, many captures made, and many rescues. As soon as Sir Frank van Halle and Sir John Lendal, who were in Auberoche, heard the noise, and perceived the banners and pennons of their friends, they hastened to arm themselves, and all those that were with them; when, mounting their horses, they sallied out of the fortress, made for the plain, and dashed into the thickest of the combat, to the great encouragement of the English.

Why should I make a long story of it? All those who were of the Count de Lisle's party were discomfited, and almost all taken prisoners or slain. Scarcely any would have escaped, if night had not closed so soon. Nine earls and viscounts were made prisoners, and so many barons, knights, and squires, that there was not a man at arms among the English that had not for his share two or three. This battle before Auberoche was fought on the eve of St. Laurence's Day, in the year 1344. The English treated their prisoners like friends: they received many upon their promises to surrender themselves by a certain day at Bordeaux or Bergerac. The English retired into Auberoche; and the Earl of Derby entertained at supper the greater part of the prisoners, — earls, viscounts, barons, and knights. They gave thanks and praises to God for having enabled them to overcome upward of ten thousand men, when they themselves were not more than one thousand, including every one; and to rescue the town of Auberoche, in which were their friends, that must have been captured in two days' time. On the next morning, a little after sunrise, the Earl of Pembroke arrived with three hundred lances and four thousand archers. He had been informed of the event of the battle as they came along, and said to the Earl of Derby, "Certainly, cousin, you have neither been courteous, nor behaved honorably, to fight my enemies without waiting for me, seeing that you had sent for me ; and you might have been assured that nothing should have prevented my coming to you." The earl replied, " Fair cousin, we were very anxious for your arrival, and we waited for you from the morning until vespers. When we saw no appearance of your coming, we dared not wait longer ; for, had our enemies been informed of our arrival, they would have had the advantage over us. But now, thanks to God, we have conquered them, and we pray of you to help us in conducting them to Bordeaux." They remained that day and night in Auberoche : on the next day early they were armed and mounted, and set off, leaving there a Gascon knight in their interest, as governor, named the Lord Alexander of Chaumont. They took the road to Bordeaux, and carried with them the greater part of their prisoners.

CHAPTER XXXVII.

THE EARL OF DERBY TAKES DIFFERENT TOWNS IN GASCONY, IN HIS ROAD TOWARD LA RÉOLE.

THE Earl of Derby and his army, upon their arrival at Bordeaux, were received with very great rejoicings : the inhabitants thought they never could enough testify their joy to the earl and to Sir Walter Manny for their enterprise, in which the Count de Lisle and more than two hundred knights were made prisoners. The winter passed over without any action taking place in Gascony that is worthy of being recorded. Easter, which may be reckoned the beginning of the year 1345, was about the middle of May; and the Earl of Derby, who had tarried all the winter in Bordeaux, collected a very large body of men at arms and archers, and declared he would make an expedition to La Réole, where the French had fixed their headquarters. He went the first day from Bordeaux to Bergerac, where he found the Earl of Pembroke ready with his troops. These two noblemen, with their forces, remained for three days in Bergerac, and on the fourth departed. When they were got into the open country they halted their men, counted them, and found that they had about a thousand men at arms and two thousand archers. They pushed forward until they came to a castle called St. Basile, to which they laid siege. Those within, considering that the principal barons of Gascony were prisoners, and that they had no expectations of receiving succors from any place, resolved to swear fealty to King Edward of England. The Earl of Derby continued his route, and took the road toward Aiguillon; but before he arrived there he came to the castle of Rochemilon, which was well provided with soldiers and artillery; nevertheless the earl ordered it to be vigorously assaulted. As the English advanced to the attack, those within threw down upon them stones, bars of iron, and pots full of hot lime, by which many were slain and wounded who adventured themselves too rashly.

When the Earl of Derby perceived that his men were laboring in vain, and getting themselves killed without any advantage, he sounded a retreat. On the morrow he

ordered the peasants to bring great quantities of brushwood, fagots, straw, and turf, and to throw them all into
the ditches of the castle, and plenty of earth with them.
When a part of the ditch was so filled that one might get
to the foot of the walls, he assembled three hundred archers, well armed and in battle-array, and sent before them
two hundred countrymen, covered with shields, having
large pickaxes and hooks : while these first were employed
in picking the walls, the archers made such good use of
their bows that no one dared to show himself on the battlements. This lasted the greatest part of the day, when
the pickaxe-men made so large a breach in the walls, that
ten men might enter abreast. The inhabitants of the
town and castle were quite confounded : some fled toward
the church, and others by a back way out of the town.
The fortress was immediately taken and pillaged, and all
the garrison were put to death, excepting such as had
taken refuge in the church, whom the Earl of Derby pardoned, for they had submitted to his mercy. The earl
placed in the castle a fresh garrison, under the command
of two English captains, Richard Willes and Robert Scot ;
and then he came before Monsegur, where he ordered his
men to prepare huts for themselves and horses : he continued before it fifteen days.

The governor of the town was Sir Hugh de Bastefol,
and there never passed a day without some assault being
made upon it. They sent for large machines from Bordeaux and Bergerac ; and the stones which they cast into
the town destroyed roofs, tiles, and the principal buildings.
The Earl of Derby sent every day to let them know, that,
if they suffered the town to be stormed, every one would
be put to the sword ; but, if they would render obedience
to the King of England, he would pardon them, and treat

them like friends. The townsmen would cheerfully have
surrendered, and they went to the governor to consult
him, and to sound his intentions ; who answered them by
ordering them to the battlements, for that he had provision of every sort in sufficiency to hold out for half a year
if it were necessary. They left him in apparent good
humor ; but about the time of vespers they seized him,
and closely confined him, assuring him, at the same time,
he should never be set at liberty if he did not assist them
to make some terms with the Earl of Derby. When he
had sworn that he would do every thing in his power, they
let him go : he went directly to the barriers of the town,
and made signs that he wished to speak with the Earl of
Derby. Sir Walter Manny being present came to the
governor, who said to him, " Sir Walter Manny, you ought
not to be surprised if we shut our gates against you, for
we have sworn fealty to the King of France ; but not perceiving any one coming from him to stop your career, and
believing that you will still proceed further, — for these
reasons, in behalf of myself and the inhabitants of this
town, we wish you would allow us these terms : namely,
that no hostilities be carried on against us for the space
of one month ; and if in that time the King of France or
the Duke of Normandy come into this country in such
force as to give you battle, we then shall hold ourselves
free from our engagement ; but, if neither of them come,
we will then enter under the obedience of the King of
England."

Sir Walter Manny went to relate this proposal to the
Earl of Derby, who acceded to it upon condition that
there should not in the mean time be any repairs made to
the fortifications of the town, and that, if any of the English army should want provisions, they might be at liberty

to purchase them. Upon this there were sent twelve of the principal citizens as hostages, who were ordered to Bordeaux. The English refreshed themselves with provisions from the town, but none were suffered to enter it. They then continued their march, burning and destroying all the country as far as Aiguillon, the governor of which place came out to meet the earl, and surrendered the town and castle to him, on condition of their lives and fortunes being spared; to the great astonishment of all the country, for it was one of the strongest castles in the world, and almost impregnable. When the squire who had thus surrendered Aiguillon came to Toulouse, which is seventeen leagues distant, the townsmen arrested him on suspicion of treason, and hung him. This castle is situated on the point between two navigable rivers. The earl ordered it to be re-victualled, and the fortifications repaired, in order to its being fit to receive him on his return, and that it might serve for a secure guard to his other possessions. He gave the command of it to Sir John de Gombry. He then came to a castle called Segart, which he took by storm, and put all the foreign soldiers he found in it to death: from thence he came to the town of La Réole.

CHAPTER XXXVIII.

THE EARL OF DERBY LAYS SIEGE TO LA RÉOLE, WHICH SURRENDERS TO HIM.

WHEN the Earl of Derby was arrived at La Réole, he encompassed it closely all round, erecting towers in the plains, and near to every road, that no provision of any kind could enter it. He caused it to be assaulted almost every day. This siege took up much of the summer; and, when the time had expired which those of Monsegur had fixed for surrendering themselves, the Earl of Derby sent thither, and the inhabitants of the town became liegemen to the earl, who in all these cases was the representative of the King of England. Even Sir Hugh de Bastefol served under the earl with the men of Monsegur, for a certain salary, which he received from the said earl, for himself and his fellow-soldiers. The English who were besieging La Réole had lain before it more than nine weeks, and had constructed two large towers of great beams of wood, three stories high: each tower was placed on wheels, and covered over with prepared leather, to shelter those within from fire and from the arrows. In each story were one hundred archers. These two towers, by dint of men's force, were pushed close to the walls of the town; for during the time they were building they had filled up the ditches, so that these towers could easily pass over them. Those that were in them began immediately to shoot so well and quick, that none dared to appear upon the battlements unless he were well armed, or had a shield. Between these two towers were posted two hundred men with pickaxes and bars, to make a breach in the walls; which they did, and cast away the stones. The inhabitants, seeing this, came upon the walls, and inquired for some of the chiefs of the army to speak to them. The Earl of Derby, being informed of it, sent thither Sir Walter Manny and the Lord Stafford, who found the townsmen willing to surrender the town, on condition of their lives and fortunes being spared.

When the governor, Sir Agos de Bans, a Provençal, found that the inhabitants wanted to surrender the town, he retired into the castle of La Réole with his fellow-soldiers ; and, while this treaty was going on, he had conveyed into it great quantities of wine and other provision. He then ordered the gates to be fastened, and said he would never surrender in so shameful a manner. The two knights returned to the Earl of Derby, and related to him that the townsmen were desirous of surrendering upon the terms above named ; the earl sent them back, to know what the governor's intentions were respecting the castle. They returned with the answer, that he had shut himself up in the castle, and would not yield it. After a little consideration the earl said, " Well, well, let us have compassion on the inhabitants : by means of the town, we shall soon gain the castle." The knights again went to the townsmen, and received their submissions. They all came out to the plain, and, presenting the keys of the town to the earl, said, " Dear sir, from this day forward, we acknowledge ourselves as your loyal subjects, and place ourselves, in every respect, under the obedience of the King of England." They swore by their heads, that they would not in any manner assist or succor those in the castle, but, on the contrary, distress them all in their power. The earl forbade, under pain of death, that any ·hurt should be done toward the inhabitants of La Réole. He then entered it with his army, and, surrounding the castle, erected all his machines against it ; but they did little mischief, for the castle was very high and built of a hard stone. It was erected a long time since by the Saracens, who laid the foundations so strong, and with such curious workmanship, that the buildings of our time cannot be compared to it. When the earl found that his machines had no effect, he commanded them to desist ; and, as he was not without miners in his army, he ordered them to undermine the ditches of the castle so that they might pass beneath. This was not soon done, however.

CHAPTER XXXIX.

Sir Walter Manny finds in La Réole the Sepulchre of his Father.

WHILE they were lying before this castle, and miners only could be employed, Sir Walter Manny was reminded of his father, who formerly had been murdered in his journey from St. James of Compostella; he had heard in his infancy that he had been buried in La Réole or that neighborhood. He therefore made inquiries in the town, if there were any one who could inform him of the truth of this matter; and offered a hundred crowns to him who should conduct him to the spot. This brought forward an old man, who said to Sir Walter Manny, "Certainly, sir: I think I can lead you to the place where your father was buried, or very near to it." Sir Walter replied, "If you prove your words true I will stick to my bargain, and even go beyond it."

To explain this matter more clearly, you must know that there was formerly a bishop of Cambray, a Gascon, and of the families of Buc and Mirefoix; and, during the time of his holding that see, a magnificent tournament was held at Cambray, where there were upwards of five hundred knights. A knight from Gascony tilted with the Lord of Manny, the father of Sir Walter: the Gascon knight was so roughly handled and wounded that he never enjoyed his health afterwards, but died. His death was laid to the door of the Lord of Manny, and the bishop and his kindred vowed revenge for it. Two or three years after, some good-hearted people endeavored to reconcile them; and peace was agreed to, on condition that the Lord of Manny should make a pilgrimage to St. James of Compostella by way of penance.

During the time of this journey the Earl Charles of Valois, brother to King Philip the Fair, was besieging La Réole, and had been there some time; for it appertained, as well as many other cities and towns, to the King of England, the father of him who besieged Tournay: so that the Lord of Manny, on his return, went to visit the Earl Charles of Valois, — as William Earl of Hainault had married the Lord Charles's daughter, — and showed him his letters, for in these parts he was as king of France. It chanced one night, as he was returning to his lodgings, that he was watched and waylaid by the kindred of him on whose account he had performed this pilgrimage, and was murdered at a small distance from the Earl Charles's hotel. No one knew positively who had done this deed, but the relations of the Gascon knight above mentioned were very strongly suspected: however, they were so powerful that it was passed over and excused, for none took the part of the Lord of Manny. The Earl of Valois had him buried immediately in a small chapel which at that time was without the walls of La Réole; and, when the Earl of Valois had conquered the town, this chapel was enclosed in it. The old man remembered all these circumstances perfectly well, for he had been present when the Lord of Manny was interred. When Sir Walter came to the spot where his father had been buried, with his aged conductor, he found there a small tomb of marble which his servants had erected over him; and the old man said, "You may be perfectly assured that your father was buried and lies under this tomb." Sir Walter then caused the inscription, which was in Latin, to be read to him by a clerk, and found that the old man had told him the truth. Two days afterwards he had the tomb opened, took out the bones of his father, and, placing them in a coffin, sent them to Valenciennes in the county of Hainault, where they were again buried in the church of the Frères Mineurs, near the choir. He ordered masses to be said, and to be continued yearly.

CHAPTER XL.

The Earl of Derby conquers the Castle of La Réole.

THE Earl of Derby was more than eleven weeks besieging the castle of La Réole : the miners, however, made such advances, that they had got under one of the courts of the castle; but they could not undermine the donjon, for it was built on too hard a rock. The Lord Agos de Bans, the governor, then told his companions they were undermined, and in great danger; who were much alarmed at it, and said, "Sir, you will be in equal peril with ourselves, if you cannot find some method of avoiding it. You are our captain, and we ought to obey you. In truth, we have defended ourselves honorably, and no one can blame us if now we enter into a treaty. Will you therefore talk with the Earl of Derby, and know if he will accept of our surrender, sparing our lives and fortunes, seeing that we cannot at present act otherwise?" Sir Agos went down 'from the great tower, and, putting his head out of a window, made signs that he wished to speak with some one from the army. A few of the English came near him, and asked what he wanted : he replied that he would speak with the Earl of Derby or Sir Walter Manny. When this was told the earl, he said to Sir Walter Manny and to Lord Stafford, " Let us go to the fortress, and see what the governor has to say to us :" they rode therefore up to it. When Sir Agos perceived them, he saluted each very respectfully, and said, "Gentlemen, you know for fact that the King of France has sent me to this town and castle, to defend them to the best of my abilities. You know in what manner I have acquitted myself, and also that I should wish to continue it on ; but one cannot always remain in the place that pleases one best. I should therefore like to depart from hence, with my companions, if it be agreeable to you ; and, that we may have your permission, if you will spare our lives and fortunes, we will surrender this castle up to you." The earl replied, " Sir Agos, Sir Agos, you will not get off so. We know that you are very much distressed, and that we can take you whenever we please, for your castle now only stands upon props. You must surrender yourselves up unconditionally, and so shall you be received." Sir Agos, answering, said, " Certainly, sir, if we should do so, I hold you of such honor and gallantry, that you will show us every mark of favor, as you would wish the King of France should do toward any of your knights ; and, please God, you will never stain your honor and nobility for a few poor soldiers that are within here, who have gained their money with great pain and trouble, and whom I brought with me from Provence, Savoy, and Dauphiné : for know, that if the lowest of our men be not treated with mercy, as well as the highest, we will sell our lives in such a manner as none besieged ever did before. I therefore entreat of you to listen to me, and treat us like brother soldiers, that we may feel ourselves obliged to you."

The three knights withdrew to a little distance, and conversed a long time together; when, considering the gallantry of Sir Agos, that he was a foreigner, and, besides, that they could not undermine the donjon, they returned, and said to him, "Sir Agos, we shall be happy always to treat every stranger knight as a brother at arms; and if, fair sir, you and yours wish to leave the castle,' you must carry nothing with you but your arms and horses."— "Let it be so, then," replied Sir Agos. Upon this he returned to his companions, and related what he had done: they immediately armed themselves, and caparisoned their horses, of which they had only six remaining. Some purchased horses of the English, who made them pay dearly for them. Thus Sir Agos de Bans gave up the castle of La Réole, of which the English took possession; and he went to the city of Toulouse.

CHAPTER XLI.

The Earl of Derby takes Castel Moron, and afterwards Villefranche, in Perigord.

WHEN the Earl of Derby had gained possession of the town and castle of La Réole, where he had spent a long time, he pushed forward, but left there an English knight to see after the repairs, that it might be put in a similar situation as when he had come before it. The earl advanced toward Monpouillant, which he instantly ordered to be attacked the moment he arrived. There were in the castle none but the peasantry of the country, who had retired thither with their cattle, depending on the strength of the place. They defended themselves as long as they were able; but at last it was taken by escalade, though it cost the earl dear in the loss of many archers and a young English gentleman called Sir Richard Pennort, who bore the banner of the Lord Stafford. The earl gave the command of the castle and its dependencies to a squire of his own, called Thomas Lancaster, and left him with twenty archers. The earl then came to Castel Moron, which he attacked; but, finding he could not make any impression, he took up his quarters before it for that night. On the morrow morning a knight from Gascony came to him, called Sir Alexander de Chaumont, and said, "Sir, pretend to decamp with your army, leaving only a small detachment here before the town; and, from the knowledge I have of its inhabitants, I am sure they will sally forth to attack them. Your men will defend themselves as they retreat, and by placing an ambuscade under these olive-trees, which as soon as they have passed, one part of your army may fall upon their rear, and the other make for the town." The earl followed this advice, and ordered the Earl of Oxford to remain behind with only a hundred men, giving him directions what he wished to have done. He then ordered all the baggage to be packed up, and to march off, as if he were going to another place. After having posted a strong ambuscade in the valley among the olives and vines, he rode on.

When the townsmen of Castel Moron perceived that the earl and the greater part of his army were marching off, they said among themselves, "Let us hasten to arm, and sally forth to combat this handful of English that stay behind: we shall soon discomfit them, and have them at our mercy, which will bring us great honor and profit."

They all agreed to this proposal; and, hastening to arm themselves, they sallied out, to the number of about four hundred. As soon as the Earl of Oxford and his party saw them coming, they began to retreat, and the French to follow them with great eagerness: they pursued them until they had passed the ambush, when those posted there advanced upon them, calling out, "Manny forever!" for Sir Walter commanded this ambuscade. One part of his detachment fell upon those that had come from the town; and the other made for Castel Moron, where they came about midnight, and found the gates wide open, for the guards thought it was their own people returning. The first-comers therefore seized the bridge, and were soon masters of the town; for the inhabitants that had sallied out were surrounded on all sides, and either slain or made prisoners. Those that had remained in the town surrendered themselves to the Earl of Derby, who received them kindly, and, out of his nobleness of disposition, respited the town from being pillaged and burnt. He made a present of it, and all its dependencies, to Sir Alexander de Chaumont, through whose advice he had gained it. Sir Alexander made his brother, who was a squire, called Antony de Chaumont, governor; and the Earl of Derby left with him his archers, and forty infantry armed with bucklers, in order to enable him the better to guard the town. The earl then came before Villefranche, which he took by storm, as well as the castle. He made an English knight, Sir Thomas Cook, governor of it. Thus did the Earl of Derby march through every part of the country, without any one venturing out to prevent him. He conquered many different towns and castles, and his army gained so much riches, that it was marvellous to think on.

CHAPTER XLII.

JACOB VON ARTAVELD IS MURDERED AT GHENT.

JACOB VON ARTAVELD, the citizen of Ghent that was so much attached to the King of England, still maintained the same despotic power over all Flanders. He had promised the King of England that he would give him the inheritance of Flanders, invest his son the Prince of Wales with it, and make it a duchy instead of an earldom. Upon which account the king was at this period — about St. John the Baptist's Day, 1345 — come to Sluys, with a numerous attendance of barons and knights. He had brought the Prince of Wales with him, in order that Jacob von Artaveld's promises might be realized. The king remained on board his fleet in the harbor of Sluys, where he kept his court. His friends in Flanders came thither to see and visit him; and there were many conferences between the king and Jacob von Artaveld on one side, and the councils from the different capital towns on the other, relative to the agreement before mentioned; as to which, those from the country did not unite in sentiment with the king or with Von Artaveld: they declared they never would consent to such a thing.

Jacob von Artaveld remained some little time longer with the King of England, in order to be made acquainted with all his affairs: he, in return, assured him that he would bring his countrymen over to his opinion. But he deceived himself, and did wrong in staying behind and not being at Ghent at the time when the citizens who had been deputed by the corporations of the town arrived there; for as soon as they were returned, taking advantage of the absence of Von Artaveld, they collected a large meeting of high and low in the market-place, and there explained to them the subject of the late conferences at Sluys, and what the King of England had required of them through the advice of Jacob von Artaveld.

The whole assembly began to murmur against him. They said that if it pleased God they never would be pointed out, or found so disloyal as to disinherit their natural lord in favor of a stranger. They then left the market-place much discontented and angry with Artaveld. Now see how unfortunately it fell out; for if he had gone to Ghent, instead of Bruges and Ypres, and had urged upon them the cause of the King of England, they would all have consented to his wishes, as those of the two above-mentioned towns had done. But he trusted so much to his prosperity and greatness, that he thought he could recover every thing back in a little time.

When, on his return, he came to Ghent about midday, the townspeople, who were informed of the hour he was expected, had assembled in the street that he was to pass through. As soon as they saw him they began to murmur, and put their heads close together, saying, "Here comes one who is too much the master, and wants to order in Flanders according to his will and pleasure; which must not be longer borne." With this they had also spread a rumor through the town, that Jacob von Artaveld had collected all the revenues of Flanders for nine years and more; that he had kept them securely to maintain his own state, and had, during the time above mentioned, received all fines and forfeitures: of this great treasure he had sent part into England. This information inflamed

The Death of Jacob van Arteveld.

those of Ghent with rage; and as he was riding up the streets he perceived that there was something in agitation against him, for those who were wont to salute him very respectfully now turned their backs, and went into their houses. He began therefore to suspect all was not as usual; and as soon as he had dismounted, and entered his hotel, he ordered the doors and windows to be shut and fastened.

Scarcely had his servants done this, when the street which he inhabited was filled from one end to the other with all sorts of people, but especially with the lowest of mechanics. His mansion was surrounded on every side, attacked, and broken into by force. Those within did all they could to defend it, and killed and wounded many; but at last they could not hold out against such vigorous attacks, for three parts of the town were there. When Jacob von Artaveld saw what efforts were making, and how hardly he was pushed, he came to a window, and with his head uncovered began to use humble and fine language, saying, "My good people, what aileth you? Why are you so enraged against me? By what means can I have incurred your displeasure? Tell me: I will conform myself entirely to your wills." Those who heard him made answer as with one voice, "We want to have an account of the great treasures you have made away with, without any title or reason." Artaveld replied in a soft tone, "Gentlemen, be assured that I have never taken any thing from the treasures of Flanders; and if you will return quietly to your homes, and come here to-morrow morning, I will be prepared to give so good an account of them that you must be reasonably satisfied." But they cried out, "No, no! we must have it directly, you shall not thus escape from us; for we know that you have emptied the treasury, and sent it into England without our knowledge : you therefore shall suffer death." When he heard this he clasped his hands together, began to weep bitterly, and said, "Gentlemen, such as I am, you yourselves have made me. You formerly swore you would protect me against all the world; and now without any reason you want to murder me. You are certainly masters, to do it if you please ; for I am but one man against you all. Think better of it, for the love of God : recollect former times, and consider how many favors and kindnesses I have conferred upon you. You wish to give me a sorry recompense for all the generosities you have had at my hands. You are not ignorant, that, when commerce was dead in this country, it was I who restored it. I afterwards governed you in so peaceable a manner, that under my administration you had all things according to your wishes." They began to bawl out, "Come down, and do not preach to us from such a height ; for we will have an account and statement of the great treasures of Flanders, which you have governed too long without rendering any account ; and it is not proper for an officer to receive the rents of a lord, or of a country, without accounting for them." When Jacob von Artaveld saw that he could not appease or calm them, he shut the window, and intended getting out of his house the back way, to take shelter in a church adjoining ; but his hotel was already broken into on that side, and upwards of four hundred were there calling out to him. At last he was seized by them, and slain without mercy : his death-stroke was given him by a saddler called Thomas Denys.

CHAPTER XLIII.

SIR JOHN OF HAINAULT QUITS THE ALLIANCE OF ENGLAND FOR THAT
OF FRANCE.

SOON after this, King Philip of France endeavored by a treaty, through the means of the Earl of Blois, to persuade Sir John of Hainault to take part with France. In order to make him alter his opinion of the English, they made him believe that they would not pay him his subsidy for a considerable time. This put Sir John so much out of humor, that he renounced all treaties and agreements which he had entered into with England. The King of France was no sooner informed of it, than he sent to him persons sufficiently authorized, who retained him, as well as his counsel for France, at a certain salary; and he recompensed him in his kingdom with a greater revenue than he derived from England.

CHAPTER XLIV.

THE DUKE OF NORMANDY MARCHES WITH A GREAT ARMY INTO GAS-
CONY, AGAINST THE EARL OF DERBY.

THE King of France, having received information of the expeditions and conquests that the Earl of Derby had made in Gascony, issued a special summons for all nobles and others that were capable of bearing arms to assemble in the cities of Orleans and Bourges, and in that neighborhood, by a certain day.

At last these lords were all assembled, with their men, in and near Toulouse, for they were too great in numbers to be lodged in the city: they amounted, in the whole, to upward of a hundred thousand persons. This was the year of grace 1345. Soon after the feast of Christmas, the Duke of Normandy, who was the commander-in-chief of this army, set out to join it, and ordered his marshals, the Lord of Montmorency and the Lord of St. Venant, to advance with the van. They came first to the castle of Miraumont, which the English had conquered in the summer, and most vigorously assaulted it. There were within about a hundred Englishmen for its defence, under the command of John Briscoe.

With the French were the Lord Lewis of Spain, and a number of Genoese crossbow-men, that spared none. Those within could not defend themselves against so superior a force, but were taken, and the greater part of them slain, even their captain. The marshals, having recruited their battalion with fresh men, advanced farther, and came before Villefranche, in the county of Agenois. The army halted there, and surrounded it on all sides. Sir Thomas Cook, the governor, was not there, but at Bordeaux, whither the Earl of Derby had sent for him. However, those within made a vigorous defence; but in the end they were taken by storm, and the greater part of the garrison put to the sword. The army then marched toward the city of Angoulême, leaving the town and castle of Villefranche standing undemolished, and without any guard. The city of Angoulême was closely besieged: the governor of it for the King of England was Sir John Norwich.

CHAPTER XLV.

Sir John Norwich escapes from Angoulême, when that Town surrenders to the French.

THE lords of France remained for a very considerable time before Angoulême. The French overran all the country which had been conquered by the English: they created much trouble, and, whenever they found a fit opportunity, brought to their camp many prisoners and much pillage. The two brothers of Bourbon acquired great praise from all, as they were the foremost in every excursion. When Sir John Norwich, the governor of Angoulême, found that the Duke of Normandy would not break up the siege until he had gained the city, that his provisions were growing short, and that the Earl of Derby showed no signs of coming to his relief; having also perceived that the inhabitants were much inclined to the French, and would have turned to them before if they had dared, — he began to be suspicious of treason, and bethought how he could best save himself and his companions. On the eve of the Purification, he came on the battlements of the walls of the city alone, without having mentioned to any one his intentions, and made signs with his cap that he wanted to speak with some one from the army. Those who had noticed the signal came to know what he wanted: he said he wished "to speak with my lord the Duke of Normandy, or with one of his marshals." They went to inform the duke of this, who came there, attended by some of his knights. As soon as Sir John saw the duke, he pulled off his cap, and saluted him. The duke returned the salute, and said, "Sir John, how fares it with you? Are you inclined to surrender yourself?" —"I have no intentions to do that," replied Sir John; "but I could wish to entreat of you, in reverence to the feast of Our Lady, which is to-morrow, that you would grant us a truce for that day only, that neither of us may hurt the other, but remain in peace." The duke said he was willing to consent to it.

Early the next morning, which was Candlemas Day, Sir John and his companions armed themselves, and packed up all they had. They then ordered one of the gates to be opened, and issued forth; which being perceived by the army, some part of it began to put itself in motion. Sir John, upon this, rode up to them, and said, "Gentlemen, gentlemen, beware that you do no harm to us; for we have had a truce agreed on for this whole day, as you must know, by the Duke of Normandy; and we shall not touch you. If you have not been informed of it, go and inquire; for we can, upon the faith of this truce, ride and go wherever we please." This information was brought to the duke, and he was asked what was to be done; who replied, "Let them go, in God's name, whatever way they choose; for we cannot force them to stay. I will keep the promise I made them." Thus Sir John Norwich passed through the whole French army unhurt, and took the road to Aiguillon. When those who were in garrison there heard in what manner he had escaped, and saved his men, they said he had acted very cunningly.*

---

* But it is to be hoped that every young reader of Froissart will heartily despise such cunning. This act of Sir John Norwich was mean and small beyond all decent words; for he took the basest advantage of the Duke of Normandy's honorable confidence in his fidelity to the sacred obligations of a truce. — ED.

The inhabitants of Angoulême held a council on Candle-mas Day, and determined to surrender themselves to the duke. They sent persons properly authorized to treat, who managed so well, that the duke showed them mercy, and pardoned them. He entered the city and castle, where he received their homage, and appointed Sir Anthony de Villiers governor, with a hundred soldiers to defend it. The duke afterwards decamped, and came before the castle of Damazan, which he laid siege to for fourteen days. There were continued assaults; but at last it was taken, and all within it, Gascons and English, put to the sword. The duke gave this castle and its dependencies to a squire from Beausse, named the Borgne de Nully. He then came before Tonniens, which is situated on the Garonne, and which he found well provided with Gascons and English. There were many attacks and skirmishes, and he remained some time before it. However, at last they surrendered, upon condition of preserving their lives and fortunes, and to be conducted in safety to Bordeaux. When these foreigners had left it, the town entered under obedience to the duke, who staid here with his whole army, and on the banks of the Garonne, until after Easter, when he advanced toward Port St. Marie upon the same river. There were about two hundred English to defend the town and this passage, who had strongly fortified it; but they, and all within, were taken by assault. The French, after they had repaired and re-enforced it with men at arms, set out and took the road toward Aiguillon.

CHAPTER XLVI..

THE DUKE OF NORMANDY LAYS SIEGE TO AIGUILLON WITH A HUNDRED THOUSAND MEN.

THE noblemen of France, under the command of the Duke of Normandy, pushed on until they came before the castle of Aiguillon, when they encamped, and divided their forces in the extensive and handsome meadows on the banks of the river Garonne, which is navigable for great vessels. Each lord was posted with his own people, and every company by itself, according to the orders of the marshals of the army. This siege continued until the beginning of October; and there were upward of one hundred thousand men in arms, including cavalry and infantry. Those within were obliged to defend themselves against this army two or three times every day, and most commonly from noon until eve without ceasing; for there were continually pouring upon them fresh forces, Genoese or others, who gave them no repose. The chiefs of the French army found they could never attack with advantage the fortress, unless they passed the river, which was wide and deep. The duke therefore ordered a bridge to be constructed, that they might cross it. Three hundred workmen were employed at this bridge, who worked day and night. As soon as the knights who were in Aiguillon perceived that this bridge was nearly finished, and that one-half of it was completed, they prepared three vessels, in which they embarked, and, driving away the workmen and guards, instantly destroyed what had taken so much time to make. The lords of France, seeing this, got ready other vessels to attack them, in which they placed a number of men at arms, Genoese crossbow-men, and infantry, and ordered the workmen to continue their works under the support of these guards. When these workmen were thus employed, Sir Walter Manny and some of his companions embarked about noon, and, dashing upon them, made them quit their work, and run off. He soon destroyed all that they had done. This kind of skirmish was continued daily; but at last the French sent such large detachments to guard the workmen, that the bridge was completed in a good and strong manner. The army then passed over it in order of battle, and attacked the castle for the space of one whole day, but did no harm; and in the evening they retreated to their camp, where they were plentifully supplied with every thing.

Those within the castle repaired what damage had been done, for they had plenty of workmen. On the morrow the French resolved to divide their army into four divisions, the first of which should make an attack on this fortress from the dawn until about nine o'clock; the second, from that time until noon; the third, from noon till four o'clock; and the fourth division, from that time till night. This mode of attack was continued for six successive days. However, those within the castle were never so much harassed but that they could defend themselves valiantly; and their enemies gained nothing but the bridge which was before the castle. The French lords, upon this, held a council, and sent to Toulouse for eight of their largest battering-engines, and constructed four other large ones upon the spot. These twelve engines cast stones into the fortress day and night; but the besieged had taken such pains to avoid what mischief they could do, that they only destroyed the roofs of the houses. They had also made counter-engines, which played upon those of their enemies, and in a short space of time totally ruined six of them.

During this siege Sir Walter Manny made frequent excursions beyond the river, with about sixscore companions, to forage, and often returned with his booty in sight of the army. One day the Lord Charles of Montmorency had been on a foraging party, with five or six hundred men, and was conducting a great number of cattle to victual the army, when he met Sir Walter Manny under the walls of Aiguillon. They immediately began an engagement, which was very sharp, and many were killed and wounded on both sides. The French were at least five to one. News was brought of this into Aiguillon, when every one sallied out for the fastest, and the Earl of Pembroke with the foremost; they dashed into the midst of them, and found Sir Walter Manny unhorsed, and surrounded by his enemies, but fighting most valiantly. He was directly rescued and remounted. During the heat of the engagement, the French hastened to drive off the cattle to a place of safety, or they would have lost them; for the English were coming in crowds to succor their countrymen, and, falling upon the French vigorously, they put them to flight, rescued those they had made prisoners, and captured also many from them. The Lord Charles de Montmorency had great difficulty to escape, and retreated as fast as he could, quite discomfited. When it was over, the English returned to Aiguillon.

Such skirmishes frequently happened, for scarcely a day passed without some engagement. The French, having one day drawn out their army, ordered those noblemen that were from Toulouse, Carcassonne, and Beaucaire, and their dependencies, to make an attack with their men, from the morning until noon ; and those from Rouergue, Cahors, and Agenois, to continue it from their retreat until the evening. The duke promised to any of his soldiers who should gain the drawbridge of the castle a reward of a hundred golden crowns. The duke, in order to assist this attack, commanded a number of vessels and barges to come down the river, in which many embarked to cross it, while the remainder passed over the bridge. Those in the castle made a gallant defence ; but at last some of the French got into a small boat, and, passing under the bridge, fastened strong hooks and chains to the drawbridge, with which they pulled so lustily, that they broke the iron chains which held the bridge, and forced it down.

The French, so eager were they to gain the promised reward, leaped upon the bridge in such haste that they tumbled over each other. The besieged flung down upon them stones, hot lime, large beams, and boiling water, so that many were hurt and drowned in the ditches. The bridge, however, was taken, though it cost them more than it was worth. But they could not gain the gate : therefore, as it was late, they returned to their camp, for they had need of rest ; and those within the castle sallied out, and repaired the bridge, making it stronger than ever.

On the next day two principal engineers came to the duke, and said, if he would find them wood and workmen they would build for him four such high towers, as, when they were advanced to the walls of the castle, should overtop them. The duke commanded all the carpenters of the country to be sent for, and handsomely paid. These four towers were constructed, and placed on the decks of four large vessels ; but they took a long time in making, and cost much money. Those ordered upon this attack embarked on board the vessels; and, when they were about half way over the river, the besieged let off four martinets, which they had newly constructed to defend themselves against these towers. These four martinets cast such large stones, and so very rapidly, that the men at arms in the towers were much hurt by them; and, having no means to shield themselves, they returned back as fast as they were able. But in their retreat one of the vessels foundered and sunk : the greater number of those that were on board were drowned, which was a great pity, as they were chiefly valiant knights who were eager to distinguish themselves. When the duke found that this scheme did not answer his expectations, he ordered them to disembark from the three remaining vessels. He was at a loss what plan to follow, by which he could gain the castle of Aiguillon ; for he had vowed he would never quit the place until he was master of it and the garrison, unless the king his father ordered otherwise. The lords therefore advised him to send the Constable of France and the Earl of Tancarville to Paris, to inform King Philip of the state of the siege, and to know if the king wished the Duke of Normandy to continue before Aiguillon until he had through famine made himself master of it, since he could not gain it by force.

The King of England, having heard how much pressed his people were in the castle of Aiguillon, determined to lead a great army into Gascony. He set about making his preparations, summoned all the vassals in his kingdom, and collected forces from whatever quarter he could, that were willing to enter into his pay. About this time Sir Godfrey de Harcourt, who had been banished from France, arrived in England. He was received by the king in his palace ; and he assigned over to him a handsome estate in England, to maintain him suitable to his rank. Soon after this the king assembled a large fleet of ships at Southampton, and sent thither his men at arms and his archers. About St. John the Baptist's Day, 1346, the king took leave of the queen, and, setting out, left her to the care of his cousin the Earl of Kent. He appointed the Lord Percy, and the Lord Neville of Raby, the Archbishop of York, the Bishop of Durham, and the Bishop of Lincoln, to be his lieutenants for the northern parts of his kingdom; and he did not take so many forces out of the realm but that there was a sufficiency of men at arms left to defend it, should there be occasion. He took the road to Southampton, where he tarried until he had a favorable wind, when he embarked with his whole army. On board the king's ship were the Prince of Wales and Sir Godfrey de Harcourt: the other lords, earls, and barons embarked with their men, as they had been ordered. There might be about four thousand men at arms, and ten thousand archers, not including the Irish and the Welsh, who followed the army on foot.

When they embarked,* the weather was as favorable as the king could wish, to carry him to Gascony; but on the third day the wind was so contrary, that they were driven upon the coasts of Cornwall, where they cast anchor, and remained for six days and six nights. During this time the king altered his mind with respect to going toward Gascony, through the advice and representations of Sir Godfrey de Harcourt, who convinced him that it would be more for his interest to land in Normandy, by such

---

* Boys who accompany King Edward on this expedition will be glad to know, at the outset, that they are not to be fobbed off with a few skirmishes and a retreat of both armies — as on the preceding ones. In fact, we are now on the way to fight the great battle of Crecy. — ED.

words as these: " Sir, that province is one of the most
fertile in the world; and I will answer on my head that
you may land in any part of it you shall please without
hinderance, for no one will think of opposing you. The
Normans have not been accustomed to the use of arms;
and all the knighthood that would have otherwise been
there are at present with the duke before Aiguillon. You
will find in Normandy rich towns and handsome castles
without any means of defence, and your people will gain
wealth enough to suffice them for twenty years to come.
Your fleet may also follow you up the river Orne as far
as Caen. I therefore entreat you will listen and give
belief to what I say." The king, who at that time was in
the flower of his youth, and who desired nothing better
than to combat his enemies, paid much attention to what
Sir Godfrey de Harcourt, whom he called cousin, had
said. He commanded his sailors to steer straight for
Normandy, and ordered the flag of the admiral, the Earl
of Warwick, to be hoisted on board his ship: he took the
lead, as admiral of the fleet, and made for Normandy with
a very favorable wind. The fleet anchored near to the
shores of Coutantin, and the king landed at a port called
La Hogue St. Vast. News of his arrival was soon spread
abroad: it was told all over the country, that the English
had landed with a very great army. Messengers were
instantly despatched to Paris, to the king, from the towns
of Coutantin. He had already been informed that the
King of England had embarked a numerous army, and
was on the coasts of Normandy and Brittany; but he was
not sure for what particular port he intended to make.
As soon, therefore, as he heard the English had landed,
he sent for his constable, the Earl of Guignes, and the
Earl of Tancarville, who were just come from Aiguil-

lon, and ordered them to set off directly for Caen, to defend that place and the neighborhood against the English.

CHAPTER XLVII.

THE KING OF ENGLAND MARCHES INTO NORMANDY WITH HIS ARMY IN THREE BATTALIONS.

WHEN the fleet of England was all safely arrived at La Hogue, the king leaped on shore first; but by accident he fell, and with such violence that the blood gushed out of his nose. The knights that were near him said, "Dear sir, let us entreat you to return to your ship, and not think of landing to-day, for this is an unfortunate omen." The king instantly replied, "For what? I look upon it as very favorable, and a sign that the land is desirous of me."

His people were much pleased with this answer. The king and his army lay that night upon the sands. In the mean time they disembarked their baggage, armor, and horses; and there was a council held, to consider how they could act most advantageously. The king created two marshals of his army: one was Sir Godfrey de Harcourt, the other the Earl of Warwick; and he made the Earl of Arundel his constable. He ordered the Earl of Huntington to remain with his fleet, with a hundred or sixscore men at arms, and four hundred archers. He then held another council respecting the order of march, and determined to divide the army into three battalions, one of which should advance on his right, following the seacoast, and another on his left; and he himself, with the prince his son and the main body, in the centre.

Every night the marshal's battalion was to retire to the quarters of the king. They then began their march, as they had resolved upon. Those who were on board the fleet coasted shores, and took every vessel, great and small, they met with. Both the armies of sea and land went forward until they came to a strong town called Barfleur, which they soon gained, the inhabitants having surrendered immediately for fear of losing their lives; but that did not prevent the town from being pillaged and robbed of gold, silver, and every thing precious that could be found therein. There was so much wealth that the boys of the army set no value on gowns trimmed with fur. They made all the townsmen quit the place, and embarked them on board the fleet; for they did not choose that after they had continued their march they should collect together, and attack them.

After the town of Barfleur had been pillaged, but not burnt, they spread themselves over the country, near the seacoast, where they did whatever they pleased, for there were none to oppose them. They advanced until they came to a considerable and wealthy town called Cherbourg, which they burnt and pillaged in part; but they could not conquer the castle, as it was too strong and well garrisoned with men at arms: they therefore passed on, and came before Montbourg, near Valogues, which they pillaged and then set fire to. In this manner did they plunder and burn a great many towns in that country, and acquired so much riches that it would have been difficult to count their wealth.

CHAPTER XLVIII.

THE KING OF FRANCE COLLECTS A LARGE FORCE TO OPPOSE THE KING OF ENGLAND.

THUS, while the English were burning and destroying great part of Normandy, the King of France was not idle, but had issued out his summons to the Lord John of Hainault, who came to him with a powerful company of knights from Hainault and elsewhere : he also sent to every earl, baron, and knight that were dependent on him. They obeyed his summons in such numbers as France had not seen for a hundred years ; but, as those in foreign countries were at great distances, they were long in arriving, and the King of England had overrun and destroyed the whole district of Coutantin in Normandy to its great detriment.

When King Philip first heard of the destruction the King of England was making in his realm, he swore that the English should never return without his having combated with them, and that the mischief they had done to his people should be dearly paid for. He hastened, therefore, to despatch his letters. He sent first to his good friends in the empire, because they were at the greatest distance ; and also to the gallant King of Bohemia, whom he so much loved ; and to the Lord Charles of Bohemia, his son, who had then the title of King of Germany, which he had obtained, as was well known, through the influence of his father and the King of France, and he had already quartered the arms of the empire. King Philip entreated of them to come speedily to his assistance, for he was impatient to meet the English who were despoiling his kingdom. These lords had no intention of excusing themselves, but set about collecting a large body of men at arms from Germany, Bohemia, and Luxembourg, and came to the King of France with a powerful army. The King of France wrote also to the Duke of Lorraine, who came to serve him with upward of three hundred lances. The Earl of Savoy, the Earl of Saltzburg, the Earl of Flanders, and Earl William of Namur, came also to King Philip, each of them with a very handsome company.

You have before heard the manner of the King of England's march : the two marshals on the right and left, and the King and Prince of Wales in the centre. They advanced by short marches, and every day they encamped between ten and twelve o'clock. They found the country so abounding with provisions, that they had no need to seek for forage, except wines, of which there was a reasonable quantity. It is not to be wondered at, if the people of the country were alarmed and frightened, for they had never seen any men at arms, and knew nothing of war or battles : they therefore fled before the English, as soon as ever they heard they were coming, leaving their houses and barns quite full, for they had neither means nor art to save them.

The King of England and Prince of Wales had in their battalion about three thousand men at arms, six thousand archers, ten thousand infantry, without counting those that were under the marshals; and they marched on in the manner I have before mentioned, burning and destroying the country, but without breaking their line of battle. They did not turn toward Coutances, but advanced to St. Lô in Coutantin, which in those days was a very rich and commercial town, and worth three such towns as Coutances. In the town of St. Lô was much drapery, and many wealthy inhabitants; among them you might count eight or nine score that were engaged in commerce. When the King of England was come near to the town, he encamped: he would not lodge in it for fear of fire. He sent, therefore, his advanced guard forward, who soon conquered it at a trifling loss, and completely plundered it. No one can imagine the quantity of riches they found in it, nor the number of bales of cloth. If there had been any purchasers, they might have bought enough at a very cheap rate.

The English then advanced toward Caen, which is a much larger town, stronger, and fuller of draperies and all other sorts of merchandise, rich citizens, noble dames and damsels, and fine churches. In particular, there are two very rich monasteries, one dedicated to St. Stephen, and the other to the Trinity. The castle is situated on one side of the town: it is the handsomest in all Normandy; and Sir Robert de Blargny was governor, with a garrison of three hundred Genoese.

In the heart of the town were the Earl of Eu and of Guignes, the Constable of France, and the Earl of Tancarville, with a crowd of men at arms. The king rode on very prudently, and, having united his three battalions, he took up his quarters for that night in the fields, two short leagues from Caen, near a town called Estreham, where there is a haven. He ordered the Earl of Huntington, whom he had made admiral of his fleet, to sail for that place. The Constable of France, and the other lords who were assembled in Caen, watched it well that night; and on the morrow they armed themselves and all the inhabitants. After they were drawn out, the constable and the

Earl of Tancarville ordered that no one should leave the town, but should guard well the bridge, the gates, and the river. They gave up the suburbs to the English, because they were not enclosed ; and they thought they should find sufficient employment to guard the town, which was only defended by the river. The townsmen, however, said they would march out into the plains, as they were in sufficient force to fight with the English. When the constable perceived their willingness, he said, "It shall be so, then ; but, in God's name, you shall not fight without me." They then marched out of the town in handsome order, and made a show as if they would fight valiantly, and risk their lives upon the event.

CHAPTER XLIX.

THE BATTLE OF CAEN. — THE ENGLISH TAKE THE TOWN.

ON this day the English rose very early, and made themselves ready to march to Caen : the king heard mass before sunrise, and afterwards mounting his horse, with the Prince of Wales and Sir Godfrey de Harcourt (who was marshal and director of the army, and through whose advice the king had undertaken this expedition), marched forward in order of battle. The battalion of the marshals led the van, and came near to the handsome town of Caen.

When the townsmen, who had taken the field, perceived the English advancing with banners and pennons flying in abundance, and saw those archers whom they had not been accustomed to, they were so frightened that they betook themselves to flight, and ran for the town in great disorder, without regarding the constable and the men at arms who were with them. The English pursued them eagerly; which, when the constable and the Earl of Tan-carville saw, they gained a gate at the entrance of the bridge in safety, and a few knights with them, for the English had already entered the town.

Some knights and squires of the French, who knew the road to the castle, made for it; and the governor, Sir Robert de Blargny, received them all. As the castle was very large, and plentifully victualled, those were safe that could get there.

The English, who were after the runaways, made great havoc; for they spared none. When the constable, and those that had taken refuge with him within the gate of the bridge, looked round them, and saw the great slaughter the English were making (for they gave no quarter), they began to fear lest they should fall into the hands of some of those archers, who would not know who they were. But they perceived a knight who had but one eye, named Sir Thomas Holland (whom they had formerly known in Prussia and Grenada), coming toward them, in company with five or six other knights: they called to him, and asked if he would take them as his prisoners. Sir Thomas and his company advanced to the gate, and, dismounting, ascended to the top, with sixteen others, where he found the above-mentioned knights, and twenty-five more, who surrendered themselves to Sir Thomas.

Having left a sufficient guard over them, he mounted his horse, rode through the streets, and prevented many acts of cruelty; as did also other knights and squires, to whom several of the citizens owed their lives. It was fortunate for the English that it was ebb-tide in the river, which admits large vessels, and the water very still, so that they could pass and repass beside the bridge. Those inhabitants who had taken refuge in the garrets flung down from them in these narrow streets stones, benches, and whatever they could lay hands on, so that they killed and wounded upwards of five hundred of the English; which so enraged the King of England, when he received the reports in the evening, that he ordered the remainder of the inhabitants to be put to the sword, and the town burnt. But Sir Godfrey de Harcourt said to him, "Dear sir, assuage somewhat of your anger, and be satisfied with what has already been done. You have a long journey yet to make before you arrive at Calais, whither it is your intention to go; and there are in this town a great number of inhabitants who will defend themselves obstinately in their houses, if you force them to it: besides, it will cost you many lives before the town can be destroyed, which may put a stop to the expedition to Calais, and that will not redound to your honor. Therefore be sparing of your men, for in a month's time you will have a call for them; as it cannot otherwise happen but that your adversary King Philip must soon come to give you battle, and you may meet with many difficulties, assaults, and skirmishes, that will find full employment for the number of, and even more if we could get them. We are complete masters of the town, without any more slaughter; and the inhabitants, and all they possess, are at our disposal." The king replied, "Sir Godfrey, you are our marshal: therefore order as you please; for this time we do not wish to interfere."

Sir Godfrey then rode through the streets, his banner displayed before him, and ordered in the king's name that no one should dare, under pain of immediate death, to insult or hurt man or woman of the town, or attempt to set fire to it. Several of the inhabitants, on hearing this proclamation, received the English into their houses ; and others opened their coffers to them, giving up their all since they were assured of their lives. However, there were, in spite of these orders, many atrocious thefts and murders committed. The English continued masters of the town for three days. In this time they amassed great wealth, which they sent in barges down the river of Estreham to St. Saveur, two leagues off, where their fleet was. The Earl of Huntington made preparations, therefore, with the two hundred men at arms and his four hundred archers, to carry over to England their riches and prisoners. The king purchased from Sir Thomas Holland and his companions the Constable of France and the Earl of Tancarville, and paid down twenty thousand nobles for them.

CHAPTER L.

THE ENGLISH COMMIT GREAT DEPREDATIONS IN NORMANDY. — SIR GOD-
FREY DE HARCOURT ENCOUNTERS THE MEN AT ARMS OF AMIENS, ON
THEIR WAY TO PARIS, AND KING EDWARD MARCHES INTO PICARDY.

WHEN the king had finished his business in Caen, and had sent his fleet to England loaded with cloths, jewels, gold and silver plate, and a quantity of other riches, and upward of sixty knights, with three hundred able citizens, prisoners ; he then left his quarters, and continued his march as before, his two marshals on his right and left, burning and wasting all the flat country.

They pushed forward until they came to Poissy, where the bridge was also destroyed ; but the beams and other parts of it were lying in the river. The king remained here five days, while they were repairing the bridge, so that his army might pass over without danger. His marshals advanced very near to Paris, and burnt St. Germain-en-Laye, La Montjoie, St. Cloud, Boulogne near Paris, and Bourg la Reine. The Parisians were much alarmed, for Paris at that time was not enclosed. King Philip upon this began to stir ; and, having ordered all the pent-houses in Paris to be pulled down, went to St. Denis, where he found the King of Bohemia, the Lord John of Hainault, the Duke of Lorraine, the Earl of Flanders, the Earl of Blois, and great multitudes of barons and knights, ready to receive him. When the Parisians learned that the king was on the point of quitting Paris, they came to him, and, falling on their knees, said, "Ah, sire and noble king, what are you about to do? to leave your fine city of Paris?" The king replied, "My good people, do not be afraid : the English will not approach you nearer than they have done." He thus spoke in answer to what they had said, — that "our enemies are only two leagues off : as soon as they shall know you have quitted us, they will come hither directly ; and we are not able to resist them ourselves, nor shall we find any to defend us. Have the kindness, therefore, sire, to remain in your good city of Paris to take care of us." · The king replied, "I am going to St. Denis, to my army ; for I am impatient to pursue the English, and am resolved to fight with them at all events."

The King of England remained at the nunnery of Poissy to the middle of August, and celebrated there the feast of the Virgin Mary. He sat at table in his scarlet robes without sleeves, trimmed with furs and ermines. He afterwards took the field, and his army marched as before : Sir Godfrey de Harcourt, one of his marshals, had the command of the vanguard, with five hundred men at arms, and about thirteen hundred archers. By accident he fell in with a large party of the citizens of Amiens on horseback, who were going to King Philip at Paris, in obedience to his summons. He immediately attacked them with those under his command; but they made a good defence, as they were very numerous and well armed, and had four knights from Amiens with them. The engagement lasted a long time, and many were slain at the onset; but at last those from Amiens were overthrown, killed, or taken prisoners. The English seized all their baggage and arms, and found many valuables; for they were going to the king excellently well equipped, and had but just quitted their city. Twelve hundred were left dead on the spot. The King of England entered the country of Beauvais, destroying all the flat country; and took up his quarters in a rich abbey called St. Messien, near to Beauvais, where he lodged one night. The morrow, as he was on his march, he by chance turned his head round, and saw the abbey all in flames; upon which he instantly ordered twenty of those who had set fire to it to be hung, as he had most strictly forbidden that any church should be violated, or monastery set on fire. He passed near Beauvais without attacking it, — for he was anxious to be as careful of his men and artillery as possible, — and took up his quarters at a small town called Milly. The two marshals passed so near to Beauvais, that they advanced to attack it, and skirmish with the townsmen at the barriers, and divided their forces into three battalions. This attack lasted until the afternoon; for the town was well fortified and provided with every thing, and the bishop was also there, whose exertions were of more service than those of all the rest. When the English found they could not gain any thing, they set fire to the suburbs, which they burnt quite close to the gates of the town, and then came, toward evening, to where the king was.

The next day the king and his whole army marched forward, burning and wasting all the country as they went, and lay that night at a village called Grandvillier. On the morrow he passed near to Argis : his scouts not finding any one to guard the castle, he attacked and burnt it, and, passing on, destroyed the country, and came to Poix, which was a handsome town with two castles. The lords of both were absent, and no one was there but two handsome daughters of the Lord of Poix. In order more effectually to guard them, they brought them to the king, who, as in honor bound, entertained them most graciously. He inquired whither they would wish to go. They answered, to Corbie, to which place they were conducted in safety. The King of England lay that night in the town of Poix. The inhabitants of Poix, as well as those of the castle, had a conference with the marshals of the army, in order to save the town from being plundered and burnt. They offered to pay, as a ransom, a certain number of florins the ensuing day, as soon as the army should have marched off. On the morrow morning the king and army departed, except some few who remained behind, by order of the marshals, to receive the ransom from the townsmen. When the inhabitants were assembled together, and considered the small number of the English who were left with them, they resolved to pay nothing, told them so, and directly fell upon them. The English defended themselves gallantly, and sent after the army for succor. When Lord Reginald Cobham and Sir Thomas Holland, who commanded the rear-guard, were told of this, they cried out, " Treason ! treason !" and returned back to Poix, where they found their countrymen still engaged with the townsmen. Almost all the inhabitants were slain, the town was burnt, and the two castles razed to the ground. The English then followed the king's army, which was arrived at Airaines, where he had ordered the troops to halt, and to quarter themselves for that night, strictly commanding, under pain of death, that no harm should be done to the town or inhabitants by theft or otherwise; for he wished to remain there a day or two in order to gain information where he could best cross the river Somme, — which he was under the necessity of doing, as you will shortly hear.

CHAPTER LI.

THE KING OF FRANCE PURSUES THE KING OF ENGLAND, IN THE COUNTRY OF BEAUVAIS.

I WISH now to return to King Philip, whom we left at St. Denis with his army, which was increasing every day. He marched off with it, and pushed forward until he came to Coppigny les Guises, which is three leagues distant from Amiens, where he halted. The King of England, who was still at Airaines, was much embarrassed how to cross the Somme, which was wide and deep, as all the bridges had been broken down, and their situations were well guarded by men at arms. The two marshals, at the request of the king, followed the course of the river, in order if possible to find a passage for the army: they had with them a thousand men at arms and two thousand archers. They passed by Lompré, and came to Pont de Remy, which they found defended by numbers of knights, squires, and people of the country. The English dis-

mounted, and attacked the French from the very dawn of
the morning until near ten o'clock ; but the bridge was so
well fortified and guarded, that they could not gain any
thing : so they departed, and went to a large town called
Fontaines-sur-Somme, which they completely plundered
and burnt, as it was quite open.   They next came to
another town, called Long, in Ponthieu ; but they could
not gain the bridge, so well was it guarded.   They then
rode on to Pecquigny, but found the town, castle, and
bridge so well garrisoned that it was impossible to pass.
In this manner had the King of France ordered all the
bridges and fords of the river Somme to be guarded, to prevent the King of England from crossing it with his army ;
for he was resolved to force them to fight when he should
see the most favorable opportunity, or else to starve them.

The two marshals, having thus in vain followed the
course of the Somme, returned to the King of England,
and related to him that they were unable to find a passage
anywhere.   That same evening the King of France took
up his quarters at Amiens, with upward of one hundred
thousand men.   The King of England was very pensive :
he ordered mass before sunrise, and his trumpets to sound
for decamping.   All sorts of people followed the marshals'
banners, according to the orders the king had issued the
preceding day ; and they marched through the country of
Vimeu, drawing near to the good town of Abbeville.   In
their march they came to a town where a great number
of country-people had assembled, trusting to some small
fortifications which were thrown up there ; but the English conquered the town as soon as they came to it, and
all that were within.   Many of the townsmen and those
from the adjoining country were slain or taken prisoners.
The king lodged that night in the great hospital.

The King of France set out from Amiens, and came to Airaines about noon : the English king had quitted it about ten o'clock. The French found there provisions of all sorts ; meat on the spits, bread and pastry in the ovens, wine in barrels, and even some tables ready spread, for the English had left it in very great haste. The King of France fixed his quarters there, to wait for his nobles and their retinue. The King of England was in the town of Oisemont. When his two marshals returned in the evening, after having overrun the country as far as the gates of Abbeville, and . St. Valery, where they had a smart skirmish, the King of England summoned a council, and ordered many prisoners, whom his people had made in the districts of Ponthieu and Vimeu, to be brought before him.

The king most courteously asked if any of them knew a ford below Abbeville, where he and his army could pass without danger ; and added, "Whoever will show us such a ford shall have his liberty, and that of any twenty of his fellow-soldiers whom he may wish to select." There was among them a common fellow whose name was Gobin Agace, who answered the king, and said, " Sir, I promise you, under peril of my life, that I will conduct you to such a place, where you and your whole army may pass the river Somme without any risk. There are certain fordable places where you may pass twelve men abreast twice in the day, and not have water above your knees ; but, when the tide is in, the river is full and deep, and no one can cross it : when the tide is out, the river is so low that it may be passed on horseback or on foot without danger. The bottom of this ford is very hard, of gravel and white stones, over which all your carriages may safely pass, and from thence is called Blanchetaque. You must therefore set out early, so as to be at the ford before sunrise." —

"Friend," replied the king, "if I find what thou hast just said to be true, I will give thee and all thy companions their liberty; and I will besides make thee a present of a hundred nobles." The king gave orders for every one to be ready to march at the first sound of his trumpet, and to proceed forward.

CHAPTER LII.

The Battle of Blanchetaque, between the King of England and Sir Godémar du Fay.

THE King of England did not sleep much that night, but, rising at midnight, ordered his trumpet to sound. Very soon every thing was ready; and, the baggage being loaded, they set out from the town of Oisemont about daybreak, and rode on, under the guidance of Gobin Agace, until they came to the ford of Blanchetaque about sunrise; but the tide was at that time so full, they could not cross. The king, however, determined to wait there for those of his army who were not yet come up; and he remained until after ten o'clock, when the tide was gone out. The King of France, who had his scouts all over the country, was informed of the situation of the King of England: he imagined he should be able to shut him up between Abbeville and the Somme, and then take him prisoner, or force him to fight at a disadvantage. From the time of his arrival at Amiens, he had ordered a great baron of Normandy, called Sir Godémar du Fay, to guard this ford of Blanchetaque, at which the English must cross and nowhere else. Sir Godémar had set out, in obedience to this order, and had with him altogether one thousand

men at arms and six thousand foot, with the Genoese.
He had passed St. Ricquier in Ponthieu, and from there
came to Crotoy, where this ford was. He had collected
in his march great numbers of the country-people. The
townsmen of Abbeville had also accompanied him, excellently well appointed : they had arrived at the passage before the English. They were in all fully twelve thousand
men. Among them were two thousand who had jackets
resembling wagoners' frocks, called *torriquiaux.*

On the arrival of the English army, Sir Godémar du
Fay drew up his men on the banks of the river to defend
the ford. The King of England, however, did not for
this give up his intention of crossing ; but, as soon as the
tide was sufficiently gone out, he ordered his marshals to
dash into the water, in the name of God and St. George.
The most doughty and the best-mounted leaped in first,
and in the river the engagement began : many on both
sides were unhorsed into the water. There were some
knights and squires from Artois and Picardy, in the pay
of Sir Godémar, who, in hope of preferment and to acquire honor, had posted themselves at this ford ; and they
appeared to be equally fond of tilting in the water as on
dry land.

The French were drawn up in battle-array near the
narrow pass leading to the ford, and the English were
much annoyed by them as they came out of the water to
gain the land ; for there were among them Genoese crossbow-men, who did them much mischief. On the other
hand, the English archers shot so well together, that they
forced the men at arms to give way. At this ford of
Blanchetaque many gallant feats of arms were performed
on each side ; but in the end the English crossed over,
and, as they came on shore, hastened to the fields. After

the king, the prince, and the other lords had crossed, the French did not long keep their order, but ran for the fastest. When Sir Godémar du Fay found his army was discomfited, he saved himself as quickly as he could, and many with him ; some making for Abbeville, others for St. Ricquier. The infantry, however, could not escape, and there were numbers of those from Abbeville, Arras, Montreuil, and St. Ricquier, slain or taken prisoners. The pursuit lasted more than a league. The English had scarcely gained the opposite bank, when some of the light-horse of the French army, particularly those belonging to the King of Bohemia and Sir John of Hainault, advanced on the rear, took from them some horses and accoutrements, and slew several on the bank who were late in crossing. The King of France had set out from Airaines that morning, thinking to find the English on the banks of the Somme. When news was brought to him of the defeat of Sir Godémar and his army, he immediately halted, and demanded of his marshals what was to be done. They answered, "You can only cross the river by the bridge of Abbeville, for the tide is now in at Blanchetaque." The King of France therefore turned back, and took up his quarters at Abbeville. The King of England, when he had crossed the Somme, gave thanks to God for it, and began his march in the same order he had done before. He called to him Gobin Agace, gave him and his companions their freedom without ransom, and ordered the hundred nobles of gold to be presented him, as well as a good horse. The king continued his march, thinking to take up his quarters at a good and large town called Noyelle, situated hard by ; but when he was informed that it belonged to the Countess d'Aumale, sister to the late Robert d'Artois, he sent to assure the inhabitants, as well as all the farmers belong-

ing to her, that they should not be hurt. He marched farther on, but his two marshals rode to Crotoy near the
sea : they took the town, and burnt it. In the harbor they
found many ships and other vessels laden with wines from
Poitou, Saintonge, and La Rochelle. They ordered the
best to be carried to the English army ; then one of the
marshals pushed forward, even as far as the gates of
Abbeville, and returned by St. Ricquier, following the
seashore to the town of St. Esprit de Rue.

These two battalions of the marshals came on a Friday,
in the afternoon, to where the king was ; and they fixed
their quarters, all three together, near Crecy in Ponthieu.
The King of England, who had been informed that the
King of France was following him in order to give him
battle, said to his people, "Let us post ourselves here ;
for we will not go farther before we have seen our enemies. I have good reason to wait for them on this spot,
as I am now upon the lawful inheritance of my lady-
mother, which was given her as her marriage-portion ; and
I am resolved to defend it against my adversary Philip de
Valois." Inasmuch as his forces were not more than one-
eighth as many as those of the King of France, his marshals fixed upon the most advantageous situation ; and the
army went and took possession of it. He then sent his
scouts toward Abbeville, to learn if the King of France
meant to take the field this Friday; but they returned, and
said they saw no appearance of it : upon which he dismissed his men to their quarters, with orders to be in
readiness by times in the morning, and to assemble in the
same place. The King of France remained all Friday in
Abbeville, waiting for more troops. He sent his marshals,
the Lord of St. Venant, and Lord Charles of Montmorency, out of Abbeville to examine the country, and get

some certain intelligence of the English. They returned
about vespers, with the information that the English were
encamped on the plain. That night the King of France
entertained at supper in Abbeville all the princes and
chief lords. There was much conversation relative to
war; and the king entreated them after supper, that they
would always remain in friendship with each other, — that
they would be friends without jealousy, and courteous
without pride. The king was still expecting the Earl of
Savoy, who ought to have been there with a thousand
lances, as he had been well paid for them at Troyes in
Champaign three months in advance.

CHAPTER LIII.

THE ORDER OF BATTLE OF THE ENGLISH AT CRECY, WHO WERE DRAWN UP IN THREE BATTALIONS ON FOOT.

THE King of England, as I have mentioned before,
encamped this Friday in the plain, for he found the
country abounding in provisions; but if they should have
failed he had plenty in the carriages which attended on
him. The army set about furbishing and repairing their
armor; and the king gave a supper that evening to the
earls and barons of his army, when they made good cheer.
On their taking leave, the king remained alone with the
lords of his bedchamber: he retired into his oratory, and,
falling on his knees before the altar, prayed to God, that,
if he should combat his enemies on the morrow, he might
come off with honor. About midnight he went to bed;
and, rising early the next day, he and the Prince of Wales
heard mass, and took the communion. The greater part

King Edward III. praying in his Tent the Night before the Battle of Crecy.

of his army did the same, confessed, and made suitable preparations. After mass the king ordered his men to arm themselves, and assemble on the ground he had before selected. He had enclosed a large park near a wood in the rear of his army, in which he placed all his baggage-wagons and horses; and this park had but one entrance. His men at arms and archers remained on foot.

The king afterwards ordered, through his constable and his two marshals, that the army should be divided into three battalions. In the first he placed the young Prince of Wales, and with him the Earls of Warwick and Oxford, Sir Godfrey de Harcourt, the Lord Reginald Cobham, Lord Thomas Holland, Lord Stafford, Lord Manley, the Lord Delaware, Sir John Chandos, Lord Bartholomew Burgherst, Lord Robert Neville, Lord Thomas Clifford, the Lord Bourchier, the Lord Latimer, and many other knights and squires whom I cannot name. There might be in this first division about eight hundred men at arms, two thousand archers, and a thousand Welshmen. They advanced in regular order to their ground, each lord under his banner and pennon, and in the centre of his men. In the second battalion were the Earl of Northampton, the Earl of Arundel, the Lords Ross, Willoughby, Basset, St. Albans, Sir Lewis Tufton, Lord Multon, the Lord Loccels, and many others; amounting in all to about eight hundred men at arms and twelve hundred archers. The third battalion was commanded by the king, and was composed of about seven hundred men at arms and two thousand archers.

The king then mounted a small palfrey, having a white wand in his hand, and attended by his two marshals on each side of him: he rode a foot's pace through all the ranks, encouraging and entreating the army that they would guard his honor, and defend his right. He spoke this so sweetly, and with such a cheerful countenance, that all who had been dispirited were directly comforted by seeing and hearing him. When he had thus visited all the battalions, it was near ten o'clock : he retired to his own division, and ordered them all to eat heartily, and drink a glass after.

They ate and drank at their ease ; and, having packed up pots, barrels, &c., in the carts, they returned to their battalions, according to the marshals' orders, and seated themselves on the ground, placing their helmets and bows before them, that they might be the fresher when their enemies should arrive.

CHAPTER LIV.

The Order of the French Army at Crecy.

THAT same Saturday the King of France rose be-times, and heard mass in the monastery of St. Peter's in Abbeville, where he was lodged. Having ordered his army to do the same, he left that town after sunrise. When he had marched about two leagues from Abbeville, and was approaching the enemy, he was advised to form his army in order of battle, and to let those on foot march forward, that they might not be trampled on by the horses. The king upon this sent off four knights, the Lord Moyne of Bosthberg, the Lord of Noyer, the Lord of Beaujeu, and the Lord of Aubigny, who rode so near to the English that they could clearly make out their position. The English plainly perceived that they were come to reconnoitre them : however, they took no notice of it, but suffered them to return unmolested. When the King of France saw them coming back, he halted his army ; and the knights, pushing through the crowds, came near the king, who said to them, "My lords, what news?" They looked at each other without opening their mouths, for neither chose to speak first. At last the king addressed himself to the Lord Moyne, who was attached to the King of Bohemia, and had performed very many gallant deeds, so that he was esteemed one of the most valiant knights in Christendom. The Lord Moyne said, " Sir, I will speak, since it pleases you to order me, but under the correction of my companions. We have advanced far enough to reconnoitre your enemies. Know, then, that they are drawn up in three battalions, and are waiting for you. I would advise, for my part (submitting, however, to better counsel), that you halt your army here, and quarter them for the night ; for before the rear shall come up, and the army be properly drawn out, it will be very late, your men will be tired and in disorder, while they will find your enemies fresh and properly arrayed. On the morrow you may draw up your army more at your ease, and may reconnoitre at leisure as to the part where it will be most advantageous to begin the attack ; for be assured they will wait for you." The king commanded that it should be so done; and the two marshals rode, one toward the front and the other toward the rear, crying out, " Halt banners, in the name of God and St. Denis!" Those that were in the front halted; but those behind said they would not halt until they were as far forward as the front. When the front perceived the rear pressing on, they pushed forward ; and neither the king nor the marshals could stop them, but they marched without any order until they came in sight of their enemies. As soon as the foremost rank saw them, they fell back at once in great disorder; which alarmed those in the rear, who thought they had been fighting. There was then space and room enough for them to have passed forward, had they been willing: some did so, but others remained shy. All the roads between Abbeville and Crecy were covered with common people, who, when they were come within three leagues of their enemies, drew their swords, bawling out, "Kill, kill!" and with them were many great lords that were eager to make show of their courage. There is no man, unless he had been present, that can imagine, or describe truly, the confusion of that day; especially the bad management and disorder of the French, whose troops were beyond number. What I know, and shall relate in this book, I have learned chiefly from the English,—who had well observed the confusion they were in, —and from those attached to Sir John of Hainault, who was always near the person of the King of France.

CHAPTER LV.

The Battle of Crecy, between the Kings of France and of England.

THE English, who were drawn up in three divisions and seated on the ground, seeing their enemies advance, rose undauntedly up, and fell into their ranks. That of the prince was the first to do so, whose archers were formed in the manner of a portcullis, or harrow, and the men at arms in the rear. The Earls of Northampton and Arundel, who commanded the second division, had posted themselves in good order on his wing to succor the prince, if necessary.

You must know that these kings, earls, barons, and lords of France did not advance in any regular order, but one after the other, or any way most pleasing to themselves. As soon as the King of France came in sight of the English, his blood began to boil, and he cried out to his marshals, " Order the Genoese forward, and begin the battle, in the name of God and St. Denis ! " There were about fifteen thousand Genoese crossbow-men ; but they were quite fatigued, having marched on foot that day six leagues, completely armed and with their crossbows. They told the constable they were not in a fit condition to do any great things that day in battle. The Earl of Alençon, hearing this, said, " This is what one gets by employ-ing such scoundrels, who fall off when there is any need for them." During this time a heavy rain fell, accompanied by thunder and a very terrible eclipse of the sun ; and before this rain a great flight of crows hovered in the air over all those battalions, making a loud noise. Shortly afterwards it cleared up, and the sun shone very bright ; but the Frenchmen had it in their faces, and the English at their backs. When the Genoese were somewhat in order, and approached the English, they set up a loud shout in order to frighten them ; but they remained quite still, and did not seem to attend to it. They then set up a second shout, and advanced a little forward ; but the English never moved.

They hooted a third time, advancing with their cross-bows presented, and began to shoot. The English archers then advanced one step forward, and shot their arrows with such force and quickness, that it seemed as if it snowed. When the Genoese felt these arrows, which

pierced their arms, heads, and through their armor, some
of them cut the strings of their crossbows, others flung
them on the ground, and all turned about and retreated
quite discomfited. The French had a large body of men
at arms on horseback, richly dressed, to support the Genoese. The King of France, seeing them thus fall back,
cried out, "Kill me those scoundrels ; for they stop up
our road, without any reason." Then you should have
seen the above-mentioned men at arms lay about them,
killing all they could of these runaways.

The English continued shooting as vigorously and
quickly as before. Some of their arrows fell among the
horsemen, who were sumptuously equipped, and, killing
and wounding many, made them caper and fall among
the Genoese, so that they were in such confusion they
could never rally again.   In the English army there were
some Cornish and Welshmen on foot, who had armed
themselves with large knives : these, advancing through
the ranks of the men at arms and archers, who made way
for them, came upon the French when they were in this
danger, and, falling upon earls, barons, knights, and
squires, slew many ; at which the King of England was
afterwards much displeased. The valiant King of Bohemia was slain there. He was called Charles of Luxembourg, for he was the son of the gallant king and emperor Henry of Luxembourg. Having heard the order of
the battle, he inquired where his son the Lord Charles
was : his attendants answered that they did not know, but
believed he was fighting. The king said to them, "Gentlemen, you are all my people, my friends and brethren at
arms this day : therefore, as I am blind, I request of you
to lead me so far into the engagement that I may strike
one stroke with my sword." The knights replied, they

The Blind King of Bohemia dead on the Battle-field of Crecy.

would directly lead him forward; and, in order that they might not lose him in the crowd, they fastened all the reins of their horses together, and put the king at their head, that he might gratify his wish, and advanced toward the enemy. The Lord Charles of Bohemia, who already signed his name as King of Germany, and bore the arms, had come in good order to the engagement; but, when he perceived that it was likely to turn out against the French, he departed, and I do not well know what road he took. The king his father rode in among the enemy, and made good use of his sword; for he and his companions fought most gallantly. They advanced so far that they were all slain; and on the morrow they were found on the ground, with their horses all tied together.

The Earl of Alençon advanced in regular order upon the English, to fight with them, as did the Earl of Flanders in another part. These two lords with their detachments, coasting, as it were, the archers, came to the prince's battalion, where they fought valiantly for a length of time. The King of France was eager to march to the place where he saw their banners displayed; but there was a hedge of archers before him. He had that day made a present of a handsome black horse to Sir John of Hainault, who had mounted on it a knight of his called Sir John de Fusselles, that bore his banner; which horse ran off with him, and forced his way through the English army, and, when about to return, stumbled and fell into a ditch, and severely wounded him. He would have been dead if his page had not followed him round the battalions, and found him unable to rise: he had not, however, any other hinderance than from his horse, for the English did not quit the ranks that day to make prisoners. The page alighted, and raised him up; but he did not return the way he came, as he would have found it difficult from the crowd. This battle, which was fought on the Saturday between La Broyes and Crecy, was very murderous and cruel, and many gallant deeds of arms were performed that were never known. Toward evening many knights and squires of the French had lost their masters: they wandered up and down the plain, attacking the English in small parties. They were soon destroyed; for the English had determined that day to give no quarter, or hear of ransom from any one.

Early in the day some French, Germans, and Savoyards had broken through the archers of the prince's battalion, and had engaged with the men at arms; upon which the second battalion came to his aid, and it was time, for otherwise he would have been hard pressed. The first division, seeing the danger they were in, sent a knight in great haste to the King of England, who was posted upon an eminence near a windmill. On the knight's arrival he said, "Sir, the Earl of Warwick, the Lord Reginald Cobham, and the others who are about your son, are vigorously attacked by the French; and they entreat that you would come to their assistance with your battalion, for, if their numbers should increase, they fear he will have too much to do." The king replied, "Is my son dead, unhorsed, or so badly wounded that he cannot support himself?" — "Nothing of the sort, thank God," rejoined the knight; "but he is in so hot an engagement that he has great need of your help." The king answered, "Now, Sir Thomas, return to those that sent you, and tell them from me not to send again for me this day, or expect that I shall come, let what will happen, as long as my son has life: and say that I command them to let the boy win his spurs; for I am determined, if it please God, that all the glory and honor of this day shall be given to him and to those into whose care I have intrusted him." The knight returned to his lords, and related the king's answer, which mightily encouraged them, and made them repent they had ever sent such a message.

It is a certain fact, that Sir Godfrey de Harcourt, who was in the prince's battalion, having been told by some of the English that they had seen the banner of his brother engaged in the battle against him, was exceedingly anxious to save him ; but he was too late, for he was left dead on the field, and so was the Earl of Aumarle, his nephew. On the other hand, the Earls of Alençon and of Flanders were fighting lustily under their banners, and with their own people ; but they could not resist the force of the English, and were there slain, as well as many other knights and squires that were attending on or accompanying them. The Earl of Blois, nephew to the King of France, and the Duke of Lorraine, his brother-in-law, with their troops, made a gallant defence ; but they were surrounded by a troop of English and Welsh, and slain in spite of their prowess. The Earl of St. Pol and the Earl of Auxerre were also killed, as well as many others. Late after vespers, the King of France had not more about him than sixty men, every one included. Sir John of Hainault, who was of the number, had once remounted the king, for his horse had been killed under him by an arrow : he said to the king, "Sir, retreat while you have an opportunity, and do not expose yourself so simply : if you have lost this battle, another time you will be the conqueror." After he had said this, he took the bridle of the king's horse, and led him off by force, for he had before entreated of him to retire. The king rode on until he came to the castle of La Broyes, where he found the gates shut, for it was very dark. The king ordered the governor of it to be summoned : he came upon the battlements, and asked who it was that called at such an hour. The king answered, "Open, open, governor : it is the fortune of France." The governor, hearing the king's voice, immediately descended, opened the gate, and let down the bridge. The king and his company entered the castle ; but he had only with him five barons, — Sir John of Hainault, the Lord Charles of Montmorency, the Lord of Beaujeu, the Lord of Aubigny, and the Lord of Montfort. The king would not bury himself in such a place as that, but, having taken some refreshments, set out again with his attendants about midnight, and rode on under the direction of guides who were well acquainted with the country, until about daybreak he came to Amiens, where he halted. This Saturday the English never quitted their ranks in pursuit of any one, but remained on the field, guarding their position, and defending themselves against all who attacked them. The battle was ended at the hour of vespers.

[There can be no better opportunity than this celebrated chapter affords to show the young reader how Froissart's Chronicles looked. both in their first English guise, and in the original old French. It is, therefore, repeated here in both versions.

The first is especially valuable as an example of how our language looked and sounded during the first quarter of the sixteenth century. The translator, John Bourchier, Lord Berners. was a notable soldier and statesman, as well as a scholar. He came of a good family : his grandfather was son of Anne, granddaughter of King Edward the Third. He was born about 1467 ; in due time went to college, fought in the French wars, travelled on the Continent, became a favorite of King Henry the Eighth, was employed in honorable embassies, became chancellor of the exchequer, and finally passed his quiet age as governor of Calais. It was at the request of King Henry the Eighth that he translated Froissart into English, though he evidently loved our fine old writer on his own account, and speaks thus in his quaint preface: ". . . Whan I advertysed and remembred the manyfolde comodyties of hystorie, howe benefyciall it is to mortall folke, and eke howe laudable and merytoryous a deed it is to write hystories, fixed my mynde to do some thyng therein; and ever whan this ymaginacyon came to me, I volved, tourned, and redde many volumes and bokes, conteyning famouse histories; and amonge all other, I redde diligently the four volumes or bokes of sir Johan Froyssart of the countrey of Heynaulte, written in the Frenche tonge, whiche I iudged comodyous, necessarie, and profytable to be hadde in Englysshe, sithe they treat of the famous actes done in our parties; . . . and specially they redounde to the honoure of Englysshemen."

Accordingly, under the "gracyous suppertacyon" of the king, he made his translation, the first volume of which was printed by Pyason in the year 1523, announcing itself thus: "Here begynnith the firste volum of Syr John Froissart: of the Cronycles of Englande, Fraunce, Spayne, Portyugale, Scotlande, Bretaine, Flaunders: and other places adjoynynge. Translated oute of Frenche into oure maternall Englysshe tongue, by John Bouchier, knyghte, lorde Berners: At the commandement of oure moste hyghe redouted Soveraygne lorde kynge Henrye the VIII, kynge of Englaunde, Fraunce, and Irelande, defendour of the faith: and of the church of Englande and also of Irelande in earth the supreme heade."

I earnestly hope that this following chapter of what may perhaps fairly be called the first classic in modern English prose may tempt some young reader hereafter to study Berners more carefully, and to re-infuse, under his influence, the old fire and color and brightness into the pale and often pitiful sentences of our current style. — S. L.]

Of the batayle of Cressy bytwene the kyng of England and the frenche kyng.

CAP. CXXX.

THENGLYSSHMEN who were in thre batayls, lyeing on the grounde to rest them, assone as they saw the frenchmen aproche, they rose upon their fete, fayre and easely, without any hast, and arranged their batayls: the first, which was the princes batell, the archers there stode in manner of a herse,* and the men of armes in the botome ot

---

* French for *a harrow.*

the batayle.   Therle of Northāpton,* and therle of Arundell, with the
second batell, were on a wyng in good order, redy to confort the
princes batayle, if nede were.   The lordes and knyghtes of France,
cāe * not to the assemble togyder in good order, for some cāe before,
and some came after, in such hast and yvell order, yᵗ † one of thē *
dyd trouble another : whan the french kyng sawe the englysshmen, his
blode chaunged, and sayde to his marshals, make the genowayes go
on before, and begynne the batayle in the name of god and saynt
Denyse ; ther were of the genowayes crosbowes, about a fiftene thousand, but they were so wery of goyng a fote that day, a six leages,
armed with their crosbowes, that they sayde to their constables, we
be not well ordred to fyght this day, for we be not in the case to do
any great dede of armes, we have more nede of rest : these wordes
came to the erle of Alanson, who sayd, a man is well at ease to be
charged wᵗ ‡ suche a sorte of rascalles, to be faynt and fayle now at
moost nede.   Also the same season there fell a great rayne, and a
clyps, with a terryble thunder, and before the rayne, ther came fleyng
over both batayls, a great nombre of crowes, for feare of the tempest comynge.   Than anone the eyre beganne to wax clere, and the
sonne to shyne fayre and bright, the which was right in the french-
mens eyen and on the englysshmens backes.   Whan the genowayes
were assembled toguyder, and beganne to aproche, they made a great
leape and crye, to abasshe thenglysshmen, but they stode styll, and
styredde not for all that; thañe the genowayes agayne the seconde
tyme made another leape, and a fell crye, and stepped forward a lytell,
and thenglysshmen remeued not one fote ; thirdly agayne they leapt
and cryed, and went forthe tyll they come within shotte ; thañe they
shotte feersly with their crosbowes ; than thenglysshe archers stept
forthe one pase, and lette fly their arowes so hotly, and so thycke, that
it semed snowe : when the genowayes felte the arowes persynge
through heedes, armes, and brestes, many of them cast downe their
crosbowes, and dyde cutte their strynges, and retourned dysconfited.
Whan the frenche kynge sawe them flye away, he sayd, slee these
rascals, for they shall lette and trouble us without reason : then ye
shulde have sene the men of armes dasshe in among them, and
kylled a great nombre of them; and ever styll the englysshmen shot

---

* The mark "-" over a letter denotes an *m* or an *n* added : thus "cāe" = *came ;*
" thē" = *them.*
    † yᵗ = *that.*   ‡ wᵗ = *with.*

where as they sawe thyckest preace; the sharpe arowes ranne into the men of armes, and into their horses, and many fell, horse and men, amōge * the genowayes; and when they were downe, they coude not relyve agayne, the preace was so thycke, that one overthrewe another. And also amonge the englysshemen there were certayne rascalles that went a fote, with great knyves, and they went in among the men of armes, and slewe and murdredde many as they lay on the grounde, bothe erles, baronnes, knyghtes, and squyers, whereof the kyng of Englande was after dyspleased, for he had rather they had bene taken prisoners. The valyant kyng of Behaygne, called Charles of Luzenbourge, sonne to the noble emperour Henry of Luzenbourge, for all that he was nyghe blynde, whan he understode the order of the batayle, he sayde to them about hym, where is the lorde Charles my son, his men sayde, sir, we can not tell, we thynke he be fyghtynge; than he sayde, sirs, ye ar my men, my companyons, and frendes in this iourney. I requyre you bring me so farre forwarde, that I may stryke one stroke with my swerde: they sayde they wolde do his commande ment, and to the intent that they shulde not lese hym in the prease, they tyed all their raynes of their bridelles eche to other, and sette the kynge before to acomplysshe his desyre, and so thei went on their ennemyes; the lorde Charles of Behaygne, his sonne, who wrote hymselfe kyng of Behaygne, and bare the armes, he came in good order to the batayle, but whañe he sawe that the matter wente awrie on their partie, he departed, I can not tell you whiche waye; the kynge his father was so farre forewarde that he strake a stroke with his swerde, ye and mo than foure, and fought valyantly, and so dyde his company, and they advētured themselfe so forwarde, that they were ther all slayne, and the next day they were founde in the place about the kyng, and all their horses tyed eche to other. The erle of Alansone came to the batayle right ordynotlye, and fought with thenglysshmen; and the erle of Flaunders also on his parte; these two lordes with their cōpanyes coosted the englysshe archers, and came to the princes batayle, and there fought valyantly longe. The frenche kynge wolde fayne have come thyder whanne he sawe their baners, but there was a great hedge of archers before hym. The same day the frenche kynge hadde gyven a great blacke courser to sir Johan of Heynault, and he made the lorde Johan of Fussels to ryde on hym, and to bere his banerre; the same horse tooke the bridell in the tethe, and brought hym

* = *amonge.*

through all the currours of thēglysshmen, and as he wolde have retourned agayne, he fell in a great dyke, and was sore hurt, and had
ben ther deed, and his page had not ben,* who folowed hym through
all the batayls, and sawe wher his maister lay in the dyke, and had
none other lette but for his horse, for thenglysshmen wolde not yssue
out of their batayle, for takyng of any prisoner; thañe the page
alyghted and relyved his maister, than he went not backe agayn yͤ
same way that they came, there was to many in his way. This batayle
bytwene Broy and Cressy, this saturday, was right cruell and fell, and
many a feat of armes done, that came not to my knowledge; in the
night, dyverse knyghtes and sqyers lost their maisters, and sometyme
came on thenglysshmen, who receyved them in suche wyse, that they
were ever nighe slayne, for there was none taken to mercy nor to
raunsome, for so the englysshmen were determyned : in the mornyng
the day of the batayle, certayne frenchemen and almaygnes † perforce
opyned the archers of the princes batayle, and came and fought with
the men of armes hande to hande : than the seconde batayle of thenglysshmen came to socour the princes batayle, the whiche was tyme,
for they had as than moche ado; and they with yͤ prince sent a mes-
sanger to the kynge, who was on a lytell wyndmyll hyll; than the
knyght sayd to the kyng, sir, therle of Warwyke. and therle of Cāfort,
sir Reynolde Cobham, and other, suche as be about the prince your
sorne, ar feersly fought with all, and are sore handled, wherfore they
desyre you, that you and your batayle wolle come and ayde them, for
if the frenchmen encrease, as they dout they woll, your sonne and
they shall have much ado. Than the kynge sayde, is my sonne deed
or hurt, or on the yerthe felled; no sir, quoth the knyght, but he is
hardely matched, wherfore he hath nede of your ayde. Well, sayde
the kyng, retourne to hym, and to them that sent you hyther, and say
to them, that they sende no more to me for any adventure that falleth,
as long as my sonne is alyve; and also say to thē, that they suffre hym
this day to wynne his spurres, for if god be pleased, I woll this iourney be his, and the honoure thereof, and to them that be aboute hym.
Than the kynght retourned agayn to thē, and shewed the kynges
wordes, the which gretly encouraged them, and repoyned in that they
had sende to the kynge as they dyd. Sir Godfray of Harecourt, wolde
gladly that the erle of Harecourt, his brother, myght have bene saved,

---

* That is, *had been there dead if* (and = *an*) *it had not been for his page.*
† *almaygnes = Allemands = Germans.*

for he hard say by thē that sawe his baner, howe that he was ther in
the felde on the french partie, but sir Godfray coude not come to
hym betymes, for he was slayne or he coude cōe at hym, and so was
also the erle of Almare, his nephue. In another place, the erle of
Alenson, and therle of Flaunders, fought valyantly, every lorde under
his owne baner; but finally, they coude not resyst agaynt the puys-
sance of the englysshemen, and so ther they were also slayne, and
dyvers other knyghtes and sqyers. Also therle Lewes of Bloyes,
nephue to the frenche kyng, and the duke of Lorayne, fought under
their baners, but at last they were closed in among a cōpany of englysshmen and walsshemen, and there were slayne, for all their prowes.
Also there was slayne, the erle of Ausser, therle of saynt Poule. and
many other. In the evenynge, the frenche kynge, who had lefte about
hym no mo than a threscore persons, one and other, wherof sir John
of Heynalt was one, who had remounted ones the kynge, for his horse
was slayne with an arowe, thā he sayde to the kynge, sir, departe
hense, for it is tyme, lese not yourselfe wylfully, if ye have losse at
this tyme, ye shall recover it agayne another season : and soo he toke
the kynges horse by the brydell, and ledde hym away in a maner perforce : than the kyng rode tyll he came to the castell of Broy, the
gate was closed, bycause it was by that tyme darke; than the kynge
called the captayne, who came to the walles, and sayd, who is that
calleth there this tyme of night, than the kynge sayde, open your
gate quickely, for this is the fortune of Fraunce : the captayne knewe
than it was the kyng, and opyned the gate, and let downe the bridge;
than the kyng entred. and he had with hym but fyve baronnes, sir
Johan of Heynault, sir Charles of Momorency, the lorde of Beauiewe,
the lorde Dobegny, and the lorde of Mountfort : the kynge wolde not
tary there, but drāke and departed thense about mydnyght, and so
rode by suche guydes as knewe the countrey, tyll he came in the
mornynge to Amyense, and there he rested. This saturday, the englysshemen never departed fro their batayls for chasynge of any man,
but kept styll their felde, and ever defended themselfe agaynst all
such as came to assayle them : this batayle ended aboute evynsonge
tyme.

COMMENT LE ROI DE FRANCE COMMANDA À SES MARÉCHAUX FAIRE COMMENCER LA BATAILLE PAR LES GÉNOIS : ET COMMENT LES DITS GÉNOIS FURENT TOUS DÉCONFITS.

Il n'est nul homme, tant fut présent à cette journée, ni eut bon loisir d'aviser et imaginer toute la besogne ainsi qu'elle alla, qui en sut ni put imaginer, ni recorder la vérité, specialement de la partie des François, tant y eut pauvre arroy et ordonnance en leurs courois (disposition) ; et ce que j'en sais, je l'ai su le plus par les Anglois, qui imaginèrent bien leur convenant (ordre), et aussi par les gens Messire Jean de Hainaut, qui fut toujours de-lez (près) le roi de France.

Les Anglois qui ordonnés étoient en trois batailles, et qui sévient jus (bas) à terre tout bellement, sitôt qu'ils virent les François approcher, ils se levèrent moult ordonnément, sans nul effroi, et se rangèrent en leurs batailles, celle du prince tout devant, leurs archers mis en manière d'une herse, et les gens-d'armes au fond de la bataille. Le comte de Northampton et le comte d'Arundel et leur bataille, qui faisoient la seconde, se tenoient sur aile bien ordonnément et avisés et pourvus pour conforter le prince, si besoin étoit. Vous devez savoir que ces seigneurs, rois, ducs, comtes, barons François ne vinrent mie jusques là tous ensemble, mais l'un devant, l'autre derrière, sans arroy et sans ordonnance. Quand le roi Philippe vint jusques sur la place où les Anglois étoient de là arrêtés et ordonnés, et il les vit, le sang lui mua, car il les héoit (haïssoit) et ne se fut adonc nullement refrené (retenu) ni abstenu d'eux combattre ; et dit à ses maréchaux : "Faites passer nos Génois devant et commencer la bataille, au nom de Dieu et de monseigneur St. Denis." Là avoit, de ces dits Génois arbalétriers, environ quinze mille qui eussent eu aussi cher néant que commencer adonc la bataille ; car ils étoient durement las et travaillés (fatigués) d'aller à pied ce jour plus de six lieues, tous armés, et de leurs arbalétres porter ; et dirent adonc à leurs connétables (commandants) qu'ils n'étoient mie adonc ordonnés de foire nul grand exploit de bataille.

Ces paroles volèrent jusques au comte d'Alençon, qui en fut durement courrucé et dit : "On se doit bien charger de telle ribaudaille qui faillent (manquent) au besoin."

Entrementes (pendant) que ces parols couroient et que ces Génois se reculoient et se détnoient (différoient) descendit une pluie du ciel, si grosse et si épaisse que merveilles, et un tonnerre, et un esclistre (eclair) moult grand et moult horrible.

Paravant cette pluie, pardessus les batailles, autant d'un côté que d'autre, avoient volé si grand' foison de courbeaux que sans nombre, et demeué le plus grand tempêtes du monde. Là disoient aucuns sages chevaliers que c'étoit un signe de grand' bataille et de grand' effusion de sang.

Après toutes ces choses se commença l'air à éclaircir et le soleil à luire bel et clair. Si l'avoient les François droit en l'œil et les Anglois par derrière. Quand les Génois furent tous recueillis et mis ensemble, et ils durent approcher leurs ennemis, ils commencèrent à crier si très haut que ce fut merveilles, et le firent pour ébahir les Anglois ; mais les Anglois se tinrent tous cois, ni oncques n'en firent semblant. Secondement encore crièrent eux ainsi, et puis allèrent un petit pas avant ; et les Anglois restoient tous cois, sans eux mouvoir de leur pas. Tiercement encore crièrent moult haut et moult clair, et passèrent avant, et tendirent leurs arbalétres et commencèrent à traire (tirer). Et ces archers d'Angleterre, quand ils virent cette ordonnance, passèrent un pas en avant, et puis firent voler ces sagettes (flèches) de grand' façon, qui entrèrent et descendirent si ouniement (à la fois) sur ces Génois que ce sembloit neige. Les Génois qui n'avoient pas appris à trouver tels archers que sont ceux d'Angleterre, quand ils sentirent ces sagettes (flèches) qui leur perçoient bras, têtes et ban-levre, furent tantôt déconfits et confèrent les plusieurs les cordes de leurs arcs et les aucuns les jetoient jus (à bas) ; si se mirent aussi de retour.

Entre eüx et les François avoît une grand' haie de gens d'armes, montés et parés moult richement, qui regardoient le convenant (disposition) des Génois ; si que quand ils cuidèrent (crurent) retourner, ils ne peuvent, car le roi de France, par grand mautalent (mécontentement), quand il vit leur pauvre arroy, et qu'ils se déconfisoient ainsi, commanda et dit : " Or tôt, tuez toute cette ribaudaille, car ils nous empêchent la voie sans raison." Là vissiez gens d'armes en tous lez (côtés) entre eux férir et frapper sur eux, et les plusieurs trébucher et cheoir parmi eux, qui oncques puis ne se relevèrent. Et toujours traioirent (tiroient) les Anglois en la plus grand' presse, qui rien ne perdoient de leur trait ; car ils empalloient et féroient parmi le corps ou parmi les membres gens et chevaux qui là chéoient (tomboient) et trebuchoient à grand meschef ; et ne pouvoient être relevés, si ce n'étoit par force et par grand' aide de gens. Ainsi se commença la bataille entre la Broye et Crécy en Ponthieu, ce samedi à heure de vespres.

CHAPTER LVI.

THE ENGLISH ON THE MORROW AGAIN DEFEAT THE FRENCH.

WHEN, on the Saturday night, the English heard no more hooting or shouting, nor any more crying out to particular lords or their banners, they looked upon the field as their own, and their enemies as beaten. They made great fires, and lighted torches because of the obscurity of the night. King Edward then came down from his post, who all that day had not put on his helmet, and, with his whole battalion, advanced to the Prince of Wales, whom he embraced in his arms, and kissed, and said, "Sweet son, God give you good perseverance : you are my son, for most loyally have you acquitted yourself this day. You are worthy to be a sovereign." The prince bowed down very low, and humbled himself, giving all the honor to the king his father. The English, during the night, made frequent thanksgivings to the Lord for the happy issue of the day, and without rioting; for the king had forbidden all riot or noise. On the Sunday morning there was so great a fog that one could scarcely see the distance of half an acre. The king ordered a detachment from the army, under the command of the two marshals, consisting of about five hundred lances and two thousand archers, to make an excursion, and see if there were any bodies of French collected together. The quota of troops from Rouen and Beauvais had, this Sunday morning, left Abbeville and St. Ricquier in Ponthieu, to join the French army, and were ignorant of the defeat of the preceding evening. They met this detachment, and, thinking they must be French, hastened to join them.

As soon as the English found who they were, they fell upon them, and there was a sharp engagement ; but the French soon turned their backs, and fled in great disorder. There were slain in this flight, in the open fields, under hedges and bushes, upward of seven thousand ; and, had it been clear weather, not one soul would have escaped.

A little time after, the same party fell in with the Archbishop of Rouen, and the great Prior of France, who were also ignorant of the discomfiture of the French ; for they had been informed that the king was not to fight before Sunday. Here began a fresh battle, for these two lords were well attended by good men at arms : however, they could not withstand the English, but were almost all slain, with the two chiefs who commanded them, very few escaping. In the course of the morning the English found many Frenchmen who had lost their road on the Saturday, and had lain in the open fields, not knowing what was become of the king or their own leaders. The English put to the sword all they met ; and it has been assured to me for fact, that of foot-soldiers sent from the cities, towns, and municipalities, there were slain, this Sunday morning, four times as many as in the battle of Saturday.

CHAPTER LVII.

THE ENGLISH NUMBER THE DEAD SLAIN AT THE BATTLE OF CRECY.

THIS detachment, which had been sent to look after the French, returned as the king was coming from mass, and related to him all that they had seen and met with. After he had been assured by them that there was not any appearance of the French collecting another army, he sent to have the numbers and condition of the dead examined.

He ordered on this business Lord Reginald Cobham, Lord Stafford, and three heralds to examine their arms, and two secretaries to write down all the names. They took much pains to examine all the dead, and were the whole day in the field of battle, not returning but just as the king was sitting down to supper. They made to him a very circumstantial report of all they had observed, and said they had found eighty banners, the bodies of eleven princes, twelve hundred knights, and about thirty thousand common men.

The English halted there that day, and on the Monday morning prepared to march off. The king ordered the bodies of the principal knights to be taken from the ground, and carried to the monastery of Montenay, which was hard by, there to be interred in consecrated ground. He had it proclaimed in the neighborhood, that he should grant a truce for three days, in order that the dead might be buried. He then marched on, passing by Montrieul-sur-mer.

His marshals made an excursion as far as Hesdin, and burnt Vaubain and Serain; but they could make nothing of the castle, as it was too strong and well guarded. They lay that Monday night upon the banks of the Canche, near Blangy. The next day they rode toward Boulogne, and burnt the towns of St. Josse and Neufchatel: they did the same to Estaples, in the country of the Boulonois. The whole army passed through the forest of Hardelou, and the country of the Boulonois, and came to the large town of Wisant, where the king, prince, and all the English lodged ; and, having refreshed themselves there one whole day, they came on the Thursday before the strong town of Calais.

CHAPTER LVIII.

The King of England lays Siege to Calais. — The Poorer Sort of the Inhabitants are sent out of it.

A BURGUNDY knight named Sir John de Vienne was governor of Calais ; and with him were Sir Arnold d'Andreghen, Sir John de Surie, Sir Bardo de Bellebourne, Sir Geoffrey de la Motte, Sir Pepin de Were, and many other knights and squires. On the king's arrival before Calais, he laid siege to it, and built, between it and the river and bridge, houses of wood ; they were laid out in streets, and thatched with straw or broom ; and in this town of the king's there was every thing necessary for an army, besides a market-place, where there were markets every Wednesday and Saturday for butchers' meat, and all other sorts of merchandise : cloth, bread, and every thing else, which came from England and Flanders, might be had there, as well as all comforts, for money. The English made frequent excursions to Guines and its neighborhood, and to the gates of St. Omer and Boulogne, from whence they brought great booties back to the army. The king made no attacks upon the town, as he knew it would be only lost labor, and he was sparing of his men and artillery ; but said he would remain there so long that he would starve the town into a surrender, unless the King of France should come there to raise the siege. When the governor of Calais saw the preparations of the King of England, he collected together all the poor inhabitants, who had not laid in any store of provisions, and, one Wednesday morning, sent upward of seventeen hundred men, women, and children out of the town. As they were passing through the English army, they asked them why they had left the town. They replied, because they had nothing to eat. The king upon this allowed them to pass through in safety, ordered them a hearty dinner, and gave to each two sterlings, as charity and alms; for which many of them prayed earnestly for the king.

CHAPTER LIX.

The Duke of Normandy raises the Siege of Aiguillon.

THE Duke of Normandy, whom we left before Aiguillon, which he was besieging, while Sir Walter Manny and the other knights were within it, made, about the middle of August, a skirmish before the castle, which increased so much that almost his whole army was engaged in it. Near about this time, the Lord Philip of Burgundy, Earl of Artois and of Boulogne, and cousin-german to the duke, arrived. He was a very young knight. As soon as this skirmish commenced, he armed himself, and, mounting a handsome steed, stuck spurs into him in order to hasten to the combat; but the horse, taking the bit between his teeth, ran off with him, and in crossing a ditch fell into it, upon the knight, who was so grievously bruised that he never recovered, and in a short time died. Soon afterwards the King of France sent to his son the Duke of Normandy, to lay all other things aside, and raise the siege, in order to return directly into France to defend his inheritance against the English. The duke upon this demanded advice from the earls and barons there present, for he had vowed he would never move from thence until he had the castle, and all within it, in his power ; but they assured him, since the king his father had so expressly ordered him to return, he might comply without any forfeiture of his honor. On the morrow at break of day, therefore, the French decamped, and, trussing up tents and baggage with great haste, took the road for France.

The knights who were in Aiguillon, seeing this, armed themselves, and, mounting their horses, sallied forth (the pennon of Sir Walter Manny taking the lead), fell upon the French, who were scarcely all marched off, cut down and slew numbers, and took upward of forty prisoners, whom they brought back to the castle. From them they learned the successful campaign the King of England had made in France, and that at present he was laying siege to Calais. Before the King of France left Amiens, after the battle of Crecy, to go for Paris, he was so much enraged against Sir Godémar du Fay, for not having done his duty in defending the ford of Blanchetaque, by which means the English had entered Ponthieu, that he had determined to hang him ; to which many of his council also were inclined, for they were desirous that Sir Godémar should make some amends, by his death, for the defeat the king had suffered at Crecy, and called him traitor. But Sir John of Hainault excused him, and averted the king's anger, by saying that it would have been difficult for him to have resisted the English army, when all the flower of the French nobility could do nothing. Soon after this the Duke of Normandy arrived in France, where he was joyfully received by his parents the king and queen.

CHAPTER LX.

SIR WALTER MANNY, BY MEANS OF A PASSPORT, RIDES THROUGH FRANCE FROM AIGUILLON TO CALAIS.

ABOUT this time Sir Walter Manny had a conversation with a great knight from Normandy, whom he detained as his prisoner, and asked him what sum he was willing to pay for his ransom. The knight replied, "Three thousand crowns." Upon this Sir Walter said, "I know you are related to the Duke of Normandy, much beloved by him, and one of his privy councillors. I will let you free upon your honor, if you will go to the duke, and obtain from him a passport for myself and twenty others, that we may ride through France as far as Calais, paying courteously for whatever we may want. If therefore you obtain this from the king, I shall hold you free from your ransom, and also be much obliged to you; for I have a great desire to see the King of England, and will not remain in any town more than one night. If you cannot accomplish it, you will return in a month to this fortress, as to your prison." The knight set out for Paris, and having obtained from the duke the passport, returned with it to Sir Walter at Aiguillon, who acquitted him of his ransom. Sir Walter shortly afterwards set out with twenty horse, and took his road through Auvergne. He told everywhere who he was, and, at every place he stopped, showed his passport, and was directly set at liberty; but at Orleans he was arrested, although he showed his papers, and from thence conducted to Paris, where he was confined in the prison of the Châtelet.

When the Duke of Normandy heard of it, he went immediately to the king, and remonstrated with him on the
subject, because Sir Walter Manny had had his passport
through his means ; and demanded that he should as soon
as possible be set at liberty, otherwise it would be said
that he had betrayed him. The king answered that he
intended putting him to death, for he looked upon him as
one of his greatest enemies. Upon which the duke said,
that, if he put his intentions in execution, he would
never bear arms against the King of England, and would
prevent all those dependent on him from doing the same.
Very high words passed between them ; and he left the
king, declaring he would never serve in any of his armies
so long as Walter Manny should remain in prison.

Things remained in this situation a long time. There
was a knight from Hainault, named Sir Mansart d'Aisnes,
who was eager to serve Sir Walter, but had great difficulty
in getting access to the Duke of Normandy : however, at
last the king was advised to let Sir Walter out of prison,
and to pay him all his expenses. The king would have
Sir Walter to dine with him in the Hotel de Nerle at
Paris, when he presented him with gifts and jewels to
the amount of a thousand florins. Sir Walter accepted
of them upon condition that when he got to Calais he
should inform the king, his lord, of it ; and if it were
agreeable to his pleasure he would keep them, otherwise
he would send them back. The king and duke said he
had spoken like a loyal knight. Sir Walter then took
leave of them, rode on by easy day's journeys to Hainault, and remained, to refresh himself, three days in
Valenciennes. He arrived at Calais, where he was well
received by the King of England, who, upon being informed by Sir Walter of the presents he had from the

King of France, said, "Sir Walter, you have hitherto most loyally served us, and we hope you will continue to do so. Send back to King Philip his presents, for you have no right to keep them: we have enough, thank God, for you and ourselves, and are perfectly well disposed to do you all the good in our power for the services you have rendered us." Sir Walter took out all the jewels, and, giving them to his cousin the Lord of Mansac, said, "Ride into France, to King Philip, and recommend me to him; and tell him that I thank him many times for the fine jewels he presented me with, but that it is not agreeable to the will and pleasure of the King of England, my lord, that I retain them." The knight did as he was commanded; but the King of France would not take back the jewels: he gave them to the Lord of Mansac, who thanked the king for them, and had no inclination to refuse them.

CHAPTER LXI.

The King of Scotland, during the Siege of Calais, invades England.

I HAVE been silent some time respecting the King of Scotland, but until this moment I have not had any thing worth relating; for, as I have said before, mutual truces had been granted between him and the King of England, which had not been infringed. During the time the King of England was carrying on the siege of Calais, the Scots determined to make war upon him, thinking it a good opportunity to be revenged for the many disasters he had brought on them. England had at that time very few men at arms, as the king had a great number with him before Calais, as well as in his other armies in Brittany, Poitou, and Gascony. The King of France took great pains to foment this war, in order that the English might have so much to employ them at home as would oblige them to raise the siege of Calais, and return to England.

King David issued his summons for a parliament to be holden at Perth; which was attended by the earls, prelates, and barons of Scotland, who were unanimous for invading England as speedily as possible. Raynold, Lord of the Isles, who governed the wild Scots, and whom alone they obeyed, was sent to, and entreated to attend the parliament. He complied with the request, and brought three thousand of the wildest of his countrymen with him. When all the Scots were assembled, they amounted together to about forty thousand combatants; but they could not make their preparations so secretly as to prevent news of it coming to the knowledge of the Queen of England, who had taken up her residence in the North, near the borders. She wrote and sent summons to all that were attached to England to come to York by a certain day. Many men at arms and archers who had remained at home put themselves in motion, and advanced to Newcastle-upon-Tyne, which the queen had appointed as the final place of rendezvous. In the mean while, the Scots set out from Perth, and advanced the first day to Dunfermline; the next day they crossed a small arm of the sea; but the king went to Stirling, crossed the water on the morrow, and came to Edinburgh. Here they halted, and numbered their men. There were full three thousand knights and squires, well armed, and thirty thousand others, mounted on galloways. They marched to Roxburgh, the first fortress belonging to the English on their road, under the command of the Lord William Montacute,

who had lately erected it against the Scots. This castle
is handsome, and very strong: the Scots therefore passed
on without attacking it, and took up their quarters on the
banks of a river between Precy and Lincolle, whence
they began to destroy and burn the country of Cumber-
land. Some of their scouts advanced as far as York,
where they burnt all without the walls and down the river,
and returned to their army, within one day's march of
Newcastle.

CHAPTER LXII.

The Battle of Neville's Cross.

THE Queen of England, who was very anxious to defend her kingdom and guard it from all disturbers,
in order to show that she was in earnest about it came
herself to Newcastle-upon-Tyne. She took up her residence there, to wait for the forces she expected from
different parts of the kingdom. The Scots, who were informed that Newcastle was the place of rendezvous of the
English army, advanced thither, and sent their vanguard
to skirmish near the town; who, on their return, burnt
some hamlets adjoining to it. The smoke and flames
came into the town, which made the English impatient to
sally out upon those who had done this mischief; but
their leaders would not permit them. On the morrow the
King of Scotland, with full forty thousand men, including
all sorts, advanced within three short English miles of
Newcastle, and took up his quarters on the land of the
Lord Neville. He sent to inform the army in the town,
that, if they were willing to come forth, he would wait for

them, and give them battle. The barons and prelates of England sent for answer, that they accepted his offer, and would risk their lives with the realm of their lord and king. They sallied out, in number about twelve hundred men at arms, three thousand archers, and seven thousand other men, including the Welsh. The Scots posted themselves opposite to the English, and each army was drawn out in battle-array.

The Queen of England came to the place where her army was, and remained until it was drawn out in four battalions. The first was under the command of the Bishop of Durham and the Lord Percy; the second, under the Archbishop of York and the Lord Neville; the third, under the Bishop of Lincoln and Lord Mowbray; the fourth was commanded by Lord Baliol, governor of Berwick, the Archbishop of Canterbury, and the Lord Roos. Each battalion had its just proportion of men at arms and archers, as was expedient. The queen now advanced among them, and entreated them to do their duty well in defending the honor of their lord and king, and urged them, for the love of God, to fight manfully. They promised her that they would acquit themselves loyally, to the utmost of their power, and perhaps better than if the king had been there in person. The queen then took her leave, and recommended them to the protection of God and St. George. The two armies were soon after in motion, and the archers on each side began to shoot; but those of the Scots did not long continue it, while the English shot incessantly. When the battalions were got into close combat, the engagement was sharp and well fought.

The battle began about nine o'clock, and lasted until noon. The Scots had very hard and sharp axes, with which they dealt deadly blows; but at last the English gained the field, though it cost them dear by the loss of their men. On the part of the Scots, there fell in the field the Earl of Sys, the Earl Dostre, the Earl Patris, the Earl of Furlant, the Earl Dastredure, the Earl of Mar, the Earl John Douglas, Sir Alexander Ramsay who bore the king's banners, and many other barons, knights, and squires. The King of Scotland was taken prisoner, fighting most gallantly, and badly wounded before he was captured by a squire of Northumberland named John Copeland; who, as soon as he got him, pushed through the crowd, and with eight other companions rode off, and never stopped until he was distant from the field of battle about fifteen miles. He came about vespers to Ogle Castle, on the river Blythe, and there declared that he would not surrender his prisoner, the King of Scotland, to man or woman, except to his lord the King of England. That same day were taken prisoners the Earls of Murray and March, Lord William Douglas, Lord Robert de Wersy, the Bishops of Aberdeen and St. Andrews, and many other barons and knights. There were about fifteen thousand slain, and the remainder saved themselves as well as they could. This battle was fought near Newcastle, in the year 1346, on a Saturday preceding Michaelmas Day.

[The old ballad of "Durham Feilde" sings the battle of Neville's Cross described in the foregoing chapter, calling it "Durham Field" after the Bishop of Durham, who led the English. The poem is divided into two parts, of which only the second is here given on account of its length. The First Part relates, in true old-servant style, how the King of Scotland was informed that the King of England was gone into France with all his soldiers, leaving none behind but "Shepherds and millers, And priests with shaven crowns;"

whereupon " the King of Scots in a study stood," and resolved to seize such a favorable moment to overrun England in the absence of its king. He calls together his lords, and in a boastful mood proceeds to divide out the whole of England among them, as if he had nothing to do but march forward and take possession. Presently, however, his army is confronted with " the comminaltye of litle England ; " the King of Scots brags that

> " They be but English knaves,
>   But shepherds and millers both,
>   And mass priests with their staves ; "

and sends his herald to view them. When the herald returns,

> " Who leads those lads ? " said the King of Scots,
>   " Thou herald, tell thou me."
> The herald said, " The Bishop of Durham
>   Is captain of that companye ;
> For the Bishop hath spread the King's banner,
>   And to battell he buskes him boune." *
> " I sweare by St. Andrewe's bones," saies the King,
>   " I'll rapp that priest on the crowne ! "

But presently a very different tale is told in

PART II.

> The King looked towards litle Durham,
>   & that hee well beheld,
> that the Earle Percy was well armed,
>   with his battell axe entred the feild.

> the King looket againe towards litle Durham,
>   4 ancyents † there see hee ;
> there were to ‡ standards, 6 in a valley,
>   he cold not see them with his eye.

> My Lord of yorke was one of them,
>   my lord of Carlile was the other ;

---

* That is, *makes him ready.* † *Ensigns.* ‡ *Two.*

& my Lord ffluwilliams,
 the one came with the other.

the Bishopp of Durham commanded his men,
 & shortlye he them bade,
'that never a man shold goe to the feild to fight
 til he had served his god.'

500 priests said masse that day
 in durham in the feild;
& afterwards, as I hard say,
 they bare both speare & sheeld.

the Bishopp of Durham orders himselfe to fight
 with his battell axe in hand;
he said, "this day now I will fight
 as long as I can stand!"

"& soe will I," sayd my Lord of Carlile,
 "in this faire morning gay;"
"& soe will I," said my Lord ffluwilliams,
 "for Mary, that myld may."*

our English archers bent their bowes
 shortlye and anon,
they shott over the Scottish oast
 & scantlye toucht a man.

"hold downe your hands," sayd the Bishopp of Durham,
 "my archers good & true."
the 2ᵈ shoote that thé † shott
 full sore the Scottes itt rue.

the Bishopp of Durham spoke on hye
 that both partyes might heare,
"be of good cheere, my merrymen all,
 the Scotts flyen,‡ & changen there cheere!"

* *Mild maid,*—the Virgin Mary. † *They.* ‡ *Fly.*

but as thé saidden, soe thé didden,
   they fell on heapes hye;
our Englishmen laid on with their bowes
   as fast as they might dree.

The King of Scotts in a studye stood
   amongst his companye,
an arrow stoke him thorrow the nose
   & thorrow his armorye.

The King went to a marsh side
   & light beside his steede,
and leaned him down on his sword hilt,
   to let his nose bleede.

there followed him a yeoman of merry England,
   his name was John of Coplande;
"yeeld thee Traytor!" saies Coplande then,
   "thy liffe lyes in my hand."

"how shold I yeeld me?" sayes the King,
   "& thou art noe gentleman."
"noe, by my troth," sayes Copland there,
   "I am but a poore yeoman;

"what art thou better then I, Sir King?
   tell me if that thou can!
what art thou better then I, Sir King,
   now we be but man to man?"

the King smote angerly at Copland then,
   angerly in that stonde;
& then Copland was a bold yeoman,
   & bore the King to the ground.

he sett the King upon a Palfrey,
   himselfe upon a steede,
he tooke him by the bridle rayne,
   towards London he can * him Lead.

        * *'gan,*—began.

& when to London that he came,
   the King from ffrance was new come home.
& there unto the King of Scottes
   he sayd these words anon,

" how like you my shepards & my millers,
   my priests with shaven crownes?"
" by my fayth, they are the sorest fighting men
   that ever I mett on the ground;

" there was never a yeoman in merry England
   but he was worth a Scottish knight!"
" I,* by my troth," said King Edward, & laughe,
   " for you fought all against the right."

but now the Prince of merry England
   worthilye under his Sheelde
hath taken the King of ffrance
   at Poytiers in the ffeelde.

the Prince did present his father with that food,†
   the lovely King off ffrance,
& fforward of his Iourney he is gone:
   god send us all good chance!

" you are welcome, brothers!" sayd the King of Scotts,
   to the King of ffrance,
   " for I am come hither too soone;
Christ leeve that I had taken my way
   unto the court of Roone!"

" & soe wold I," said the King of ffrance,
   " when I came over the streame,
that I had taken my Iourney
   unto Ierusalem."

Thus ends the battell of ffaire Durham
   in one morning of may,

   * *Ay*,—yea.   † *Feod*,—one who owes fealty.

the battell of Cressey, & the battle of Potyers,
All within one monthes day.

then was welthe and welfare in mery England,
Solaces, game, & glee,
& every man loved other well,
& the King loved good yeomanrye

but God that made the grasse to growe,
& leaves on greenwoode tree,
now save & keepe our noble King,
& maintaine good yeomanry!

ffinis.]

CHAPTER LXIII.

JOHN COPELAND TAKES THE KING OF SCOTLAND PRISONER, AND RECEIVES GREAT ADVANTAGES FROM IT.

WHEN the Queen of England, who had remained in Newcastle, heard that her army had gained the day, she mounted her palfrey, and went to the field of battle. She was informed that the King of Scotland had been made prisoner by a squire of the name of John Copeland, but who had ridden off with him, they could not tell whither. The queen ordered that a letter should be written, commanding him to bring the King of Scots to her, and telling him that he had not done what was agreeable to her in carrying off his prisoner without leave. All that day the queen and army remained on the field of battle which they had won, and on the morrow returned to Newcastle.

When the letter from the queen was presented by a

knight to John Copeland, he answered that he would not give up his prisoner, the King of Scots, to man or woman, except to his own lord the King of England; that they might depend on his taking proper care of him, and he would be answerable for guarding him well. The queen upon this wrote letters to the king, which she sent off to Calais. She therein informed him of the state of his kingdom. The king then ordered John Copeland to come to him at Calais; who, having placed his prisoner under good guards, in a strong castle on the borders of North-umberland, set out, and, passing through England, came to Dover, where he embarked, and landed near Calais. When the King of England saw the squire, he took him by the hand, and said, "Ha! welcome, my squire, who by his valor has captured my adversary the King of Scot-land." John Copeland, falling on one knee, replied, "If God, out of his great kindness, has given me the King of Scotland, and permitted me to conquer him in arms, no one ought to be jealous of it; for God can, when he pleases, send his grace to a poor squire, as well as to a great lord. Sir, do not take it amiss if I did not sur-render him to the orders of my lady the queen; for I hold my lands of you, and my oath is to you, not to her, except it be through choice." The king answered, "John, the loyal service you have done us, and our esteem for your valor, is so great, that it may well serve you as an excuse; and shame fall upon all those that bear you any ill-will. You will now return home, and take your pris-oner the King of Scotland, and convey him to my wife; and by way of remuneration I assign lands, as near your house as you can choose them, to the amount of five hun-dred pounds sterling a year, for you and your heirs; and I retain you as a squire of my body and of my household." John Copeland left Calais the third day after his arrival, and returned to England. When he was come home he assembled his friends and neighbors, and, in company with them, took the King of Scots, and conveyed him to York, where he presented him, in the name of the king, to the queen, and made such handsome excuses that she was satisfied.

When the queen had sufficiently provided for the defence of the city of York, the castle of Roxburgh, the city of Durham, and the town of Newcastle-upon-Tyne, as well as for all the borders, and had appointed the Lords Percy and Neville governors of Northumberland to take proper care of it, she set out from York, and returned to London. She ordered the King of Scots, the Earl of Murray, and the other prisoners, to be confined in the Tower of London; and, having placed a sufficient guard over them, set out for Dover, where she embarked, and with a favorable wind arrived before Calais three days preceding the feast of All Saints. The king, upon her arrival, held a grand court, and ordered magnificent entertainments for all the lords who were there, but more especially for the ladies; as the queen had brought a great many with her, who were glad to accompany her, in order to see fathers, brothers, and friends, that were engaged at this siege of Calais.

CHAPTER LXIV.

THE YOUNG EARL OF FLANDERS IS BETROTHED, THROUGH THE CON-
STRAINT OF THE FLEMINGS, TO THE DAUGHTER OF THE KING OF
ENGLAND.—HE ESCAPES TO FRANCE IN A SUBTLE MANNER.

THE siege of Calais lasted a long time, during which
many gallant feats of arms and adventures happened. But it is not possible for me to relate the fourth
part of them; for the King of France had posted so many
men at arms in the fortresses, and on the borders of the
counties of Guines, Artois, Boulogne, round to Calais,
and had such numbers of Genoese, Normans, and others
in vessels on the sea, that none of the English could
venture abroad on horseback or on foot, to forage, without meeting some of these parties. There were frequent
skirmishes near the gates and ditches of the town, which
never ended without several being killed and wounded:
sometimes one side gained the advantage, and sometimes
the other. The King of England and his council studied
night and day to invent new engines more effectually to
annoy the town; but the inhabitants were equally alert to
destroy their effect, and exerted themselves so much that
they suffered nothing from them. However, no provisions could be brought into the place but by stealth,
and by the means of two mariners who were guides to
such as adventured. One was named Marant, and the
other Mestriel: both of them resided in Abbeville. By
their means the town of Calais was frequently victualled,
and by their boldness they were often in great danger,
many times pursued and almost taken; but they escaped,

and slew and wounded many of the English. The siege
lasted all the winter. The king had a great desire to keep
on good terms with the municipalities of Flanders, because he thought that through them he should the more
easily obtain his end. He made, therefore, frequent
protestations of friendship to them, and gave them to
understand, that, after he should have succeeded at Calais, he would reconquer for them Lisle, Douay, and all
their dependencies: so that the Flemings, believing in
such promises, put themselves in motion about the time
that the king was in Normandy, whence he came to Crecy
and Calais; and they laid siege to Bethune. They had
chosen for their commander the Lord Oudart de Renty,
who had been banished from France, and had closely besieged the town and much damaged it by their attacks.
But there were within four knights for the King of
France, who well defended it: their names were Sir
Geoffry de Chargny, the Lord Eustace de Ribeaumont,
the Lord Baudoin d'Anequin, and Lord John de Landas.
The town of Bethune was so well defended, that the
Flemings conquered nothing: they returned, therefore, to
Flanders, not having been more successful than before.

When the King of England was come to Calais, he did
not cease sending flattering messengers and promises to
the municipalities of Flanders, to preserve their friendship, and lessen their opinion of the King of France, who
was taking great pains to acquire their affections. The
King of England would have gladly seen the Earl Lewis
of Flanders, who at that time was but fifteen years old,
married to his daughter Isabella, and set so many engines
to work among the Flemings that they acceded to it;
which mightily rejoiced the king, for he imagined that
by this marriage he would easily govern that country.

The Flemings also thought that this alliance would enable them more effectually to resist the French; and that it would be more profitable to be connected with the King of England than with the King of France. Their young earl, however, who had been educated with the royal family of France, and who at the time was in that kingdom, would not agree to it, and declared frankly that he would never take to wife the daughter of him who had slain his father. On the other hand, Duke John of Brabant was very eagerly trying to make a match between the earl and his daughter, and promised to obtain for him the full enjoyment of Flanders, by fair or foul means. The duke also gave the King of France to understand, that, if the marriage took place, he would manage the Flemings, that they should attach themselves to him in preference to the King of England. Upon the strength of these promises, the King of France consented to the marriage of the Earl of Flanders with the Duke of Brabant's daughter. After the duke had obtained this consent, he sent messengers to all the principal citizens of the great towns in Flanders; who colored the union with so many specious reasons, that the councils of the principal towns sent to the earl, and informed him that if he would come to Flanders and follow their advice, they would be his true friends, and would give up to him all royalties, rights, and jurisdictions, in a greater degree than any earl had hitherto been possessed of. The earl was advised to go to Flanders, where he was joyfully received; and the chief towns made him rich and handsome presents.

As soon as the King of England was informed of this, he sent the Earls of Northampton and Arundel, and Lord Reginald Cobham, into Flanders; who managed matters so well with the leading men in the place, and with the corporations, that they were more desirous their lord should marry a daughter of the King of England, than the daughter of the Duke of Brabant : they very affectionately entreated their lord so to do, and supported it by many strong and good arguments (which would be too tedious to detail here), insomuch that those of the Duke of Brabant's party could say nothing to the contrary. The earl, how ever, would not consent to it, notwithstanding their fair speeches and arguments ; but repeated his former declara tion, that he would never marry the daughter of him who had killed his father, were he to have a moiety of the kingdom of England for her dower. When the Flemings heard this, they said their lord was too much of a French man, and very ill-advised; and that he must not expect any good from them, since he would not listen to their counsels. They arrested him, and confined him, — though not a close prisoner, — and told him he should never have his liberty until he would pay attention to their advice. They added, that if the late earl his father had not loved the French so much, but had listened to them, he would have been the greatest prince in Christendom, and would have recovered Lisle, Bethune, and Douay, and been alive at this day.

While all this was passing, the King of England still held on the siege of Calais. He kept his court there at Christmas in a right royal manner ; and in the ensuing Lent the Earl of Derby, the Earl of Pembroke, the Earl of Oxford, and many knights and squires who had crossed the sea with them, returned from Gascony.

The Earl of Flanders was for a long time in danger from the Flemings, and, being a prisoner, was perfectly weary of it. He therefore made them understand that he was willing to follow their advice, for he could receive more advantages from them than from those in any other country. These words pleased the Flemings much : they gave him his liberty, and allowed him to partake of one of his favorite amusements, hawking, of which he was very fond. It happened one day, in the same week that he was to espouse the English princess, he went out a-hawking : the falconer fled his hawk at a heron, and the earl did the same with his. The two hawks pursued their game, and the earl galloped off, as if following them, crying, " Hoye, hoye ! " When he was at some distance from his keepers, and in the open fields, he stuck spurs into his horse, and made such speed that he was soon out of sight. He did not stop until he was got into Artois, where he was safe. He then went to King Philip in France, and related to him and his nobles his adventures, who told him he had acted wisely; but the English, on the contrary, accused him of betraying and deceiving them.

CHAPTER LXV.

The King of England prevents the Approach of the French Army to raise the Siege of Calais, and the Town surrenders.

THE King of England, who found he could not conquer Calais but by famine, ordered a large castle to be constructed of strong timbers, in order to shut up the communication with the sea ; and he directed it to be built and embattled in such a manner that it could not be destroyed. He placed it between the town and the sea, and fortified it with all sorts of warlike instruments, and garrisoned it with forty men at arms and two hundred archers, who guarded the harbor and port of Calais so closely that nothing could go out or come into the town without being sunk or taken. By this means he more sorely aggrieved the Calesians than by any thing he had hitherto done, and sooner brought famine among them.

I will now relate what the King of England had done, and was doing, when he saw with what a prodigious force the King of France was come to raise the siege of Calais, which had cost him so much money and labor. He knew that the town was so nearly famished, that it could hold out but a very short time : therefore it would have sorely hurt him to have been forced at that time to raise it. He considered that the French could neither approach his army nor the town of Calais but by two roads, — the one by the downs along the seashore, the other higher up the country, which, however, was full of ditches and bogs ; and there was but one bridge, called the bridge of Nieullet, by which they could be crossed. He posted, therefore, his fleet along the shore, as near as he could to the downs, and provided it with plenty of every warlike engine, so that the French could not pass that way. He sent the Earl of Derby, with a sufficient force of men at arms and archers, to guard the bridge of Nieullet. The French therefore were prevented from advancing thither, unless they attempted crossing the marshes between Sangate and the sea, which were impassable. There was also, nearer to Calais, a high tower, which was guarded by thirty archers from England ; and they had fortified it with double ditches, as a stronger defence of the passage over the downs. When the French had taken up their quarters on the hill of Sangate, those from Tournay, who might amount to about fifteen hundred men, advanced toward this tower ; the garrison shot at them, and wounded some ;

but the men of Tournay crossed the ditches, and reached the foot of the tower with pickaxes and bars. The engagement was then very sharp, and many of the Tournay men were killed and wounded; but in the end the tower was taken and thrown down, and all that were within it put to the sword.

The King of France sent his two marshals, the Lord of Beaujeu and the Lord of St. Venant, to examine the country, and see where the army could pass, in order to fight with the English; but, after they had well examined all the passes, they returned, and told the king there was not any possibility of doing it but with infinite loss of men. Things remained in this state that day and the following night; but on the morrow, after the King of France had heard mass, he sent to the King of England the Lord Geoffry de Chargny, the Lord Eustace de Ribeaumont, Sir Guy de Nesle, and the Lord of Beaujeu, who, as they rode along, observed how strongly all the passes were guarded. They were allowed to proceed freely, for so the King of England had ordered, and praised very much the dispositions of the Earl of Derby, who was posted at the bridge of Nieullet, over which they passed. They rode on until they came where the king was, whom they found surrounded by his barons and knights. They all four dismounted, and advanced toward the king with many reverences; then the Lord Eustace de Ribeaumont said, "Sir, the King of France informs you, through us, that he is come to the hill of Sangate in order to give you battle, but he cannot find any means of approaching you: he therefore wishes you would assemble your council, and he will send some of his, that they may confer together, and fix upon a spot where a general combat may take place." The King of England was advised to make his answer as follows : "Gentlemen, I perfectly understand the request you have made me from my adversary, who wrongfully keeps possession of my inheritance, which weighs much upon me. You will therefore tell him from me, if you please, that I have been on this spot near a twelvemonth ; this he was well informed of, and, had he chosen it, might have come here sooner ; but he has allowed me to remain so long, that I have expended very large sums of money, and have done so much that I must be master of Calais in a very short time. I am not therefore inclined, in the smallest degree, to comply with his request, or to gratify his convenience, or to abandon what I have gained, or what I have been so anxious to conquer. If, therefore, neither he nor his army can pass this way, he must seek out some other road." The four noblemen then returned, and were escorted as far as the bridge of Nicullet, and related to the King of France the King of England's answer.

The King of France, perceiving he could not in any way succeed, decamped on the morrow, and took the road to Amiens, where he disbanded all his troops, the men at arms as well as those sent from the different towns. When the Calesians saw them depart, it gave them great grief. Some of the English fell on their rear, and captured horses, and wagons laden with wine and other things, as well as some prisoners ; all which they brought to their camp before Calais.

After the departure of the King of France, with his army, from the hill of Sangate, the Calesians saw clearly that all hopes of succor were at an end ; which occasioned them so much sorrow and distress that the hardiest could scarcely support it. They entreated, therefore, most earnestly, the Lord John de Vienne, their governor, to mount upon the battlements, and make a sign that he wished to hold a parley. The King of England, upon hearing this, sent to him Sir Walter Manny and Lord Basset. When they were come near, the Lord de Vienne said to them, "Dear gentlemen, you, who are very valiant knights, know that the King of France, whose subjects we are, has sent us hither to defend this town and castle from all harm and damage : this we have done to the best of our abilities. All hopes of help have now left us, so that we are most exceedingly straitened ; and, if the gallant king your lord have not pity upon us, we must perish with hunger. I therefore entreat that you would beg of him to have compassion on us, and to have the goodness to allow us to depart in the state we are in, and that he will be satisfied with having possession of the town and castle, with all that is within them, as he will find therein riches enough to content him." To this Sir Walter Manny replied, "John, we are not ignorant of what the king our lord's intentions are, for he has told them to us. Know, then, that it is not his pleasure you should get off so ; for he is resolved that you surrender yourselves solely to his will, to allow those whom he pleases their ransom, or to put them to death ; for the Calesians have done him so much mischief, and have, by their obstinate defence, cost him so many lives and so much money, that he is mightily enraged." The Lord de Vienne answered, "These conditions are too hard for us. We are but a small number of knights and squires, who have loyally served our lord and master, as you would have done, and have suffered much ill and disquiet ; but we will endure more than any man ever did in a similar situation, before we consent that the smallest boy in the town should fare worse than the best. I therefore once more entreat you, out of compassion, to return to the King of England, and beg of him to have pity on us : he will, I trust, grant you this favor ; for I have such an opinion of his gallantry as to hope that, through God's mercy, he will alter his mind." The two lords returned to the king, and related what had passed. The king said he had no intentions of complying with the request, but should insist that they surrendered themselves unconditionally to his will. Sir Walter replied, "My lord, you may be to blame in this, as you will set us a very bad example ; for, if you order us to go to any of your castles, we shall not obey you so cheerfully, if you put these people to death ; for they will retaliate upon us in a similar case." Many barons who were then present supported this opinion. Upon which the king replied, "Gentlemen, I am not so obstinate as to hold my opinion alone against you all. Sir Walter, you will inform the governor of Calais that the only grace he must expect from me is, that six of the principal citizens of Calais march out of the town, with bare heads and feet, with ropes around their necks, and the keys of the town and castle in their hands. These six persons shall be at my absolute disposal, and the remainder of the inhabitants pardoned."

Sir Walter returned to the Lord de Vienne, who was waiting for him on the battlements, and told him all that he had been able to gain from the king. "I beg of you," replied the governor, "that you would be so good as to remain here a little, while I go and relate all that has passed to the townsmen ; for, as they have desired me to undertake this, it is but proper they should know the result of it." He went to the market-place, and caused the bell to be rung ; upon which all the inhabitants, men and women, assembled in the town-hall. He then related to them what he had said, and the answers he had received; and that he could not obtain any conditions more favorable, to which they must give a short and immediate answer. This information caused the greatest lamentations and despair, so that the hardest heart would have had compassion on them. Even the Lord de Vienne wept bitterly.

After a short time the most wealthy citizen of the town, by name Eustace de St. Pierre, rose up and said, "Gentlemen, both high and low, it would be a very great pity to suffer so many people to die through famine, if any means could be found to prevent it; and it would be highly meritorious in the eyes of our Saviour, if such misery could be averted. I have such faith and trust in finding grace before God, if I die to save my townsmen, that I name myself as first of the six." When Eustace had done speaking, they all rose up and almost worshipped him: many cast themselves at his feet with tears and groans. Another citizen, very rich and respected, rose up, and said he would be the second to his companion Eustace; his name was John Daire. After him, James Wisant, who was very rich in merchandise and lands, offered himself as companion to his two cousins; as did Peter Wisant his brother. Two others then named themselves, which completed the number demanded by the King of England. The Lord John de Vienne then mounted a small hackney, for it was with difficulty that he could walk, and conducted them to the gate. There was the greatest sorrow and lamentation all over the town; and in such manner were they attended to the gate, which the governor ordered to be opened, and then shut upon him and the six citizens, whom he led to the barriers, and said to Sir Walter Manny, who was there waiting for him, "I deliver up to you, as governor of Calais, with the consent of the inhabit-

How the Six Citizens of Calais delivered themselves up to the English King.

ants, these six citizens; and I swear to you that they were, and are at this day, the most wealthy and respectable inhabitants of Calais. I beg of you, gentle sir, that you would have the goodness to beseech the king that they may not be put to death." — "I cannot answer for what the king will do with them," replied Sir Walter; "but you may depend that I will do all in my power to save them." The barriers were opened, when these six citizens advanced toward the pavilion of the king, and the Lord de Vienne re-entered the town.

When Sir Walter Manny had presented these six citizens to the king, they fell upon their knees, and with uplifted hands said, "Most gallant king, see before you six citizens of Calais, who have been capital merchants, and who bring you the keys of the castle and of the town. We surrender ourselves to your absolute will and pleasure, in order to save the remainder of the inhabitants of Calais, who have suffered much distress and misery. Condescend, therefore, out of your nobleness of mind, to have mercy and compassion upon us." All the barons, knights, and squires, that were assembled there in great numbers, wept at this sight. The king eyed them with angry looks (for he hated much the people of Calais, for the great losses he had formerly suffered from them at sea), and ordered their heads to be stricken off. All present entreated the king, that he would be more merciful to them; but he would not listen to them. Then Sir Walter Manny said, "Ah, gentle·king, let me beseech you to restrain your anger: You have the reputation of great nobleness of soul : do not therefore tarnish it by such an act as this, nor allow any one to speak in a disgraceful manner of you. In this instance all the world will say you have acted cruelly, if you put to death six such respectable persons, who, of their own free will, have surrendered themselves to your mercy, in order to save their fellow-citizens." Upon this the king gave a wink, saying, "Be it so," and ordered the headsman to be sent for; for that the Calesians had done him so much damage, it was proper they should suffer for it. The Queen of England fell on her knees, and with tears said, "Ah, gentle sir, since I have crossed the sea with great danger to see you, I have never asked you one favor: now I most humbly ask as a gift, for the sake of the Son of the blessed Mary, and for your love to me, that you will be merciful to these six men." The king looked at her for some time in silence, and then said, "Ah, lady, I wish that you had been anywhere else than here. You have entreated in such a manner that I cannot refuse you. I therefore give them to you, to do as you please with them." The queen conducted the six citizens to her apartments, and had the halters taken from round their necks, after which she new-clothed them, and served them with a plentiful dinner. She then presented each with six nobles, and had them escorted out of the camp in safety.

CHAPTER LXVI.

The King of England re-peoples Calais.

THE king, after he had presented these six citizens to the queen, called to him Sir Walter Manny, and his two marshals, — the Earls of Warwick and Stafford, — and said to them, "My lords, here are the keys of the town and castle of Calais: go and take possession of them. You will put into prison the knights you may find there, but you will send out of the town all the other inhabitants, and all soldiers that may have come there to serve for pay; as I am resolved to re-people the town with English alone." These three noblemen, with only one hundred men, went and took possession of Calais, and from the gates sent to prison the Lord John de Surie, the Lord John de Vienne, the Lord John de Bellebourne, and other knights. They then ordered every sort of arms to be brought, and piled in a heap in the market-place. They sent out of the town all ranks of people, retaining only one priest, and two other old men, that were well acquainted with the customs and usages of Calais, in order to point out the different properties; and gave directions for the castle to be prepared for lodging the king and queen, and different hotels for their attendants. When this had been done, the king and queen mounted their steeds, and rode toward the town, which they entered at the sound of trumpets, drums, and all sorts of warlike instruments.

The king gave to Sir Walter Manny, Lord Stafford, Lord Warwick, Sir Bartholomew Burghersh, and other knights, very handsome houses in Calais, that they might re-people it; and his intentions were, to send thither, on his return to England, thirty-six substantial citizens, with all their wealth, and to exert himself in such a manner that the inhabitants of the town should be wholly English: which he afterwards accomplished. The new town and fortifications, which had been built before Calais, were destroyed, as well as the castle upon the harbor; and the great boom which was thrown across was brought into the town. The king posted different persons to guard the gates, walls, and towers of the town; and what had been damaged he got repaired, which, however, was not soon done. The Lord John de Vienne and his companions were sent to England: they remained in London about half a year, and then were ransomed. In my opinion, it was a melancholy thing for the inhabitants of both sexes, of the town of Calais, thus to be sent abroad, with their children, from their inheritances, leaving every thing behind: for they were not allowed to carry off any of their furniture or wealth; and they received no assistance from the King of France, for whom they had lost their all. They did, however, as well as they were able; and the greater part went to St. Omer.

The Cardinal Guy de Boulogne, who was come into France as ambassador, and was with his cousin King Philip in the city of Amiens, labored so earnestly, that he obtained a truce between the two kings and their adherents, which was to last for two years.

CHAPTER LXVII.

A ROBBER OF THE NAME OF BACON DOES MUCH MISCHIEF IN LANGUEDOC, AND A PAGE OF THE NAME OF CROQUART TURNS ROBBER.

ALL this year of the truce, the kings remained at peace. But Lord William Douglas, and the Scots, who had taken refuge in the forest of Jedworth, carried on the war against the English, wherever they could meet with them. Those in Gascony, Poitou, and Saintonge, as well French as English, did not observe the truce any better, but conquered towns and castles from each other, by force or intrigue, and ruined and destroyed the country, day and night. There were frequently gallant deeds of arms performed, with alternate success.

Poor rogues took advantage of such times, and robbed both towns and castles ; so that some of them, becoming rich, constituted themselves captains of bands of thieves. There were among them those worth forty thousand crowns. Their method was, to mark out the particular towns or castles, a day or two's journey from each other : they then collected twenty or thirty robbers, and, travelling through by-roads in the night-time, entered the town or castle they had fixed on about daybreak, and set one of the houses on fire. When the inhabitants perceived it, they thought it had been a body of forces sent to destroy them, and took to their heels as fast as they could. The town of Donzere was treated in this manner ; and many other towns and castles were taken, and afterwards ransomed. Among other robbers in Languedoc, one had marked out the strong castle of Cobourne in Limosin, which is situated in a very strong country. He set off in the night-time, with thirty companions, and took and destroyed it. He seized also the Lord of Cobourne, whom he imprisoned in his own castle, and put all his household to death. He kept him in prison until he ransomed himself for twenty-four thousand crowns, paid down. The robber kept possession of the castle and dependencies, which he furnished with provisions, and thence made war upon all the country round about. The King of France, shortly afterwards, was desirous of having him near his person. He purchased the castle for twenty thousand crowns, appointed him his usher at arms, and heaped on him many other honors. The name of this robber was Bacon ; and he was always mounted on handsome horses, of a deep roan color, or on large palfreys, apparelled like an earl, and very richly armed ; and this state he maintained as long as he lived.

There were similar disorders in Brittany; and robbers carried on the like methods of seizing and pillaging different towns and castles, and then selling them back again to the country at a dear rate; by which means many of their leaders became very rich. Among others there was one of the name of Croquart, who was originally but a poor boy, and had been page to the Lord d'Ercle in Holland. When this Croquart arrived at manhood, he had his discharge, and went to the wars in Brittany, where he attached himself to a man at arms, and behaved very well. It happened, that in some skirmish his master was taken and slain; when, in recompense for his prowess, his companions elected him their leader, in the place of his late master. He then made such profit by ransoms, and the taking of towns and castles, that he was said to be worth full forty thousand crowns, not including his horses, of which he had twenty or thirty, very handsome and strong, and of a deep roan color. He had the reputation of being the most expert man at arms of the country, was chosen to be one of the thirty that engaged against a similar number, and was the most active combatant on the side of the English. King John of France made him the offer of knighting him, and marrying him very richly, if he would quit the English party, and promised to give him two thousand livres a year; but Croquart would never listen to it. It chanced one day, as he was riding a young horse which he had just purchased for three hundred crowns, and was putting him to his full speed, that the horse ran away with him, and, in leaping a ditch, stumbled into it, and broke his master's neck. Such was the end of Croquart.

CHAPTER LXVIII.

SIR AYMERY DE PAVIE PLOTS WITH SIR GEOFFRY DE CHARGNY TO
SELL THE TOWN OF CALAIS.

AT this time Sir Geoffry de Chargny was stationed
at St. Omer, to defend the frontier; and in every
thing touching war he acted as if he had been king. He
bethought himself, that as Lombards are very poor, and
by nature avaricious, he would attempt to recover the
town of Calais by means of Aymery de Pavie the governor; and as, from the terms of the truce, the inhabitants of the towns of St. Omer and Calais might go to
each place to sell their different merchandises, Sir Geoffry
entered into a secret treaty with Sir Aymery, and succeeded so far that he promised to deliver up the town on
receiving twenty thousand crowns. The King of England, however, got intelligence of it, and sent to Aymery
the Lombard orders to cross the sea immediately, and
come to him at Westminster. He obeyed; for he could
not imagine that the king knew of his treason, it had been
so secretly carried on. When the king saw the Lombard,
he took him aside, and said, "Thou knowest that I have
intrusted to thee what I hold dearest in this world, except
my wife and children: I mean the town and castle of
Calais, which thou hast sold to the French, and for which
thou deservest death." The Lombard flung himself on
his knees, and said, "Ah, gentle king, have mercy on
me, for God's sake! All that you have said is very true;
but there is yet time to break the bargain, for hitherto I
have not received one penny." The king had brought up

this Lombard from a child, and much loved him : he replied, "Aymery, it is my wish that you continue on this
treaty : you will inform me of the day that you are to
deliver up Calais, and on these conditions I promise you
my pardon." The Lombard then returned to Calais, and
kept every thing secret. In the mean time Sir Geoffry
de Chargny thought himself sure of having Calais, and
issued out privately his summons for five hundred lances.
The greater part were ignorant where he intended to lead
them, for it was only known to a few barons. I do not
believe he had even informed the King of France of his
plan, as he would have dissuaded him from it on account
of the truce. The Lombard had consented to deliver up
the town to him the last night of the year, with which
he made the King of England acquainted by means of
his brother.

CHAPTER LXIX.

THE BATTLE OF CALAIS, BETWEEN THE KING OF ENGLAND, UNDER THE
BANNER OF SIR WALTER MANNY, WITH SIR GEOFFRY DE CHARGNY
AND THE FRENCH.

WHEN the King of England was informed of this,
and knew that the day was for a certainty fixed, he
set out from England with three hundred men at arms
and six hundred archers. He embarked at Dover, and
came so privately to Calais, that no one knew of his being
there. He placed his men in ambuscade in the rooms
and towers of the castle, and said to Sir Walter Manny,
"Sir Walter, I will that you be the chief of this enterprise ; and I and my son will fight under your banner."
Sir Geoffry de Chargny had left St. Omer the latter end

of December, with all the forces he had collected; and
arrived near to Calais about midnight, the last day of the
month. He halted there for his rear to come up, and sent
forward two of his squires, who found Sir Aymery waiting
for them. They asked if it were time for Sir Geoffry to
advance: the Lombard answered that it was. The two
squires upon this returned to Sir Geoffry, who marched
his men in battle-array over the bridge of Nieullet. He
then sent forward twelve of his knights, with one hundred men at arms, to take possession of the castle of
Calais; for he thought, if he had possession of the castle,
he should soon be master of the town, considering what
strength he had with him; and in a few days time he
could have as much more, should there be occasion. He
gave orders for twenty thousand crowns to be delivered
to Sir Odoart de Renty, who was in this expedition, for
him to pay to the Lombard; and Sir Geoffry remained
in the plain in silence, his banner displayed before him,
with the rest of his army; for his intention was to enter
the town by one of its gates, otherwise he would not
enter it at all.

The Lombard had let down the drawbridge of the castle, and opened one of the gates, through which his detachment entered unmolested; and Sir Odoart had given
him the twenty thousand crowns in a bag, — who said
he supposed they were all there, for he had not time
to count them, as it would be day immediately. He
flung the bag of crowns into a room, which he locked,
and told the French he would conduct them to the great
tower, that they might the sooner be masters of the
castle: in saying this he advanced on, and, pushing back
the bolt, the door flew open. In this tower was the King
of England with two hundred lances, who sallied forth,

with swords and battle-axes in their hands, crying out,
"Manny, Manny, to the rescue! What! do these Frenchmen think to conquer the castle of Calais with such a
handful of men!" The French saw that no defence
could save them, so they surrendered themselves prisoners; and scarcely any of them were wounded. They
were made to enter this tower, whence the English had
sallied, and there shut in. The English quitted the castle,
and, forming themselves in array, mounted their horses
(for they knew the French were mounted), and made for
the gate leading to Boulogne. Sir Geoffry was there
with his banner displayed (his arms were three escutch-
eons argent on a field gules), and he was very impatient
to be the first that should enter Calais. He said to those
knights who were near him, that, if this Lombard delayed opening the gate, they should all die with cold.
"In God's name," replied Sir Pepin de Werre, "these
Lombards are a malicious sort of people: perhaps he is
examining your florins, lest there should be any false ones,
and to see if they be right in number." During this conversation the King of England and his son advanced,
under the banner of Sir Walter Manny. There were
many other banners also there, such as the Earl of
Suffolk's, the Lord Stafford's, Lord John Montacute's
(brother to the Earl of Salisbury), the Lord John Beauchamp's, the Lord Berkeley's, the Lord de la Waae. All
these were barons having banners; and no more than
these were in this expedition.

The great gates were soon opened, and they all sallied
out. When the French saw this, and heard the cries of
"Manny to the rescue!" they found they had been betrayed; and Sir Geoffry said to those around them,
"Gentlemen, if we fly, we shall lose all: it will be more

advantageous for us to fight valiantly, in the hopes that the day may be ours." — " By St. George," said some of the English, who were near enough to hear it, " you speak truth : evil befall him who thinks of flying!" They then retreated a little, and dismounted, driving their horses away, to avoid being trampled on. When the King of England saw this, he halted the banner under which he was, and said, "I would have the men drawn up here in order of battle ; and let a good detachment be sent toward the bridge of Nieullet, for I have heard that there is posted a large body of French on horseback and on foot." Six banners and three hundred archers left his army, and made for the bridge of Nieullet, where they found the Lord Moreau de Fiennes, and the Lord of Crequi, who guarded it. There were also posted, between the bridge and Calais, the crossbow-men from St. Omer and Aire, who had that day sharp work. More than six hundred were slain or drowned; for they were immediately discomfited, and pursued to the river. It was then scarcely daybreak. The knights of Picardy maintained this post some time, and many gallant actions were performed ; but the English kept increasing from the town, when, on the contrary, the French fell off: so that, when they found they could not longer keep the bridge, those that had horses mounted them, and betook themselves to flight. The English immediately pursued them, and many were overthrown : but those that were well mounted escaped ; among them were the Lords de Fiennes, de Crequi, de Sempy, de Lonchinleich, and the Lord of Namur. Many were taken through their own hardiness, who might otherwise have saved themselves. When it was broad daylight, that each could see the other, some knights and squires collected themselves together, and vigorously attacked the English, insomuch that several of the French made good prisoners, that brought them much profit.

We will now speak of the King of England, who was there incognito under Sir Walter Manny's banner. He advanced with his men on foot, to meet the enemy, who were formed in close order, with their pikes, shortened to five feet, planted out before them. The first attack was very sharp and severe. The king singled out Sir Eustace de Ribeaumont, who was a strong and hardy knight. He fought a long time marvellously well with the king, so that it was a pleasure to see them : but by the confusion of the engagement they were separated ; for two large bodies met where they were fighting, and forced them to break off their combat. On the side of the French there was excellent fighting by Sir Geoffry de Chargny, Sir John de Landas, Sir Hector and Sir Gavin Ballicul, and others ; but they were all surpassed by Sir Eustace de Ribeaumont, who that day struck the king twice down on his knees : at last, however, he was obliged to surrender his sword to the king, saying, "Sir knight, I surrender myself your prisoner, for the honor of the day must fall to the English." All that belonged to Sir Geoffry de Chargny were either slain or captured : among the first were Sir Henry du Bois and Sir Pepin de Werre : Sir Geoffry and the rest were taken prisoners. The last that was taken, and who in that day excelled all, was Sir Eustace de Ribeaumont. This business was finished under the walls of Calais, the last day of December, toward morning, in the year of grace 1348.

CHAPTER LXX.

THE KING OF ENGLAND PRESENTS A CHAPLET OF PEARLS TO SIR
EUSTACE DE RIBEAUMONT.

WHEN the engagement was over, the king returned
to the castle in Calais, and ordered all the prisoners
to be brought before him. The French then knew for the
first time that the King of England had been there in person, under the banner of Sir Walter Manny. The king
said he would, this evening of the new year, entertain
them all at supper in the castle. When the hour for supper was come, the tables spread, and the king and his
knights dressed in new robes, as well as the French, —
who, notwithstanding they were prisoners, made good
cheer, for the king wished it should be so, — the king
seated himself at table, and made those knights do the
same around him in a most honorable manner. The gallant Prince of Wales, and the knights of England, served
up the first course, and waited on their guests. At the
second course they went and seated themselves at another
table, where they were served and attended on very quietly.

When supper was over, and the tables removed, the
king remained in the hall, among the English and French
knights, bareheaded, except a chaplet of fine pearls which
was round his head. He conversed with all of them ; but
when he came to Sir Geoffry de Chargny his countenance
altered, and, looking at him askance, he said, "Sir Geoffry,
I have but little reason to love you, when you wished to
seize from me by stealth, last night, what had given me so
much trouble to acquire, and has cost me such sums of

money. I am, however, rejoiced to have caught you thus in attempting it. You were desirous of gaining it cheaper than I did, and thought you could purchase it for twenty thousand crowns ; but, through God's assistance, you have been disappointed." He then passed on, and left Sir Geoffry standing, without having a word to say for himself. When he came to Sir Eustace de Ribeaumont, he assumed a cheerful look, and said with a smile, "Sir Eustace, you are the most valiant knight in Christendom, that I ever saw attack his enemy, or defend himself. I never yet found any one in battle, who, body to body, had given me so much to do as you have done this day. I adjudge to you the prize of valor above all the knights of my court, as what is justly due to you." The king then took off the chaplet, which was very rich and handsome, and, placing it on the head of Sir Eustace, said, "Sir Eustace, I present you with this chaplet, as being the best combatant this day, either within or without doors ; and I beg of you to wear it this year for love of me. I know that you are lively and amorous, and love the company of ladies and damsels : therefore say, wherever you go, that I gave it to you. I also give you your liberty, free of ransom ; and you may set out to-morrow, if you please, and go whither you will."

CHAPTER LXXI.

The Sea-Fight off Sluys. (From the Manuscript in the Hafod Library.)

ABOUT this period there was much ill-will between the King of England and the Spaniards, on account of some infractions and pillages committed at sea by the latter. It happened at this season, that the Spaniards who had been in Flanders with their merchandise were informed they would not be able to return home without meeting the English fleet. The Spaniards did not pay much attention to this intelligence : however, after they had disposed of their goods, they amply provided their ships from Sluys with arms and artillery, and all such archers, crossbow-men, and soldiers as were willing to receive pay. The King of England hated these Spaniards greatly, and said publicly, "We have for a long time spared these people, for which they have done us much harm, without amending their conduct : on the contrary, they grow more arrogant; for which reason they must be chastised as they repass our coasts." His lords readily assented to this proposal, and were eager to engage the Spaniards. The king therefore issued a special summons to all gentlemen who at that time might be in England, and left London. He went to the coast of Sussex, between Southampton and Dover, which lies opposite to Ponthieu and Dieppe, and kept his court in a monastery, whither the queen also came. At this time and place that gallant knight Lord Robert de Namur, who was lately returned from beyond sea, joined the king : he came just in time to be one of this armament, and the king was exceedingly pleased at his arrival. On finding that he was not too late to meet the Spaniards on their return, the king, with his nobles and knights, embarked on board his fleet ; and he was never attended by so numerous a company in any of his former expeditions at sea.

When the Spaniards had completed their cargoes, and laden their vessels with linen cloths, and whatever they imagined would be profitable in their own country, they embarked on board their fleet at Sluys. They knew they should meet the English, but were indifferent about it; for they had marvellously provided themselves with all sorts of warlike ammunition, such as bolts for crossbows, cannon, and bars of forged iron to throw on the enemy, in hopes, with the assistance of great stones, to sink him. When they weighed anchor, the wind was favorable for them: there were forty large vessels of such a size, and so beautiful, it was a fine sight to see them under sail. Near the top of their masts were small castles, full of flints and stones, and a soldier to guard them; and there also was the flagstaff, from whence fluttered their streamers in the wind, that it was pleasant to look at them. If the English had a great desire to meet them, it seemed as if the Spaniards were still more eager for it, as will hereafter appear. The Spaniards were full ten thousand men, including all sorts of soldiers they had enlisted when in Flanders: this made them feel sufficient courage not to fear the combat with the King of England, and whatever force he might have at sea. Intending to engage the English fleet, they advanced with a favorable wind until they came opposite to Calais. The King of England, being at sea, had very distinctly explained to all his knights the order of battle he would have them follow. He had appointed the Lord Robert de Namur to the command of a ship called "Le Salle du Roi," on board of which was all his household. The king posted himself in the forepart of his own ship. He was dressed in a black velvet jacket, and wore on his head a small hat of beaver, which became him much. He was that day, as I was told by those who were present, as joyous as he ever was in his life, and ordered his minstrels to play before him a German dance which Sir John Chandos had lately introduced. For his amusement he made the same knight sing with his minstrels, which delighted him greatly. From time to time he looked up to the castle on his mast, where he had placed a watch to inform him when the Spaniards were in sight. While the king was thus amusing himself with his knights, who were happy in seeing him so gay, the watch, who had observed a fleet, cried out, "Ho! I spy a ship; and it appears to me to be a Spaniard." The minstrels were silenced, and he was asked if there were more than one; soon after he replied, "Yes: I see two, three, four, and so many, that, God help me, I cannot count them." The king and his knights then knew they must be the Spaniards. The trumpets were ordered to sound, and the ships to form a line of battle for the combat; as they were aware, that, since the enemy came in such force, it could not be avoided. It was, however, rather late, about the hour of vespers. The king ordered wine to be brought, which he and his knights drank; when each fixed their helmets on their heads. The Spaniards now drew near. They might easily have refused the battle, if they had chosen it; for they were well freighted, in large ships, and had the wind in their favor. They could have avoided speaking with the English, if they had willed; but their pride and presumption made them act otherwise. They disdained to sail by, but bore instantly down on them, and commenced the battle.

When the King of England saw from his ship their order of battle, he ordered the person who managed his vessel, saying, "Lay me alongside the Spaniard who is bearing down on us; for I will have a tilt with him." The master dared not disobey the king's order, but laid his ship ready for the Spaniard, who was coming full sail. The king's ship was large and stiff: otherwise she would have been sunk, for that of the enemy was a great one, and the shock of their meeting was more like the crash of a torrent or tempest. The rebound caused the castle in the king's ship to encounter that of the Spaniard, so that the mast of the latter was broken, and all in the castle fell with it into the sea, when they were drowned. The English vessel, however, suffered, and let in water; which the knights cleared, and stopped the leak, without telling the king any thing of the matter. Upon examining the vessel he had engaged lying before him, he said, "Grapple my ship with that; for I will have possession of her." His knights replied, "Let her go her way: you shall have better than her." That vessel sailed on; and another large ship bore down, and grappled with chains and hooks to that of the king. The fight now began in earnest, and the archers and crossbows on each side were eager to shoot and defend themselves. The battle was not in one place, but in ten or twelve at a time. Whenever either party found themselves equal to the enemy, or superior, they instantly grappled, when grand deeds of arms were performed. The English had not any advantage; and the Spanish ships were much larger and higher than their opponents, which gave them a great superiority in shooting and casting stones and iron bars on board their enemy, which annoyed them exceedingly. The knights on board the king's ship were in danger of sinking, for the leak still admitted water: this made them more eager to conquer the vessel they were grappled to. Many gallant deeds were done; and at last they gained the ship, and flung all they found in it overboard, having quitted their own ship. They continued the combat against the Spaniards, who fought valiantly, and whose crossbow-men shot such bolts of iron as greatly distressed the English.

This sea-fight between the English and Spaniards was

well and hardly fought; but, as night was coming on, the English exerted themselves to do their duty well, and discomfit their enemies. The Spaniards, who are used to the sea, and were in large ships, acquitted themselves to the utmost of their power. The young Prince of Wales and his division were engaged apart: his ship was grappled by a great Spaniard, when he and his knights suffered much; for she had so many holes, that the water came in very abundantly, and they could not by any means stop the leaks, which gave the crew fears of her sinking. They therefore did all they could to conquer the enemy's ship, but in vain; for she was very large, and excellently well defended. During this danger of the prince, the Duke of Lancaster came near, and, as he approached, saw he had the worst of the engagement, and that his crew had too much on their hands, for they were bailing out water: he therefore fell on the other side of the Spanish vessel, with which he grappled, shouting, "Derby to the rescue!" The engagement was now very warm, but did not last long, for the ship was taken, and all the crew thrown overboard, not one being saved. The prince, with his men, instantly embarked on board the Spaniard; and scarcely had they done so when his own vessel sunk, which convinced them of the imminent danger they had been in.

The engagement was in other parts well contested by the English knights, who exerted themselves; and need there was of it, for they found those who feared them not. Late in the evening, the "Salle du Roi," commanded by Lord Robert de Namur, was grappled by a large Spaniard, and the fight was very severe. The Spaniards were determined to gain this ship; and, the more effectually to succeed in carrying her off, they set all their sails, took advantage of the wind, and, in spite of what Lord Robert and his crew could do, towed her out of the battle; for the Spaniard was of a more considerable size than the Lord Robert's ship, and therefore she more easily conquered. As they were thus towed, they passed near the king's ship, to whom they cried out, "Rescue the 'Salle du Roi,'" but were not heard, for it was dark; and, if they were heard, they were not rescued. The Spaniards would have carried away with ease this prize, if it had not been for a gallant act of one Hanequin, a servant to the Lord Robert, who, with his drawn sword on his wrist, leaped on board the enemy, ran to the mast, and cut the large cable which held the mainsail, by which it became unmanageable; and with great agility he cut other four principal ropes, so that the sails fell on the deck, and the course of the ship was stopped. Lord Robert, seeing this, advanced with his men, and, boarding the Spaniard sword in hand, attacked the crew so vigorously that all were slain or thrown overboard, and the vessel won.

I cannot speak of every particular circumstance of this engagement. It lasted a considerable time; and the Spaniards gave the King of England and his fleet enough to do. However, at last victory declared for the English: the Spaniards lost fourteen ships, the others saved themselves by flight. When it was completely over, and the king saw he had none to fight with, he ordered his trumpets to sound a retreat, and made for England. They anchored at Rye and Winchelsea a little after nightfall, when the king, the Prince of Wales, the Duke of Lancaster, the Earl of Richmond, and other barons, disembarked, took horses in the town, and rode to the mansion where the queen was, scarcely two English leagues distant. The queen was mightily rejoiced on seeing her lord and children. She had suffered that day great affliction from her doubts of success; for her attendants had seen from the hills of the coast the whole of the battle, as the weather was fine and clear, and had told the queen, who was very anxious to learn the number of the enemy, that the Spaniards had forty large ships. She was therefore much comforted by their safe return. The king, with those knights who had attended him, passed the night in revelry with the ladies, conversing of arms and amours. On the morrow the greater part of his barons who had been in this engagement came to him. He greatly thanked them for all the services they had done him, before he dismissed them; when they took their leave, and returned every man to his home.

CHAPTER LXXII.

The Death of King Philip, and Coronation of his Son King John.

IN the beginning of August, in the year 1350, Raoul de Cahours, and many other knights and squires, to the number of one hundred and twenty men at arms, or thereabouts, combated with the commander for the King of England in Brittany, called Sir Thomas Daggeworth, before the castle of Aurai. Sir Thomas and all his men were slain, to the amount of about a hundred men at arms. On the 22d of August in the same year, King Philip of France departed this life at Nogent-le-Roi, and was carried to Notre Dame in Paris. The twenty-sixth day of September ensuing, John, eldest son of King Philip, was crowned king, on a Sunday, at Rheims. His wife, Queen Jane, was also crowned at the same time.

CHAPTER LXXIII.

THE KING OF FRANCE ISSUES OUT A SUMMONS FOR ASSEMBLING AN
ARMY TO COMBAT THE PRINCE OF WALES, WHO WAS OVERRUNNING
THE PROVINCE OF DERBY.

WHEN King John of France had re-conquered all
the towns and castles in Lower Normandy, which
belonged to the King of Navarre, whom he detained in
prison, he returned to the city of Paris. He had not been
long there before he heard that the Prince of Wales, with
his whole army, had invaded his kingdom,* and was advancing toward the fertile country of Berry. When this
was told him, the king said, with an oath, that he would
immediately set out after him, and give him battle
wherever he should find him. He issued out a special
summons to all nobles and others who held fiefs under
him, that they should not, under any pretence whatever,
absent themselves without incurring his highest displeasure, but, immediately on the receipt of these letters, set
out to meet him on the borders of Touraine and Blois;
for he was determined to fight the English. The king, to
hasten the business, marched from Paris, — for he had at
this time a large body of men at arms in the field, — and
went to Chartres, to gain more certain intelligence of the
enemy. He remained there some time; and great crowds
of troops and men at arms came to him from the different
countries of Auvergne, Berry, Burgundy, Lorraine, Hai-

---

* The narrative has advanced five years since the last chapter. King
John keeps his oath: he "sets out after" the prince, and in a short time
brings on the great battle of Poitiers. — ED.

nault, Vermandois, Picardy, Brittany, and Normandy. They passed through the town on their arrival, to show their musters, and took up their quarters in the fields, according to the orders of the two marshals, the Lord John de Clermont and Lord Arnold d'Andreghen. The king gave orders for all the towns in Anjou, Poitou, Maine, and Touraine, to be well garrisoned, and provided with all things, — especially those on the borders, by which it was hoped the English would pass, — that they might be enclosed, and cut off from any subsistence for themselves and horses. In spite of this, however, the prince, who had with him two thousand men at arms and six thousand archers, rode on at his ease, and collected everywhere provisions in plenty. They found the country of Auvergne, which they had entered and overrun, very rich, and all things in great abundance ; but they would not stop there, as they were desirous of combating their enemies.

They marched toward Romorantin. The King of France sent into Berry three gallant barons, — the Lord of Craon, the Lord of Boucicault, and the Hermit of Chaumont, — to defend the frontiers, and to observe the motions of the English. They had with them three hundred lances ; and, skirting the borders of the province, they followed them for six days, without finding any opportunity of intercepting or of attacking the enemy : such good and close order did the English maintain on their march. The French therefore had recourse to an ambuscade, near to Romorantin, in a wonderfully narrow spot which the English were obliged to pass. That same day there left the prince's army, from the battalion of the marshals, by permission of the prince, the Lord Bartholomew Burghersh, the Lord of Muyssidan, a Gascon, the

Lord Petiton Courton, the Lord Delawar, the Lord Basset, Sir Walter Pavely, Sir Richard Pontchardan, Sir Nesle Loring, the young Lord Despencer, Sir Eustace and Sir Sanchez d'Ambreticourt, with about two hundred combatants, in order to push forward to Romorantin. They passed through the ambuscade of the French without molestation; but, the moment they were clear of it, the French, who were mounted on excellent and well-dressed horses, stuck spurs into them to overtake them. The English, who had got far forward, hearing the sound of horses' feet, turned round, and found it was the enemy. They immediately halted, to wait for the French, who advanced on a gallop, fully determined what to do, with their lances in their rests. The English, seeing them thus charge full speed, opened on each side, and let them pass through, so that no more than five or six were unhorsed. They then closed their ranks, and fell upon the rear of the French. This engagement was very sharp: many knights and squires were unhorsed, raised up again, and rescued on both sides. It lasted a long time, and no one could tell, so valiantly was it disputed, to which side victory would incline, when the battalion of the marshals appeared in sight. The French first noticed it, as it marched, skirting along a wood, and immediately thought of saving themselves as fast as they could, taking the road to Romorantin. The English followed on full gallop, overthrowing all they could, without sparing themselves or their horses. The slaughter was great, and many were killed and unhorsed. One-half of them, however, got safe into the castle of Romorantin, whose gates were opened to receive them. There the three barons saved themselves, as well as some knights and squires who were the best mounted. The town of Romorantin was taken on the first arrival of the English; for it was not fortified. The remainder of the French endeavored to escape by getting into the castle.

CHAPTER LXXIV.

THE PRINCE OF WALES TAKES THE CASTLE OF ROMORANTIN.

WHEN the Prince of Wales was informed that his people had been engaged, he hastened the march of his army toward Romorantin, and, when he entered the town, found it full of men, who were studying how they could take the castle. The prince called Sir John Chandos, and ordered him to go and hold a parley with those in the castle. Sir John went to the barriers, and made a sign that he wished to speak with some one: those upon guard inquired his name, by whom he was sent, and then went to inform their masters; upon which the Lord of Boucicault and the Hermit of Chaumont came down to the bars. When Sir John saw them, he saluted them, and said, "Gentlemen, I am sent to you by my lord the prince, who wishes, as it appears to me, to behave courteously toward his enemies; and thus says, that, if you will surrender the castle and yourselves, he will show you mercy, and give you good company." The Lord of Boucicault replied, "We have no sort of inclination to accept of such terms, nor to commit such an act of folly without any necessity; for we are determined to defend ourselves." Upon this they parted; and the prince ordered his men to quarters, for the next day he meant to attack the castle. They were therefore commodiously lodged in the town of Romorantin, and close about it.

On the next morning the men at arms prepared themselves; and the archers advanced under their respective
banners, and made a sharp attack upon the castle. The
archers, who had posted themselves on the ditches, shot
so justly, that scarcely any one dared to show himself on
the battlements. Some got upon hurdles and doors, with
pickaxes and mattocks in their hands, and swam over the
ditch, when they began to undermine the walls. Those
within flung down upon them large stones and pots of
hot lime. On this occasion there was slain, on the part
of the English, a squire called Remond de Gederlach,
who belonged to the division of the Captal de Buch.
The attack lasted the whole day, with little intermission.
The English retreated, toward night, to their quarters, in
order to take care of the wounded; and on the morrow at
sunrise the marshals' trumpets sounded. All who were
ordered for this assault got themselves in readiness: the
Prince of Wales himself attended in person, and by his
presence mightily encouraged the English. A squire, of
the name of Bernard, was killed close at his side, by a
stone thrown from the castle; upon which the prince
swore he would never move from that place until he had
the castle and all in it in his power, and immediately
ordered re-enforcements to the assault.

Some of the wisest thought that they might use lances
and arrows forever in vain; and therefore they ordered
cannons to be brought forward, to throw aquereaux and
Greek fire * into the lower court of the castle, so that it
was all in a blaze. The fire increased so much, that it

---

* Some say it was composed of sulphur, naphtha, pitch, gum, and bitu-
men; others, that the ingredients are not now known. It was invented by
Callinicus of Heliopolis, in the seventh century, to destroy the ships of the
Saracens. — ED.

gained a large tower which was covered with thatch. When those within the castle found that they must either surrender themselves, or perish by fire, the Lord of Craon, the Lord of Boucicault, and the Hermit of Chaumont, came down from the castle, and surrendered themselves to the prince, who made them ride and attend him, as his prisoners. Many other knights and squires who were in the castle were set at liberty, and the castle was destroyed.

CHAPTER LXXV.

THE KING OF FRANCE LEADS A GREAT ARMY TO THE BATTLE OF POITIERS.

AFTER the taking of the castle of Romorantin, and the above-mentioned knights, the prince and his army marched forward as before, burning and destroying the country, in his approach to Anjou and Touraine. The King of France, who had resided at Chartres, set out from that place, and came to Blois, where he remained two days. He then came to Amboise, and then to Loches, where he heard that the English were in Touraine, taking the road for their return through Poitou ; for the English army was constantly observed by some able and expert knights of France and Burgundy, who sent the king particular information of its movements. The King of France then advanced to La Haye, in Touraine. His army had crossed the Loire by the bridges of Orleans, Mehun, Samur, Blois, and Tours, and wherever else they could. There were such numbers of good and able men, that they were at least twenty thousand men at arms, without reckoning the others : there were twenty-five dukes and earls, and upward of sixscore banners. The four young sons of the king were also with him, — Charles, Duke of Normandy; the Lord Lewis, who was afterwards Duke of Anjou; the Lord John, since Duke of Berry; and the Lord Philip, the younger, who was afterwards Duke of Burgundy.

On the other hand, the Prince of Wales and his army were ignorant of the exact motions of the French; but they supposed they were not far distant, for their foragers found great difficulties in procuring forage, of which the whole army was in extreme want. They repented of the great waste they had made in Berry, Anjou, and Touraine, and that they had not more amply provisioned themselves.

It happened on this Friday, from the King of France in person passing the bridge of Chauvigny, and the great crowds which attended him, that three great barons of France, the Lord of Auxerre, the Lord Raoul de Joigny, and the Earl of Joigny, were obliged to remain all that day in the town of Chauvigny, and a part of their people with them: the others passed over without baggage or armor except what they had on their backs. On the Saturday morning they dislodged, crossed the bridge, and followed the army of the king, which was about three leagues off. They made for the open fields and the heaths, which were surrounded by woods, in order to arrive at Poitiers. This same Saturday the prince decamped from a village hard by, and sent forward a detachment to seek adventures, and to bring some intelligence of the French. They consisted of about sixty men, well armed and mounted for the occasion. Among the knights were Sir Eustace d'Ambreticourt and Sir John de Guistelles. By accident they got on the heaths surrounded by the woods above mentioned. The French soon saw they were enemies : they fixed on their helmets, and unfurled their banners as quickly as they were able ; when, fixing their lances in their rests, they stuck spurs to their horses.

The English no sooner perceived these Frenchmen, who were about two hundred lances, than they allowed themselves to be pursued, as the prince and his army were not far distant ; they therefore wheeled about, and made for the rutty road through the wood. The French chased them with shouts and a great noise, and, as they galloped on, fell in with the army of the prince, which had halted among the heaths to wait for their companions. The Lord Raoul de Joigny, and those under his banner, were advanced so far that they came right upon the banner of the prince. The engagement was very sharp, and Sir Raoul fought well : however, he was made prisoner, as were the Earl of Joigny, the Viscount de Breuse, and the Lord of Chauvigny : the greater part were either slain or captured. By these the prince learnt that the King of France had marched forward, and that he could not return without fighting him. Upon which he collected all the stragglers, and ordered that no one, under pain of death, should advance or skirmish before the battalion of the marshals. They marched on this Saturday, from about nine o'clock until vespers, when they came within small leagues of Poitiers. The Captal de Buch, Sir Haymenon de Pomiers, Sir Bartholomew Burghersh, and Sir Eustace d'Ambreticourt were ordered to advance, and observe where the French were encamped. These knights, with two hundred men well armed and mounted on their best steeds, set out, and soon perceived the French king's army. All the plain was covered with men at arms, and these English could not refrain from attacking the rear of the French: they unhorsed many, and took some prisoners, insomuch that the main army began to be in motion. News was brought of this to the King of France, as he was on the point of entering the city of Poitiers: upon which he turned back, and ordered his whole army to do the same, and make for the open fields, so that it was very late before they were quartered. The English detachment returned to the prince, and related to him the appearance of the French, that they were in immense numbers. The prince, on hearing this, said, "God help us! we must now consider which will be the best manner to fight them the most advantageously." This night the English were quartered in a very strong position, among vineyards and hedges; and both armies were well guarded.

CHAPTER LXXVI.

The Disposition of the French before the Battle of Poitiers.

ON the Sunday morning, the King of France, who was very impatient to combat the English, ordered a solemn mass to be sung in his pavilion; and he and his four sons received the communion. Mass being over, there came to him the Duke of Orleans, the Duke of Bourbon, the Earl of Ponthieu, the Lord James de Bourbon, the Duke of Athens, constable of France, the Earl of Tancarville, the Earl of Saltzburg, the Earl of Dammartin, the Earl of Ventadour, and many barons of France, as well as other great lords who held fiefs in the neighborhood, such as my Lord of Clermont, Sir Arnold d'An-dreghen, marshal of France, the Lord de St. Venant, the Lord John de Landas, the Lord Eustace de Ribeaumont, the Lord de Fiennes, the Lord Geoffry de Chargny, the Lord of Châtillon, the Lord of Sully, the Lord of Nesle, Sir Robert de Duras, and many more, according to a summons they had received for a council. They were a considerable time debating: at last it was ordered, that the whole army should advance into the plain, and each lord should display his banner, and push forward in the name of God and St. Denis. Upon this the trumpets of the army sounded, and every one got himself ready, mounted his horse, and made for that part of the plain where the king's banner was planted and fluttering in the wind. There might be seen all the nobility of France, richly dressed out in brilliant armor, with banners and pennons gallantly displayed; for all the flower of the French nobility were there : no knight nor squire, for fear of dishonor, dared to remain at home. By the advice of the constable and the marshals, the army was divided into three battalions, each consisting of sixteen thousand men at arms, who had before shown themselves men of tried courage. The Duke of Orleans commanded the first battalion, where there were thirty-six banners and twice as many pennons. The second was under the command of the Duke of Normandy and his two brothers, the Lord Lewis and Lord John. The King of France commanded the third.

While these three battalions were forming, the king called to him the Lord Eustace de Ribeaumont, the Lord John de Landas, and the Lord Guiscard de Beaujeu, and said to them, " Ride forward, as near the English army as you can, and observe their countenance, taking notice of

their numbers, and examine which will be the most advantageous manner for us to combat them, whether on horseback or on foot." The three knights left the king to obey
his commands. The king was mounted upon a white
palfrey, and, riding to the head of his army, said aloud,
"You, men of Paris, Chartres, Rouen, and Orleans, have
been used to threaten what you would do to the English
if you could find them, and wished much to meet them in
arms. Now that wish shall be gratified: I will lead you to
them; and let us see how you will revenge yourselves for
all the mischief and damage they have done you. Be
assured we will not part without fighting." Those who
heard him replied, "Sir, through God's assistance, we
will most cheerfully meet them." At this instant the
three knights returned, and, pushing through the crowd,
came to the king, who asked what news they had brought.
Sir Eustace de Ribeaumont, whom his companions had
requested to be their spokesman, answered, "Sir, we have
observed accurately the English. They may amount, according to our estimate, to about two thousand men at
arms, four thousand archers, and fifteen hundred footmen.
They are in a very strong position, but we do not imagine
they can make more than one battalion: nevertheless
they have posted themselves with great judgment, have
fortified all the road along the hedge-side, and lined the
hedges with part of their archers; for, as that is the only
road for an attack, one must pass through the midst of
them. This lane has no other entry; and it is so narrow,
that scarcely can four men ride through it abreast. At
the end of this lane, amid vines and thorns, where it is impossible to ride or march in any regular order, are posted
the men at arms, on foot; and they have drawn up before
them their archers, in the manner of a harrow, so that it

will be no easy matter to defeat them." The king asked
in what manner they would advise him to attack them.
"Sir," replied Sir Eustace, "on foot: except three hundred of the most expert and boldest of your army, who
must be well armed and excellently mounted, in order to
break, if possible, this body of archers; and then your battalions must advance quickly on foot, attack the men at
arms hand to hand, and combat them valiantly. This is
the best advice that I can give you; and, if any one know
a better, let him say it." The king replied, "Thus shall
it be, then;" and in company with his two marshals he
rode from battalion to battalion, and selected, in con-
formity to their opinions, three hundred knights and
squires of the greatest repute in his army, each well armed
and mounted on the best of horses. Soon after, the battalion of the Germans was formed, who were to remain on
horseback to assist the marshals: they were commanded
by the Earls of Saltzburg, Neydo, and Nassau.

King John was armed in royal armor, and nineteen
others like him. He had given his eldest son in charge to
the Lord of St. Venant, the Lord of Landas, and the Lord
Theobald de Bodenay. The Lord Geoffry de Chargny
carried the banner of France, as being the most valiant
and prudent knight of the army. The Lord Reginald de
Quenolle,* surnamed the Archpriest, wore the full armor
of the young Earl of Alençon.

---

* It was Arnaut (i.e., Arnold) de Cervolle who was surnamed the Archpriest. — ED.

CHAPTER LXXVII.

The Cardinal de Perigord endeavors to make Peace between the King of France and the Prince of Wales, previous to the Battle of Poitiers.

WHEN the battalions of the King of France were drawn up, and each lord posted under his proper banner, and informed how they were to act, it was ordered, that all those who were armed with lances should shorten them to the length of five feet, that they might be the more manageable, and that every one should take off his spurs. As the French were on the point of marching to their enemies, the Cardinal de Perigord, who had left Poitiers that morning early, came full gallop up to the king, making a low reverence, and entreated him, with uplifted hands, for the love of God, to halt a moment, that he might speak to him. He thus began: "Most dear sire, you have here with you all the flower of knighthood of your kingdom, against a handful of people, such as the English are, when compared to your army: you may have them upon other terms than by a battle; and it will be more honorable and profitable to you to gain them by these means than to risk such a fine army and such noble persons as you have now with you. I therefore beseech you, in all humility, and by the love of God, that you will permit me to go to the prince, and remonstrate with him on the dangerous situation he is in." The king answered, " It is very agreeable to us ; but make haste back again."

All this Sunday the cardinal rode from one army to the other, and was very anxious to reconcile the two parties.

Many proposals were made. At last they declared that if the Prince of Wales, and one hundred of his knights, did not surrender themselves prisoners to the King of France, he would not allow them to pass on without an engagement. The prince and his army disdained accepting such conditions. The Cardinal de Perigord, not being able by any means to reconcile the king and prince, returned to Poitiers late in the evening. That same day the French kept in their quarters, where they lived at their ease, having plenty of provisions; while the English, on the other hand, were but badly off, nor did they know whither to go for forage, as they were so straitly kept by the French, they could not move without danger. This Sunday they made many mounds and ditches round where the archers were posted, the better to secure them.

On Monday morning the prince and his army were soon in readiness, and as well arrayed as on the former day. The French were also drawn out by sunrise. The cardinal, returning again that morning, imagined that, by his exhortations, he could pacify both parties; but the French told him to return where he pleased, and not attempt bringing them any more treaties or pacifications, else worse might betide him. When the cardinal saw that he labored in vain, he took leave of the King of France, and set out toward the Prince of Wales, to whom he said, " Fair son, exert yourself as much as possible, for there must be a battle : I cannot by any means pacify the King of France." The prince replied, that such were the intentions of him and his party ; "and God defend the right." The cardinal then took leave of him, and returned to Poitiers.

The arrangement of the prince's army, in respect to the battalions, was exactly the same as what the three knights

before named had related to the King of France, except
at this time he had ordered some valiant and intelligent
knights to remain on horseback, similar to the battalion of
the French marshals, and had also commanded three hundred men at arms, and as many archers on horseback, to
post themselves on the right, on a small hill, that was not
too steep nor too high ; and, by passing over its summit,
to get round the wing of the Duke of Normandy's battalion, who was in person at the foot of it. These were all
the alterations the prince had made in his order of battle :
he himself was with the main body, in the midst of the
vineyards ; the whole completely armed, with their horses
near them, if there should be occasion for them. They
had fortified and enclosed the weaker parts, with their
wagons and baggage.

I wish to name some of the most renowned knights
who were with the Prince of Wales. There were Thomas
Beauchamp, Earl of Warwick ; John Vere, Earl of Oxford ;
William Montacute, Earl of Salisbury ; Robert Hufford,
Earl of Suffolk ; Ralph, Lord Stafford, the Earl of Stafford ; the Lord Richard Stafford, brother to the Earl ; Sir
John Chandos ; the Lord Reginald Cobham ; the Lord
Edward Spencer ; the Lord James Audley, and his
brother the Lord Peter ; the Lord Thomas Berkeley (son
of the Lord Maurice Berkeley, who died at Calais nine
years before) ; Ralph, Lord Basset, of Drayton ; John,
Lord Warren (eldest son to John Plantagenet, late Earl of
Warren, Strathern, and Surrey, by his first lady, Maude
de Hereford) ; Peter, Lord Mauley, the sixth of the name ;
the Lord John Willoughby de Eresby ; the Lord Bartholomew de Burghersh ; the Lord William Felton, and the
Lord Thomas Felton his brother ; the Lord Thomas
Bradestan ; Sir Walter Pavely ; Sir Stephen Cossington ;

Sir Matthew Gournay; Sir William de la More, and other English. From Gascony, there were the Lord of Pumiers; the Lord d'Albret; the Captal de Buch; the Lord John de Chaumont; the Lord de l'Esparre; the Lord of Rosen; the Lord of Cousen; the Lord de Montferrand; the Lord de Landulas; the Lord Souldich de la Traine, and many more whom I cannot remember. Of Hainaulters, there were Sir Eustace d'Ambreticourt; the Lord John de Guystelle, and two other strangers; the Lord Daniel Phaselle, and Lord Denys de Morbeque. The whole army of the prince, including every one, did not amount to eight thousand; when the French, counting all sorts of persons, were upward of sixty thousand combatants, among whom were more than three thousand knights.

CHAPTER LXXVIII.

THE BATTLE OF POITIERS, BETWEEN THE PRINCE OF WALES AND THE KING OF FRANCE.

WHEN the Prince of Wales saw, from the departure of the cardinal without being able to obtain any honorable terms, that a battle was inevitable, and that the King of France held both him and his army in great contempt, he thus addressed himself to them: "Now, my gallant fellows, what though we be a small body when compared to the army of our enemies? do not let us. be cast down on that account, for victory does not always follow numbers, but where Almighty God pleases to bestow it. If, through good fortune, the day shall be ours, we will gain the greatest honor and glory in this world: if the contrary should happen, and we be slain, I have a father

and beloved brethren alive, and you all have some relations or good friends, who will be sure to revenge our
deaths.　I therefore entreat you to exert yourselves, and
combat manfully ; for, if it please God and St. George,
this day you shall see me a good knight."　By such words
and arguments as these the prince harangued his men, as
did the marshals, by his orders ; so that they were all in
high spirits.　Sir John Chandos placed himself near the
prince, to guard and advise him ; and never, during that
day, would he on any account quit his post.

The Lord James Audley remained also a considerable
time near him ; but, when he saw that they must certainly
engage, he said to the prince, "Sir, I have ever served
most loyally my lord your father, and yourself, and shall
continue to do so as long as I have life.　Dear sir, I must
now acquaint you, that formerly I made a vow, if ever I
should be engaged in any battle where the king your
father, or any of his sons, were, that I would be the foremost in the attack, and the best combatant on his side, or
die in the attempt.　I beg, therefore, most earnestly, as a
reward for any services I may have done, that you would
grant me permission honorably to quit you, that I may
post myself in such wise to accomplish my vow."　The
prince granted this request, and, holding out his hand to
him, said, "Sir James, God grant that you may this day
shine in valor above all other knights !"　The knight then
set off, and posted himself at the front of the battalion,
with only four squires whom he had detained with him, to
guard his person.　This Lord James was a prudent and
valiant knight ; and by his advice the army had thus been
drawn up in order of battle.　Lord James began to advance, in order to fight with the battalion of the marshals.
In like manner Sir Eustace d'Ambreticourt took great

pains to be the first to engage, and was so, or near it ; and, at the same time that Lord James Audley was pushing forward to seek his enemies, it thus befell Sir Eustace. I mentioned before that the Germans, attached to the French interest, were drawn up in one battalion on horseback, and remained so, to assist the marshals. Sir Eustace d'Ambreticourt, being mounted, placed his lance in its rest, and, fixing his shield, stuck spurs into his horse, and galloped up to this battalion. A German knight, called Lord Lewis von Coucibras (who bore for arms five roses, gules, on a shield argent, while those of Sir Eustace were ermine, three humets, in pale gules), perceiving Sir Eustace quit his army, left his battalion, that was under the command of Earl John of Nassau, and made up to him. The shock of their meeting was so violent, that they both fell to the ground. The German was wounded in the shoulder, so that he could not rise again so nimbly as Sir Eustace, who, when upon his legs, after he had taken breath, was hastening to the knight that lay on the ground ; but five German men at arms came upon him, struck him down, and made him prisoner. They led him to those that were attached to the Earl of Nassau, who did not pay much attention to him, nor do I know if they made him swear himself their prisoner ; but they tied him to a car with some of their harness.

The engagement now began on both sides ; and the battalion of the marshals was advancing before those who were intended to break the battalion of the archers, and had entered the lane where the hedges on both sides were lined by the archers, who, as soon as they saw them fairly entered, began shooting with their bows in such an excellent manner, from each side of the hedge, that the horses, smarting under the pain of the wounds made by

their bearded arrows, would not advance, but turned about,
and by their unruliness threw their masters, who could
not manage them, nor could those that had fallen get up
again for the confusion : so that this battalion of the
marshals could never approach that of the prince. However, there were some knights and squires that were so
well mounted, that, by the strength of their horses, they
passed through, and broke the hedge, but, in spite of their
efforts, could not get up to the battalion of the prince.
The Lord James Audley, attended by his four squires,
had placed himself, sword in hand, in front of this battalion, much before the rest, and was performing wonders.
He had advanced through his eagerness so far, that he
engaged the Lord Arnold d'Andreghen, Marshal of France,
under his banner, when they fought a considerable time,
and the Lord Arnold was roughly enough treated. The
battalion of the marshals was soon after put to the rout
by the arrows of the archers, and the assistance of the
men at arms, who rushed among them as they were struck
down, and seized and slew them at their pleasure. The
Lord Arnold d'Andreghen was there made prisoner, but
by others than the Lord James Audley or his four squires ;
for that knight never stopped to make any one prisoner
that day, but was the whole time employed in fighting and
following his enemies. In another part, the Lord John
Clermont fought under his banner as long as he was able ;
but, being struck down, he could neither get up again, nor
procure his ransom : he was killed on the spot. Some
say this treatment was owing to his altercation on the
preceding day with Sir John Chandos.

In a short time this battalion of the marshals was
totally discomfited ; for they fell back so much on each
other, that the army could not advance, and those who

were in the rear, not being able to get forward, fell back upon the battalion commanded by the Duke of Normandy, which was broad and thick in the front, but it was soon thin enough in the rear; for, when they learnt that the marshals had been defeated, they mounted their horses, and set off. At this time a body of English came down from the hill, and, passing along the battalions on horse-back, accompanied by a large body of archers, fell upon one of the wings of the Duke of Normandy's division. To say the truth, the English archers were of infinite service to their army; for they shot so thickly and so well, that the French did not know which way to turn themselves to avoid their arrows: by this means they kept advancing by little and little, and gained ground. When the men at arms perceived that the first battalion was beaten, and that the one under the Duke of Normandy was in disorder, and beginning to open, they hastened to mount their horses, which they had, ready prepared, close at hand. As soon as they were all mounted, they gave a shout of, "St. George for Guienne!" and Sir John Chandos said to the prince, "Sir, sir, now push forward, for the day is ours: God will this day put it in your hand. Let us make for our adversary the King of France; for, where he is, will lie the main stress of the business. I well know that his valor will not let him fly; and he will remain with us, if it please God and St. George. But he must be well fought with; and you have before said that you would show yourself this day a good knight." The prince replied, "John, get forward: you shall not see me turn my back this day, but I will always be among the foremost." He then said to Sir Walter Woodland, his banner-bearer, "Banner, advance, in the name of God and St. George." The knight

obeyed the commands of the prince. In that part the
battle was very hot and greatly crowded.   Many a one
was unhorsed ; and you must know that whenever any one
fell he could not get up again unless he were quickly
and well assisted. As the prince was thus advancing
upon his enemies, followed by his division, and upon the
point of charging them, he perceived the Lord Robert
de Duras lying dead near a small bush on his right hand,
with his banner beside him, and ten or twelve of his
people ; upon which he ordered two of his squires and
three archers to place the body upon a shield, carry it to
Poitiers, and present it from him to the Cardinal of
Perigord, and say that "I salute him by that token."
This was done ; for he had been informed how the suite
of the cardinal had remained in the field of battle in arms
against him, which was not very becoming, nor a fit deed
for churchmen to do, as they, under pretext of doing good
and establishing peace, pass from one army to the other :
they ought not therefore to take up arms on either side.
These, however, had done so, at which the prince was
much enraged, and for this had sent the cardinal his
nephew Sir Robert de Duras, and was desirous of striking
off the head of the castellan of Amposta, who had been
made prisoner, notwithstanding he belonged to the cardinal ; but Sir John Chandos said, "My lord, do not think
of such things at this moment, when you must look to
others of the greatest importance.   Perhaps the cardinal
may excuse himself so well, that you will be convinced
he was not to blame."

The prince, upon this, charged the division of the Duke
of Athens ; and very sharp the encounter was, so that
many were beaten down.   The French, who fought in
large bodies, cried out, "Montjoye St. Denis !" and the

English answered them with, "St. George for Guienne!"
The prince next met the battalion of Germans, under the
command of the Earl of Saltzburg, the Earl of Nassau,
and the Earl of Neydo; but they were soon overthrown
and put to flight. The English archers shot so well, that
none dared to come within reach of their arrows, and they
put to death many who could not ransom themselves.
The three above-named earls were slain there, as well as
many other knights and squires attached to them. In the
confusion Sir Eustace d'Ambreticourt was rescued by his
own men, who remounted him: he afterwards performed
many gallant deeds of arms, and made good captures that
day.

When the battalion of the Duke of Normandy saw the
prince advancing so quick upon them, they bethought
themselves how to escape. The sons of the king, the
Duke of Normandy, the Earl of Poitiers, the Earl of
Touraine, who were very young, too easily believed what
those under whose management they were placed said to
them: however, the Lord Guiscard d'Angle and Sir John
de Saintré, who were near the Earl of Poitiers, would not
fly, but rushed into the thickest of the combat. The three
sons of the king, according to the advice given them,
galloped away, with upward of eight hundred lances who
had never been near the enemy, and took the road to
Chauvigny. When the Lord John de Landas, who with
the Lord Theobald de Bodenay and the Lord of St.
Venant were the guardians of the Duke of Normandy,
had fled with him a good league, they took leave of him,
and besought the Lord of St. Venant not to quit him until
they were all arrived at a place of safety; for by doing
thus he would acquire more honor than if he were to
remain on the field of battle. On their return they met

the division of the Duke of Orleans, quite whole and
unhurt, who had fled from behind the rear of the king's
battalion. True it is, there were many good knights and
squires among them, who, notwithstanding the flight of
their leaders, had much rather have suffered death than
the smallest reproach. The king's battalion advanced in
good order to meet the English; many hard blows were
given with swords, battle-axes, and other warlike weapons.
The King of France, with the Lord Philip his youngest
son, attacked the division of the marshals, the Earls of
Warwick and Suffolk. There were also with the marshals
some Gascons, such as the Captal de Buch, the Lord of
Pumiers, the Lord Amery de Charree, the Lord of Lan-
guran, the Lord de l'Estrade. The Lord John de Landas
with the Lord Theobald de Bodenay, returning in good
time, dismounted, and joined the battalion of the king.
On one side the Duke of Athens, constable of France,
was engaged with his division; and a little higher up the
Duke of Bourbon, surrounded with good knights from the
Bourbonois and Picardy. Near to these were the men of
Poitou, the Lord de Pons, the Lord de Partenay, the Lord
de Dampmaire, the Lord de Montabouton, the Lord de
Surgeres, the Lord John de Saintré, the Lord Guiscard
d'Angle, the Lord d'Argenton, the Lord de Linieres, the
Lord de Montrande, the Viscount de Rochechouart, the
Earl of Aulnoy. Many others were also engaged, such as
the Lord James de Beaujeu, the Lord of Chateau-Villain,
and other knights and squires from Burgundy. In another part were the Earls of Vantadour and Montpensier,
the Lord James de Bourbon, the Lord John d'Artois
and the Lord James his brother, the Lord Arnold de Cervolle, surnamed the Archpriest, armed as the young Earl
of Alençon. There were also from Auvergne the Lord de

Marcueil, the Lord de la Tour, the Lord de Chalenton, the Lord de Montagu, the Lord de Rochefort, the Lord de la Chaire, the Lord d'Achon; and from Limousin the Lord de Linal, the Lord de Naruel, and the Lord Pierre de Buffiere. From Picardy there were the Lord William de Merle, the Lord Arnold de Renneval, the Lord Geoffry de St. Dizier, the Lord de Chauny, the Lord de Hely, the Lord de Monsant, the Lord de Hagnes, and many others. The Lord Douglas from Scotland was also in the king's battalion, and for some time fought very valiantly; but, when he perceived that the discomfiture was so complete on the side of the French, he saved himself as fast as he could; for he dreaded so much being taken by the English, that he had rather have been slain.

The Lord James Audley, with the assistance of his four squires, was always engaged in the heat of the battle. He was severely wounded in the body, head, and face; and, as long as his strength and breath permitted him, he maintained the fight, and advanced forward. He continued to do so until he was covered with blood: then, toward the close of the engagement, his four squires, who were as his body-guard, took him, and led him out of the engagement, very weak and wounded, toward a hedge, that he might cool and take breath. They disarmed him gently as they could, in order to examine his wounds, dress them, and sew up the most dangerous.

King John, on his part, proved himself a good knight; and, if the fourth of his people had behaved as well, the day would have been his own. Those, however, who had remained with him acquitted themselves to the best of their power, and were either slain or taken prisoners. Scarcely any who were with the king attempted to escape. In this engagement, upward of two hundred knights and squires were killed or captured. A band of Norman knights still kept up the battle in another part of the field; and of these Sir Guinenton de Chambly and Sir Baudrin de la House were slain. Many others were discomfited, who were fighting in small bodies.

CHAPTER LXXIX.

Two Frenchmen, running away from the Battle of Poitiers, are pursued by two Englishmen, who are themselves made Prisoners.

AMONG the battles, skirmishes, flights, and pursuits which happened in the course of this day, an adventure befell Sir Edward de Roucy which I cannot omit relating in this place. He had left the field of battle, as he perceived the day was irrecoverably lost; and, not wishing to fall in the hands of the English, was got about a league off, when he was pursued by an English knight, his lance in rest, who cried to him, "Sir knight, turn about! you ought to be ashamed thus to fly." Upon this Sir Edward halted, and the Englishman attacked him, thinking to fix his lance in his target; but he failed, for Sir Edward turned the stroke aside, nevertheless he did not miss his own: with his spear he hit his enemy so violent a blow on the helmet, that he was stunned, and fell to the ground, where he remained senseless. Sir Edward dismounted, and, placing his lance on his breast, told him he would certainly kill him if he did not surrender himself his prisoner, rescued or not. The Englishman surrendered, and went with Sir Edward, who afterwards ransomed him.

It happened that in the midst of the general pursuit, a

squire from Picardy, named John de Helennes, had quitted
the king's division, and, meeting his page with a fresh
horse, had mounted him, and made off as fast as he could.
At that time there was near to him the Lord of Berkeley,
a young knight, who for the first time had that day displayed his banner: he immediately set out in pursuit of
him. When the Lord of Berkeley had followed him for
some little time, John de Helennes turned about, put his
sword under his arm in the manner of a lance, and thus
advanced upon the Lord Berkeley, who, taking his sword
by the handle, flourished it, and lifted up his arm in order
to strike the squire as he passed. John de Helennes, seeing the intended stroke, avoided it, but did not miss his
own ; for, as they passed each other, by a blow on the arm
he made Lord Berkeley's sword fall to the ground. When
the knight found that he had lost his sword, and that the
squire had his, he dismounted, and made for the place
where his sword lay ; but he could not get there before
the squire gave him a violent thrust which passed through
both his thighs, so that, not being able to help himself, he
fell to the ground. John upon this dismounted, and, seizing the sword of the knight, advanced up to him, and
asked him if he were willing to surrender. The knight
required his name. "I am called John de Helennes,"
said he ; "what is your name?"—"In truth, companion,"
replied the knight, "my name is Thomas, and I am Lord
of Berkeley, a very handsome castle situated on the River
Severn, on the borders of Wales." — "Lord of Berkeley,"
said the squire, "you shall be my prisoner : I will place
you in safety, and take care you are healed, for you appear
to me to be badly wounded." The knight answered, "I
surrender myself willingly, for you have loyally conquered
me." He gave him his word that he would be his pris-

oner, rescued or not. John then drew his sword out of the knight's thighs, and the wounds remained open; but he bound them up tightly, and, placing him on his horse, led him a foot-pace to Châtelherault. He continued there, out of friendship to him, for fifteen days, and had medicines administered to him. When the knight was a little recovered, he had him placed in a litter, and conducted him safe to his house in Picardy, where he remained more than a year before he was quite cured, though he continued lame; and when he departed he paid for his ransom six thousand nobles, so that this squire became a knight by the great profit he got from the Lord of Berkeley.

CHAPTER LXXX.

The Manner in which King John was taken Prisoner at the Battle of Poitiers.

KING JOHN himself did wonders: he was armed with a battle-axe, with which he fought and defended himself. The Earl of Tancarville, in endeavoring to break through the crowd, was made prisoner close to him; as were also Sir James de Bourbon, Earl of Ponthieu, and the Lord John d'Artois, Earl of Eu. In another part, a little farther off, the Lord Charles d'Artois and many other knights and squires were captured by the division under the banner of the Captal de Buch. The pursuit continued even to the gates of Poitiers, where there was much slaughter and overthrow of men and horses; for the inhabitants of Poitiers had shut their gates, and would suffer none to enter: upon which account there was great butchery on the causeway, before

The Surrender of King John of France.

the gate, where such numbers were killed or wounded, that several surrendered themselves the moment they spied an Englishman; and there were many English archers who had four, five, or six prisoners.

The Lord of Pons, a powerful baron in Poitou, was slain there, as were several other knights and squires. The English and Gascons poured so fast upon the king's division, that they broke through the ranks by force; and the French were so intermixed with their enemies, that at times there were five men attacking one gentleman. The Lord of Pompadour and the Lord Bartholomew de Brunes were there captured. The Lord de Chargny was slain, with the banner of France in his hands, by the Lord Reginald Cobham; and afterwards the Earl of Dammartin shared the same fate.

There was much pressing at this time, through eagerness to take the king; and those who were nearest to him, and knew him, cried out, "Surrender yourself, surrender yourself, or you are a dead man." In that part of the field was a young knight from St. Omer, who was engaged by a salary in the service of the King of England: his name was Denys de Morbeque: who for five years had attached himself to the English, on account of having been banished in his younger days from France for a murder committed in an affray at St. Omer. It fortunately happened for this knight that he was at the time near to the King of France, when he was so much pulled about: he by dint of force (for he was very strong and robust) pushed through the crowd, and said to the king in good French, "Sire, sire, surrender yourself." The king, who found himself very disagreeably situated, turning to him asked, "To whom shall I surrender myself? to whom? Where is my cousin the Prince of Wales? if I could see him, I would speak to him." — "Sire," replied Sir Denys, "he is not here; but surrender yourself to me, and I will lead you to him." — "Who are you?" said the king. "Sire, I am Denys de Morbeque, a knight from Artois; but I serve the King of England, because I cannot belong to France, having forfeited all I possessed there." The king then gave him his right-hand glove, and said, "I surrender myself to you." There was much crowding and pushing about, for every one was eager to cry out, "I have taken him." Neither the king nor his youngest son Philip were able to get forward, and free themselves from the throng.

The Prince of Wales, who was as courageous as a lion, took great delight that day to combat his enemies. Sir John Chandos, who was near his person, and had never quitted it during the whole of the day, nor stopped to make prisoners, said to him toward the end of the battle, "Sir, it will be proper for you to halt here, and plant your banner on the top of this bush, which will serve to rally your forces, that seem very much scattered; for I do not see any banners or pennons of the French, nor any considerable bodies able to rally against us; and you must refresh yourself a little, as I perceive you are very much heated." Upon this the banner of the prince was placed on a high bush: the minstrels began to play, and trumpets and clarions to do their duty. The prince took off his helmet; and the knights attendant on his person, and belonging to his chamber, were soon ready, and pitched a small pavilion of crimson color, which the prince entered. Liquor was then brought to him and the other knights who were with him: they increased every moment; for they were returning from the pursuit, and stopped there surrounded by their prisoners.

As soon as the two marshals were come back, the prince asked them if they knew any thing of the King of France: they replied, "No, sir, not for a certainty; but we believe he must be either killed or made prisoner, since he has never quitted his battalion." The prince then, addressing the Earl of Warwick and Lord Cobham, said, "I beg of you to mount your horses, and ride over the field, so that on your return you may bring me some certain intelligence of him." The two barons, immediately mounting their horses, left the prince, and made for a small hillock, that they might look about them: from their stand they perceived a crowd of men at arms on foot, who were advancing very slowly. The King of France was in the midst of them, and in great danger; for the English and Gascons had taken him from Sir Denys de Morbeque, and were disputing who should have him, the stoutest bawling out, "It is I that have got him!"—"No, no," replied the others, "we have him." The king, to escape from this peril, said, "Gentlemen, gentlemen, I pray you conduct me and my son in a courteous manner to my cousin the prince; and do not make such a riot about my capture, for I am so great a lord that I can make all sufficiently rich." These words, and others which fell from the king, appeased them a little; but the disputes were always beginning again, and they did not move a step without rioting. When the two barons saw this troop of people, they descended from the hillock, and, sticking spurs into their horses, made up to them. On their arrival, they asked what was the matter: they were answered, that it was the King of France, who had been made prisoner, and that upward of ten knights and squires challenged him at the same time, as belonging to each of them. The two barons then pushed through the crowd by main force, and ordered all to draw aside. They commanded, in the name of the prince, and under pain of instant death, that every one should keep his distance, and not approach unless ordered or desired so to do. They all retreated behind the king; and the two barons, dismounting, advanced to the king with profound reverences, and conducted him in a peaceable manner to the Prince of Wales.

CHAPTER LXXXI.

THE PRINCE OF WALES MAKES A HANDSOME PRESENT TO THE LORD JAMES AUDLEY, AFTER THE BATTLE OF POITIERS.

SOON after the Earl of Warwick and the Lord Reginald Cobham had left the prince, as has been above related, he inquired from those knights who were about him of Lord James Audley, and asked if any one knew what was become of him. "Yes, sir," replied some of the company: "he is very badly wounded, and is lying in a litter hard by." — "By my troth," replied the prince, "I am sore vexed that he is so wounded. See, I beg of you, if he be able to bear being carried hither: otherwise I will come and visit him." Two knights directly left the prince, and, coming to Lord James, told him how desirous the prince was of seeing him. "A thousand thanks to the prince," answered Lord James, "for condescending to remember so poor a knight as myself." He then called eight of his servants, and had himself borne in his litter to where the prince was. When he was come into his presence, the prince bent down over him, and embraced him, saying, "My Lord James, I am bound to honor you very much; for by your valor this day you have acquired glory and renown above us all, and your prowess has proved you the bravest knight." Lord James replied, "My lord, you have a right to say whatever you please, but I wish it were as you have said. If I have this day been forward to serve you, it has been to accomplish a vow that I had made, and it ought not to be thought so much of." — "Sir James," answered the prince, "I and all the rest of us deem you the bravest knight on our side in this battle; and to increase your renown, and furnish you withal to pursue your career of glory in war, I retain you henceforward, forever, as my knight, with five hundred marks of yearly revenue, which I will secure to you from my estates in England." — "Sir," said Lord James, "God make me deserving of the good fortune you bestow upon me!" At these words he took leave of the prince, as he was very weak, and his servants carried him back to his tent. He could not have been at a great distance, when the Earl of Warwick and Lord Reginald Cobham entered the pavilion of the prince, and presented the King of France to him. The prince made a very low obeisance to the king, and gave him as much comfort as he was able, which he knew well how to administer. He ordered wine and spices to be brought, which he presented to the king himself, as a mark of his great affection.

When the Lord James Audley was brought back to his tent, after having most respectfully thanked the prince for his gift, he did not remain long before he sent for his brother Sir Peter Audley, the Lord Bartholomew Burghersh, Sir Stephen Coffington, Lord Willoughby of Eresby, and Lord William Ferrers of Groby: they were all his relations. He then sent for his four squires that had attended upon him that day, and, addressing himself to the knights, said, "Gentlemen, it has pleased my lord the prince to give me five hundred marks as a yearly inheritance; for which gift I have done him very trifling bodily service. You see here these four squires, who have always served me most loyally, and especially in this day's engagement. What glory I may have gained has been through their means, and by their valor; on which account I wish to reward them. I therefore give and resign into their hands the gift of five hundred marks, which my lord the prince has been pleased to bestow on me, in the same form and manner that it has been presented to me. I disinherit myself of it, and give it to them simply, and without a possibility of revoking it." The knights present looked on each other, and said, "It is becoming the noble mind of Lord James to make such a gift;" and then unanimously added, "May the Lord God remember you for it! We will bear witness to this gift to them wheresoever and whensoever they may call on us." They then took leave of him; when some went to the Prince of Wales, who that night was to give a supper to the King of France from his own provisions: for the French had brought vast quantities with them, which were now fallen into the hands of the English, many of whom had not tasted bread for the last three days.

CHAPTER LXXXII.

THE PRINCE OF WALES ENTERTAINS THE KING OF FRANCE AT SUPPER, THE EVENING AFTER THE BATTLE.

WHEN evening was come, the Prince of Wales gave a supper in his pavilion to the King of France, and to the greater part of the princes and barons who were prisoners. The prince seated the King of France and his son the Lord Philip at an elevated and well-covered table: with them were Sir James de Bourbon, the Lord John d'Artois, the Earls of Tancarville, of Estampes, of Dammartin, of Graville, and the Lord of Partenay. The other knights and squires were placed at different tables. The prince himself served the king's table, as well as the others, with every mark of humility, and would not sit down at it, in spite of all his entreaties for him so to do, saying that he was not worthy of such an honor, nor did it appertain to him to seat himself at the table of so great a king, or of so valiant a man as he had shown himself by his actions that day. He added also with a noble air, "Dear sir, do not make a poor meal because the Almighty God has not gratified your wishes in the event of this day; for be assured that my lord and father will show you every honor and friendship in his power, and will arrange your ransom so reasonably that you will henceforward always remain friends. In my opinion, you have cause to be glad that the success of this battle did not turn out as you desired; for you have this day acquired such high renown for prowess, that you have surpassed all the best knights on your side. I do not, dear sir, say this to flatter you; for all those of our side who have seen and observed the actions of each party have unanimously allowed this to be your due, and decree you the prize and garland for it." At the end of this speech there were murmurs of praise heard from every one; and the French said the prince had spoken nobly and truly, and that he would be one of the most gallant princes in Christendom, if God should grant him life to pursue his career of glory.

CHAPTER LXXXIII.

THE PRINCE OF WALES RETURNS TO BORDEAUX, AFTER THE BATTLE
OF POITIERS.

WHEN they had supped and sufficiently regaled
themselves, each departed to his lodging with the
knights and squires they had captured. Those that had
taken them asked what they could pay for their ransoms
without much hurting their fortunes, and willingly believed whatever they told them; for they had declared
publicly, that they did not wish to deal harshly with any
knight or squire, that his ransom should be so burdensome
as to prevent his following the profession of arms, or
advancing his fortune. Toward morning, when these
lords had heard mass, and had eaten and drunk a little,
while the servants were packing up or loading the baggage, they decamped and advanced toward Poitiers.

That same night the Lord of Roye had entered the city
of Poitiers with a hundred lances that had not been engaged in the battle; for, having met the Duke of Normandy near Chauvigny, he had commanded him to march
for Poitiers, and to guard it until he should receive other
orders. When the Lord of Roye had entered Poitiers, he
ordered the gates, towers, and walls to be well watched
that night, on account of the English being so near; and
on the morning he armed all sorts of people, and posted
them wherever he judged most convenient for the defence
of the town. The English, however, passed by without
making any attempt upon it; for they were so laden with
gold, silver, jewels, and great prisoners, that they did

not attack any fortress in their march, but thought they should do great things if they were able to convey the King of France and his son, with all their booty, in safety to the city of Bordeaux. They returned therefore, by easy marches, on account of their prisoners and heavy baggage, never advancing more than four or five leagues a day. They encamped early, and marched in one compact body, without quitting the road, except the division of the marshals, who advanced in front, with about five hundred men at arms, to clear the country. They met with no resistance anywhere; for the whole country was in a state of consternation, and all the men at arms had retreated into the strong fortresses.

During this march the Prince of Wales was informed how Lord James Audley had made a present of his pension of five hundred marks to his four squires. He sent for him. Lord James was carried in his litter to the presence of the prince, who received him very graciously, and said to him, "Sir James, I have been informed, that after you had taken leave of me, and were returned to your tent, you made a present to your four squires of the gift I presented to you. I should like to know, if this be true, why you did so, and if the gift were not agreeable to you." — "Yes, my lord," answered Lord James, "it was most agreeable to me; and I will tell you the reasons which induced me to bestow it on my squires. These four squires who are here have long and loyally served me on many great and dangerous occasions; and, until the day that I made them this present, I had not any way rewarded them for all their services; and never in this life were they of such help to me as on that day. I hold myself much bound to them for what they did at the battle of Poitiers; for, dear sir, I am but a single man, and can do no more than my powers admit; but through their aid and assistance I have accomplished my vow, which for a long time I had made, and by their means was the first combatant, and should have paid for it with my life if they had not been near to me. When, therefore, I consider their courage and the love they bear to me, I should not have been courteous nor grateful if I had not rewarded them. Thank God! my lord, I have a sufficiency for my life to maintain my state; and wealth has never yet failed me, nor do I believe it ever will. If, therefore, I have in this acted contrary to your wishes, I beseech you, dear sir, to pardon me; for you will be ever as loyally served by me, and my squires to whom I gave your present, as heretofore." The prince answered, "Sir James, I do not in the least blame you for what you have done, but, on the contrary, acknowledge your bounty to your squires, whom you praise so much. I readily confirm your gift to them, but I shall insist upon your accepting of six hundred marks upon the same terms and conditions as the former gift."

The Prince of Wales and his army kept advancing without meeting any obstacle; and, having passed through Poitou and Saintonge, came to Blaye, where he crossed the Garonne, and arrived in the good city of Bordeaux. It is not possible to relate all the feasts and entertainments which the citizens and clergy of Bordeaux made for the prince, and with what joy they received him and the King of France. The prince conducted the king to the monastery of St. Andrew, where they were both lodged; the king on one side, and the prince on the other. The prince purchased from the barons, knights, and squires of Gascony the ransoms of the greater part of the French earls who were there, and paid ready money for them. There were many meetings and disputes among the knights and squires of Gascony, and others, relative to the capture of the King of France. On this account Denys de Morbeque truly and by right of arms claimed him. He challenged another squire of Gascony, named Bernard de Trouttes, who had declared that he had an equal right to him. There was much disputing between them before the prince and the barons present; and, as they had engaged to fight each other, the prince put them under an arrest until they should be arrived in England, and forbade any thing more being said on the subject till they were in the presence of the king his father. However, as the King of France gave every assistance to Sir Denys in support of his claim, and leaned more to him than to any of the other claimants, the prince ordered two thousand nobles to be given privately to Sir Denys in order to enable him the better to support his rank.

Soon after the prince's arrival at Bordeaux the Cardinal de Perigord came thither, as, it was said, ambassador from the pope. It was upward of a fortnight before the prince would speak to him, on account of the castellan of Amposta and his people having been engaged against him at the battle of Poitiers. The prince believed that the cardinal had sent them thither; but the cardinal, through the means of his relations, the Lord of Chaumont, the Lord of Montferrant, and the Captal of Buch, gave such good reasons for his conduct to the prince, that he admitted him to an audience. Having obtained this, he exculpated himself so clearly that the prince and his council were satisfied, and he regained the place he before held in the prince's affection. All his people were set at liberty at moderate ransoms : the castellan's amounted to ten thousand francs, which he paid. The cardinal soon after began to touch upon the deliverance of King John ; but

I shall say little on that head, as nothing was done in the business. The prince, with his Gascons and English, remained all that winter at Bordeaux, where was much feasting and merriment; and they foolishly expended the gold and silver they had gained. In England also there were great rejoicings when the news arrived of the affair of Poitiers and of the defeat of the French; solemn thanksgivings were offered up in all the churches, and bonfires made in every town and village. Those knights and squires who returned to England after having been in this battle were honored in preference to any others.

CHAPTER LXXXIV.

THE PRINCE OF WALES CONDUCTS THE KING OF FRANCE FROM BORDEAUX TO ENGLAND.

WHEN the season was sufficiently advanced, and every thing was ready for the prince's departure, he sent for the great barons of Gascony. He then informed them of his intention of going to England; that he should take some of them with him, and the rest he should leave in different parts of the province to guard the frontiers against the French, and should put all the cities and castles under their management, as if they were their own property. After this he nominated four of them as governors of the country until his return, — the Lords d'Albret, de l'Esparre, de Pumiers, and de Rosem. This being done, the prince embarked on board a handsome ship, and took with him a great many Gascons: among them were the Captal de Buch, Sir Aymery de Tarse, the Lord de Tarse, the Lord de Landuras, the Lord de Mucident, the Souldich de la Trane, and many others.

The King of France was in a ship by himself, in order that he might be more at his ease. In the fleet there were five hundred men at arms and two thousand archers to guard against any accidents at sea, and also because the prince had been informed before he left Bordeaux that the three estates who then governed France had raised two large armies, which were posted in Normandy and at Crotoy to meet the English and to carry off the king; but they saw nothing of them. They were eleven days and nights at sea; and on the twelfth they arrived at Sandwich, where they disembarked, and took up their quarters in the town and neighborhood. They remained there two days to refresh themselves, and on the third set out and came to Canterbury.

When the King of England was informed of their arrival, he gave orders for the citizens of London to make such preparations as were suitable to receive so great a prince as the King of France; upon which they all dressed themselves very richly in companies, and the different manufactories of cloth appeared with various pageants. The king and prince remained one day at Canterbury, where they made their offerings to the shrine of St. Thomas. On the morrow they rode to Rochester, where they reposed themselves. The third day they came to Dartford, and the fourth to London, where they were received with every honor and distinction, as indeed they had been by all the chief towns on their road.

The King of France, as he rode through London, was mounted on a white steed with very rich furniture, and the Prince of Wales on a little black hackney by his side. He rode through London, thus accompanied, to the palace of the Savoy, which was part of the inheritance of the Duke of Lancaster. There the King of France kept his household for some time; and there he was visited by the

King and Queen of England, who often entertained him sumptuously, and afterwards were very frequent in their visits, consoling him all in their power. The Cardinals de Perigord and St. Vital soon after came to England by command of Pope Innocent VI. They endeavored to make peace between the two kingdoms, which they labored hard to effect, but without success. However, by some fortunate means they procured a truce between the two kings and their allies, to last until St. John the Baptist's Day, 1359. The Lord Philip de Navarre and his allies, the Countess of Montfort, and the Duchy of Brittany, were excluded from this truce.

Shortly afterwards the King of France and all his household were removed from the Palace of Savoy to Windsor Castle, where he was permitted to hunt and hawk, and take what other diversions he pleased in that neighborhood, as well as the Lord Philip his son. The rest of the French lords remained at London; but they visited the king as often as they pleased, and were prisoners on their parole of honor.

CHAPTER LXXXV.

THE ARCHPRIEST ASSEMBLES A COMPANY OF MEN AT ARMS. — HE IS MUCH HONORED AT AVIGNON.

ABOUT this period,* a knight named Sir Arnold de Cervole, but more commonly called the archpriest, collected a large body of men at arms, who came from all

---

* After the battle of Poitiers the wretched land of France was tormented by all the ills of lawlessness. This chapter, and the next three, particularly those describing the Jacquerie, will show every boy the frenzies to which a people may be driven when the law is weak. In this case the arm of the law — King John — was wholly lacking in France. — ED.

parts, seeing that their pay would not be continued in France, and that, since the capture of the king, there was not any probability of their gaining more in that country. They marched first into Provence, where they took many strong towns and castles, and ruined the country by their robberies, as far as Avignon. Pope Innocent VI., who resided in Avignon, was much alarmed, as not knowing what might be the intentions of the archpriest, the leader of these forces; and for fear of personal insult he and the cardinals kept their household armed day and night. When the archpriest and his troops had pillaged all the country, the pope and clergy entered into treaty with him. Having received proper security, he and the greater part of his people entered Avignon, where he was received with as much respect as if he had been son to the King of France. He dined many times with the pope and cardinals, who gave him absolution from all his sins; and at his departure they presented him with forty thousand crowns to distribute among his companions. These men therefore marched away to different places, following, however, the directions of the archpriest.

CHAPTER LXXXVI.

A WELSHMAN, OF THE NAME OF RUFFIN, COMMANDS A TROOP OF THE FREE COMPANIES.

AT this time, also, there was another company of men at arms, or robbers, collected from all parts, who stationed themselves between the rivers Loire and Seine, so that no one dared to travel between Paris and Orleans, nor between Paris and Montargis, or even to remain in the country. The inhabitants on the plains had all fled to Paris and Orleans. This company had chosen for their leader a Welshman named Ruffin, whom they had knighted, and who acquired such immense riches as could not be counted. These companies advanced one day near to Paris, another day toward Orleans, another time to Chartres; and there was no town nor fortress but what was taken and pillaged, excepting such as were strongly garrisoned.

They rode over the country in parties of twenty, thirty, or forty, meeting with none to check their pillage; while, on the seacoast of Normandy, there were still a greater number of English and Navarrois, plunderers and robbers. Sir Robert Knolles was their leader, who conquered every town and castle he came to, as there was no one to oppose him. Sir Robert had followed this trade for some time, and by it gained upward of one hundred thousand crowns. He kept a great many soldiers in his pay; and, being very liberal, he was cheerfully followed and obeyed.

CHAPTER LXXXVII.

THE PROVOST OF THE MERCHANTS OF PARIS KILLS THREE KNIGHTS IN THE APARTMENT OF THE PRINCE.

DURING the time that the three estates governed the kingdom, all sorts of people united themselves together, under the name of Free Companies: they made war upon every man that was worth robbing. I must here inform you that the nobles and prelates of the realm and church began to be weary of the government and regulations of the three estates: they therefore permitted the provost of the merchants of Paris to summon some of the citizens, because they were going greater lengths than they approved of.

It happened one day, when the regent of France was in his palace at Paris, with many knights, nobles, and prelates, that the provost of the merchants collected also a great number of the common people of Paris, who were devoted to him, all wearing caps similar to his own, that they might know each other; and, attended by this crowd, the provost came to the palace. He entered the apartment of the duke,* and demanded of him, in an insolent manner, to take the management of the kingdom of France, and to govern it wisely (since it would become his by inheritance), that all those free companies who at present were overrunning the country might be prevented from doing further mischief. The duke replied that he would very willingly comply with his request if he had the means to carry it into execution, but that it more properly belonged to those who had raised and received the imposts due to the realm to perform it. I cannot pretend to say how it happened; but words increased so much, and with such warmth, that at last three of the principal counsellors of the duke were slain, and so near to him that their blood flew over his robe: he himself was in very great danger, but they had put one of their caps on his head, and he consented to pardon the death of his three knights. Two of them were knights of arms, and the other of laws. Their names were, the Lord Robert de Clermont, a gallant and magnificent knight, and the Lord de Conflans: the knight of laws was the Lord Simon de Buci.

* Of Normandy. — ED.

CHAPTER LXXXVIII.

The Commencement of the infamous Jacquerie of Beauvoisis.

SOON after the deliverance of the King of Navarre out of prison, a marvellous and great tribulation befell the kingdom of France, in Beauvoisis, Brie, upon the river Marne, in the Laonnois, and in the neighborhood of Soissons. Some of the inhabitants of the country towns assembled together in Beauvoisis, without any leader; they were not at first more than one hundred men. They said that the nobles of the kingdom of France, knights, and squires, were a disgrace to it, and that it would be a very meritorious act to destroy them all; to which proposition every one assented, and added, Shame befall him that should be the means of preventing the gentlemen from being wholly destroyed! They then, without further counsel, collected themselves in a body, and with no other arms than the staves, shod with iron, which some had, and others with knives, marched to the house of a knight who lived near, and, breaking it open, murdered the knight, his lady, and all the children, both great and small : they then burnt the house.

After this their second expedition was to the strong castle of another knight, which they took. They then murdered the lady, her daughter, and the other children, and last of all the knight himself, with much cruelty. They destroyed and burnt his castle. They did the like to many castles and handsome houses; and their numbers increased so much that they were in a short time upward of six thousand. Wherever they went, they received additions, for all of their rank in life followed them, while every one else fled, carrying off with them their ladies, damsels, and children, ten or twenty leagues distant, where they thought they could place them in security, leaving their houses with all their riches in them.

These wicked people, without leader and without arms, plundered and burnt all the houses they came to. He who committed the most atrocious actions, and such as no human creature would have imagined, was the most applauded, and considered as the greatest man among them. I dare not write the horrible and inconceivable atrocities they committed. They had chosen a king among them, who came from Clermont in Beauvoisis ; he was elected as the worst of the bad, and they denominated him Jacques Bonhomme.* These wretches burnt and destroyed in the county of Beauvoisis, and at Corbie, Amiens, and Mont-didier, upward of sixty good houses and strong castles. By the acts of such traitors in the country of Brie and there-about, it behooved every lady, knight, and squire, having the means of escape, to fly to Meaux, if they wished to preserve themselves from being insulted and afterwards murdered. The Duchess of Normandy, the Duchess of Orleans, and many other ladies, had adopted this course to save themselves. These cursed people thus supported themselves in the countries between Paris, Noyon, and Soissons, and in all the territory of Coucy, in the county of Valois. In the bishoprics of Noyon, Laon, and Sois-sons, there were upward of one hundred castles, and good houses of knights and squires, destroyed.

---

* That is, Jack Goodman. — ED.

CHAPTER LXXXIX.

THE BATTLE OF MEAUX IN BRIE, WHERE THE VILLAINS ARE DISCOM-
FITED BY THE EARL OF FOIX AND THE CAPTAL OF BUCH.

AT the time these wicked men were overrunning the
country, the Earl of Foix, and his cousin the Captal
of Buch, were returning from a croisade in Prussia. They
were informed, on their entering France, of the distress
the nobles were in; and they learnt at the city of Cha-
lons, that the Duchess of Orleans, and three hundred
other ladies, under the protection of the Duke of Orleans,
were fled to Meaux on account of these disturbances.
The two knights resolved to go to the assistance of these
ladies, and to re-enforce them with all their might, notwithstanding the Captal was attached to the English; but at
that time there was a truce between the two kings. They
might have in their company about sixty lances. They
were most cheerfully received, on their arrival at Meaux,
by the ladies and damsels; for these Jacks and peasants
of Brie had heard what number of ladies, married and
unmarried, and young children of quality, were in Meaux:
they had united themselves with those of Valois, and were
on their road thither. On the other hand, those of Paris
had also been informed of the treasures Meaux contained,
and had set out from that place in crowds. Having met
the others, they amounted together to nine thousand men:
their forces were augmenting every step they advanced.

They came to the gates of the town, which the inhabitants opened to them, and allowed them to enter: they
did so in such numbers that all the streets were quite

filled as far as the market-place, which is tolerably strong, but it required to be guarded, though the river Marne nearly surrounds it. The noble dames who were lodged there, seeing such multitudes rushing toward them, were exceedingly frightened. On this the two lords and their company advanced to the gate of the market-place, which they had opened, and marching under the banners of the Earl of Foix and Duke of Orleans, and the pennon of the Captal of Buch, posted themselves in front of this peasantry, who were badly armed. When these banditti perceived such a troop of gentlemen, so well equipped, sally forth to guard the market-place, the foremost of them began to fall back. The gentlemen then followed them, using their lances and swords. When they felt the weight of their blows, they, through fear, turned about so fast, they fell one over the other. All manner of armed persons then rushed out of the barriers, drove them before them, striking them down like beasts, and clearing the town of them; for they kept neither regularity nor order, slaying so many that they were tired. They flung them in great heaps into the river. In short, they killed upward of seven thousand. Not one would have escaped, if they had chosen to pursue them further.

On the return of the men at arms, they set fire to the town of Meaux, and burnt it; and all the peasants they could find were shut up in it, because they had been of the party of the Jacks. Since this discomfiture which happened to them at Meaux, they never collected again in any great bodies; for the young Enguerrand de Coucy had plenty of gentlemen under his orders, who destroyed them, wherever they could be met with, without mercy.

BOOK II.*

CHAPTER I.

Coronation of King Charles of France.

A S you may well imagine, nothing was spared by the nobility and great lords to add to the magnificence of the coronation of the young King Charles † of France, who was crowned at Rheims on a Sunday, in the twelfth year of his age, in the year 1380. At this solemnity there were many high and mighty lords.

The young king made his entry into the city of Rheims on the Saturday, handsomely attended by the great lords, nobility, and minstrels, at vespers. In particular, there

---

* Froissart's Chronicles having been composed in four volumes, the peculiar nature of his work makes it well to preserve this division, aside from the general advantage of giving in unaltered form, so far as possible, the parts presented. — Ed.

† This is King Charles the Sixth of France, called "the Maniac." The narrative has here advanced twenty-four years since we left King John in England, a prisoner, after the battle of Poitiers. John has died, and been succeeded by Charles V., — "the Wise," — who has reigned sixteen years, and died. We now go on to see how his successor, young Charles the Sixth, fares in his wars with Philip von Artaveld to recover the rights of the Earl of Flanders. I have chosen these special chapters because they give us lively pictures of manners and customs among a different people from those illustrated by the selections of the first book. The insurrection of Wat Tyler, of which Froissart gives such a lively account in this book, ought really to begin these first chapters, since it occurred in 1378, — two years before the coronation of King Charles, — in the reign of Richard II of England. The period covered by my extracts from this second book is therefore from 1378 to 1382, when the battle of Rosbecq was fought. — Ed.

were upward of thirty trumpets, which preceded him, and sounded so clear it was quite marvellous to hear them. There were also a great many other young squires, children of the great barons of France, whom the king on the morrow, being the day of his coronation, created knights. This Saturday the king heard vespers in the church of Our Lady, and performed his vigils in that church, according to the custom of those times, the greater part of the night. All the youths desirous of knighthood attended him, and did the same.

On the Sunday, which was All Saints' Day, the church of Our Lady was very richly decorated for the coronation; so much so, that it could not possibly have been better ordered. The Archbishop of Rheims, after having said mass with great solemnity, consecrated the king with the holy ampulla with which St. Remy had anointed Clovis, the first Christian king of the French.

Before the consecration, the king created, in front of the altar, all those young squires, knights. The office of mass was afterwards chanted by the archbishop, the king being clothed in his royal robes, and seated on an elevated throne, adorned with cloth of gold; and all the young knights were placed on low benches, covered also with the same, at his feet. In this state did they remain the whole day. The new constable, Sir Oliver de Clisson, was present: he had been named constable a few days prior to this ceremony, and performed well his charge, and every thing belonging to it. The principal barons of France were also there, so richly dressed it would be tedious to relate. The king was seated in royal majesty, with a crown on his head rich and precious beyond measure. The church of Our Lady at Rheims was so much crowded during this ceremony that one could not turn one's foot. I have heard also, that at this accession of the young king to the throne, in order to please the people of France, all impositions, aids, taxes, subsidies, and other levies, which had displeased and had much oppressed them, were abolished, greatly to the joy of the subjects.

After mass they went to the palace; but, as the hall was too small for such numbers, they erected in the court of the palace a large covered stage, on which the dinner was served. The king was seated with his five uncles of Brabant, Anjou, Berry, Burgundy, and Bourbon; but, though they were at his table, they were at a distance from him. The Archbishop of Rheims and other prelates were on his right hand. He was served by the great barons, the Lord de Coucy, the Lord de Clisson, Sir Guy de la Tremouille, the Lord High Admiral, and several others, on handsome horses, covered and decorated with gold brocade. The whole day passed in ceremonies. On the morrow many of the great barons took leave of the king and his uncles, and returned to their own country. The king went that day to dinner at the abbey of St. Thierry, two leagues from Rheims; for those monks are bound to give him this entertainment, and the city of Rheims to provide for the coronation of the king. Thus ended this noble feast. He returned to Paris, where he was grandly feasted by the Parisians at his entrance.

CHAPTER II.

A Combat between an English and a French Squire.

WE will now speak of certain knights and squires who returned to Cherbourg by land, and relate what befell them on the road. The Constable of France, who at that time resided at Château Josselin, seven leagues from Vannes, had granted passports to some English and Navarre knights of the garrison of Cherbourg, who had served under the Earl of Buckingham. Among others were Sir John Harlestone, governor of Cherbourg, Sir Evan Fitzwarren, Sir William Clinton, and Sir John Burley. They set out from Vannes, following the road to Château Josselin, for it was in their route. On their arrival they took up their quarters in the town below the castle, not intending more than to dine and continue their journey. When they had dismounted at the inn, like travellers who wished to repose themselves, the knights and squires of the castle came to visit them as brother-soldiers, who always see each other with pleasure, particularly the French and English. Among the French there was a squire of great renown in arms, who belonged to John de Bourbon, Count de la Marche, the nearest to his person of all his squires, and whom he loved the most: his name was John Boucmel. He had formerly been in garrison in Valogne with Sir William des Bordes, and in his expedition against Cherbourg. During that time he had often had words with an English squire called Nicholas Clifford, who was then present, respecting a tilting-match. In the course of the conversation which these French knights and squires held at the inn with the English, John Boucmel, recollecting Clifford, cried out, "Nicholas Clifford! ah! Nicholas, Nicholas, we have often wished and sought to perform a tilting-match; but we never could find fit opportunity or place for it. Now, as we are here before my lord constable and those gentlemen, let us perform it: I therefore demand from you three courses with a lance." — "John," replied Nicholas, "you .know that we are here but as travellers on our road, under the passport of my lord constable : what you ask from me cannot now be complied with, for I am not the principal in the passport, but under the command of these knights whom you see. If I were to stay behind, they would set out without me."—"Ha, Nicholas, do not make such excuses as these : let your friends depart, if they please, for I give you my promise, that, as soon as our tilt shall be over, I will conduct you myself within the gates of Cherbourg without loss or peril, as I can depend on my lord constable's good-will."

Nicholas said, "Now, suppose it to be as you say, and that I place my confidence in being safely conducted by you, yet you see we are travelling through the country without arms of any sort; therefore, if I were willing to arm myself, I have not wherewithal to do so." John replied, "You shall not excuse yourself that way, for I will tell you what I will do: I have plenty of arms at my command, and will order different sorts to be brought to the place where we shall tilt; and when all are laid out you shall examine them, and consider which will suit you best, for I will leave the choice to you ; and when you shall have chosen I will then arm myself."

When Nicholas saw himself so earnestly pressed, he was ashamed that those present should have heard it, and thought that since John made such handsome offers, he could not in honor refuse them; for John still added, "Make whatever arrangements you please, I will agree to them sooner than we should not have a tilting-match." Nicholas then said he would consider of it, and before his departure he would make him acquainted with his resolution ; adding, "If it will not be possible for me to comply with your request at this place, and if my lords, under whom I am, should be unwilling to assent to it, on my return to Cherbourg, if you will come to Valogne, and signify to me your arrival, I will immediately hasten thither, and deliver you from your engagement." — "No, no," said John ; "seek not for excuses : I have offered you such handsome proposals, that you cannot in honor depart without running a tilt with me, according to the demand I make." Nicholas was more enraged than before ; for he thought, and true it was, that he by such a speech greatly outraged his honor. Upon this the French returned to the castle, and the English to their inn where they dined.

When these knights had got to the castle, you may suppose they were not silent on the words which had passed between John Boucmel and Nicholas Clifford, insomuch that the constable heard of them. He considered a short time ; and, when the knights and squires of the country who were with him entreated him to interest himself that this combat might be fought, he willingly promised it. The English knights and squires, wishing to pursue their journey after dinner, went to the castle to wait on the constable ; for he was to give them seven knights to escort them the whole road through Brittany and Normandy, as far as Cherbourg.

When they were arrived at the castle, the constable received them very amicably, and then said, "I put you all under arrest, and forbid you to depart hence this day. To-morrow morning, after mass, you shall witness the combat between your squire and ours, and then you shall dine with me. Dinner over, you shall set out, and I will give you good guides to conduct you to Cherbourg." They complied with his requests, and, having drank of his wine, returned to their inn. Now the two squires consulted together, for it was fixed they should on the morrow morning engage without fail. When morning came they both

heard mass, confessed themselves, and mounted their
horses, the French being on one side, and the English on
the other ; they rode together to a smooth plain on the outside of the castle, where they dismounted.   John Boucmel
had provided there two suits of armor, according to his
promise, which were good and strong, as the occasion demanded.   Having had them displayed, he told the English
squire to make the first choice.   "No," said the Englishman, "I will not choose : you shall have the choice."
John was therefore forced to choose first, which he did,
and armed himself completely (in doing which he was
assisted) as a good man at arms should be.   Nicholas did
the same.   When they were both armed they grasped
their spears, well made with Bordeaux steel, and of the
same length ; and each took the position proper for him to
run his course with their helmets and visors closed.   They
then advanced, and when they approached pretty near
they lowered their spears, aiming them to hit each other.
At the first onset Nicholas Clifford struck with his spear
John Boucmel on the upper part of his breast ; but the
point slipped off the steel breastplate, and pierced the
hood, which was of good mail, and, entering his neck, cut
the jugular vein, and passed quite through, breaking off at
the shaft with the head ; so that the truncheon remained
in the neck of the squire, who was killed, as you may suppose.   The English squire passed on to his chair, where
he seated himself.   The French lords, who had seen the
stroke, and the broken spear in his neck, hastened to him.
They immediately took off his helmet, and drew out the
spear.   On its being extracted, he turned himself about
without uttering a word, and fell down dead.   The English
squire hurried to his relief, crying out to have the blood
stanched, but could not arrive before he expired.   Nicho-

las Clifford was then exceedingly vexed for having by ill
fortune slain a valiant and good man at arms. All who at
that time could have seen the despair of the Count de la
Marche, who had such an affection for his deceased squire,
would surely have much pitied him : he was in the greatest distress, for he esteemed him above all others.

The constable was present, and endeavored to comfort
him, saying that such things were to be expected in
similar combats. "It has turned out unfortunate for our
squire, but the Englishman could not help it." He then
addressed himself to the English : "Come, come to dinner, for it is ready." The constable led them, as I may
say against their wills, to the castle to dinner; for they
wished not to go there on account of the death of the
Frenchman.

The Count de la Marche most tenderly bewailed his
squire as he viewed his corpse. Nicholas Clifford directly
retired to his lodgings, and would not by any means dine
at the castle, as well for the great vexation he was in for
this death as on account of his relations and friends; but
the constable sent to seek for him, and it was necessary
he should comply. On his arrival the constable said, "In
truth, Nicholas, I can very well believe, and I see by your
looks, that you are much concerned for the death of John
Boucmel. But I acquit you of it, for it was no fault of
yours; and, as God is my judge, if I had been in the
situation you were in, you have done nothing more than I
would have done, as it is better to hurt one's enemy than
to be hurt by him. Such is the fate of war."

They then seated themselves at the table, and these
lords dined at their ease. After they had finished their
repast, and drank their wine, the constable called the Lord
Le Barrois des Barres, and said to him, "Barrois, prepare

yourself: I will that you conduct these Englishmen as far as Cherbourg, and that you have opened to them every town and castle, and have given to them whatever they shall be in need of." Le Barrois replied, "My lord, I shall cheerfully obey your orders."

The English then, taking leave of the constable and the knights with him, came to their lodgings, where every thing was packed up and ready. They mounted their horses, departed from Château Josselin, and rode straight to Pontorson and Mont St. Michel. They were under the escort of that gallant knight Le Barrois des Barres, who never quitted them in Brittany or Normandy until they had arrived in Cherbourg.

CHAPTER III.

The Populace of England rebel against the Nobility.

THERE happened in England great commotions among the lower ranks of the people, by which England was near ruined without resource. Never was a country in such jeopardy as this was at that period, and all through the too great comfort of the commonalty. Rebellion was stirred up as it was formerly done in France by the Jacques Bons-hommes, who did much evil, and sore troubled the kingdom of France. It is marvellous from what a trifle this pestilence raged in England. In order that it may serve as an example to mankind, I will speak of all that was done, from the information I had at the time on the subject.

It is customary in England, as well as in several other countries, for the nobility to have great privileges over the commonalty, whom they keep in bondage : that is to say, they are bound by law and custom to plough the lands of gentlemen, to harvest the grain, to carry it home to the barn, to thresh and winnow it ; they are also bound to harvest the hay, and carry it home. All these services they are obliged to perform for their lords, and many more in England than in other countries. The prelates and gentlemen are thus served. In the counties of Kent, Essex, Sussex, and Bedford, these services are more oppressive than in all the rest of the kingdom.

The evil-disposed in these districts began to rise, saying they were too severely oppressed ; that at the beginning of the world there were no slaves, and no one ought to be treated as such unless he had committed treason against his lord as Lucifer had done against God ; but they had done no such thing, for they were neither angels nor spirits, but men formed after the same likeness with their lords, who treated them as beasts. This they would not longer bear, but had determined to be free ; and, if they labored or did any other works for their lords, they would be paid for it.

A crazy priest in the county of Kent, called John Ball, who for his absurd preaching had been thrice confined in the prison of the Archbishop of Canterbury, was greatly instrumental in inflaming them with those ideas. He was accustomed every Sunday after mass, as the people were coming out of the church, to preach to them in the market-place, and assemble a crowd around him, to whom he would say, " My good friends, things cannot go on well in England, nor ever will, until every thing shall be in common ; when there shall neither be vassal nor lord, and all distinctions levelled ; when the lords shall be no more masters than ourselves. How ill they have used

us! and for what reason do they thus hold us in bondage?
Are we not all descended from the same parents, Adam
and Eve? And what can they show, or what reasons
give, why they should be more the masters than ourselves,
except, perhaps, in making us labor and work for them to
spend? They are clothed in velvets and rich stuffs ornamented with ermine and other furs, while we are forced to
wear poor cloth; they have wines, spices, and fine bread,
when we have only rye and the refuse of the straw, and, if
we drink, it must be water; they have handsome seats
and manors, when we must brave the wind and rain in our
labors in the field: but it is from our labor they have
wherewith to support their pomp. We are called slaves,
and if we do not perform our services we are beaten; and
we have not any sovereign to whom we can complain, or
who wishes to hear us and do us justice. Let us go to
the king, who is young, and remonstrate with him on our
servitude; telling him we must have it otherwise, or that
we shall find a remedy for it ourselves. If we wait on
him in a body, all those who come under the appellation
of slaves, or are held in bondage, will follow us in the
hopes of being free. When the king shall see us, we shall
obtain a favorable answer, or we must then seek ourselves
to amend our condition."

These promises stirred up those in the counties of
Kent, Essex, Sussex, and Bedford, and the adjoining
country, so that they marched toward London; and, when
they arrived near, they were upward of sixty thousand.
They had a leader called Wat Tyler, and with him were
Jack Straw and John Ball: these three were their commanders, but the principal was Wat Tyler. This Wat
had been a tiler of houses, a bad man, and a great enemy
to the nobility. When these wicked people first began to

rise, all London, except their friends, were very much frightened. The mayor and rich citizens assembled in council on hearing they were coming to London, and debated whether they should shut the gates, and refuse to admit them ; but, having well considered, they determined not to do so, as they should run the risk of having the suburbs burnt.

The gates were therefore thrown open, when they entered in troops of one to two hundred, by twenties or thirties, according to the populousness of the towns they came from ; and as they came into London they lodged themselves. But it is a truth that full two-thirds of these people knew not what they wanted, nor what they sought for : they followed one another like sheep, or like the shepherds of old who said they were going to conquer the Holy Land, and afterwards accomplished nothing. In such manner did these poor fellows and vassals come to London from distances of a hundred and sixty leagues, but the greater part from those counties I have mentioned, and on their arrival they demanded to see the king. The gentlemen of the country, the knights, and the squires began to be alarmed when they saw the people thus rise ; and if they were frightened they had sufficient reason, for less causes create fear. They began to collect together as well as they could.

The same day that these wicked men of Kent were on their road toward London, the Princess of Wales, mother to the king, was returning from a pilgrimage to Canterbury. She ran great risks from them ; for these scoundrels attacked her car, and caused much confusion, which greatly frightened the good lady lest they should do some violence to her or to her ladies. God, however, preserved her from this · and she came in one day from Canterbury to London without venturing to make any stop by the way. Her son Richard was this day in the Tower of London : thither the princess came, and found the king attended by the Earl of Salisbury, the Archbishop of Canterbury, Sir Robert de Namur, the Lord de Gomme-gines, and several more, who had kept near his person from suspicions of his subjects who were thus assembling without knowing what they wanted. This rebellion was well known to be in agitation in the king's palace before it broke out, and the country people had left their homes, to which the king applied no remedy, to the great aston-ishment of every one. In order that gentlemen and others may take example, and correct wicked rebels, I will most amply detail how this business was conducted.

CHAPTER IV.

The Populace of England commit many Cruelties on those in Official Situations.—They send a Knight as Ambassador to the King.

ON Monday preceding the feast of the Holy Sacra-ment, in the year 1381, did these people sally forth from their homes, to come to London to remonstrate with the king, that all might be made free, for they would not there should be any slaves in England. At Canterbury they met John Ball (who thought he should find there the archbishop, but he was at London), Wat Tyler, and Jack Straw. On their entrance into Canterbury, they were much feasted by every one, for the inhabitants were of their way of thinking ; and, having held a council, they resolved to march to London, and also to send emissaries across the Thames to Essex, Suffolk, Bedford, and other counties, to press the people to march to London on that side, and thus, as it were, to surround it, which the king would not be able to prevent. It was their intention that all the different parties should be collected together on the feast of the Holy Sacrament, or on the following day.

On Corpus Christi Day, King Richard heard mass in the Tower of London, with all his lords, and afterwards entered his barge, attended by the Earls of Salisbury, Warwick, and Suffolk, with other knights. He rowed down the Thames toward Rotherhithe, a manor belonging to the crown, where were upward of ten thousand men, who had come from Blackheath to see the king and to speak to him. When they perceived his barge approach, they set up such shouts and cries as if all the devils in hell had been in their company.

When the king and his lords saw this crowd of people, and the wildness of their manner, there was not one among them so bold and determined but felt alarmed : the king was advised by his barons not to land, but to have his barge rowed up and down the river. " What do ye wish for ? " demanded the king : "I am come hither to hear what you have to say." Those near him cried out with one voice, "We wish thee to land, when we will remonstrate with thee, and tell thee more at our ease what our wants are." The Earl of Salisbury then replied for the king, and said, "Gentlemen, you are not properly dressed, nor in a fit condition for the king to talk with you."

Nothing more was said ; for the king was desired to return to the Tower of London, from whence he had set out. When the people saw they could obtain nothing more, they were inflamed with passion, and went back to

Blackheath, where the main body was, to relate the answer they had received, and how the king was returned to the Tower. They all then cried out, " Let us march instantly to London." They immediately set off, and in their road thither they destroyed the houses of lawyers, courtiers, and monasteries. Advancing into the suburbs of London, which were very handsome and extensive, they pulled down many fine houses : in particular, they demolished the prison of the king, called the Marshalsea, and set at liberty all those confined within it. They did much damage to the suburbs, and menaced the Londoners at the entrance of the bridge for having shut the gates of it, saying they would set fire to the suburbs, take the city by storm, and afterwards burn and destroy it.

With respect to the common people of London, numbers were of their opinions, and, on assembling together, said, "Why will you refuse admittance to these honest men ? They are our friends, and what they are doing is for our good." It was then found necessary to open the gates, when crowds rushed in, and ran to those shops which seemed well stored with provision : if they sought for meat or drink, it was placed before them, and nothing refused, but all manner of good cheer offered, in hopes of appeasing them.

Their leaders, John Ball, Jack Straw, and Wat Tyler, then marched through London, attended by more than twenty thousand men, to the palace of the Savoy, which is a handsome building on the road to Westminster, situated on the banks of the Thames, belonging to the Duke of Lancaster : they immediately killed the porters, pressed into the house, and set it on fire. Not content with committing this outrage, they went to the house of the Knights Hospitalers of Rhodes, dedicated to St. John of

Mount Carmel, which they burnt, together with their hospital and church. They afterwards paraded the streets,
and killed every Fleming they could find, whether in
house, church, or hospital : not one escaped death. They
broke open several houses of the Lombards, taking whatever money they could lay their hands on, none daring to
oppose them. They murdered a rich citizen called Richard Lyon, to whom Wat Tyler had been formerly servant
in France ; but, having once beaten this varlet, he had
not forgotten it, and, having carried his men to his house,
ordered his head to be cut off, placed upon a pike, and
carried through the streets of London. Thus did these
wicked people act like madmen; and on this Thursday
they did much mischief to the city of London.

Toward evening they fixed their quarters in a square
called St. Catherine's, before the Tower, declaring they
would not depart thence until they should obtain from the
king every thing they wanted, and have all their desires
satisfied, and the Chancellor of England made to account
with them, and show how the great sums which had been
raised were expended ; menacing, that, if he did not render such an account as was agreeable to them, it would be
the worse for him. Considering the various ills they had
done to foreigners, they lodged themselves before the
Tower. You may easily suppose what a miserable situation the king was in, and those with him ; for at times
these rebellious fellows hooted as loud as if the devils
were in them.

About evening a council was held in the presence of
the king, the barons who were in the Tower with him, Sir
William Walworth the mayor, and some of the principal
citizens, when it was proposed to arm themselves, and
during the night to fall upon these wretches who were in

the streets, and amounted to sixty thousand, while they were asleep and drunk, for then they might be killed like flies, and not one in twenty among them had arms. The citizens were very capable of doing this, for they had secretly received into their houses their friends and servants, properly prepared to act. Sir Robert Knolles remained in his house, guarding his property, with more than sixscore companions completely armed, and would have instantly sallied forth. Sir Perducas d'Albreth was also in London at that period, and would have been of great service; so that they could have mustered upward of eight thousand men, well armed. But nothing was done, for they were too much afraid of the commonalty of London; and the advisers of the king, the Earl of Salisbury and others, said to him, "Sir, if you can appease them by fair words, it will be so much the better, and good-humoredly grant them what they ask: for, should we begin what we cannot go through, we shall never be able to recover it: it will be all over with us and our heirs, and England will be a desert." This counsel was followed, and the mayor ordered to make no movement. He obeyed, as in reason he ought. In the city of London, with the mayor, there are twelve sheriffs, of whom nine were for the king and three for these wicked people, as it was afterwards discovered, and for which they then paid dearly.

On Friday morning those lodged in the square before St. Catherine's, near the Tower, began to make themselves ready; they shouted much, and said, that, if the king would not come out to them, they would attack the Tower, storm it, and slay all in it. The king was alarmed at these menaces, and resolved to speak with them: he therefore sent orders for them to retire to a handsome meadow at Mile-end, where, in the summer, people go to amuse themselves, and that there the king would grant them their demands. Proclamation was made in the king's name for all those who wished to speak with him to go to the above-mentioned place, where he would not fail to meet them.

The commonalty of the different villages began to march thither; but all did not go, nor had they the same objects in view, for the greater part only wished for the riches and destruction of the nobles, and the plunder of London. This was the principal cause of their rebellion, as they very clearly showed; for when the gates of the Tower were thrown open, and the king, attended by his two brothers, the Earls of Salisbury, of Warwick, of Suffolk, Sir Robert de Namur, the Lords de Vertain and de Gommegines, with several others, had passed through them, Wat Tyler, Jack Straw, and John Ball, with upward of four hundred, rushed in by force, and, running from chamber to chamber, found the Archbishop of Canterbury, whose name was Simon, a valiant and wise man, and chancellor of England, who had but just celebrated mass before the king : he was seized by these rascals, and beheaded. The Prior of St. John's suffered the same fate ; and likewise a Franciscan friar, a doctor of physic, who was attached to the Duke of Lancaster, out of spite to his master ; and also a sergeant at arms of the name of John Laige. They fixed these four heads on long pikes, and had them carried before them through the streets of London : when they had sufficiently played with them, they placed them on London Bridge, as if they had been traitors to their king and country.

These scoundrels entered the apartment of the princess, and cut her bed ; which so much terrified her, that she fainted, and in this condition was by her servants and ladies carried to the river-side, when she was put into a covered boat, and conveyed to the house called the Wardrobe, where she continued that day and night like to a woman half dead, until she was comforted by the king her son, as you shall presently hear.

CHAPTER V.

THE NOBLES OF ENGLAND ARE IN GREAT DANGER OF BEING DESTROYED. —THREE OF THE PRINCIPAL LEADERS OF THE REBELS ARE PUNISHED, AND THE REST SENT BACK TO THEIR HOMES.

WHEN the king was on his way to the place called Mile-end, without London, his two brothers, the Earl of Kent, and Sir John Holland, stole off and galloped from his company, as did also the Lord de Gommegines, not daring to show themselves to the populace at Mile-end for fear of their lives.

On the king's arrival, attended by the barons, he found upward of sixty thousand men assembled from different villages and counties of England: he instantly advanced into the midst of them, saying in a pleasant manner, "My good people, I am your king and your lord: what is it you want? and what do you wish to say to me?" Those who heard him answered, "We wish thou wouldst make us free forever, us, our heirs and our lands, and that we should no longer be called slaves, nor held in bondage." The king replied, "I grant your wish: now, therefore, return to your homes and the places whence you came, leaving two or three men from each village, to whom I will order letters to be given sealed with my seal, which they shall carry back with every demand you have made fully granted; and, in order that you may be the more sat-isfied, I will direct that my banners shall be sent to every stewardship, castlewick, and corporation." These words greatly pleased the novices and well-meaning ones who were there, and knew not what they wanted, saying, "It is well said : we do not wish for more." The people were thus quieted, and began to return toward London.

The king added a few words which pleased them much : "You, my good people of Kent, shall have one of my ban-ners; and you also of Essex, Sussex, Bedford, Suffolk, Cambridge, Stafford, and Lincoln, shall each of you have one; and I pardon you all for what you have hitherto done; but you must follow my banners, and now return home on the terms I have mentioned." They unani-mously replied they would. Thus did this great assembly break up, and set out for London. The king instantly employed upward of thirty secretaries, who drew up the letters as fast as they could ; and, having sealed and deliv-ered them to these people, they departed, and returned to their own counties.

The principal mischief remained behind : I mean Wat Tyler, Jack Straw, and John Ball, who declared that though the people were satisfied, they would not thus depart; and they had more than thirty thousand who were of their mind. They continued in the city, without any wish to have their letters, or the king's seal ; but did all they could to throw the town into such confusion that the lords and rich citizens might be murdered, and their houses pil-laged and destroyed. The Londoners suspected this, and kept themselves at home, with their friends and servants, well armed and prepared, every one according to his abilities.

When the people had been appeased at Mile-end Green, and were setting off for their different towns as speedily as they could receive the king's letters, King Richard went to the Wardrobe, where the princess was in the greatest fear. He comforted her, as he was very able to do, and passed there the night.

I must relate an adventure which happened to these clowns near Norwich, and to their leader, called William Lister, who was from the county of Stafford. On the same day these wicked people burnt the palace of the Savoy, the church and house of St. John, the hospital of the Templars, pulled down the prison of Newgate, and set at liberty all the prisoners. There were collected numerous bodies from Lincolnshire, Norfolk, and Suffolk, who proceeded on their march toward London, according to the orders they had received, under the direction of Lister.

In their road they stopped near Norwich, and forced every one to join them, so that none of the commonalty remained behind. The reason why they stopped near Norwich was, that the governor of the town was a knight called Sir Robert Salle : he was not by birth a gentleman, but, having acquired great renown for his ability and courage, King Edward had created him a knight. He was the handsomest and strongest man in England. Lister 'and his companions took it into their heads they would make this knight their commander, and carry him with them, in order to be the more feared. They sent orders to him to come out into the fields to speak with them, or they would attack and burn the city. The knight, considering it was much better for him to go to them than that they should commit such outrages, mounted his horse, and went out of the town alone to hear what they had to say. When they perceived him coming, they showed him every mark of respect, and courteously entreated him to dismount and talk with them. He did dismount, and committed a great folly; for when he had so done, having surrounded him, they at first conversed in a friendly way, saying, "Robert, you are a knight, and a man of great weight in this country, renowned for your valor ; yet, notwithstanding all this, we know who you are : you are not a gentleman, but the son of a poor mason, just such as ourselves. Do you come with us, as our commander, and we will make so great a lord of you that one-quarter of England shall be under your command."

The knight, on hearing them thus speak, was exceedingly angry; he would never have consented to such a proposal; and, eying them with inflamed looks, answered, " Begone, wicked scoundrels and false traitors as you are ! Would you have me desert my natural lord for such a company of knaves as you? would you have me dishonor myself? I would much rather you were all hanged, for that must be your end." On saying this, he attempted to mount his horse; but, his foot slipping from the stirrup, his horse took fright. They then shouted out, and cried, " Put him to death!" When he heard this he let his horse go ; and, drawing a handsome Bordeaux sword, he began to skirmish, and soon cleared the crowd from about him, that it was a pleasure to see. Some attempted to close with him ; but with each stroke he gave he cut off heads, arms, feet, or legs. There were none so bold but were afraid ; and Sir Robert performed that day marvellous feats of arms. These wretches were upward of forty thousand ; they shot and flung at him such things, that, had he been clothed in steel instead of being unarmed, he must have been overpowered : however, he killed twelve of them, besides many whom he wounded. At last he

was overthrown, when they cut off his legs and arms, and
rent his body in piecemeal. Thus ended Sir Robert Salle,
which was a great pity; and, when the knights and squires
in England heard of it, they were much enraged.

On the Saturday morning the king left the Wardrobe,
and went to Westminster, where he and all the lords
heard mass in the abbey. In this church there is a
statue of Our Lady in a small chapel, that has many virtues, and performs great miracles, in which the kings of
England have much faith. The king, having paid his
devotions and made his offerings to this shrine, mounted
his horse about nine o'clock, as did the barons who were
with him. They rode along the causeway to return to
London; but when they had gone a little way he turned
to a road on the left to go from London.

This day all the rabble were again assembled, under
the conduct of Wat Tyler, Jack Straw, and John Ball, to
parley at a place called Smithfield, where, every Friday,
the horse-market is kept. They amounted to upward of
twenty thousand, all of the same sort. Many more were
in the city, breakfasting, and drinking Rhenish, Malmsey,
and Madeira wines, in taverns and at the houses of the
Lombards, without paying for any thing; and happy was
he who could give them good cheer. Those who were
collected in Smithfield had king's banners, which had been
given to them the preceding evening; and these repro-
bates wanted to pillage the city the same day, their leaders saying that hitherto they had done nothing. "The
pardons which the king has granted will not be of much
use to us; but, if we be of the same mind, we shall pillage this large, rich, and powerful town of London, before
those from Essex, Suffolk, Cambridge, Bedford, Warwick, Reading, Lancashire, Arundel, Guilford, Coventry,

Lynne, Lincoln, York, and Durham shall arrive ; for they are on the road, and we know for certain that Vaquier and Lister will conduct them hither. If we now plunder the city of the wealth that is in it, we shall have been before-hand, and shall not repent of so doing ; but, if we wait for their arrival, they will wrest it from us." To this opinion all had agreed, when the king appeared in sight, attended by sixty horse. He was not thinking of them, but in-tended to have continued his ride without coming into London : however, when he came before the Abbey of St. Bartholomew, which is in Smithfield, and saw the crowd of people, he stopped, and said he would not proceed until he knew what they wanted ; and, if they were troubled, he would appease them.

The lords who accompanied him stopped also, as was but right since the king had stopped ; when Wat Tyler, seeing the king, said to his men, "Here is the king ; I will go and speak with him : do not you stir from hence until I give you a signal." He made a motion with his hand, and added, "When you shall see me make this sign, then step forward, and kill every one except the king ; but hurt him not, for he is young, and we can do what we please with him ; for by carrying him with us through England we shall be lords of it without any opposition." There was a doublet-maker of London called John Ticle, who had brought sixty doublets, with which some of the clowns had dressed themselves ; and on his asking who was to pay, for he must have for them thirty good marks, Tyler replied, "Make thyself easy, man : thou shalt be well paid this day. Look to me for it : thou hast sufficient security for them." On saying this he spurred the horse on which he rode, and, leaving his men, galloped up to the king, and came so near that his horse's head touched the crupper of that of the king. The first words he said when he addressed the king were, "King, dost thou see all those men there?"—"Yes," replied the king: "why dost thou ask?"—"Because they are all under my command, and have sworn by their faith and loyalty to do whatever I shall order."—"Very well," said the king: "I have no objections to it." Tyler, who was only desirous of a riot, answered, "And thinkest thou, king, that those people and as many more who are in the city, also under my command, ought to depart without having had thy letters? Oh, no! we will carry them with us."—"Why!" replied the king, "so it has been ordered, and they will be delivered out one after the other; but, friend, return to thy companions, and tell them to depart from London. Be peaceable and careful of yourselves; for it is our determination that you shall all of you have your letters by villages and towns, as it had been agreed on."

As the king finished speaking, Wat Tyler, casting his eyes around him, spied a squire attached to the king's person, bearing his sword. Tyler mortally hated this squire: formerly they had had words together when the squire ill-treated him. "What! art thou here?" cried Tyler. "Give me thy dagger."—"I will not," said the squire: "why should I give it thee?" The king, turning to him, said, "Give it him, give it him;" which he did, though much against his will. When Tyler took it he began to play with it, and turn it about in his hand, and, again addressing the squire, said, "Give me that sword." —"I will not," replied the squire; "for it is the king's sword, and thou art not worthy to bear it who art but a mechanic; and if only thou and I were together thou wouldst not have dared to say what thou hast, for as large a heap of gold as this church."—"By my troth," answered

Tyler, "I will not eat this day before I have thy head."
At these words the mayor of London, with about twelve
more, rode forward, armed under their robes, and, pushing
through the crowd, saw Tyler's manner of behaving; upon
which he said, "Scoundrel, how dare you thus behave in
the presence of the king, and utter such words? It is
too impudent for such as thou." The king then began to
be enraged, and said to the mayor, "Lay hands on him."

While the king was giving this order, Tyler had addressed the mayor, saying, "Hey! in God's name, what I
have said, does it concern thee? What dost thou mean?"
— "Truly," replied the mayor, who found himself supported by the king, "does it become such a stinking
rascal as thou art to use such speech in the presence of
the king, thy natural lord? I will not live a day if thou
pay not for it." Upon this he drew a kind of cimeter
he wore, and struck Tyler such a blow on the head as
felled him to his horse's feet. When he was down he was
surrounded on all sides, so that his men could not see
him; and one of the king's squires, called John Standwich, immediately leaped from his horse, and, drawing a
handsome sword which he bore, thrust it into his belly,
and thus killed him.

His men, advancing, saw their leader dead, when they
cried out, "They have killed our captain: let us march to
them, and slay the whole." On these words they drew up
in a sort of battle-array, each man having his bent bow
before him. The king certainly hazarded much by this
action, but it turned out fortunate; for, when Tyler was
on the ground, he left his attendants, ordering not one to
follow him. He rode up to these rebellious fellows, who
were advancing to revenge their leader's death, and said to
them, "Gentlemen, what are you about? You shall have

no other captain but me : I am your king ; remain peaceable." When the greater part of them heard these words, they were quite ashamed, and those inclined to peace began to slip away. The riotous ones kept their ground, and showed symptoms of mischief, and as if they were resolved to do something.

The king returned to his lords, and asked them what should next be done. He was advised to make for the fields ; for the mayor said that "to retreat or fly would be of no avail. It is proper we should act thus, for I reckon that we shall very soon receive assistance from London, —that is, from our good friends who are prepared and armed, with all their servants in their houses." While things remained in this state, several ran to London, and cried out, "They are killing the king ! They are killing the king and our mayor !" Upon this alarm every man of the king's party sallied out toward Smithfield and to the fields whither the king had retreated ; and there were instantly collected from seven to eight thousand men in arms.

Among the first came Sir Robert Knolles and Sir Perducas d'Albreth well attended ; and several of the aldermen with upward of six hundred men at arms, and a powerful man of the city called Nicholas Bramber, the king's draper, bringing with him a large force, who, as they came up, ranged themselves in order on foot on each side of him. The rebels were drawn up opposite them : they had the king's banners, and showed as if they intended to maintain their ground by offering combat. The king created three knights : Sir William Walworth, mayor of London, Sir John Standwich, and Sir Nicholas Bramber. The lords began to converse among themselves, saying, "What shall we do ? We see our enemies, who would willingly have murdered us if they had gained the upper hand." Sir Robert Knowles advised immediately to fall on them and slay them; but the king would not consent, saying, "I will not have you act thus: you shall go and demand from them my banners. We shall see how they will behave when you make this demand, for I will have them by fair or foul means."—"It is a good thought," replied the Earl of Salisbury.

The new knights were therefore sent, who, on approaching, made signs for them not to shoot, as they wished to speak with them. When they had come near enough to be heard, they said, "Now attend: the king orders you to send back his banners, and we hope he will have mercy on you." The banners were directly given up, and brought to the king. It was then ordered, under pain of death, that all those who had obtained the king's letters should deliver them up. Some did so, but not all. The king, on receiving them, had them torn in their presence. You must know that from the instant when the king's banners were surrendered these fellows kept no order; but the greater part, throwing their bows to the ground, took to their heels, and returned to London.

Sir Robert Knolles was in a violent rage that they were not attacked, and the whole of them slain; but the king would not consent to it, saying he would have ample revenge on them, — which in truth he afterwards had.

Thus did these people disperse and run away on all sides. The king, the lords, and the army returned in good array to London, to their great joy. The king immediately took the road to the Wardrobe to visit the princess his mother, who had remained there two days and two nights under the greatest fears, as indeed she had cause. On seeing the king her son, she was mightily rejoiced, and said, "Ha, ha, fair son! what pain and anguish have I not suffered for you this day!"—"Certainly, madam," replied the king: "I am well assured of that; but now rejoice and thank God, for it behooves us to praise him, as I have this day regained my inheritance and the kingdom of England which I had lost."

The king remained the whole day with his mother. The lords retired to their own houses. A proclamation was made through all the streets, that every person who was not an inhabitant of London, and who had not resided there for a whole year, should instantly depart; for that, if there were any found of a contrary description on Sunday morning at sunrise, they would be arrested as traitors to the king, and have their heads cut off. After this proclamation had been heard, no one dared to infringe it, but all departed instantly to their former homes quite discomfited. John Ball and Jack Straw were found hidden in an old ruin, thinking to steal away; but this they could not do, for they were betrayed by their own men. The king and the lords were well pleased with their seizure: their heads were cut off, as was that of Tyler, and fixed on London Bridge in the place of those gallant men whom they beheaded on the Thursday. The news of this was sent through the neighboring counties, that those might hear of it who were on their way to London, according to the orders these rebels had sent them; upon which they instantly returned to their homes without daring to advance farther.

CHAUCER'S BALLADE SENT TO KING RICHARD.

Somtyme the worlde was so stedfast and stable,

man's *held*
That mannes worde was holde obligacioun ;

it *false* *deceiving*
And now hyt is so fals and disceyvable

deed (as concluding or binding a man)
That worde and dede, as in conclusyoun,

Is *like* *nothing* *upside-down*
Ys lyke noothyng ; for turned up-so-doun

all *meed (gain)*
Is alle this worlde, for mede and wilfulnesse,

lack
That alle is loste for lakke of stedfastnesse.

What maketh this worlde to be so variable

(desire, that folk have, to be in dissension)
But luste, that folke hav in dissensioun ?

among *now* *held* *unfit*
For amonges us nowe a man is holde unhable,

if (unless) can *some* *collusion*
But yf he kan, by somme collusyoun,

neighbor
Do his neghbor wronge or oppressioun.

wretchedness
What causeth this but wilfulle wrecchednesse,

all *is* *lack*
That alle ys loste for lakke of stedfastnesse ?

Truth *reason*
Trouthe is put doun, resoun is holden fable ;

Virtue *hath* *no*
Vertu hathe now noo dominacioun ;

Pity *is* *merciful*
Pitee exiled, noo man ys merciable ;

Through covetousness *blinded*
Thurgh covytyse is blente discrecioun ;

The worlde hath made permutacioun

From right *from truth* *fickleness*
Fro ryht to wrong, fro trouthe to fikelnesse,

That alle ys lost for lakke of stedfastnesse.

LENVOYE.

O Prince desire to be honourable ;

<u>Cherish</u>
Cherysshe thy folke, and hate extorsioun ;

<u>Suffer</u>
Suffre nothing that may be reprovable

<u>estate</u>   <u>done</u>
To thyn estaate, doon in thy regioun ;

<u>sword</u>
Shew forth the swerde of castigacioun ;

<u>Dread (fear)</u>   <u>truth</u>
Drede God, do law, love trouthe and worthinesse,

<u>wed</u>   <u>folk</u>   <u>again</u>
And wedde thy folke ayeyne to stedfastnesse.

CHAPTER VI.

The Earl of Flanders again lays Siege to Ghent.

WHILE the affairs you have heard were passing in England, there was no intermission in the wars which the Earl of Flanders was carrying on against Ghent, and which those citizens waged against him. You know that Philip von Artaveld was chosen commander in Ghent, through the recommendation of Peter du Bois, who advised him, when in office, to become cruel and wicked to be the more feared. Philip did not forget this doctrine, for he had not long been governor of Ghent before he had twelve persons beheaded in his presence: some said they were those who had been principally concerned in the murder of his father, and thus he revenged himself on them.

Philip von Artaveld began his reign with great power, and made himself beloved and feared by many, more especially by those who followed the profession of arms: for, to gain their favor, he refused them nothing; every thing

was abandoned to them. I may be asked how the Ghent
men were able to carry on this war; and I will answer
to the best of my ability, according to the information I
received. They were firmly united among themselves, and
maintained the poor, each according to his means: thus,
by being so firmly united, they were of great force. Besides, Ghent, taken all together, is one of the strongest
towns in the world, provided Brabant, Zealand, and Holland be not against it; but, in case these countries were
leagued with Flanders, they would be shut up, surrounded,
and starved.

This whole winter of 1382, the Earl and country of
Flanders had so much constrained Ghent, that nothing
could enter the place by land or water: he had persuaded
the Duke Brabant and Duke Albert to shut up their countries so effectually, that no provisions could be exported
thence but secretly and with a great risk to those who
attempted it. It was thought by the most intelligent, that
it could not be long before they perished through famine,
for all the storehouses of corn were empty, and the people
could not obtain bread for money: when the bakers had
baked any, it was necessary to guard their shops, for the
populace who were starving would have broken them
open. It was melancholy to hear these poor people (for
men, women, and children of good substance were in this
miserable plight) make their daily complaints and cries to
Philip von Artaveld, their commander-in-chief. He took
great compassion on them, and made several very good
regulations, for which he was much praised. He ordered
the granaries of the monasteries and rich men to be
opened, and divided the corn among the poor at a fixed
price. By such means he gave comfort to the town of
Ghent, and governed it well. Sometimes there came to

them in casks flour and baked bread from Holland and Zealand, which were of great assistance; for, had they not been thus succored by those countries, they would have been much sooner defeated.

The Earl of Flanders determined to lay siege to Ghent once more, but with a much superior army to what he had hitherto brought against it; for he declared he would invade the Quatre Metiers, and burn and destroy them, as they had been too active in assisting Ghent. The earl therefore signified his intentions to all the principal towns in Flanders, that they might be ready in time. Immediately after the procession at Bruges, he was to march from hence, to lay siege to Ghent and destroy it. He wrote also to those knights and squires who were dependent on him in Hainault, to meet him at Bruges at the appointed day, or even eight days before.

CHAPTER VII.

The Earl of Flanders sends a Harsh Answer to those who wished to mediate a Peace between him and Ghent.

NOTWITHSTANDING all these summons, levies, and orders, which the Earl of Flanders was issuing, the Duchess of Brabant, Duke Albert, and the Bishop of Liege exerted themselves so much, that a meeting of their councils, to consider of the means of establishing a peace, was ordered to be held in the city of Tournay. The Earl of Flanders, at the request of these lords and the Duchess of Brabant, although he intended to act contrary, gave his terms of accommodation; and these conferences were fixed for the end of Easter, at Tournay, in the year 1382.

Twelve deputies came from the bishopric of Liege and the chief towns, with Sir Lambert de Perney, a very discreet knight. The Duchess of Brabant sent her council thither, and some of the principal inhabitants from the great towns. Duke Albert met likewise his council from Hainault, his bailiff, Sir Simon de Lalain, with others. All these came to Tournay in Easter-week; and Ghent sent also twelve deputies, of whom Philip von Artaveld was the head. The inhabitants of Ghent had resolved to accede to whatever terms their deputies should agree on, with the exception that no one was to be put to death; but that, if it pleased the earl their lord, he might banish from Ghent, and the country of Flanders, all those who were disagreeable to him, and whom he might wish to punish, without any possibility of their return. This resolution they had determined to abide by; and Philip von Artaveld was willing, if he should have angered the earl ever so little during the time he was governor of Ghent, to be one of the banished men for life, out of the regard he had for the lower ranks of people. Certain it is, that, when he set out from Ghent for Tournay, men, women, and children cast themselves before him on their knees, and with uplifted hands besought him, that, at whatever cost it might be, he would bring them back peace; and, from the pity he felt for them, he had agreed to act as I have just related.

CHAPTER VIII.

WHEN Philip von Artaveld and his companions returned to Ghent, great crowds of the common people, who only wished for peace, were much rejoiced on his arrival, and hoped to hear from him good news. They went out to meet him, saying, "Ah, dear Philip von Artaveld, make us happy: tell us what you have done, and how you have succeeded." Philip made no answer to these questions, but rode on, holding down his head: the more silent he was, the more they followed him, and were the more clamorous. Once or twice, as he was advancing to his house, he said, "Get you to your homes, and may God preserve you from harm! To-morrow morning be in the market-place by nine o'clock, and there you shall hear every thing." As they could not obtain any other answer, the people were exceedingly alarmed.

You may easily imagine, when the day so eagerly expected was come, in which Philip was to report what had passed in the conferences at Tournay, that all the inhabitants of Ghent were early in the market-place. It was on a Wednesday morning, and the time of meeting nine o'clock. Philip von Artaveld, Peter du Bois, Peter le Nuitre, Francis Atremen, and the other chiefs came there; and, having entered the town-hall, they ascended the staircase, when Philip, showing himself from the windows, thus spoke : " My good friends, the Lord de Raseflez, the Lord de Gontris, Sir John Villames, and the provost of Harlebecque, came to Tournay, where they very graciously informed us of the will of the earl, and the only means of putting an end to this war. They declared his final terms for peace between him and the inhabitants of Ghent were, that every male inhabitant, excepting priests and monks, from the age of sixteen to that of sixty, should march out of the town in their shirts, with bare heads and feet, and halters about their necks, and should thus go two leagues or more to the plains of Burlesquans, where they would meet the Earl of Flanders, attended by such whom he may choose to bring with him ; and that, when he should see us in this situation, with joined hands, crying out for mercy, he would, if he pleased, take compassion on us. But I could not learn from his council, that there was the least plea of justice to put to death such numbers of people as would be there that day. Now consider if you will have peace on these terms."

When Philip had done speaking, it was a melancholy sight to behold men, women, and children, bewailing, with tears, their husbands, fathers, brothers, and neighbors.

Those who were near him, and had most distinctly heard what he had said, replied, " Ah, dear lord, we put our whole confidence in you : what would you advise us ? for we will do whatever you think will be most for our advantage." — " By my faith, then," said Philip, " I would advise that we all march in arms against my lord. We shall find him at Bruges ; and, when he hears of our coming, he will sally forth, and fight with us ; for the pride of those in Bruges and about his person, who excite him day and night against us, will urge him to the combat. If God shall, through his mercy, grant that we gain the field, and defeat our enemies, our affairs will be instantly retrieved, and we shall be the most respected people in the universe. If we be defeated, we shall die honorably, and God will have pity on us ; and thus the remainder of the inhabitants of Ghent will escape and be pardoned by the earl our lord."

At these words they all shouted out, "We will follow this plan, and no other!" Philip then said, "My good gentlemen, since you are thus resolved, return home, and get ready your arms; for in the course of to-morrow I am determined to march for Bruges : the remaining longer here will not be to our advantage. Within five days we shall know if we be to die, or to live with honor. I will order the constables of the different parishes to go from house to house, and choose the best armed and those most fit for the service."

Immediately after the meeting broke up, and every one returned home to make ready, each according to his abilities. They kept the gates of the town so closely shut that no person whatever was suffered to come in or go out before Thursday afternoon, when those who were to march on the expedition were prepared, — in all about five thousand men, and not more. They loaded about two hundred carts with cannon and artillery, and only seven with provisions; that is, five with bread and two with wine, for there were but two tuns of wine in the town. You may judge from this to what straits they had been reduced.

It was a miserable spectacle to see those who went and those who remained. These last said to them, "Good friends, you see what you leave behind; but never think of returning unless you can do so with honor, for you will not find any thing here. The moment we hear of your defeat or death, we will set fire to the town, and perish in the flames, like men in despair." Those who were marching out replied, by way of comforting them, "What you say is very just. Pray God for us; for we place our hopes in him, and trust he will assist you, as well as us, before our return."

Thus did these five thousand men of Ghent march off with their slender stores, and encamped about a league from Ghent, but touched not their provision, taking up with what they could find in the country. On Friday they marched the whole day, and then meddled not with their stores; but their scouts picked up some few things in the country, with which they made shift, and fixed their quarters that evening a long league from Bruges. They halted there, considering it a proper place to wait for their enemies, for there were in front two extensive marshes, which were a good defence on one side; and they fortified themselves on the others with the carriages, and thus passed the night.

CHAPTER IX.

THE ORDER OF BATTLE OF THE GHENT MEN. — THEY DEFEAT THE EARL OF FLANDERS AND THE MEN OF BRUGES. — THE MEANS BY WHICH THIS WAS BROUGHT ABOUT.

THE Saturday was a fine bright day; and, being the feast of the Holy Cross, the inhabitants of Bruges, according to custom, made their usual processions. News was soon brought to Bruges, that the Ghent army was near at hand; so that every one began to murmur until the earl heard it, as well as those about his person. He was much surprised, and said, "See how the wickedness

of these mad and foolish people of Ghent leads them to
their destruction : indeed, it is time this war should be put
an end to." His knights and others instantly waited on
him, whom he very graciously received, and said, "We
will go and fight these wicked people : however, they
show courage in preferring death by the sword rather than
famine." They determined to send out three men at arms
to examine the force and situation of the enemy. The
Marshal of Flanders ordered three valiant squires on this
service, whose names were Lambert de Lambres, Damas
de Buffy, and John de Béart : they set out, mounted on
the finest horses in the town, and advanced toward the
Ghent army. While this was going forward, every person
in Bruges made himself ready, and showed the most eager
desire to sally forth and combat the men of Ghent ; of
whom I will now say a word, and of the manner in which
they had drawn themselves up.

On the Saturday morning, Philip von Artaveld ordered
his whole army to pay their devotions to God, and masses
to be said in different places (for there were with them
several monks), that every man should confess himself and
make other becoming preparations, and that they should
pray to God with that truth, as people looking to him
alone for mercy. All this was done, and mass celebrated
in seven different places. After each mass was a sermon,
which lasted an hour and a half. The monks and priests
endeavored, by their discourses, to show the great simili-
tude between them and the people of Israel, whom Pha-
raoh, king of Egypt, detained so long in slavery ; and
who, through God's grace, were delivered, and conducted
by Moses and Aaron into the land of promise, while Pha-
raoh and the Egyptians were drowned. "In like manner,
my good people," preached the monks, "have you been

kept in bondage by your lord, the Earl of Flanders, and by your neighbors of Bruges, whom you are now to meet, and by whom you will, without doubt, be combated, for your enemies are in great numbers, and have little fear of your force. But do not you mind this ; for God, who can do all things, and is acquainted with your situation, will have mercy on you : therefore, think of nothing but what you have left behind, for you well know that every thing is lost if you be defeated. Sell yourselves well and valiantly ; and, if you must die, die with honor. Do not be alarmed if great numbers issue forth from Bruges against you ; for victory is not to the multitude, but whither God shall please to send it, and by his grace it has been often seen, as well by the Maccabees as the Romans, that those who fought manfully, and confided in God, discomfited the greater number. Besides, you have justice and reason on your side in this quarrel, which ought to make you feel yourselves bold and better comforted." In such words as these the priests had been ordered to preach to the army, and with these discourses they were well pleased. Three parts of them communicated, and all showed great devotion and much fear in God.

After the sermons the whole army assembled round a small hill, on which Philip von Artaveld placed himself in order to be the better heard, and harangued them very ably, explaining to them every point in which they were justified in this war ; and how Ghent had frequently sought pardon from the earl, and never could obtain it without submitting to conditions too hard for the town and its inhabitants ; that now they had advanced so far, they could not retreat ; and that, if they would consider, they would see nothing could be gained, were they to return, for all they had left behind were in sorrow and misery. They ought not, therefore, to think of Ghent, their wives and children who were in it, but to act in such manner as was becoming their honor. Philip von Artaveld addressed many more fine speeches to them, for he was very eloquent, and had words at command, which was fortunate for him; and toward the end he added, "My good friends, you see here all your provision: divide it among you fairly, like brethren, without any disturbance; for, when it is gone, you must conquer more if you wish to live."

At these words they drew up very regularly, and unloaded the carts, when the bags of bread were given out to be divided by constable-wicks, and the two tuns of wine placed on their bottoms; and there they moderately breakfasted, each man having a sufficiency at that time, — after which breakfast they found themselves more determined, and active on their feet, than if they had eaten more. This repast being over, they put themselves in order, and retired within their ribaudeaus. These ribaudeaus are tall stakes, with points shod with iron, which they were always accustomed to carry with them. They fixed them in front of their army, and enclosed themselves within.

The three knights who had been sent by the earl to reconnoitre found them in this situation. They approached the entrances of these ribaudeaus; but the Ghent men never moved, and rather seemed rejoiced to see them. They returned to Bruges, where they found the earl in his palace, surrounded by many knights, waiting for them, to hear what intelligence they had brought back. They pushed through the crowd, and came near the earl, when they spoke aloud, for the earl wished all present to hear, and said they had advanced so close to the Ghent army, that they might have shot at them if they had so chosen, but they left them in peace; and that they had seen their banners, and the army enclosed within their ribaudeaus. "And what are their numbers, think ye?" said the earl. They answered, that, as near as they could guess, they might be from five to six thousand. "Well," said the earl, "now let every one instantly get ready; for I will give them battle, and this day shall not pass without a combat." At these words the trumpet sounded in Bruges, when every one armed himself, and made for the market-place. As they came, they drew up under their proper banners, as they had usually done, in bands and constable-wicks.

Many barons, knights, and men at arms drew up before the palace of the earl. When all was ready, and the earl armed, he came to the market-place, and was much pleased to see such numbers in battle-array. They then marched off (for none dared disobey his commands), and in order of battle made for the plain. The men at arms afterwards issued forth from Bruges. It was a handsome sight, for there were upward of forty thousand armed heads; and thus horse and foot advanced in proper order, near to the place where the Ghent men were, and then halted. It was late in the afternoon when the earl and his army arrived, and the sun going down. One of the knights said to the earl, "My lord, you now see your enemies: they are but a handful of men in comparison with your army, and as they cannot escape, do not engage them this day, but wait for to-morrow, when you will have the day before you: you will, besides, have more light to see what you are about; and they will be weaker, for they have not any thing to eat."

The earl approved much this advice, and would willingly have followed it; but the men of Bruges, impatient to begin the fight, would not wait, saying they would soon

defeat them and return back to their town.   Notwithstanding the orders of the men at arms (for the earl had not
less than eight hundred lances, knights, and squires), the
Bruges men began to shoot and to fire cannons.

The Ghent men, being collected in a body on an eminence, fired at once three hundred cannon ; after which
they turned the marsh, and placed the Bruges men with
the sun in their eyes, which much distressed them, and
then fell upon them, shouting out, "Ghent!"   The moment the men of Bruges heard the cannon and the cry of
Ghent, and saw them marching to attack them in front,
they, like cowards, opened their ranks, and, letting the
Ghent men pass without making any defence, flung down
their staves, and ran away.   The Ghent men were in close
order, and, perceiving their enemies were defeated, began
to knock down and kill on all sides.   They advanced with
a quick step, shouting, "Ghent!" and saying, "Let us
pursue briskly our enemies, who are defeated, and enter
the town with them : God eyes us this day with looks of
pity."

They followed those of Bruges with so much courage,
that, whenever they knocked down or killed any one, they
marched on without halting or quitting the pursuit, while
the men of Bruges fled with the haste of a defeated army.
I must say that at this place there were multitudes of
slain, wounded, and thrown down, for they made no defence ; and never were such cowardly wretches as those of
Bruges, or who more weakly or recreantly behaved themselves, after their insolence when they first took the field.
Some may wish to excuse them by supposing there might
have been treason, which caused this defeat.   This was
not so ; but such poor and weak conduct fell on their own
heads.

CHAPTER X.

WHEN the Earl of Flanders and the men at arms saw
that by the miserable defence of the men of Bruges
they had caused their own defeat, and that there was not
any remedy for it, for every man was running away as fast
as he could, they were much surprised, and began to be
alarmed for themselves, and to make off in different directions. It is true, that, had they seen any probability of
recovering the loss which the Bruges men were suffering,
they would have done some deeds of arms by which they
might have rallied them a little ; but they saw it was hope-
less, for they were flying to Bruges in all directions, and
neither the son waited for the father, nor the father for
his child.

The men at arms therefore began to break their ranks.
Few had any desire to return to Bruges, for the crowd
was so great on the road thither, that it was painful to see
and hear the complaints of the wounded and hurt. The
men of Ghent were close at their heels, shouting out,
" Ghent, Ghent ! " knocking down all that obstructed
them. The greater part of the men at arms had never
before been in such peril : even the earl was advised to
make for Bruges, and to have the gates closed and guarded,
so that the Ghent men should not be able to force them,
and become masters of the town. The Earl of Flanders
saw no help for his men, who were flying on all sides ; and,
as it was now dark night, followed this advice, and took

the road to Bruges, his banner displayed before him. He
entered the gates one of the first, with about forty others,
for no more had followed him.   He ordered the guards to
defend the gates if the Ghent men should come hither;
and then rode to his palace, from whence he issued
a proclamation that every person, under pain of death,
should assemble in the market-place. The intention of
the earl was to save the town by this means; but it did
not succeed, as you shall hear.

While the earl was in his palace, and had sent the clerks
of the different trades from street to street to hasten the
inhabitants to the market-place in order to preserve the
city, the men of Ghent, having closely pursued their enemies, entered the town with them, and instantly made
for the market-place, without turning to the right or left,
where they drew themselves up in array.   Sir Robert
Mareschaut, one of the earl's knights, had been sent to
the gates to see they were guarded; but, while the earl
was planning means for defending the town, Sir Robert
found a gate flung off its hinges, and the Ghent men
masters of it.   Some of the citizens said to him, "Robert,
Robert, return and save yourself, if you can, for the
Ghent men have taken the town."   The knight returned
as speedily as he could to the earl, whom he met coming
out of his palace on horseback, with a number of torches.
The knight told him what he had heard; but notwithstanding this, the earl, anxious to defend the town, advanced toward the market-place, and as he was entering
it with a number of torches, shouting, "Flanders for the
Lyon! Flanders for the earl!" those near his horse and
about his person, seeing the place full of Ghent men, said,
"My lord, return; for if you advance farther you will be
slain, or at the best made prisoner by your enemies, as

they are drawn up in the square and are waiting for you."

They told him truth ; for the Ghent men, seeing the great blaze of torches in the street, said, "Here comes my lord, here comes the earl : how he falls into our hands !" Philip von Artaveld had given orders to his men, that, if the earl should come, every care was to be taken to preserve him from harm, in order that he might be carried alive and in good health to Ghent, when they should be able to obtain what peace they chose. The earl had entered the square, near where the Ghent men were drawn up, when several people came to him and said, "My lord, do not come further ; for the Ghent men are masters of the market-place and of the town, and if you advance you will run a risk of being taken. Numbers of them are now searching for their enemies from street to street ; and many of the men of Bruges have joined them, who conduct them from hotel to hotel to seek those whom they want. You cannot pass any of the gates without danger of being killed, for they are in their possession ; nor can you return to your palace, for a large rout of Ghent men have marched thither."

When the earl heard this speech, which was heart-breaking as you may guess, he began to be much alarmed, and to see the peril he was in. He resolved to follow the advice of not going further, and to save himself if he could, which was confirmed by his own judgment. He ordered the torches to be extinguished, and said to those about him, " I see clearly that affairs are without remedy : I therefore give permission for every one to depart, and save himself in the best manner he can." His orders were obeyed. The torches were put out, and thrown in the streets ; and all who were in company with the earl separated and went away. He himself went to a by-street, where he was disarmed by his servant, and, throwing down his clothes, put on his servant's, saying, "Go about thy business, and save thyself if thou canst; but be silent if thou fall into the hands of my enemies, and if they ask any thing about me do not give them any information." — "My lord," replied the valet, "I will sooner die."

The Earl of Flanders thus remained alone, and it may be truly said he was in the greatest danger; for it was over with him if he had at that hour, by any accident, fallen into the hands of the mob, who were going up and down the streets, searching every house for the friends of the earl; and whomsoever they found they carried before Philip von Artaveld and the other captains in the market-place, when they were instantly put to death. It was God alone who watched over him, and delivered him from this peril; for no one had ever before been in such imminent danger, as I shall presently relate. The earl inwardly bewailed his situation from street to street at this late hour; for it was a little past midnight, and he dared not enter any house, lest he should be seized by the mobs of Ghent and Bruges. Thus, as he was rambling through the streets, he at last entered the house of a poor woman, a very unfit habitation for such a lord, as there were neither halls nor apartments, but a small house, dirty and smoky, and as black as jet: there was only in this place one poor chamber, over which was a sort of garret that was entered by means of a ladder of seven steps, where, on a miserable bed, the children of this woman lay.

The earl entered this house with fear and trembling, and said to the woman, who was also much frightened, "Woman, save me: I am thy lord, the Earl of Flanders; but at this moment I must hide myself, for my enemies are in pursuit of me; and I will handsomely reward thee for the favor thou showest me." The poor woman knew him well, for she had frequently received alms at his door; and had often seen him pass and repass when he was going to some amusement or hunting. She was ready with her answers, in which God assisted the earl; for, had she delayed it ever so little, they would have found him in conversation with her by the fireside. "My lord, mount this ladder, and get under the bed in which my children sleep." This he did, while she employed herself by the fireside, with another child in a cradle.

The Earl of Flanders mounted the ladder as quickly as he could, and, getting between the straw and the coverlet, hid himself, and contracted his body into as little space as possible. He had scarcely done so, when some of the mob of Ghent entered the house. One of them took a candle, and mounted the ladder, and, thrusting his head into the place, saw nothing but the wretched bed in which the children were asleep. He looked all about him, above and below, and then said to his companions, "Come, come, let us go: we only lose our time here."

The Earl of Flanders, hearing all this conversation as he lay hid, you may easily imagine, was in the greatest fear of his life. In the morning he could have said he was one of the most powerful princes in Christendom, and that same night he felt himself one of the smallest. One may truly say that the fortunes of this world are not stable. It was fortunate for him to save his life; and this miraculous escape ought to be to him a remembrance his whole lifetime.

CHAPTER XI.

I WAS informed, and believe my authority good, that on the Sunday evening, when it was dark, the Earl of Flanders escaped from Bruges. I am ignorant how he accomplished it, or if he had any assistance, but some I believe he must have had. He got out of the town on foot, clad in a miserable jerkin, and when in the fields was quite joyous, as he might then say he had escaped from the utmost peril. He wandered about at first, and came to a thornbush to consider whither he should go; for he was unacquainted with the roads or country, having never before travelled on foot. As he lay thus hid under the bush, he heard some one talk, who by accident was one of his knights, that had married a bastard daughter of his: his name was Sir Robert Mareschaut. The earl, hearing him talk as he was passing, said to him, "Robert, art thou there?" The knight, who well knew his voice, replied, "My lord, you have this day given me great uneasiness in seeking for you all round Bruges: how were you able to escape?" — "Come, come, Robert," said the earl: "this is not a time to tell one's adventures: endeavor to get me a horse, for I am tired with walking, and take the road to Lille, if thou knowest it." — "My lord," answered the knight, "I know it well." They then travelled all night and the morrow till early morn, before they could procure a horse. The first beast they could find was a mare belonging to a poor man in a village. The earl mounted the mare, without saddle or bridle, and, travelling all Monday, came, toward evening, to the castle of Lille, whither a great part of his knights who had escaped from the battle of Bruges had retired. They had got off as well as they could, some on foot, others on horseback : but all did not follow this road ; some went by water to Holland and Zealand, where they remained until they received better news.

CHAPTER XII.

The Duke of Burgundy instigates his Nephew King Charles to make War on Ghent and its Allies, as well in Revenge for the burnt Villages as to assist in the Recovery of Flanders for the Earl, who was his Vassal.

THE Duke of Burgundy was not forgetful of the engagements he had entered into with his lord and father the Earl of Flanders. He set out from Bapaume attended by Sir Guy de la T-rémouille and Sir John de Vienne, Admiral of France, who were very desirous the earl should be assisted. These two were the principal persons of his council. They continued their journey until they arrived at Senlis, where the king was with his two uncles of Berry and Bourbon. When he found an opportunity, he drew his brother the Duke of Berry aside, and explained to him how the Ghent men, in the insolence of their pride, were endeavoring to be masters everywhere, and to destroy all gentlemen ; that they had already burnt and pillaged part of the kingdom of France, which was much to the prejudice and dishonor of the realm, and ought not to be patiently borne.

The king entered the apartments where his uncles were,

with a falcon on his wrist : he was struck with the duke's last words, and said with much good-humor, "What were you speaking of, my fair uncles, at this moment, with so much earnestness ? I should like to hear it, if it be proper for me to know." — "Yes, my lord," answered the Duke of Berry ; "for what we were discussing personally concerns you. Your uncle, my brother of Burgundy, has just been complaining to me of the Flemings. Those villains of Flanders have driven the earl their lord out of his country, and all the gentlemen. They are now, to the amount of a hundred thousand men, besieging Oudenarde, under a captain called Philip von Artaveld, an Englishman for courage, who has sworn he will never break up the siege until he has had his will on those of the town, unless you shall force him to it. This reservation he has made. Now, what do you say to this ? will you assist your cousin of Flanders to regain his inheritance, of which peasants, in their pride and cruelty, have deprived him ?" — "By my faith, my dear uncles," replied the king, "I have a very great inclination so to do, and in God's name let us march thither. I wish for nothing more than to try my strength in arms, for never hitherto have I had armor on. It is necessary, therefore, if I wish to reign with honor and glory, that I learn the art of war." The two dukes were well pleased at hearing the king thus speak out. The Duke of Bourbon now came, having been sent for by them ; and they related to him all you have heard, and how eager the king was to march to Flanders, with which he was much pleased.

CHAPTER XIII.

CHARLES THE SIXTH, KING OF FRANCE, FROM A DREAM, CHOOSES A
FLYING HART FOR HIS DEVICE.

IT happened that during the residence of the young
king Charles at Senlis, as he was sleeping in his bed a
vision appeared to him. He thought he was in the city
of Arras, where until then he had never been, attended
by all the flower of knighthood of his kingdom; that the
Earl of Flanders came there to him, and placed on his
wrist a most beautiful and elegant pilgrim-falcon, saying,
"My lord, in God's name I give this falcon to you for the
best that was ever seen, the most indefatigable hunter,
and the most excellent striker of birds." The king was
much pleased with the present, and said, "Fair cousin, I
give you my thanks." He then thought he turned to the
Constable of France, who was near him, and said, "Sir
Oliver, let you and I go to the plains, and try this elegant
falcon which my cousin of Flanders has given me;" when
the constable answered, "Well, let us go." Then each
mounted their horses, and went into the fields, taking the
falcon with them, where they found plenty of herons to fly
him at. The king said, "Constable, cast off the falcon, and
we shall see how he will hunt." The constable let him fly,
and the falcon mounted so high in the air they could
scarcely see him : he took the direction toward Flanders.
"Let us ride after my bird," said the king to the constable ;
"for I will not lose him." The constable assented ; and
they rode on, as it appeared to the king, through a large
marsh, when they came to a wood, on which the king cried

out, "Dismount, dismount! we cannot pass this wood on horseback." They then dismounted, when some servants came and took their horses. The king and the constable entered the wood with much difficulty, and walked on until they came to an extensive heath, where they saw a falcon chasing herons, and striking them down; but they resisted, and there was a battle between them. It seemed to the king that his falcon performed gallantly, and drove the birds before him so far that he lost sight of him. This much vexed the king, as well as the impossibility of following him; and he said to the constable, "I shall lose my falcon, which I shall very much regret; for I have neither lure nor any thing else to call him back." While the king was in this anxiety he thought a beautiful hart, with two wings, appeared to issue out of the wood, and come to this heath, and bend himself down before the king, who said to the constable as he regarded this wonder with delight, "Constable, do you remain here; and I will mount this hart that offers himself to me, and follow my bird." The constable agreed to it; and the young king joyfully mounted the hart, and went seeking the falcon. The hart, like one well tutored to obey the king's pleasure, carried him over the tops of the highest trees, when he saw his falcon striking down such numbers of birds that he marvelled how he could do it. It seemed to the king that, when the falcon had sufficiently flown and struck down enough of the herons, he called him back; and instantly, as if well taught, he perched on the king's wrist, when it seemed to him that after he had taken the falcon by its lure, and given him his reward, the hart flew back again over the wood, and replaced the king on the same heath whence he had carried him, and where the constable was waiting, who was much rejoiced at his return.

On his arrival he dismounted : the hart returned to the wood, and was no more seen. The king then, as he imagined, related to the constable how well the hart had carried him, and that he had never rode so easy before in his life ; and also the goodness of his falcon, who had struck down such numbers of birds : to all which the constable willingly listened. The servants then seemed to come after them with their horses, which, having mounted, they followed a magnificent road that brought them back to Arras. The king at this part awakened, much astonished at the vision he had seen, which was so imprinted on his memory that he told it to some of his attendants who were waiting in his chamber. The figure of this hart was so agreeable to him, that he could not put it out of his imagination ; and this was the cause why, on this expedition to Flanders against the Flemings, he took a flying hart for his device.

CHAPTER XIV.

KING CHARLES, AT THE INSTIGATION OF THE EARL OF FLANDERS, WHO WAS PRESENT, ASSEMBLES HIS ARMY IN ARTOIS AGAINST THE FLEMINGS. — PHILIP VON ARTAVELD GUARDS THE PASSES INTO FLANDERS.

THE King of France, like one who was desirous of marching to Flanders to abase the pride of the Flemings, as his predecessors had formerly done, set his secretaries at work, and sent his letters and summons by messengers to all parts of his kingdom, ordering every one to hasten to Arras without delay, accoutred each according to his rank in the best manner he was able ; for, if it were God's pleasure, he was determined to fight the Flemings in their own country.

No lord of his realm disobeyed; but all sent orders to their vassals, and marched from the most distant countries, such as Auvergne, Rouergue, Toulousain, Gascony, Poitou, Limousin, Saintonge, and Brittany: others came from the Bourbonois, Forêts, Burgundy, Dauphiné, Savoy, Bar, and Lorrain, and from all parts of France and its dependencies, to Arras. The assemblage of such numbers of men at arms was a wonderful, beautiful sight. The Earl of Flanders resided at Hêdin, and heard daily, from the King of France and the Duke of Burgundy, of the great levies which were making, and in consequence issued a proclamation throughout Artois forbidding any one, under pain of losing his life and fortune, to withdraw any thing whatever from house, fortress, or town; for he was desirous that the men at arms who were marching to Artois should have the advantage of being served with whatever was in the Low Countries.

The King of France came into Artois, where he remained. Men at arms came to him from all quarters, and so handsomely equipped, it was a fine sight to see: they quartered themselves as they arrived in the plains, and found all the barns quite full and well furnished. The Earl of Flanders came to Arras, which greatly pleased the king and his lords: he performed his homage in the presence of those peers who were there, for the county of Artois, and the king accepted him as his vassal. His majesty then addressed him, saying, "Fair cousin, if it please God and St. Denis, we will restore you to your inheritance of Flanders, and will abate the pride of Philip von Artaveld and the Flemings so effectually, that they shall never again have it in their power to rebel." — "My lord," replied the earl, "I have full confidence in it; and you will acquire such honor and glory that as long as the world lasts you will be praised, for certainly the pride of the Flemings is very great."

Philip, while at the siege of Oudenarde, was informed of every thing, and that the King of France was marching a large army against him, though he pretended not to believe it; and said to his people, "By what means does this young king think to enter Flanders? He is as yet too young by a year to imagine he can frighten us by his assembling an army. I will have the entrances so well guarded that it shall not be in their power for this year to cross the river Lis." He sent to Ghent for the Lord de Harzelles. On his arrival, he said to him, "Lord de Harzelles, you hear how the King of France is making preparations to destroy us. We must have a council on this subject. You shall remain here, and I will go to Bruges to learn surer intelligence, and to encourage the citizens of the principal towns. I will go to establish such garrisons on the river Lis, and at the chief passes, that the French shall not be able to advance through them."

CHAPTER XV.

SEVERAL KNIGHTS OF THE PARTY OF THE EARL OF FLANDERS, HAVING PASSED PONT-AMENIN, ARE DEFEATED AND KILLED ON THEIR ATTEMPT TO REPASS IT, THE FLEMINGS HAVING BROKEN DOWN THE BRIDGE. —PHILIP, HEARING THIS NEWS WHEN AT YPRES, MAKES USE OF IT TO ENCOURAGE THE INHABITANTS.

WHILE these preparations were going forward, and during the residence of the King of France at Arras, great bodies of men at arms were assembling in the Tourneois, Artois, and castlewick of Lille and its neigh-

borhood. Some knights and squires who resided at Lille
and thereabout resolved to perform feats of arms that
should gain them renown, chiefly through the exhortations
of the Haze de Flanders. They collected about sixscore
knights and squires, and crossed the river Lis at Pont-
Amenin, which was not then broken down, two leagues
from Lille. They rode for the town of Harle, which they
surprised ; and, after slaying many in the town and environs, they drove the remainder out of the town. Their
cries were heard in the neighboring villages ; the inhabitants of which sounded their alarm-bells, and marched
toward Harle and Pont-Amenin, whence the cries seemed
to come.

When the Haze, Sir John Jumont, the Constable de
Vuillon, Sir Henry Duffle, and the other knights and
squires, had sufficiently alarmed the country, they thought
it was time for them to retreat, and set out on their return,
intending to repass the bridge; but they found it strongly
occupied by Flemings, who were busily employed in destroying it ; and when they had broken down any parts
they covered them with straw, that the mischief might
not be perceived. The knights and squires at this moment arrived, mounted on the best of horses, and found
upward of two thousand peasants drawn up in a body
without the town, prepared to advance upon them. The
gentlemen, on seeing this, formed ; and, having fixed their
lances on their rests, those best mounted instantly charged
this body of peasants, with loud shouts. The Flemings
opened their ranks through fear, but others say through
malice ; for they well knew the bridge would not bear
them, and they said among themselves, "Let us make
way for them, and we shall soon see fine sport."

The Haze de Flanders and his companions, desirous to

get away (for any further stay would be against them), galloped for the bridge, which was now too weak to bear any great weight: however, the Haze and some others had the courage and good luck to pass over, — they might be about thirty, — but, as others were following, the bridge broke down under them. Horses and riders were over-thrown, and both perished together. Those behind, see-ing this misfortune, were thunderstruck, and knew not whither to fly to save themselves. Some leaped into the river, intending to swim, but they were not able thus to escape. Great slaughter ensued; for the Flemings fell upon them, and killed them easily and without pity. They made several leap into the water, and they were drowned. Sir John de Jumont narrowly escaped, for the bridge broke under him, but by great agility of body he saved himself: he was, however, badly wounded on the head and body by arrows, and it was six weeks before he recovered. At this unfortunate action were killed the Constables de Vuillon, de Bouchars, de St. Hilaire, and more drowned: Sir Henry Duffle was slain. Including drowned and killed, there were upward of sixty; and very fortunate were those who escaped. Great numbers re-turned wounded from this enterprise. News was carried to the lords of France at Arras, of their countrymen hav-ing lost the day, and that the Haze de Flanders had con-ducted this foolish expedition. He was pitied by some, but by others not. Those who had been most accustomed to arms said they had acted ill, to cross a river that was not fordable, attack a large town, and enter an enemy's country, and return the way they had come, without hav-ing established guards on the bridge. It was not an enterprise planned by prudent men at arms, who were desirous of success; but, since they planned their enterprise with so much self-sufficiency, they had suffered from the consequence.

This affair passed off, and was soon forgotten. Philip departed from Bruges, and came to Ypres, where he was most joyfully received. Peter du Bois went to Commines, where all the inhabitants of the flat country were assembled, and instantly began his preparations for defence, loosening the planks of the bridge, so that, if there should be occasion, it could immediately be pulled down; but he was unwilling totally to destroy the bridge, lest the inhabitants of the adjacent flat country might suffer, who daily crossed it with their cattle in droves, to place them in greater security on that side of the Lis. The whole country was so much covered with them, it was marvellous to see.

The day Philip von Artaveld came to Ypres, news arrived of the defeat of the French at Pont-Amenin, and that the Haze had been nearly taken. Philip was mightily rejoiced at this, and said with a smile, to encourage those near, "By the grace of God, and the just cause we are engaged in, it will all end so; and never shall this king, if he should be so foolishly advised to cross the Lis, return again to France."

Philip was five days in Ypres, and harangued the people in the open market-place, to encourage them and to keep them steady to their engagements, telling them that the King of France was coming to destroy them without the least shadow of right. "Good people," said Philip, "do not be alarmed if he should march against us; for he will never be able to cross the river Lis, as I have had all the passes well guarded, and have ordered Peter du Bois to Commines with a large body of men: he is a loyal man, and one who loves the honor of Flanders; and

Peter le Nuitre I have sent to Warneton. All the other bridges on the Lis are broken down, and there is neither pass nor ford which they can cross but at these two towns. I have also heard from our friends whom we sent to England. In a short time we shall receive considerable succors from thence, as we have made a strong alliance with them. Keep up, therefore, valiantly your hopes, for our honor shall be unsullied; and observe punctually what you have promised and sworn to us in the good town of Ghent, which has had such trouble and difficulty to maintain the rights and franchises of Flanders. Now let all those who are determined to remain steady to the cause, according to the oath they took, gallantly lift up their hands to heaven as a token of loyalty."

At these words all who were in the market-place, and who had heard the speech, held up their hands as a sign of their loyalty. After this Philip descended from the scaffold on which he had harangued, and returned to his house, where he remained the whole day. On the morrow he and his attendants mounted their horses, and went toward Oudenarde, where the siege was still going on, notwithstanding the news of the French; but on passing through Courtray he rested two days.

CHAPTER XVI.

THE ORDER OF THE FRENCH ARMY IN ITS MARCH TO FLANDERS, AFTER THEY HAD HEARD THE BRIDGES WERE BROKEN AND GUARDED.

WE will for a while leave Philip von Artaveld, and speak of the young King of France, who resided at Arras, and who, as he showed, had a great desire to enter

Flanders to lower the pride of the Flemings; and was daily increasing his army by the arrival of men at arms from all quarters. On the third day of November, he came to Seclin, where he halted. A council was held in the presence of the Constable of France, and the Marshals of France, Burgundy, and Flanders, to consider how they should proceed. The common report in the army was the impossibility to enter Flanders in case the passes of the river should be strongly guarded. It rained, besides, at this time continually, and was so exceedingly cold that they could not advance. Some of the wisest said it was wrong to undertake such an expedition at this season of the year, and to bring the king so far into such a country. They ought not to have united before the summer to carry the war into Flanders, for the king had never been so far in his life.

This river Lis is so difficult to cross, that except at certain places it cannot be passed. There are no fords, and the country it runs through is so very marshy, horses cannot approach it. There were many debates among these lords on this subject; and those who knew the country said, "Certainly, at such a season as this, it will not be right to advance into that country, nor can we go into the territories of Cassel, Surnes, or Verthes."—"And what road shall we then take?" cried the constable. Upon which the Lord de Coucy said, "I would propose that we march to Tournay, and there cross the Scheld, and take the road toward Oudenarde. This road is very easy, and we shall engage with our enemies. After passing the Scheld, we shall not have any thing to stop us before Tournay. We may thus arrive before Oudenarde, and punish Philip von Artaveld. We can have daily refreshments of provisions come to us from Hainault, and follow us down the river from Tournay." This speech of the Lord de Coucy was well attended to, and supported by several for some time : but the constable and marshals were more inclined to follow the course of the Lis, to seek a shorter passage, than to march to the right or left by a longer road ; and they urged strong reasons for it, saying, " If we look for any other road but the straight one, we do not show ourselves good men at arms ; at least it is our duty to examine if we cannot pass the river above or below this pass of Commines, which is guarded. Besides, if we retreat, our enemies will rejoice and be encouraged : their forces will increase, and they will say that we fly from them. There is also another point which ought to be considered : we are ignorant what has been the success of the ambassadors they sent to England; for if, by any treaty, assistance should come to them from that quarter, they will give us much trouble. It is therefore better that we get rid of this business in Flanders as speedily as possible, than be thus long in determining upon it. Let us instantly, and with courage, march toward Commines, and God will assist us."

This plan was unanimously adopted. During the time these lords were assembled, they considered how they should form their battalions ; and selected those who were to march on foot with the constable in the vanguard, in order to clear the roads for the army to pass and march in a line, and to act as scouts to observe and find out their enemies. They also chose those who were to be in the king's battalion, regulated the arms with which they should serve, and appointed proper persons to carry the oriflamme of France and to guard it; and likewise determined of what numbers the wings were to be composed, and how many were to be in the rear-guard. All these things they

debated and arranged. When these points had been settled, and they could not think of any thing more that was
necessary to be done, the council broke up, and every one
retired to his lodgings. Those lords and barons who had
not been present were informed of the regulations, and the
manner in which they were to act from henceforward. It
was this day ordered, that the king should on the morrow
dislodge from Seclin, march through Lille without halting,
and take up his quarters at Margnette l'Abbayee; and that
the vanguard should pass on to Commines and Warneton,
and do the most they could in the course of the day.
This being settled, the master of the crossbows, in con-
junction with the constable and marshals, unanimously
appointed Sir Josse de Haluyn and the Lord de Ram-
bures to the command of the infantry, who were to clear
the roads by cutting down hedges and forests, filling up
valleys, and every thing else that might be necessary.
Their numbers amounted to seventeen hundred and sixty.

In the vanguard were the Marshals of Flanders, France,
and Burgundy, who had under their command seventeen
hundred men at arms and seven hundred crossbows, besides four thousand infantry whom the earl had given to
them, armed with large shields and other weapons. It
was also ordered that the Earl of Flanders and his battalion, consisting of about sixteen hundred men at arms,
knights, squires, and infantry, should march on the wings
of the vanguard to re-enforce it, should it be necessary. It
was likewise ordered that the king's battalion should march
between the vanguard and the battalion of the Earl of
Flanders, and that the king's three uncles, Berry, Burgundy, and Bourbon, should be in it; and also the Count
de la Marche, Sir James de Bourbon, his brothers, the
Count de Clermont, the Dauphin d'Auvergne, the Count

de Dampmartin, the Count de Sancerre, Sir John de Boulogne, to the amount of six thousand men at arms, two
thousand Genoese crossbows, and others.

The rear-guard was to consist of two thousand men at
arms and two hundred archers ; the commanders of which
were the Lord John d'Artois, Count d'Eu, the Lord Guy,
Count de Blois, Sir Waleran, Count de St. Pol, Sir William, Count de Harcourt, the Lord de Chatillon, and the
Lord de Sere.

Sir Peter de Villiers was appointed to bear the oriflamme,
attended by four knights, whose names were Sir Robert le
Baveux, Sir Morice de Sancourt, Sir Guy de Tresiquidi,
and Brandon de la Heuse : Le Borgne de Ruet and Le
Borgne de Montdoulcet were named to guard the banner.

It is proper to be known, that the lords who had planned
this expedition had determined they would never return to
France until they had engaged Philip von Artaveld and
his forces ; and it was for this reason they had drawn up
their battalions as ready for the combat on the morrow.
The Lords d'Albreth, de Coucy, and Sir Hugh de Hanlon
were ordered to form the battalions, and place them in
array. Sir William de Bannes and the Lord de Champ-
reny were appointed marshals to attend to the quarters of
the king and his battalion.

It was also ordered, that on the day of battle no one
but the king and eight valiant men appointed to attend his
person should be on horseback. The names of these
eight men were as follows : the Lord de Raineval, Le Bègue
de Villaines, Sir Aymemon de Pommiers, Sir Enguerrant
de Haluyn, the Viscount d'Acy, Sir Guy le Baveux, Sir
Nicholas de Pennel, and Sir William des Bourdes. The
Lord de Raineval and Sir Enguerrant de Haluyn were to
take post in front of the king ; Le Bègue de Villaines and

the Viscount d'Acy (who is called in several places hereafter the Viscount d'Aunoy) were to place themselves on
each side; and Sir Aymemon de Pommiers, Sir Nicholas
de Pennel, Sir Guy le Baveux, and Sir William des
Bourdes were to take post in the rear. It was likewise
ordered, that on the day of battle Sir Oliver de Clisson,
Constable of France, and Sir William de Poitiers, should
advance on horseback, to reconnoitre and observe the appearance of the enemy.

CHAPTER XVII.

SOME FEW OF THE FRENCH, NOT BEING ABLE TO CROSS THE LIS AT
THE BRIDGE OF COMMINES, FIND MEANS OF DOING SO BY BOATS AND
OTHER CRAFT, UNKNOWN TO THE FLEMINGS.

THE orders above mentioned were punctually obeyed;
and the vanguard dislodged on the morrow, marching in order of battle toward Commines. They found the
roads well made, for the Lord de Fransures and Sir Josse
de Haluyn had paid great attention to them: this was
on the Monday. When the Constable and Marshals of
France, with the vanguard, arrived at the bridge of Commines, they were forced to halt; for it was so completely
destroyed, that it was not in the power of man to repair it
if any opposition should be made when they were attempting it, as the Flemings were in great force on the opposite
side of the river, and ready to defend the pass against all
who might wish to attack them: they were upward of nine
thousand, under the command of Peter du Bois and others,
who showed good inclinations to repulse any attempt.
Peter du Bois had placed himself on the causeway, at the

end of the bridge, with a battle-axe in his hand; and the Flemings were drawn up on each side.

The Constable of France and the lords with him, having considered the situation, thought it impossible to pass the river at that place unless the bridge were rebuilt; they ordered their servants to follow the course of the river, and examine its banks for about a league up and down. When they returned, they informed their masters, who were waiting for them, they had not been able to find any place where the cavalry could pass. Upon hearing this, the constable was much vexed, and said, "We have been badly advised to take this road: better would it have been for us to have gone to St. Omer than remain in this danger, or to have crossed the Scheld at Tournay, as the Lord de Coucy advised, and to have marched straight to Oudenarde and fought our enemies, since it is both our duty and inclination to combat them; and they are so presumptuous, they would have waited for us at their siege." The Lord Louis Sancerre then said, "I am of opinion that we fix our quarters here for this day, and lodge our army, should it arrive, as well as we are able; and that we send to Lille to seek for boats and hurdles, that may come down the river, with which to-morrow we can throw a bridge from these fine meads, and cross over; for we have no other alternative." Upon this Sir Josse de Haluyn said, "My lord, we have been informed that there will be great difficulties between this and Lille; for the river Menyn, on which all boats must pass to come hither, has been obstructed by large beams thrown across it by the Flemings who are in those parts: they have totally destroyed the bridge, and we learn it is impossible for any vessels or boats to pass." — "I know not, then," added the constable, "what we can now do. It will be better for us to take the road to Aire, and cross the Lis at that place, since we are unable to do so here."

During the time the Constable and Marshals of France and Burgundy were in this dilemma at the bridge of Commines, several knights and squires silently withdrew, with the intent to hazard some gallant deeds of arms, and attempt to cross the river, whatever it might cost them. They meant likewise to combat the Flemings in their intrenchments, and open a passage, as I shall now relate. While the vanguard was on its march from Lille to Commines, the Lord de St. Py, and some other knights from Hainault, Flanders, Artois, and even France, had held a council without the knowledge of the constable or marshals. They said, "We will procure two or three boats, which we will launch into the river Lis, at a sheltered place below Commines, and will fix posts on each side of the river where it is not wide, to fasten cords to. We shall by this means soon convey over a large body of men; and by marching on the rear of our enemies we may attack them, and if victorious we shall gain the reputation of valiant men at arms." After they had thus determined in council, the Lord de St. Py exerted himself so much that he procured from Lille a boat and cords, with every other necessary article. On the other hand, Sir Herbeaux de Belleperche and Sir John de Roye, who were companions in this expedition, had also caused a boat to be brought. Sir Henry de Manny, Sir John de Malatrait, and Sir John Chauderon, Bretons, who had been of this council, had likewise provided one, and followed the preceding companies.

The Lord de St. Py was the first who arrived at the river with his boat, cords, and fastenings. They fixed a strong stake, to which they tied the cord: three varlets then crossed over, and the boat, with the cords, being launched, they fixed on the opposite side another strong post, to which they fastened the other end of the cord; and, this being done, they returned with the boat to their master. It happened that the Constable and Marshals of France were at that time at the bridge of Commines, pondering how they could discover a passage. They were then informed of the intentions of the Lord de St. Py and the other knights; upon which the constable, addressing himself to the Lord Louis de Sancerre, said, "Marshal, go and see what they are doing, and, if it be possible to cross the river in the manner they propose, add some of our men to theirs."

Just as these knights were preparing to embark, the Marshal of France came thither, attended by a large company of knights and squires. They made way for him, as was right. He stopped on the bank, and with pleasure saw the arrangement of the boats. The Lord de St. Py, addressing him, said, "My lord, is it agreeable to you that we should cross here?"—"I am very well pleased with it," replied the marshal; "but you are running great risks: for if our enemies, who are at Commines, should know your intentions, they would do you great mischief."—"My lord," answered the Lord de St. Py, "nothing venture, nothing win: in the name of God and St. George we will cross over, and before to-morrow evening will fall suddenly on our enemies, and attack them." The Lord de St. Py then placed his pennon in the boat, and was the first who stepped into it: he was followed by nine others, who were as many as the boat could hold, and instantly, by means of the cord they held, crossed over. When disembarked, in order to prevent themselves from being discovered, they entered a small alder-grove, where they lay hidden. Those on the bank, by means of the cord, drew the boat back. The Count de Conversant, Lord d'Anghien, embarked with his banner, with the Lord de Vertain his brother, and seven others. These nine then passed, and the third time others followed them.

The two other boats now arrived that belonged to Sir Herbaut de Belleperche, Sir John de Roye, and the Bretons; which were launched in the same manner the first had been. These knights then crossed, and none but determined men at arms did the same. It was a pleasure to see with what eagerness they embarked: at times a great crowd was pushing who should cross first, so that if the Marshal of France had not been there, who kept them in proper order, accidents would have happened from their overloading the boats.

News was brought to the constable and the lords of France at the bridge of Commines, how their people were crossing the river, when he said to the Seneschal de Rieux, "Go and examine this passage, I beg of you, and see if our people be passing as they tell us." The Lord de Rieux was never happier than when he had this commission, and, clapping spurs to his horse, hastened thither with his whole company, to the amount of full forty men at arms. When he arrived at the passage where one hundred and fifty of his countrymen had already crossed, he immediately dismounted, and said he would also pass the river. The Marshal of France would not refuse him; and intelligence was sent to the constable, that his cousin the Lord de Rieux had crossed. The constable mused a little, and then said, "Make the crossbows shoot, and skirmish with the Flemings who are on the other side of the bridge, to occupy their attention, and prevent them from observing our people; for, if they should have any notion what

they are about, they will fall upon them, destroy the passage, and kill all those who have crossed; and I would
much rather die than that should happen."

Upon this, the crossbows and infantry advanced.
There were among them some who flung hand-grenades,
which, bursting, cast out bolts of iron beyond the bridge,
even as far as the town of Commines. The skirmish now
began to be very sharp; and the vanguard, by their movements, seemed determined to cross the bridge if they
could. The Flemings, being shielded up to their noses,
made a good appearance, and defended themselves well.
Thus passed this day, which was a Monday, in skirmishing; and it was soon dark, for at that season the days are
very short. The boats, however, continued to carry over
men at arms in great numbers, who on their landing hid
themselves in the alder-wood, waiting for more.

You may easily guess what perils they were in; for,
had those in Commines gained the least intelligence of
them, they must have had them at their mercy, and conquered the greater part, besides taking the boats; but,
God favored the other party, and consented that the pride
of the Flemings should be humbled.

CHAPTER XVIII.

A SMALL BODY OF FRENCH, HAVING CROSSED THE LIS, DRAW UP IN BATTLE-ARRAY BEFORE THE FLEMINGS.

I MAINTAIN that all men of understanding must hold
this enterprise of the boats, and passage of men at
arms, as a deed of superior valor and enterprise. Toward
evening the knights and squires of the vanguard were

eager to cross with their companions; so that late in this
Monday evening there were, on the Flanders side of the
river, about four hundred men at arms, all the flower of
knighthood, for no varlet was suffered to cross.

The Lord Louis de Sancerre, seeing so many gallant
men (sixty banners and thirty pennons), said he should
think himself to blame if he remained behind. He then
entered the boats, with his knights and squires; and the
Lord de Hangest, &c., crossed at the same time. When
they were all assembled, they said, "It is time to march
toward Commines, to look at our enemies, and see if we
cannot make our quarters good in the town." Upon this
they tightened their arms, buckled their helmets on their
heads in a proper manner, and, advancing through the
marshes which are contiguous to the river, marched in
order of battle, with banners and pennons displayed, as
if they were immediately to engage. The Lord de St. Py
was the principal conductor and commander-in-chief, because he knew the country better than any of the others.

As they were thus marching in close order, in their
way toward the town, Peter du Bois and the Flemings
were drawn up on the causeway; when, casting their eyes
toward the meads, they saw this body of men at arms
approaching. They were exceedingly astonished, and demanded from Peter du Bois, "By what devil of a road
have these men at arms come? and how have they crossed
the Lis?" He replied, "They must have crossed in boats,
and we have known nothing of the matter; for there is
neither bridge nor passable ford over the Lis between this
and Courtray."—"What shall we do?" said some of them
to Peter du Bois: "shall we offer them battle?"—"By
no means," replied Peter: "let them advance, but we will
remain in our strength and in our place: we are on high

ground, and they on low, so that we have great advantage over them ; and, if we descend to meet them in the plain, we shall lose it. Let us wait until the night become more obscure, and then we will consider how we had best act. They are not of force sufficient to withstand us in battle ; and, besides, we are acquainted with all the roads of the country, of which they must be ignorant." This advice was followed ; for the Flemings never budged from their post, but remained steady at the foot of the bridge, drawn up in order of battle on the causeway, in silence, and, by their appearance, seemed as if they had not noticed what was passing. Those who had crossed the river continued advancing slowly through the marshes, following the course of it as they approached Commines.

The Constable of France, on the opposite side of the water, saw his men at arms, with banners and pennons fluttering in the wind, drawn up in a handsome small battalion, and marching toward Commines. On seeing this his blood began to run cold from the great dread he had of their being defeated ; for he knew the Flemings were in great force on that side of the water. In the excess of rage he cried out, "Ah, St. Ives ! ha, St. George ! ha, Our Lady ! what do I see there ? I see in part the flower of our army, who are most unequally matched. I would rather have died than have witnessed this. Ah ! Sir Louis de Sancerre, I thought you more temperate and better taught than I see you now are : how could you have hazarded so many noble knights and squires and men at arms against ten or twelve thousand men, who are proud, presumptuous, and well prepared, and who will show them no mercy, while we are unable, if there should be a necessity, to aid them ? Ah, Rohan ! ah, Laval ! ah, Rieux ! ah, Beaumanoir ! ah, Longueville ! ah, Rochfort ! ah,

Manny! ah, Malatrait! ah, Conversant! ah, such a one and such a one!—how afflicted am I for you all, when, without consulting me, you have run into such imminent danger! Why am I Constable of France? for if you be conquered I shall incur all the blame, and they will say I ordered you on this mad enterprise." The constable, before he heard that such numbers of valiant men had crossed, had forbidden any of those near him to pass the river; but, when he saw the appearance of those who had passed, he said aloud, "I give free liberty for all who wish it to cross, if they be able."

At these words the knights and squires stepped forth, seeking means to cross the bridge; but it was soon night, and they were forced to leave off their attempt, though they had begun to lay planks on the beams, and even some had placed their targets to make a road: so that the Flemings who were in Commines had enough to do to watch them, and were puzzled how to act, for on the one hand they saw below the bridge, in the marshes, a large body of men at arms who had halted with their lances advanced before them, and to whom great re-enforcements were coming, and, on the other, those of the vanguard on the opposite side of the bridge were constantly skirmishing with them, and exerting themselves lustily to repair the bridge.

In this situation were the French who had that evening crossed over in boats. They had halted on the marshes, in mud and filth up to their ankles. Now consider what must have been their courage and difficulties, when in these long winter-nights they thus remained a whole night with their arms and helmets on, with their feet in the mire, and without any sort of refreshments. Certainly, I say, they are worthy of great renown; for they were but a handful of men in comparison with the Flemings in Commines and in that neighborhood. They dared not therefore advance to attack them, and for this reason had halted, saying among themselves, " Let us stop here until it be daylight, when we shall have a sight of these Flemings who quit not the advantage of their intrenchments ; but at last they will not fail to come to us, and when near we will shout our war-cries with a loud voice, each his own cry, or the cry of his lord, notwithstanding all our lords may not have joined us. By this means we shall frighten them, when we will fall on them with a thorough good will. It is in the power of God, and within the compass of our own ability, to defeat them ; for they are badly armed, while our spears and swords are of well-tempered steel from Bordeaux ; and the habergeons they wear will be a poor defence, and cannot prevent our blows from penetrating through them." With such hopes as these did those who had passed the river comfort themselves, and remain in silence during the night.

CHAPTER XIX.

THE FRENCH WHO HAD CROSSED THE LIS DEFEAT, WITH GREAT SLAUGHTER, PETER DU BOIS AND THE FLEMINGS. — THE VANGUARD OF THE FRENCH ARMY REPAIR AND PASS OVER THE BRIDGE OF COMMINES.

PETER DU BOIS, knowing these men at arms were in the marshes joining Commines, was not perfectly at his case, for he was uncertain what might be the event. He had, however, under his command, six or seven thousand men, to whom, during the night, he had thus spoken :

"The men at arms who have crossed the river to fight with us are neither of iron nor steel. They have labored hard this whole day, and have been all night standing in these marshes, so that it is possible that toward daybreak they will be overpowered with sleep. While they are in this situation, we will come slyly to attack them. Our numbers are sufficient to surround them, but, when we have so done, let no one dare to rush upon them, but remain silent; for, when it shall be proper time for you to act, I will inform you." To this command of Peter they all promised obedience. On the other hand, the barons, knights, and squires, who had remained in the marshes so near the enemy, were far from being comfortable: some of them were up to their ankles in mud, and others half way up their legs. But their eagerness and joy, on gaining this pass with so much honor (for very gallant deeds of arms were likely to ensue), made them forget all their pains and difficulties. If it had been in summer-time, instead of the seventh day of November, they would have enjoyed it; but now the ground was cold, muddy, and dirty, and the nights were long. At times also it rained heavily on their heads; but it ran off, as they had their helmets on, and every thing prepared for the combat, and were only waiting for the enemy to come and attack them. The great attention they paid to be in readiness kept up their spirits, and made them almost forget their situation.

The Lord de St. Py full loyally acquitted himself in this expedition, as a scout and observer of what the Flemings were doing, though he was the commander-in-chief. He was continually on the lookout, and went privily to reconnoitre their motions. On his return he said to his companions in a low voice, "Now up: our enemies are very quiet. Perhaps they will advance on us at daybreak:

therefore be on your guard, and prepare to act." He would then return again to see if any thing were going forward, and then come back to tell what he had observed. This he continued to do until the hour which the Flemings had fixed upon to attack them. It was on the point of day when they began their march in close order, without uttering a word. The Lord de St. Py, who was on the watch, no sooner saw this manœuvre than he found they were in earnest, and, hastening to his companions, said to them, "Now, my lords, be alert: we have but to do our utmost, for our enemy is on his march, and will be instantly here. These barons of new date are advancing slowly, and think to catch and surprise us: show yourselves true men at arms, for we shall have a battle." As the Lord de St. Py uttered these words, the knights and squires, with great courage, seized their long Bordeaux spears, and, having grasped them with a hasty will, placed themselves in as good order as any knights or squires could devise.

When the Flemings advanced to the combat, the knights and squires began to utter their war-cries, insomuch that the constable and vanguard, who had not yet crossed the bridge, heard them, and said, "Our friends are engaged: may God help them! for at this moment we are unable to give them any assistance." Peter du Bois marched in front, and was followed by his Flemings; but, when they approached the French, they were received on the sharp points of their long Bordeaux spears, to which their coats of mail made not more resistance than if they had been of cloth thrice doubled; so that they passed through their bodies, heads, and stomachs.

When the Flemings felt these sharp spears which impaled them, they fell back, and the French advancing gained ground upon them; for there were none so hardy but that feared their strokes. Peter du Bois was one of the first who was wounded, and run through by a lance. It came quite out at his shoulder: he was also wounded on the head, and would have been instantly slain if it had not been for the body-guard he had formed, of thirty stout varlets, who, taking him in their arms, carried him as quickly as they could out of the crowd. The mud from the causeway to Commines was so deep that all these people sunk in it up to the middle of their legs. The men at arms, who had been long accustomed to their profession, drove down and slew the Flemings without let or hinderance: they shouted, "St. Py forever!" "Laval," "Sancerre," "Anghien!" and the war-cries of others who were there. The Flemings were panic-struck, and began to give way, when they saw these knights attack them so vigorously, and pierce them through with their spears. They retreated, and, falling back on each other, were followed by the French, who marched through them or around them, always attacking the thickest bodies. They no more spared killing them than if they had been so many dogs; and they were in the right, for, had the Flemings conquered, they would have served them the same.

The Flemings, finding themselves thus driven back, and that the men at arms had won the causeway and bridge, counselled together to set fire to the town, in hopes it would cause the French to retreat, or enable them to collect their people. This was executed, and fire set to several houses, which were instantly in flames; but they were disappointed in thinking by this to frighten the French, for they pursued them as valiantly as before, fighting and slaying them on the ground, or in the houses whither they had retreated. Upon this the Flemings made for the open plain, where they collected in a body. They sent to Vertain, Poperingue, Bergues, Rollers, Mesieres, Warneton, and the other neighboring towns, to urge them to come to their assistance at Commines. Those who fled, and the inhabitants of the villages near Commines, began to set their bells a-ringing, which clearly showed there was an engagement going forward. Some of them, however, began to slacken, and others to occupy themselves in saving what they could of their goods, and to carry them to Ypres or Courtray. Women and children ran thither, leaving their houses full of furniture, cattle, and grain. Others again marched in haste toward Commines, to help their countrymen who were fighting.

While this was passing, and those valiant knights who had crossed the Lis in boats were so gallantly engaged, the constable and vanguard were busily employed in attempting to repair the bridge and cross it. There was a very great throng, for the constable had given permission for all to pass it who could. There was much danger for those who crossed it first; and the lords who did so were obliged to step on targets thrown on the beams of the bridge. When they had crossed, they began to strengthen the bridge, for they found the planks lying on the ground, which they put in their proper places. During the night two wagon-loads of hurdles were brought, which were of great use to them, so that shortly it was made as strong as ever. On Tuesday the whole vanguard passed, took possession of the place, and, as they crossed, fixed their quarters in the town.

Those of the vanguard who were in Commines drove out the Flemings. There were slain of them in the streets and fields about four thousand, not including those killed in the pursuit, in windmills, and in monasteries, whither they had fled for shelter; for, as soon as the Bretons had crossed, they mounted their horses, and began a chase after the Flemings, and overran the country, which was then rich and plentiful.

CHAPTER XX.

THE KING OF FRANCE CROSSES THE LIS AT THE BRIDGE OF COMMINES. — THE TOWN OF YPRES SURRENDERS TO HIM. — THE KING OF FRANCE LODGES IN YPRES. — PETER DU BOIS PREVENTS BRUGES FROM SURRENDERING TO THE KING. — PHILIP VON ARTAVELD ASSEMBLES HIS FORCES TO COMBAT THE FRENCH.

WE will now return to the King of France, and say how he went on. When intelligence was brought him of Commines being conquered, that the Flemings were dispersed, and the bridge rebuilt, he set out from the abbey of Marquette where he had lodged, and marched with his whole army in battle-array, as was befitting him to do, toward Commines. The king and his uncles arrived at Commines on Tuesday, and took up their lodgings in the town; from whence the vanguard had marched for the hill of Ypres, where they had fixed their quarters. On the Wednesday morning the king advanced to the hill of Ypres, where he remained until the baggage and the remainder of his army should cross the river at Commines or at Warneton; for there were very numerous trains, and multitudes of horses.

While the king and his whole army were on Mount Ypres, many markets were there held, and plenty of pillage was sold to those of Lille, Douay, and Tournay, indeed, to all who wished to buy. A piece of cloth of Vexin, Malines, Poperingue, or Commines, was sold for one franc. People were clothed there too cheaply. Some

Bretons and other pillagers, determined on gain, went in large bodies, and loaded carts and horses with their booty of cloths, linen, knives, money in gold and silver, dishes and plates of silver, wherever they found them, which they sent, well packed up, to a place of safety on the other side of the Lis, or by their servants into France.

The king and all the lords came to Ypres, where they quartered themselves as well as they could, and in as great numbers as the town would hold. They remained there to refresh themselves four or five days.

We will now return to Philip, and say what he was doing. Being eager to combat the King of France, as he plainly showed, he ordered, on his arrival at Ghent, every man capable of bearing arms, after leaving a sufficient garrison in the town, to follow him. All obeyed; for he gave them to understand that by the grace of God they would defeat the French, be lords of Ghent, and rank as sovereigns among other nations. Philip von Artaveld carried with him about ten thousand men as the arriere-ban : he had before sent to Bruges, Damme, Ardembourg, Sluys, to the seacoasts, the Quatre Mestiers, and constable-wicks of Grammont, Dendremonde, and Alost, and had raised from those places about thirty thousand more. He and his whole army were quartered one night before Oudenarde : on the morrow they marched away, and came before Courtray : he had with him about fifty thousand men. The King of France received intelligence that Philip von Artaveld was approaching, and, as it was said, with full sixty thousand men. Upon this the vanguard set off from Ypres, under the command of the Constable and Marshals of France, and encamped a league and a half from Ypres, between Rollers and Rosebecque. On the morrow the king and all the lords, with the main battalion and rear-guard, quartered themselves there also. I must say that these lords, while they were in the field, suffered greatly; for it was in the heart of winter, the beginning of December, and it rained every day. They slept on the roads every night, for they were in daily and hourly expectation of a battle: it was commonly said in the army, "They will come to-morrow;" which they believed, from the news the foragers brought when they returned from their excursions.

The king was quartered in the midst of his army. The lords of France were much vexed at Philip for delaying, for they were very impatient of being out in such bad weather. It should be known, that with the king were all the flower of French knighthood: it was therefore highly presumptuous in Philip von Artaveld and the Flemings to think of fighting with them; for if they had been satisfied with continuing their siege of Oudenarde, and had slightly intrenched themselves, the French, considering the wetness of the season, would never have marched to seek them; and, if they had done so, they would have combated them under the greatest disadvantages. But Philip was so vain of the good fortune he had met with at Bruges, that he thought nothing could withstand him, and he hoped he should be lord of the world. No other thoughts had he, and was nothing afraid of the King of France nor his army; for, if he had entertained any fears, he would not have done that which he did, as you shall hear related.

CHAPTER XXI.

PHILIP VON ARTAVELD, HAVING ENTERTAINED HIS CAPTAINS AT SUP-
PER, GIVES THEM INSTRUCTIONS HOW THEY ARE TO ACT ON THE
MORROW AT THE BATTLE OF ROSEBECQUE.

PHILIP VON ARTAVELD, with his whole army, on
the Wednesday evening preceding the battle, was
encamped. in a handsome position, tolerably strong,
between a ditch and grove, and with so good a hedge
in front that they could not easily be attacked. It was
between the hill and town of Rosebecque where the king
was quartered. That same evening Philip gave a magnificent supper to his captains at his quarters; for he had
wherewithal to. do so, as his provisions followed him.
When the supper was over, he addressed them in these
words: "My fair gentlemen, you are my companions in
this expedition, and I hope to-morrow we shall have something to do; for the King of France, who is impatient to
meet and fight with us, is quartered at Rosebecque. I
therefore beg of you to be loyal, and not alarmed at any
thing you shall see or hear; for we are combating in a just
cause, to preserve the franchises of Flanders, and for our
right. Admonish your men to behave well, and draw them
up in such manner that, by this means and our courage, we
may obtain the victory. To-morrow, through God's grace,
we shall not find any lord to combat with us, or any who
will dare take the field, unless he mean to remain there;
and we shall gain greater honor than if we could have
depended on the support of the English; for, if they had
been with us, they alone would have gained all the reputa-

tion. The flower of the French nobility is with the king, for he has not left one behind : order, therefore, your men not to grant quarter to any one, but to kill all who fall in their way. By this means we shall remain in peace; for I will and command, under pain of death, that no prisoners be made, except it be the King of France. With regard to the king, I wish to support him, as he is but a child, and ought to be forgiven ; for he knows not what he does, and acts according as he is instructed : we will carry him to Ghent, and teach him Flemish : but as for dukes, earls, and other men at arms, kill them all. The common.people of France will never be angry with us for so doing ; for they wish, as I am well assured, that not one should ever return to France, and it shall be so."

When these Flemish captains had retired, and all gone to their quarters to repose, the night being far advanced, those upon guard fancied they heard a great noise toward the Mont d'Or. Some of them were sent to see what it could be, and if the French were making any preparations to attack them in the night. On their return they reported that they had been as far as the place whence the noise came, but that they had discovered nothing. This noise, however, was still heard, and it seemed to some of them that their enemies were on the mount about a league distant.

Philip arose, and, wrapping himself in a gown, took a battle-axe, and went out of his tent to listen to this noise. It seemed to him as if there were a great tournament. He directly returned to his tent, and ordered his trumpet to be sounded to awaken the army. As soon as the sound of the trumpet was heard, it was known to be his. Those of the guard in front of the camp armed themselves, and sent some of their companions to Philip to know what he

wished to have done, as he was thus early arming himself.
On their arrival, he wanted to send them to the part
whence the noise had come, to find out what it could be;
but they reported that that had already been done, and
that there was no cause found for it. Philip was much
astonished; and they were greatly blamed, that, having
heard a noise toward the enemy's quarters, they had remained quiet. "Ha," said they to Philip, "in truth we
did hear a noise toward the Mont d'Or, and we sent to
know what it could be; but those who had been ordered
thither reported that there was nothing to be found or
seen. Not having seen any positive appearance of a
movement of the enemy, we were unwilling to alarm the
army lest we should be blamed for it." This speech of the
guard somewhat appeased Philip; but in his own mind he
marvelled much what it could be. Some said it was the
devils of hell running and dancing about the place where the
battle was to be, for the abundance of prey they expected.

Neither Philip von Artaveld nor the Flemings were
quite at their ease after this alarm. They were suspicious
of having been betrayed and surprised. They armed
themselves leisurely with whatever they had, made large
fires in their quarters, and breakfasted comfortably, for
they had victuals in abundance. About an hour before
day, Philip said, "I think it right that we march into the
plain, and draw up our men; because, should the French
advance to attack us, we ought not to be unprepared, nor
in disorder, but properly drawn up like men, knowing well
what we are to do." All obeyed this order, and, quitting
their quarters, marched to the heath beyond the grove.
There was in front a wide ditch newly made, and in their
rear quantities of brambles, junipers, and shrubs. They
drew up at their leisure in this strong position, and formed

one large battalion, thick and strong. By the reports from the constables they were about fifty thousand, all chosen men, who valued not their lives. Among them were about sixty English archers, who, having stolen away from their companions at Calais, to gain greater pay from Philip, had left behind them their armor in their quarters.

Every thing being arranged, each man took to his arms. The horses, baggage, women, and varlets were dismissed; but Philip von Artaveld had his page mounted on a superb courser, worth five hundred florins, which he had ordered to attend him, to display his state, and to mount if a pursuit of the French should happen, in order that he might enforce the commands which he had given to kill all. It was with this intention that Philip had posted him by his side. Philip had likewise from the town of Ghent about nine thousand men, well armed, whom he placed near his person; for he had greater confidence in them than any of the others: they therefore, with Philip at their head with banners displayed, were in front; and those from Alost and Grammont were next; then the men from Courtray, Bruges, Damme, Sluys, and the Franconate. They were armed, for the greater part, with bludgeons, iron caps, jerkins, and with gloves of iron-work. Each man had a staff with an iron point, and bound round with iron. The different townsmen wore liveries and arms, to distinguish them from one another. Some had jackets of blue and yellow, others wore a welt of black on a red jacket, others chevroned with white on a blue coat, others green and blue, others lozenged with black and white, others quartered red and white, others all blue. Each carried the banners of their trades. They had also large knives hanging down from their girdles. In this state they remained, quietly waiting for day, which soon came.

CHAPTER XXII.

PHILIP VON ARTAVELD AND HIS FLEMINGS QUIT THE STRONG POSITION
THEY HAD TAKEN IN THE MORNING, TO ENCAMP ON MONT D'OR,
NEAR TO YPRES.—THE CONSTABLE AND ADMIRAL OF FRANCE, WITH
SIR WILLIAM OF POITIERS, SET OUT TO RECONNOITRE THEIR SITUA-
TION.

ON the Thursday morning all the men at arms of the
army, the vanguard, the rear-guard, and the king's
battalion, armed themselves completely, except their helmets, as if they were about to engage; for the lords well
knew the day could not pass without a battle, from the
reports of the foragers on the Wednesday evening, who
had seen the Flemings on their march demanding a battle.
The King of France heard mass, as did the other lords,
who all devoutly prayed to God that the day might turn
out to their honor. In the morning there was a thick
mist, which continued so long that no one could see the
distance of an acre: the lords were much vexed at this,
but they could not remedy it.

After the king's mass, which had been attended by the
constable and other great lords, it was ordered that those
valiant knights Sir Oliver de Clisson, Constable of France,
Sir John de Vienne, Admiral of France, and Sir William
de Poitiers, who had been long used to arms, should reconnoitre the position of the Flemings, and report to the
king and his uncles the truth of it; during which time
the Lord d'Albreth and Sir Hugh de Châtillon were
employed in forming the battalions. These three knights,
leaving the king, set off on the flower of their steeds, and
rode toward that part where they thought they should find

the Flemings, and toward the spot where they had encamped the preceding night.

You must know that on the Thursday morning, when
the thick mist came on, the Flemings having, as you have
before heard, marched before daybreak to this strong
position, had there remained until about eight o'clock,
when, not seeing nor hearing any thing of the French,
their numbers excited in them pride and self-sufficiency,
and their captains, as well as others, began thus to talk
among themselves: "What are we about, thus standing
still, and almost frozen with cold? Why do we not advance with courage, since such is our inclination, and seek
our enemies to combat them? We remain here to no
purpose, for the French will never come to look for us.
Let us at least march to Mont d'Or, and take advantage
of the mountain." Many such speeches were made, and
they all consented to march to Mont d'Or, which was
between them and the French. In order to avoid the
ditch in their front, they turned the grove, and entered
the plain. While they were thus on their march round the
grove, the three knights came so opportunely that they
reconnoitred them at their ease, and rode by the side of
their battalions, which were again formed within a bow-
shot from them. When they had considered them on the
left, they did the same on the right, and thus carefully and
fully examined them. The Flemings saw them plainly,
but paid not any attention to them; nor did any one quit
his ranks. The three knights were well mounted, and so
much used to this business that they cared not for them.
Philip said to his captains, "Our enemies are near at
hand: let us draw up here in battle-array for the combat.
I have seen strong appearances of their intentions: for
these three horsemen who pass and repass have reconnoitred us, and are still doing so."

The Three Knights reconnoitring the Flemings in the Mist.

Upon this the Flemings halted on the Mont d'Or, and formed in one thick and strong battalion; when Philip said aloud, "Gentlemen, when the attack begins, remember our enemies were defeated and broken at the battle of Bruges by our keeping in a compact body. Be careful not to open your ranks, but let every man strengthen himself as much as possible, and bear his staff right before him. You will intermix your arms, so that no one may break you, and march straight forward with a good step, without turning to the right or left; and act together, so that, when the conflict begins, you may throw your bombards and shoot with your crossbows in such manner that our enemies may be thunderstruck with surprise."

When Philip had formed his men in battle-array, and told them how to act, he went to the wing of his army in which he had the greatest confidence. Near him was his page on the courser, to whom he said, "Go, wait for me at that bush out of bow-shot; and, when thou shalt see the discomfiture of the French and the pursuit begin, bring me my horse, and shout my cry; they will make way for thee to come to me, for I wish to be the first in the pursuit." The page, on these words, left his master, and did as he had ordered him. Philip placed near him, on the side of this wing, forty English archers whom he had in his pay. Now, if it be considered how well Philip had arranged this business, I am of opinion (and in this I am joined by several others) that he well knew the art of war; but in one instance, which I will relate, he acted wrong. It was in quitting the first strong position he had taken in the morning; for they would never have sought to fight him there, as it would have been too much to their disadvantage; but he wished to show that his people were men of courage, and had little fear of their enemies.

CHAPTER XXIII.

THE BATTLE OF ROSEBECQUE, BETWEEN THE FRENCH AND FLEM-
INGS. — PHILIP VON ARTAVELD IS SLAIN, AND HIS WHOLE ARMY
DEFEATED.

THE three knights returned to the King of France and to his battalions, which had already been formed and were marching slowly in order of battle; for there were many prudent and brave men, who had been long accustomed to arms, in the vanguard, in the king's battalion, and in the rear-guard, who knew well what they were to do, for they were the flower of chivalry in Christendom. Way was made for them; and the Lord de Clisson spoke first, bowing to the king from his horse, and taking off the beaver he wore, saying, "Sire, rejoice: these people are our own, and our lusty varlets will fight well with them." — "Constable," replied the king, "God assist you! Now advance, in the name of God and St. Denis." The knights before mentioned as the king's body-guard now drew up in good order. The king created many new knights, as did different lords in their battalions, so that several new banners were displayed.

It was ordered, that when the engagement was about to commence, the battalion of the king, with the oriflamme of France, should march to the front of the army, that the van and rear guards should form the two wings as speedily as possible, and by this means enclose and straiten the Flemings, who were drawn up in the closest order, and gain a great advantage over them. Notice of this intended movement was sent to the rear-guard, of which the

Count d'Eu, the Count de Blois, the Count de St. Pol, the Count de Harcourt, the Count de Châtillon, and the Lord de la Gere were commanders. The young Lord de Haurel displayed his banner this day before the Count de Blois, who also knighted Sir Thomas d'Istre, and Sir James de Hameth. According to the report of the heralds, there were this day created four hundred and sixty-seven knights.

The Lord de Clisson, Sir John de Vienne, and Sir William de Langres, having made their report to the king, left him, and went to their post in the vanguard. Shortly afterwards the oriflamme was displayed by Sir Peter de Villiers, who bore it. Some say (as they find it written) that it was never before displayed against Christians, and that it was a matter of great doubt during the march whether it should be displayed or not. However, the matter having been fully considered, they resolved to display it, because the Flemings followed opinions contrary to that of Pope Clement, and called themselves Urbanists; for which the French said they were rebellious and out of the pale of the Church. This was the principal cause why it had been brought and displayed in Flanders.

The oriflamme was a most excellent banner, and had been sent from heaven with great mystery: it is a sort of gonfalon, and is of much comfort in the day of battle to those who see it. Proof was made of its virtues at this time; for all the morning there was so thick a fog. that with difficulty could they see each other, but the moment the knight had displayed it, and raised his lance in the air, this fog instantly dispersed, and the sky was as clear as it had been during the whole year. The lords of France were much rejoiced when they saw this clear day, and the sun shine, so that they could look about them on all sides.

It was a fine sight to view these banners, helmets, and beautiful emblazoned arms : the army kept a dead silence, not uttering a sound, but eyed a large battalion of Flemings before them, who were marching in a compact body, with their staves advanced in the air, which looked like spears ; and so great were their numbers, they had the appearance of a wood. The Lord d'Estonnenort told me that he saw (as well as several others), when the oriflamme was displayed, and the fog had dispersed, a white dove fly many times round the king's battalion. When it had made several circles, and the engagement was about to begin, it perched on one of the king's banners : this was considered as a fortunate omen.

The Flemings advanced so near, that they commenced a cannonade with bars of iron, and quarrels headed with brass. Thus was the battle begun by Philip and his men against the king's battalion, which at the outset was very sharp ; for the Flemings, inflamed with pride and courage, came on with vigor, and, pushing with shoulders and breasts like enraged wild boars, they were strongly interlaced, one with the other, that they could not be broken, nor their ranks forced. By this attack of cannons and bombards, the Lord d'Albaruin, banneret, Morlet de Haruin, and James Doré, on the side of the French, were first slain, and the king's battalion obliged to fall back. But the van and rear guards pushed forward, and, by enclosing the Flemings, straitened them much. Upon the two wings these men at arms made their attack, and, with their well-tempered lances of Bordeaux, pierced through their coats of mail to the flesh. All who were assailed by them drew back to avoid the blows, for never would those that escaped return to the combat. By this means, the Flemings were so straitened that they could not use their staves to defend themselves. They lost both strength and breath, and, falling upon one another, were stifled to death without striking a blow.

Philip von Artaveld was surrounded, wounded by spears, and beaten down, with numbers of the Ghent men, who were his guards. When Philip's page saw the ill success of his countrymen, being well mounted on his courser, he set off, and left his master, for he could not give him any assistance, and returned toward Courtray, on his way to Ghent. When the Flemings found themselves enclosed on two sides, there was an end to the business, for they could not assist each other. The king's battalion, which had been somewhat disordered at the beginning, now recovered. The men at arms knocked down the Flemings with all their might. They had well-sharpened battle-axes, with which they cut through helmets, and disbrained heads : others gave such blows with leaden maces, that nothing could withstand them. Scarcely were the Flemings overthrown before the pillagers advanced, who, mixing with the men at arms, made use of the long knives they carried, and finished slaying whoever fell into their hands, without more mercy than if they had been so many dogs. The clattering on the helmets, by the axes and leaden maces, was so loud, that nothing else could be heard for the noise. I was told, that if all the armorers of Paris and Bruxelles had been there working at their trade, they could not have made a greater noise than these combatants did on the helmets of their enemies ; for they struck with all their force, and set to their work with the greatest good-will. Some, indeed, pressed too forward into the crowd, and were surrounded and slain : in particular, Sir Louis de Gousalz, a knight from Berry, and Sir Fleton de Reniel. There were several more, which was a great pity ;

but in such a battle as this, where such numbers are engaged, it is not possible for victory to be obtained without being dearly bought; for young knights and squires, eager to gain renown, willingly run into perils in hopes of honor.

The crowd was now so great, and so dangerous for those enclosed in it, that the men at arms, if not instantly assisted, could not raise themselves when once down. By this were several of the French killed and smothered; but they were not many, for, when in danger, they helped each other. There was a large and high amount of the Flemings who were slain; and never was there seen so little blood spilt at so great a battle, where such numbers were killed. When those in the rear saw the front fail, and that they were defeated, they were greatly astonished, and began to throw away their staves and armor, to disband, and fly toward Courtray and other places, not having any care but to save themselves if possible. The Bretons and French pursued them into ditches, alder-groves, and heaths, where they fought with and slew them. Numbers were killed in the pursuit, between the field of battle and Courtray, whither they were flying in their way to Ghent.

This battle on Mont d'Or took place the twenty-seventh day of November, on the Thursday before Advent, in the year of grace 1382; and at that time the King of France was fourteen years of age.

CHAPTER XXIV.

THE NUMBER OF SLAIN AT THE BATTLE OF ROSEBECQUE, AND PURSUIT
AFTERWARDS. — PHILIP VON ARTAVELD IS HANGED AFTER HE WAS
DEAD.

THUS were the Flemings defeated on Mont d'Or, their
pride humbled, and Philip von Artaveld slain; and
with him nine thousand men from Ghent and its dependencies (according to the report of the heralds) on the
spot, not including those killed in the pursuit, which
amounted to twenty-five thousand more. This battle,
from the beginning to the defeat, did not last more than
half an hour.

When the King of France arrived at his camp, where
his magnificent pavilion of red silk had been pitched, and
when he had been disarmed, his uncles, and many barons
of France, came, as was right, to attend him. Philip von
Artaveld then came into his mind, and he said, "If Philip
is dead or alive, I should like to see him." They replied,
they would have a search made for him. It was proclaimed through the army, that whoever should discover
the body of Philip von Artaveld should receive one hundred francs. Upon this the varlets examined the dead,
who were all stripped, or nearly so; and Philip through
avarice was so strictly sought after, that he was found by
a varlet, who had formerly served him some time, and who
knew him perfectly. He was dragged before the king's
pavilion. The king looked at him for some time, as did
the other lords. He was turned over and over to see if
he had died of wounds, but they found none that could

have caused his death. He had been squeezed in the crowd, and, falling into a ditch, numbers of Ghent men fell upon him, who died in his company. When they had sufficiently viewed him, he was taken from thence, and hanged on a tree. Such was the end of Philip von Artaveld.

BOOK III.*

CHAPTER I.

IN order to know the truth of distant transactions, without sending upon the inquiry any other in place of myself, I took an opportunity of visiting that high and redoubted prince Gaston Phœbus, Count de Foix and de Béarn; for I well knew, that if I were so fortunate as to be admitted into his household, and to remain there in quiet, I could not choose a situation more proper to learn the truth of every event, as numbers of foreign knights and squires assembled there from all countries, attracted by his high birth and gentility. It fell out just as I had imagined.

I told this my intention to my very renowned lord the Count de Blois, and also the journey I wished to undertake, who gave me letters of recommendation to the Count de Foix. I began my journey, inquiring on all sides for news; and, through the grace of God, continued it, without peril or hurt, until I arrived at the count's residence, at Orthès in Béarn, on St. Catherine's Day in the year of grace 1388. The Count de Foix, as soon as he saw me,

---

* I devote my selections from this book mainly to showing the manner in which the good canon Froissart picked up matter for his Chronicles from the conversation of chance travellers as he rode on his way; together with a glimpse of the handsome person and brilliant court of the great Béarnese lord Gaston Phœbus, Count de Foix. The time is the year 1388. — ED.

gave me a hearty welcome, adding, with a smile and in good French, that he was well acquainted with me, though he had never seen me before, but he had frequently heard me spoken of. He retained me in his household, and, by means of the letters which I had brought, gave me full liberty to act as I pleased as long as I should wish to remain with him. I there learnt the greater part of those events which had happened in the kingdoms of Castile, Portugal, Navarre, Aragon, even in England, in the Bourbonnois, and every thing concerning the whole of Gascony. He himself, when I put any question to him, answered it most readily, saying that the history I was employed on would in times to come be more sought after than any other; "because," added he, "my fair sir, more gallant deeds of arms have been performed within these last fifty years, and more wonderful things have happened, than for three hundred years before."

I was thus received by the Count de Foix in his hotel, and entertained according to my pleasure. My wish was to inquire after news relative to my history; and I had at my option barons, knights, and squires, who gave me information, as well as the gallant Count de Foix himself. I will therefore illustrate, in good language, all I there learnt, to add to my materials, and to give examples to those worthies who wish to advance themselves in renown. If I have heretofore dwelt on gallant deeds, attacks, and captures of castles, towns, and forts, on hard-fought battles and skirmishes, many more will now ensue; all of which, by God's grace, I will truly narrate.

CHAPTER II.

AT the time I undertook my journey to visit the Count de Foix, reflecting on the diversity of countries I had never seen, I set out from Carcassonne, leaving the road to Toulouse on the right hand, and came to Monteroral, then to Tonges, then to Belle, then to the first town in the county of Foix ; from thence to Maisieres, to the castle of Sauredun ; then to the handsome city of Pamiers, which belongs to the Count de Foix, where I halted to wait for company that were going to Béarn, where the count resided. I remained in the city of Pamiers three days ; it is a very delightful place, seated among fine vineyards, and surrounded by a clear and broad river called the Liege. Accidentally, a knight attached to the Count de Foix, called Sir Espaign du Lyon, came thither on his return from Avignon : he was a prudent and valiant knight, handsome in person, and about fifty years of age. I introduced myself to his company, as he had a great desire to know what was doing in France. We were six days on the road travelling to Orthès. As we journeyed, the knight, after saying his orisons, conversed the greater part of the day with me, asking for news ; and when I put any questions to him he very willingly answered them. On our departure from Pamiers we crossed the mountain of Cesse, which is difficult of ascent, and passed near the town and castle of Ortingas, which belongs to the King of France, but did not enter it. We went to dine at a castle of the Count de Foix, half a league farther, called Carlat, seated on a high mountain. After dinner the knight said, "Let us ride gently : we have but two leagues of this country (which are equal to three of France) to our lodging." — "Willingly," answered I. " Now," said the knight, " we have this day passed the castle of Ortingas, the garrison of which did great mischief to all this part of the country. Peter d'Anchin had possession of it ; he took it by surprise, and has gained sixty thousand francs from France." — " How did he get so much ?" said I. " I will tell you," replied the knight. " On the feast of Our Lady, the middle of August, a fair is holden, where all the country assemble, and there is much merchandise brought thither during that time. Peter d'Anchin and his companions of the garrison of Lourde had long wanted to gain this town and castle, but could not devise the means. They had, however, in the beginning of May, sent two of their men, of very simple outward appearance, to seek for service in the town : they soon found masters who were so well satisfied with them, that they went in and out of the town whenever they pleased, without any one having the smallest suspicion of them.

"When mid-August arrived, the town was filled with foreign merchants from Foix, Béarn, and France ; and you know, when merchants meet, after any considerable absence, they are accustomed to drink plentifully together to renew their acquaintance, so that the houses of the masters of the two servants were quite filled, where they drank largely, and their landlords with them. At midnight Peter d'Anchin and his company advanced toward Ortingas, and hid themselves and horses in the wood

through which we passed. He sent six varlets with two
ladders to the town, who, having crossed the ditches where
they had been told was the shallowest place, fixed their
ladders against the walls ; the two pretended servants,
who were in waiting, assisted them (while their masters
were seated at table) to mount the walls. They were no
sooner up, than one of the servants conducted their companions toward the gate where only two men guarded the
keys : he then said to them, ' Do you remain here, and not
stir until you shall hear me whistle; then sally forth, and
slay the guards. I am well acquainted with the keys,
having more than seven times guarded the gate with my
master.'

"As he had planned, so did they execute, and hid themselves well. He then advanced to the gate, and, having
listened, found the watch drinking: he called them by
their names, for he was acquainted with them, and said,
'Open the door : I bring you the best wine you ever
tasted, which my master sends you that you may watch
the better.' Those who knew the varlet imagined he was
speaking the truth, and opened the door of the guard-
room : upon this he whistled, and his companions sallied
forth, and pushed between the door, so that they could
not shut it again. The guards were thus caught cunningly, and so quietly slain that no one knew any thing
of it. They then took the keys, and went to the gate,
which they opened, and let down the drawbridge so gently
it was not heard. This done, they sounded a horn with
one blast only, which those in ambuscade hearing, they
mounted their horses, and came full gallop over the bridge
into the town, where they took all its inhabitants, either
at table or in their beds. Thus was Ortingas taken by
Peter d'Anchin of Bigorre and his companions in Lourde."

I then asked the knight, "But how did they gain the castle?"—"I will tell you," said Sir Espaign du Lyon. "At the time the town was taken, by ill-luck the governor was absent, supping with some merchants from Carcassonne, so that he was made prisoner; and on the morrow Peter d'Anchin had him brought before the castle wherein were his wife and children, whom he frightened by declaring he would order the governor's head to be struck off if they did not enter into a treaty to deliver up the castle. It was concluded, that, if his lady would surrender, the governor should be given up to her, with permission to march unmolested away with every thing that belonged to them. The lady, who found herself in such a critical situation, through love to him who could not now defend her, in order to recover her husband and to avoid greater dangers, surrendered the castle, when the governor, his wife, and children, set out with all that belonged to them, and went to Pamiers. By this means Peter d'Anchin captured the town and castle of Ortingas; and, when they entered the place, he and his companions gained thirty thousand francs, as well in merchandise which they found there, as in good French prisoners. All those who were from the county of Foix or Béarn received their liberty, with their goods untouched.

"Peter d'Anchin held Ortingas for full five years; and he and his garrison made frequent excursions as far as the gates of Carcassonne, which is sixteen long leagues distant, greatly ruining the country, as well by the ransoms of towns which compounded, as by the pillage they made. During the time Peter d'Anchin garrisoned Ortingas, some of his companions made a sally, being desirous of gain, and came to a castle a good league off, called Le Paillier, of which Raymond du Paillier, a French knight, was the lord. They this time accomplished their enterprise, having before attempted it in vain; and, by means of a scalado, they took the castle, the knight and his lady in bed. They kept possession of it, allowing the lady and the children to depart, but detained the knight four months in his own castle, until he had paid four thousand francs for his ransom. In short, after they had sufficiently harassed the country, they sold these two castles, Ortingas and Le Paillier, for eight thousand francs, and then retired to Lourde, their principal garrison. Such feats of arms and adventures were these companions daily practising.

CHAPTER III.

FROISSART CONTINUES HIS JOURNEY. — IN TRAVELLING FROM TOURNAY TO TARBES, THE KNIGHT RELATES TO HIM HOW THE GARRISON OF LOURDE HAD A SHARP RENCOUNTER WITH THE FRENCH FROM THE ADJACENT GARRISONS.

IN the morning we mounted our horses, set out from Tournay, passed the river Lesse at a ford, and, riding toward the city of Tarbes, entered Bigorre.

I recollected what he had said some days before respecting the country of Larre and Mengeant de Lourde, and, reminding him of them, said, "My lord, you promised that when we came to the country of Larre, you would tell me more of Mengeant de Lourde, and the manner of his death." — "It is true," replied the knight: "come and ride by my side, and I will tell it you." I then pushed forward to hear him the better, when he began as follows : —

"During the time Peter d'Anchin held the castle and garrison of Ortingas, as I have before related, those of

Lourde made frequent excursions at a distance from their fort, when they had not always the advantage.

"It was told to the governor of Tarbes, a squire of Gascony, called Ernauton Biffete, how those of Lourde were overrunning and harassing the country; and he sent information of this to the Lord de Benach and to Enguerros de Lane, son of Sir Raymond, and also to the Lord de Barbasan, adding, he was determined to attack them. These knights and squires of Bigorre, having agreed to join him, assembled their men in the town of Tournay, through which the garrison of Lourde generally returned. When those of Lourde heard that the French garrisons were waiting for them at Tournay, they began to be alarmed, and called a council to determine how to conduct their pillage in safety. It was resolved to divide themselves into two parties : one, consisting of servants and pillagers, was to drive the booty, and take by-roads to Lanebourg, crossing the bridge of Tournay, and the river Lesse between Tournay and Malvoisin; the other division was to march in order of battle on the high grounds, and to make an appearance as if they meant to return by the pass of Larre below Marteras, but to fall back between Barbasan and Montgaillard, in order that the baggage might cross the river in safety. They were to meet all together at Montgaillard, from whence they would soon be at Lourde.

"The French, in like manner as those of Lourde, had called a council respecting their mode of acting. Sir Monant de Barbasan and Ernauton Biscete said, ' Since we know the men of Lourde are bringing home great plunder and many prisoners, we shall be much vexed if they escape us : let us therefore form two ambuscades, for we are enough for both.' Upon this it was ordered, that Le Bourg d'Espaign, Sir Raymond de Benach, and Enguerros de Lane, with one hundred spears, should guard the passage at Tournay, for the cattle and prisoners must necessarily cross the river; and the Lord de Barbasan and Ernauton Biscete, with the other hundred lances, should reconnoitre, if perchance they could come up with them. They separated from each other; and the Lord de Benach, and Le Bourg d'Espaign, placed themselves in ambuscade at the bridge between Tournay and Malvoisin. The other division rode to the spot where we now are, which is called the Larre, and there the two parties met. They instantly dismounted, and, leaving their horses to pasture, with pointed lances advanced, for a combat was unavoidable, shouting their cries, 'St. George for Lourde!' 'Our Lady for Bigorre!'

"They charged each other, thrusting their spears with all their strength, and, to add greater force, urged them forward with their breasts. The combat was very equal; and for some time none were struck down, as I heard from those present. When they had sufficiently used their spears, they threw them down, and with battle-axes began to deal out terrible blows on both sides. When any were so worsted or out of breath that they could not longer support the fight, they seated themselves near a large ditch full of water in the middle of the plain, when, having taken off their helmets, they refreshed themselves: this done, they replaced their helmets, and returned to the combat. I do not believe there ever was so well-fought or so severe a battle as this of Marteras in Bigorre, since the famous combat of thirty English against thirty French knights in Brittany.

"They fought hand to hand; and Ernauton de Sainte Colombe, an excellent man at arms, was on the point of being killed by a squire of the country called Guillonet de

Salenges, who had pushed him so hard that he was quite out of breath, when I will tell you what happened: Ernauton de Sainte Colombe had a servant who was a spectator of the battle, neither attacking nor attacked by any one; but, seeing his master thus distressed, he ran to him, and, wresting the battle-axe from his hands, said, 'Ernauton, go and sit down: recover yourself: you cannot longer continue the battle.' With this battle-axe he advanced upon the squire, and gave him such a blow on the helmet as made him stagger and almost fall down. Guillonet, smarting from the blow, was very wroth, and made for the servant to strike him with his axe on the head; but the varlet avoided it, and grappling with the squire, who was much fatigued, turned him round, and flung him to the ground under him, when he said, 'I will put you to death, if you do not surrender yourself to my master.'—'And who is thy master?'—'Ernauton de Sainte Colombe, with whom you have been so long engaged.' The squire, finding he had not the advantage, being under the servant, who had his dagger ready to strike, surrendered on condition to deliver himself prisoner, within fifteen days, at the castle of Lourde, whether rescued or not. Of such service was this servant to his master; and I must say, Sir John, that there was a superabundance of feats of arms that day performed, and many companions were sworn to surrender themselves at Tarbes and at Lourde. Ernauton Biscete and Le Mengeant de Sainte Basile fought hand to hand, without sparing themselves, and performed many gallant deeds, while all the others were fully employed: however, they fought so vigorously that they exhausted their strength, and both were slain on the spot. Thus fell Ernauton Biscete and Le Mengeant de Sainte Basile."

"By my faith," said I to the knight, "I have listened to

How the Bourg d'Espaign fed the Fire in the great Fire-place of the Count of Foix.

you with pleasure ; and in truth it was a very severe affair
for so small a number. But what became of those who
conducted the pillage ?" — "I will tell you," replied he.
"At the bridge of Tournay, below Malvoisin, where they
intended to cross, they found the Bourg d'Espaign in
ambuscade, who, on their arrival, sallied out upon them,
being in sufficient force. Those of Lourde could not
retreat, and were obliged to abide the event. I must truly
say that the combat was as severe and as long, if not
longer than that at Marteras. The Bourg d'Espaign performed wonders : he wielded a battle-axe, and never hit a
man with it but he struck him to the ground. He was
well formed for this, being of a large size, strongly made,
and not too much loaded with flesh. He took with his
own hand the two captains, the Bourg de Cornillac and
Perot Palatin de Béarn."

"Holy Mary!" said I to the knight, "this Bourg d'Espaign, is he so strong a man as you tell me?" — "Yes,
that he is, by my troth," said he, "and you will not find
his equal in all Gascony for vigor of body : it is for this
the Count de Foix esteems him as his brother in arms.
Three years ago I saw him play a ridiculous trick, which
I will relate to you. On Christmas Day, when the Count
de Foix was celebrating the feast with numbers of knights
and squires, as is customary, the weather was piercing
cold ; and the count had dined, with many lords, in the
hall. After dinner he rose, and went into a gallery, which
has a large staircase of twenty-four steps : in this gallery
is a chimney where is a fire kept when the count inhabits
it, otherwise not ; and the fire is never great, for he does
not like it : it is not for want of blocks of wood, for Béarn
is covered with wood in plenty to warm him if he had
chosen it, but he has accustomed himself to a small fire.

When in the gallery he thought the fire too small, for it was freezing, and the weather very sharp; and said to the knights around him, 'Here is but a small fire for this weather.' Ernauton d'Espaign instantly ran down stairs (for, from the windows of the gallery which looked into the court, he had seen a number of asses with billets of wood for the use of the house), and seizing the largest of these asses, with his load, threw him over his shoulders, and carried him up stairs, pushing through the crowd of knights and squires who were around the chimney, and flung ass and load, with his feet upward, on the dogs of the hearth; to the delight of the count, and the astonishment of all, at the strength of the squire, who had carried, with such ease, so great a load up so many steps."

This feat of strength did I hear; and all the histories of Sir Espaign du Lyon gave me such satisfaction and delight, I thought the road was much too short.

CHAPTER IV.

SIR JOHN FROISSART ARRIVES AT ORTHÈS. — AN OLD SQUIRE RELATES
TO HIM THE CRUEL DEATH OF THE ONLY SON OF THE COUNT DE FOIX.

ON the morrow we set out, and dined at Montgerbal, when having remounted, and drunk a cup at Ercie, we arrived by sunset at Orthès. The knight dismounted at his own house; and I did the same at the Hotel of the Moon, kept by a squire of the count, called Ernauton du Pin, who received me with much pleasure on account of my being a Frenchman. Sir Espaign du Lyon, who had accompanied me, went to the castle to speak with the count on his affairs. He found him in his gallery, for a little before that hour he had dined. It was a custom with the count, which he had followed from his infancy, to rise at noon, and sup at midnight.

The knight informed him of my arrival, and I was instantly sent for; for he is a lord above all others who delights to see strangers, in order to hear news. On my entering, he received me handsomely, and retained me of his household; where I staid upward of twelve weeks well entertained, as were my horses. Our acquaintance was strengthened by my having brought with me a book which I had made at the desire of Winceslaus of Bohemia, Duke of Luxembourg and Brabant. In this book, called "Le Meliâdor," are contained all the songs, ballads, roundelays, and virelays, which that gentle duke had composed, and of them I had made this collection. Every night after supper I read out to him parts; during which time neither he nor any one else spoke, for he was desirous I should be well heard, and took much delight in it. When any passages were not perfectly clear, he himself discussed them with me, not in his Gascon language, but in very good French.

I shall relate to you several things respecting him and his household, for I tarried there as long as I could gain any information. Count Gaston Phœbus de Foix, of whom I am now speaking, was at that time fifty-nine years old; and I must say, that although I have seen very many knights, kings, princes, and others, I have never seen any so handsome, either in the form of his limbs and shape, or in countenance, which was fair and ruddy, with gray and tender eyes, that gave delight whenever he chose to express affection. He was so perfectly formed, one could not praise him too much. He loved earnestly the things he ought to love, and hated those which it was becoming him so to hate. He was a prudent knight, full of enterprise and wisdom. He had never any men of abandoned character with him, reigned prudently, and was constant in his devotions. There were regular nocturnals from the Psalter, prayers from the rituals to the Virgin, to the Holy Ghost, and from the burial-service. He had every day distributed as alms, at his gate, five florins in small coin, to all comers. He was liberal and courteous in his gifts; and well knew how to take when it was proper, and to give back where he had confidence. He mightily loved dogs above all other animals, and during the summer and winter amused himself much with hunting. He never liked any foolish works nor ridiculous extravagances; and would know every month the amount of his expenditure. He chose from his own subjects twelve of the most able to receive and administer his finances: two of them had the management for two months, when they were changed for two others; and from them he selected one as comptroller, in whom he placed his greatest confidence, and to whom all others rendered their accounts. This comptroller accounted by rolls or written books, which were laid before the count. He had certain coffers in his apartment, from whence he took money to give to different knights, squires, or gentlemen, when they came to wait on him, for none ever left him without a gift; and these sums he continually increased, in order to be prepared for any event that might happen. He was easy of access to all, and entered very freely into discourse, though laconic in his advice and in his answers. He employed four secretaries to write and copy his letters; and these secretaries were obliged to be in readiness the moment he came out from his closet. He called them neither John, Walter, nor William, but his good-for-nothings, to whom he gave his letters after he had read them, either to copy, or to do any thing else he might command.

In such manner did the Count de Foix live. When he quitted his chamber at midnight for supper, twelve servants bore each a lighted torch before him, which were placed near his table, and gave a brilliant light to the apartment. The hall was full of knights and squires; and there were plenty of tables laid out for any person who chose to sup. No one spoke to him at his table, unless he first began a conversation. He commonly ate heartily of poultry, but only the wings and thighs; for in the daytime he neither ate nor drank much. He had great pleasure in hearing minstrels, as he himself was a proficient in the science, and made his secretaries sing songs, ballads, and roundelays. He remained at table about two hours; and was pleased when fanciful dishes were served up to him, which having seen, he immediately sent them to the tables of his knights and squires.

In short, every thing considered, though I had before been in several courts of kings, dukes, princes, counts, and noble ladies, I was never at one that pleased me more, nor was I ever more delighted with feats of arms, than at this of the Count de Foix.

I was very anxious to know, seeing the hotel of the count so spacious and so amply supplied, what was become of his son Gaston, and by what accident he had died, for Sir Espaign du Lyon would never satisfy my curiosity. I had made so many inquiries, that at last an old and intelligent squire informed me : —

"Gaston, the son of my lord, grew up, and became a fine young gentleman. He was married to the daughter of the Count d'Armagnac, sister to the present count and to Sir Bernard d'Armagnac; and by this union peace was insured between Foix and Armagnac. The youth might be about fifteen or sixteen years old: he was a very handsome figure, and the exact resemblance of his father in his whole form.

"He took it into his head to make a journey into Navarre, to visit his mother * and uncle ; but it was an unfortunate journey for him and for this country. On his arrival at Navarre, he was splendidly entertained ; and he staid some time with his mother. On taking leave, he could not prevail on her, notwithstanding his remonstrances and entreaties, to accompany him back ; for, the lady having asked if the Count de Foix, his father, had ordered him to bring her back, he replied that when he set out no such orders had been given ; which caused her to fear trusting herself with him. She therefore remained ; and the heir of Foix went to Pampeluna to take leave of his uncle. The king entertained him well, and detained him upward of ten days. On his departure, he made him handsome presents, and did the same by his attendants. The last gift the king gave him was the cause of his death, and I will tell you how it happened. As the youth was on the point of setting out, the king took him privately into his chamber, and gave him a bag full of powder, which was of such pernicious quality as would cause the death of any one that ate of it. 'Gaston, my fair nephew,' said the king, 'will you do what I am about to tell you? You see how unjustly the Count de Foix hates your mother, who . being my sister, it displeases me as much as it should you. If you wish to reconcile your father to your mother, you must take a small pinch of this powder, and, when you see a proper opportunity, strew it over the meat destined for

---

* His mother had been sent by her husband to bring home her dowry, in the hands of her brother the King of Navarre. The latter refused to send it ; and the lady therefore remained in his country, fearing the anger of her husband if she should return without it. — Ed.

your father's table; but take care no one sees you. The
instant he shall have tasted it, he will be impatient for his
wife, your mother, to return to him; and they will love
each other henceforward so strongly, they will never again
be separated. You ought to be anxious to see this accomplished. Do not tell it to any one; for, if you do, it will
lose its effect.' The youth, who believed every thing his
uncle the King of Navarre had told him, replied, he would
cheerfully do as he had said; and on this he departed from
Pampeluna, on his return to Orthès. His father the Count
de Foix received him with pleasure, and asked what was the
news in Navarre, and what presents and jewels had been
given him; he replied, 'Very handsome ones,' and showed
them all, except the bag which contained the powder.

"It was customary, in the hotel de Foix, for Gaston
and his bastard brother Evan to sleep in the same chamber. They mutually loved each other, and were dressed
alike, for they were nearly of the same size and age. It
fell out, that their clothes were once mixed together; and,
the coat of Gaston being on the bed, Evan, who was malicious enough, noticing the powder in the bag, said to
Gaston, 'What is this that you wear every day on your
breast?' Gaston was not pleased at the question, and
replied, 'Give me back my coat, Evan: you have nothing
to do with it.' Evan flung him his coat, which Gaston put
on, but was very pensive the whole day. Three days after,
as if God was desirous of saving the life of the Count de
Foix, Gaston quarrelled with Evan at tennis, and gave him
a box on the ear. The boy was vexed at this, and ran crying to the apartment of the count, who had just heard
mass. The count, on seeing him in tears, asked what was
the matter. 'In God's name, my lord,' replied Evan, 'Gaston has beaten me; but he deserves beating much more

than I do.'—'For what reason?' said the count, who began
to have some suspicions. 'On my faith,' said Evan, 'ever
since his return from Navarre, he wears on his breast a
bag of powder: I know not what use it can be of, nor what
he intends to do with it; except that he has once or twice
told me, his mother would soon return hither, and be more
in your good graces than ever she was.'—'Ho!' said the
count, 'hold thy tongue, and be sure thou do not mention
what thou hast just told me to any man breathing.'—'My
lord,' replied the youth, 'I will obey you.' The Count de
Foix was very thoughtful on this subject, and remained
alone until dinner-time, when he rose up, and seated himself as usual at his table in the hall. His son Gaston always placed the dishes before him, and tasted the meats.*
As soon as he had served the first dish, and done what
was usual, the count cast his eyes on him, having formed
his plan, and saw the strings of the bag hanging from his
pourpoint. This sight made his blood boil, and he said,
'Gaston, come hither: I want to whisper you something.'
The youth advanced to the table, when the count, opening
his bosom, undid his pourpoint, and with his knife cut
away the bag. The young man was thunderstruck, and
said not a word, but turned pale with fear, and began to
tremble exceedingly, for he was conscious he had done
wrong. The count opened the bag, took some of the powder, which he strewed over a slice of bread, and, calling a
dog to him, gave it him to eat. The instant the dog had
eaten a morsel, his eyes rolled round in his head, and he
died. The count on this was very wroth, and indeed had
reason. Rising from table, he would have struck his son

---

* The young readers of Froissart may remember this passage when they
come to read Chaucer's account of the young squire who "Carf byforn his
fadur at the table" (i.e., *carved before his father at the table*). — ED.

with a knife; but the knights and squires rushed in between them, saying, 'For God's sake, my lord, do not be too hasty, but make further inquiries before you do any ill to your son.' The first words the count uttered were in Gascon: 'Ho, Gaston, thou traitor! for thee, and to increase thy inheritance which would have come to thee, have I made war, and incurred the hatred of the kings of France, England, Spain, Navarre, and Aragon, and have borne myself gallantly against them; and thou wishest to murder me! Thy disposition must be infamously bad: know therefore thou shalt die with this blow.' And leaping over the table, with a knife in his hand, he would have slain him; but the knights and squires again interfered, and on their knees said to him with tears, 'Ah, ah! my lord, for Heaven's sake, do not kill Gaston: you have no other child. Let him be confined, and inquire further into the business. Perhaps he was ignorant what was in the bag, and may therefore be blameless.' — 'Well,' replied the count, 'let him be confined in the dungeon, but so safely guarded that he may be forthcoming.' The youth was therefore confined in this tower. I will tell you the cause of his death, since I have said so much on the subject. The Count de Foix had caused him to be confined in a room of the dungeon where was little light: there he remained for ten days. He scarcely ate or drank any thing of the food which was regularly brought to him, but threw it aside. The count would not permit any one to remain in the chamber to advise or comfort him: he therefore never put off the clothes he had on when he entered his prison. This made him melancholy, and vexed him, for he did not expect so much harshness: he therefore cursed the hour he was born, and lamented that he should come to such an end. On the day of his death, those who

brought him food said, 'Gaston, here is meat for you.'
He paid not any attention to it, but said, 'Put it down.'
The person who served him, looking about, saw all the
meat untouched that he had brought thither the last days :
then, shutting the door, he went to the count, and said,
'My lord, for God's sake, look to your son : he is starving
himself in his prison. I do not believe he has eaten any
thing since his confinement ; for I see all that I have
carried to him lying on one side untouched.' On hearing
this, the count was enraged, and, without saying a word,
left his apartment, and went to the prison of his son. In
an evil hour, he had in his hand a knife, with which he
had been paring and cleaning his nails ; he held it by the
blade so closely that scarcely the thickness of a groat
appeared of the point, when, pushing aside the tapestry
that covered the entrance of the prison, through ill luck,
he hit his son on a vein of his throat, as he uttered, 'Ha,
traitor, why dost thou not eat?' and instantly left the
room, without saying or doing any thing more. The youth
was much frightened at his father's arrival, and withal
exceedingly weak from fasting. The point of the knife,
small as it was, cut a vein, which as soon as he felt he
turned himself on one side, and died. The count had
barely got back again to his apartment, when the attendants of his son came, and said, 'My lord, Gaston is dead.'
—'Dead!' cried the count. 'Yes, God help me! indeed
he is, my lord.' The count would not believe it, and sent
one of his knights to see. The knight, on his return, confirmed the news. The count was now bitterly affected,
and cried out, 'Ha, ha, Gaston! what a sorry business has
this turned out for thee and me! In an evil hour didst
thou go to visit thy mother in Navarre. Never shall I
again enjoy the happiness I had formerly.' He then or-

dered his barber to be sent for, and was shaven quite bare. He clothed himself, as well as his whole household, in black. The body of the youth was borne, with tears and lamentations, to the church of the Augustine Friars at Orthès, where it was buried. Thus have I related to you the death of Gaston de Foix: his father killed him indeed, but the King of Navarre was the cause of this sad event."

BOOK IV.*

CHAPTER I.

I HAVE delayed, for a long time, speaking of a grand and noble enterprise that was undertaken by some knights of France, England, and other countries, against the kingdom of Barbary. The text of the subject I mean to proceed on says, that about this time the Genoese were reported throughout France and other countries, to be desirous of raising a large army to invade Barbary; and that all knights, squires, or men at arms, who would engage in this expedition, should be supplied with such purveyances as biscuit, fresh water, vinegar, and vessels and galleys to transport them thither.

The cause of their forming this armament was, that the Africans had attacked the country of Genoa, plundering the islands belonging to them, and carrying off such from the coasts of Genoa as were not on their guard, by which they were kept under continual alarms. They possessed also a town, situated on the sea-shore of Barbary, which

* For the sake of further variety I extract from Froissart's fourth volume a lively picture of a crusade against the Saracens. The time is the last decade of the fourteenth century; more particularly, two months of the year 1390. — ED.

is beyond measure strong, and called Africa, surrounded with high walls, gates, and deep ditches. Like as the strong town of Calais is the key to France and Flanders, and whoever is master of it may at all times enter those countries, and from thence may be sent a powerful force by sea, to do mischief to their neighbors; just so is the town of Africa the stronghold of the inhabitants of Barbary, Bugia, and Tunis, and other infidel countries. The Genoese, who are rich merchants, bore great hatred to this town; for its corsairs frequently watched them at sea, and, when strongest, fell on and plundered their ships, carrying their spoils to this town of Africa, which was, and is now, their place of deposit, and may be called their warren.

The Genoese, to put an end to such conduct, and satisfy the complaints of their subjects, that were daily made to them, determined to make their situation known to the court of France, and to offer to such knights as would undertake an expedition against the infidels, vessels of provision, with a passage thither and back free of all costs, provided that one of the king's uncles, or his brother the Duke of Touraine (who, being young, ought to labor to gain renown), would take the chief command. They likewise offered the aid of pilgrims, from foreign parts to assist them, twelve thousand select Genoese crossbows, and eight thousand infantry armed with spears and shields, all at their expense. They imagined, that as now there was a truce between France, England, and their allies, their knights would, from having nothing to do, be glad to join in this warfare, and that they should have numbers of them from those kingdoms.

When this intelligence was first brought to the French knights, they were much rejoiced, in hope of gaining honor; and the ambassadors from Genoa were told they should not return without their business being attended to, and succor afforded them, for their anxiety to extend the Christian faith was very praiseworthy. They waited at Paris, while it was under deliberation of the council who should be appointed commander-in-chief. The Duke of Touraine offered his services to the king and council; but they, as well as the Dukes of Berry and Burgundy, remonstrated, that this command was not fit for him. They considered, that as the Genoese insisted on the king's brother, or one of his uncles, taking the command, the Duke of Bourbon would be the most proper person, and that he should have for his second the Lord de Coucy. The Genoese ambassadors having received a favorable answer from the king, and certain assurances of being assisted with knights and men at arms from France, under the command of the Duke of Bourbon, in the course of the year, were greatly contented. They took leave of the king, and returned to their own country, to relate the good news, and make preparations accordingly.

Reports of an invasion of Barbary were soon spread throughout France. To some knights and squires it was agreeable, to others the contrary. All who were desirous of going thither could not, as it would have been at their own charges, for no lord paid for any but those of his own household. It was also ordered, that no one from France should make part of this expedition but such as had the king's leave, for the council wished not the realm to be void of defence; and the Genoese were expressly bound not to suffer any servants to embark, but solely such as were gentlemen, and who could be depended upon. It was, besides, meant as a compliment to the knights and squires of other nations who might wish to join in the enterprise. This regulation gave pleasure to all foreign knights who heard of it. The Duke of Bourbon, having accepted the command, sent his servants to Genoa, where they were to embark, to make the necessary preparations for him and his household. The gallant Count d'Auvergne, who was likewise of the expedition, did the same. The Lord de Coucy, Sir Guy de la Tremouille, Sir John de Vienne, and all the great barons and knights of France who had obtained leave to make part of this army, were not behindhand in sending thither purveyances suitable to their state. The Lord Philip d'Artois, Count d'Eu, Sir Philip de Bar, the Lord de Harcourt, Sir Henry d'Antoing, did so likewise. From Brittany and Normandy many great lords made preparations for this expedition to Barbary, as well as from Hainault; among the last were the Lord de Ligne and the Lord de Havreth. Several knights came from Flanders; and the Duke of Lancaster had a bastard son, called Henry de Beaufort, whom, through devotion, he sent thither. He had him well accompanied by many knights and squires of rank in England.

The Count de Foix was unwilling his bastard son, Evan of Foix, should remain behind, and had him properly attended by knights and squires, as he wished him to keep his state grandly. Every one had taken care to send beforehand all he should want; and those at the greatest distance from Genoa left their countries the middle of May, but it was about a month before all were assembled. The Genoese were well pleased on their arrival, and made handsome and rich presents to the chiefs, the better to secure their affections. As the knights arrived, they were posted adjoining each other, and, on being mustered by the marshals, amounted to fourteen hundred knights and squires. They were embarked on board of ships and galleys, that had been properly equipped for the voyage, on St. John Baptist's Day, in the year of grace 1390.

It was a beautiful sight to view this fleet, with the emblazoned banners of the different lords glittering in the sun and fluttering in the wind: and to hear the minstrels and other musicians sounding their pipes, clarions, and trumpets, whose sounds were re-echoed back by the sea. When all were embarked, they cast anchor, and remained that night at the mouth of the harbor; but the servants and horses were left behind on shore. A horse worth fifty francs was on their embarkation sold for ten, as many of the knights and squires were uncertain when, or if ever, they should return, and the keep of five horses at Genoa was upward of a franc a day: they therefore, on departing, made of them what money they could, but it was little enough.

There were about three hundred galleys to transport the men at arms and archers, and upward of one hundred vessels for the purveyances and other necessaries. On the morrow, at daybreak, they weighed anchor, and rode coastwise that and the succeeding night. The third day they made Port-fino, where they lay that night: at sunrise they rowed to Porto-Venere, and again cast anchor. The ensuing morning they weighed, and took to the deep, putting themselves under the protection of God and St. George. When they had passed the island of Elba, they encountered a violent tempest, which drove them back by Gorgona, Sardinia, and Corsica, into the Gulf of Lyons, a position always dangerous; but they could not avoid it, for the tempest was so violent, that the ablest mariner could not do any thing to prevent their running the utmost risk of destruction: they waited therefore the will of God. This storm lasted a day and night, and dispersed the fleet.

When the weather became calm, and the sea tranquil, the pilots, who were acquainted with those seas, steered as directly as they could for the island of Commeres, which is but thirty miles from the town of Africa, whither they bent their course. The masters of the vessels had held a council before they entered the Gulf of Lyons, and determined, that, should they part company, they would rendezvous at the island of Commeres, and wait there until they were all assembled. This plan was adopted; and it was upward of nine days before all were collected, so much had they been scattered.

The island of Commeres, though not large, is very pleasant. The lords there refreshed themselves, and praised God for having all met again without essential loss or damage. When on the eve of departure, the French lords, who took the lead, held a council on their future proceedings, as they were now so near the port of Africa.

CHAPTER II.

THE CHRISTIAN LORDS WEIGH ANCHOR, AND LEAVE THE ISLAND OF COMINO, IN ORDER TO LAY SIEGE TO THE TOWN OF AFRICA. — THE MANNER IN WHICH THEY CONDUCT THEMSELVES.

THEY addressed the masters of the galleys as follows : "Gentlemen, we are now on the nearest land to the strong town of Africa, whither, if it please God, we will go, and besiege it. We must therefore consult with you how we may enter the harbor and disembark. We propose to send in advance our smaller vessels, called brigandines, to amuse the enemy, while we remain at the mouth of the harbor; on the following day we will at our leisure

land, through God's grace, and encamp ourselves as near
the town as possible, out of the reach of their bricolles.*
The Genoese crossbows shall be drawn up, and ready for
defence or attack. We suppose that, on our debarkation,
a multitude of your young squires will demand to be
knighted, for increase of honor and advancement. In-
struct them gently how they ought to act, for you are very
capable of doing it; and know, gentlemen, that we are
well inclined to acquit ourselves handsomely toward you;
and, to show our eagerness to annoy the enemy, we shall
take every possible pains that this town of Africa may be
won. It has done you too great damage to be longer endured, and is, besides, the key to the empire of Barbary
and the surrounding kingdoms of Africa, Morocco, and
Bugia. Should God, of his goodness, permit us to conquer it, all the Saracens will tremble, as far as Nubia and
Syria, and we shall be everywhere talked of. With the
assistance of the princes of Christendom, who are the
nearest to us, we may re-enforce it with men, and victual it
again; so that, if once we gain possession, it will become
a place for all knights and squires to adventure themselves
in arms against the enemies of God, and conquer their
lands." — "My lords," replied the masters of the vessels,
"we shall never pretend to teach you how to act, but give
our opinions with all modesty and humility; for you are
too noble, wise, and valiant, for us to pretend to lay down
rules for your conduct." The Lord de Coucy said, "We
should, however, wish to have your opinions, for we have
observed nothing but what is praiseworthy in you; and, as
it is you who have brought us hither, to accomplish deeds
of arms, we shall never act without having your advice."
Such were the conversations held in the presence of the

* Machines for throwing stones. — ED.

Duke of Bourbon, the Count d'Eu, and some of the great barons of France, with the captains of the Genoese vessels, before they sailed for the coast of Africa.

When all was ready, and the men at arms had re-embarked on board their galleys, with a good will to meet their enemies the Saracens, the admiral gave orders for the trumpets to sound, and the fleet to get under way. The sea was now calm, and the weather fine : it was a pleasure to see the rowers force their vessels through its smooth surface, which seemed to delight in bearing these Christians to the shores of the infidels. Their fleet was numerous and well ordered ; and it was a fine sight to view their various banners and pennons, emblazoned with their arms, fluttering with the gentle gales, and glittering in the sun. Late in the evening, the Christians saw the towers of Africa, as pointed out to them by the sailors, which, as they advanced, opened more to their view. Every one was rejoiced at this sight, and not without cause, as they had in part accomplished the object of their voyage. If the Christians, on thus seeing Africa, conversed much concerning the war they were about to commence, the Saracens, who had so plainly observed them from their town, and were on the watch, did the same. They were astonished at the great number of vessels, of all descriptions, and concluded they had a very large army on board to besiege the town. They were not cast down with this, for they knew the place was strong, well fortified with towers, and plentifully stored with artillery and provisions.

On their first noticing the fleet, they sounded, according to custom, a number of bells on the towers, to alarm and inform the country that an enemy was on the coast. There were encamped near the town a large body of barbarians and infidels, whom the kings of Tunis and Bugia had sent thither to defend the coast, and prevent the Christians from making any progress into the interior of the country. The noise of the trumpets and drums announced the arrival of the Christians; and, in consequence, they formed their army according to their manner, and sent some of the ablest captains to the shore to observe the motions of the enemy, and the manner of their debarkation. They also posted their most expert men at arms on the towers and battlements of the town, that they might not be taken by surprise; for it was strong enough to resist every thing but a long siege, if they were on their guard.

As I, John Froissart, the author of these Chronicles, was never in Africa, I sought all the information I could from those knights and squires who had been on this expedition, and made several journeys to Calais to learn the truth of all that passed. [Having inquired as to the size and form of the town of Africa, some who had been there figured it out to me, and said it was in the form of a bow, like to Calais, extending its arms toward the sea. This town of Africa, at the time the lords of France and other nations were before it with an anxious desire to win it, was wonderfully strong, surrounded with high walls at proper distances. The entrance of the harbor was defended by a tower larger than the rest, on which was placed a bricolle to cast large stones and quarrels, with which it was well provided.

When the Christians approached the harbor, the walls of the town seemed to be hung with cloths or tapestry, somewhat similar in appearance to coverlets of beds. They cast anchor about one league distant from the port, where they remained until the morrow. The night was

clear and serene, for it was the month of July, about Magdalen-tide; and they made themselves comfortable, rejoi-
cing that, through God's pleasure, they had so far succeeded as to have the town of Africa now before them.

The Saracens, who were on the opposite shore watch-
ing the Christian fleet, held this night a council on their
future mode of proceeding, for they knew the town would
be besieged. They thus conversed among themselves:
"Our enemies are now arrived: they will, if they can, land,
and lay siege to Africa, which is the key to the adjoining
kingdoms. We must therefore consider well our plans for
opposing them: otherwise we shall be greatly blamed, and
especially if we should not at first dispute their landing."
It was proposed by a valiant Saracen, called Mandifer,
to resist their landing, as being the most honorable; and
to oppose them instantly with their whole force, or they
would probably have fault found with them. This was
strongly supported by many, as it seemed the most courageous plan; when an ancient Saracen began to speak, who
had great influence among them, as he showed. This lord
came from a town in Africa called Maldages, and his name
was Bellius. He gave his opinion quite contrary to that
of Mandifer, and supported it with the following reasons:
"Gentlemen, we are sent hither to guard the coast, and
defend this country; but we have no orders from the
kings of Tunis or of Bugia to attack our enemies without
having maturely considered the consequences. What I
have to propose, I will maintain by such reasons as these:
First, you must suppose that this army of Christians has
been long in preparation, and is provided with all things
necessary. Their captains, you may also believe, are perfect men at arms, as able in council as in the field, with
the greatest ardor to perform deeds of arms. If we meet

them on the shore, they will advance their Genoese cross-bows, for you may be assured they have brought numbers of them. It will be against them who have such excellent crossbows, that we must support the first attack; and we are not armed, nor have we shields to guard us against their arrows. Our men, finding themselves wounded, will draw back, and refuse the combat, so that these Genoese will make good their landing in spite of us. Their men at arms, desirous of displaying their courage, will leap from their boats, and, observing our disorder, will attack us with lances, and gain a victory. Should this happen, the town of Africa is irrecoverably lost, for any thing we can do to prevent it. Those within will be so much discouraged by our defeat, that, before our men can be rallied, the place will be taken by storm or capitulation, and be so well guarded that we shall have the greatest difficulty to regain it. The French, and those with them, are very expert and subtle in arms. I therefore maintain, that it will be more to our advantage that the enemy should be ignorant of our force at the onset; for at this moment we have not a sufficiency to offer them battle, though our strength is daily increasing. I advise, that we suffer them to disembark at their ease; for, as they have no horses to advance into the country, they will remain where they land, suspicious of our intentions.] The town of Africa is not afraid of them, nor of their attacks; for it is tolerably strong, and well provided with every thing. The air is now warm, and will be hotter. They will be exposed to the heat of the sun, while we shall be in the shade. Their provisions will be destroyed, without hopes of having a supply, if they make any long stay, and we shall have abundance from our own country: we will frequently beat up their quarters; and, should they be unfortunate in these skirmishes, they will be worn down. We must avoid all general engagements, otherwise we cannot conquer them; but we shall do it by this plan, and trusting to the climate, which is contrary to the nature of their constitutions. [They will not have any re-enforcements, and we shall have many. The extreme heat of the sun, and the fatigue they will undergo from being always armed in fear of us, will very soon bring on disorders which will carry numbers to the grave; and thus shall we be revenged without striking a blow.] Such is the plan I propose; and, if I knew of any better, I would lay it before you."

All those in the council, who had been used to arms, adopted the advice the old Saracen lord had given. It was in consequence forbidden, under pain of death, for the army to attack or skirmish with the Christians on the sea-shore; but they were ordered to remain quietly in their quarters, and suffer them to land and encamp themselves without any opposition. None dared infringe these orders. They sent a body of their archers into the town of Africa, to assist in its defence; and never made any movement until the morrow, so that the country seemed uninhabited.

The Christians having lain this night, as I have said, at anchor at the mouth of the harbor, made themselves ready the next day, which was a clear bright morning, for approaching the town, being very desirous to land. Trumpets and clarions began to sound and make a loud noise on board the different galleys and ships. When it was about nine o'clock, and the Christians had drunk a cup, and partaken of soup made of Grecian or Malmsey wines, with which they had abundantly provided themselves, to cheer their hearts and raise their spirits, they began to . execute the plan they had laid down while at the island. They sent, as it seems to me, some light vessels called

brigandines, armed with bricolles and cannons, first toward the harbor.　When they were properly drawn up
in array, they entered the haven, and saluted the town
with arrows and stones ; but the walls were hung with wet
carpeting to deaden the blows.　These brigandines entered
the port without damage, and were followed by the galleys
and other vessels in such handsome order as to make a
pleasant show.　In turning into the harbor, there was a
large castle with towers, and on one larger than the rest
was placed a bricolle, for the defence of the place, which
was not idle, but threw quarrels among the fleet.　On each
of the towers on the walls was a bricolle which shot well ;
and, to say the truth, the Saracens had laid in stores for a
long time, from the expectation of a siege.

When the Christians entered the port of Africa, to
disembark, the weather was so beautiful, and their order
so well preserved, that it was delightful to see it.　Their
trumpets and clarions made the air resound, and were
echoed back by the waves.　Many knights both from
France and from other countries now displayed their banners, and several knights were created ; the first of whom
was John, Lord de Ligny, in Hainault : he was knighted
by his cousin Sir Henry d'Antoing ; and the Lord de
Ligny there first displayed his banner, which was emblazoned with his arms on a field or, having a bend gules ; he
was accompanied by his cousin-german the Lord d'Havreth
in Hainault.　All the knights and squires disembarked in
view of the Saracens, on a Wednesday, the vigil of Magdalen Day, in the year of grace 1390, and, as they landed,
encamped according to orders from the marshals.　Thus
they took possession of the land of their enemies, who,
noticing their camp, could not avoid highly praising the
good order of it.　Those in the larger galleys, that could

not lie near the shore, were put into boats, and conveyed to land, under the banner of Our Lady. The Saracens, both within and without the town, allowed them to land peaceably, for they were not in numbers sufficient to oppose them; and the French advanced with displayed banners, on which were emblazoned their arms, to places marked out for their lodgings by the marshals.

The Duke of Bourbon, as commander-in-chief, was lodged in the centre of his army, with all honor, and powerfully guarded. The device on his banner, powdered over with flowers-de-luce, was a figure of the Virgin Mary in white, seated in the centre, and an escutcheon of Bourbon at her feet. I will name those lords of rank who were quartered on the right of the duke, looking toward the town: first Sir William de la Tremouille, and his brother, with a pennon; the Lord de Bordenay, with a banner; Sir Helion de Lignac, with a pennon; the Lord de Tours. the same. Then were placed the Hainaulters, whose standard bore the device of the Lord William of Hainault, at that time Count d'Ostrevant, eldest son of Duke Albert of Bavaria, Count of Holland, Hainault, and Zealand, which device was a harrow or, on a field gules. There was the Lord d'Havreth with his banner; the Lord de Ligny, with his; and then the Lord Philip, Count d'Artois, with his banner; the Lord de Mathefelon, with his banner; the Lord de Calan, with a pennon; the seneschal d'Eu, with the same; the Lord de Linieres, with a banner; the Lord de Thim, with the same; the Lord d'Ameval, with the same; Sir Walter de Chastillon, with a pennon; Sir John de Châteaumorant, with a banner; the brother to the Marshal de Sancerre, with a pennon; the Lord de Coucy, with his banner, and better supported than any except the Duke of Bourbon; the Lord de Licques, with a pennon;

Sir Stephen de Sancerre, with the same; and then the pennon of the King of France, blazoned with his device. Beside it was Sir John le Barrois, with his pennon ornamented with his arms; Sir William Morles, with his banner; the Lord de Longueval, with a pennon; Sir John de Roye, with a banner; the Lord de Bours, with a pennon; the Viscount d'Ausnay, with a banner; and Sir John de Vienne, Admiral of France, with his banner.

Those on the left hand of the Duke of Bourbon were, the Lord d'Ausemont, with a banner; Sir John Beaufort, bastard to the Duke of Lancaster, a banner; Sir John le Bouteiller, an Englishman, a pennon; Sir John de Crama, a banner; the Souldich de l'Estrade, a pennon; Sir John de Harcourt, a banner; the Lord Berald, Count de Clermont, and Dauphin of Auvergne, a banner, and with good array; Sir Hugh Dauphin, his brother, a pennon; the Lord de Berthencourt, a pennon; the Lord de Pierre Buffiere, a banner; the Lord de St. Semere, a banner; the Lord de Louvart, marshal of the army, a pennon; the Begue de Beausse, a pennon; the Lord de Louvy, a banner; Sir Gerard de Louvy, his brother, a pennon; the Lord de Saint-Germain, a banner; and then the pennon on a standard, with the device of the Duke of Bourbon; the Lord Philip de Bar, a banner; Sir Lewis de Poitiers, a pennon; Sir Robert de Calobre, the same; the Viscount de Les, a banner; the Lord de Nogent, the same; the Lord de Villeneuve, a pennon; Sir William de Moulin, the same; the Lord de Longwy, a pennon; Sir Angorget d'Amboise, the same; Sir Alain de la Champaigne, a pennon.

All these banners and pennons that I have named were placed in front of the camp, facing the town of Africa. But there were many knights and squires, of great courage and ability, who were quartered in the fields, whom I cannot name; and, if I could, it would take up too much space, for they were in the whole fourteen thousand, all gentlemen. This was a handsome army, able to perform many gallant deeds, and support a hard warfare, if the Saracens had ventured an attack, which they did not, contenting themselves this day with throwing large bolts, not meaning to act contrary to their plan. When the Christians were encamped, it was necessary for them to be careful of the provision they had brought; for they could not now venture to forage in this country, nor collect wood nor boughs for huts, as they would have run many risks by foolishly venturing themselves for such objects.

The knights were lodged under tents and pavilions of cloth, which they had procured at Genoa. The Genoese crossbows formed two wings, enclosing within them the principal lords; and, from their numbers, they occupied a great deal of ground, turning toward the sea-shore. All their provision was on board the vessels, and there were boats continually employed in bringing different articles from them, as they were wanted. When the inhabitants of the neighboring islands, such as Sicily and others, as well as those in the kingdom of Naples, la Puglia, and Calabria, heard the Christians were laying siege to Africa, they exerted themselves to supply them with every sort of provision: some from a desire of gain, others from affection to the Genoese. However, these purveyances did not come regularly; for at times the supply was most abundant, at others they were in great distress from want.

CHAPTER III.

THE CONDUCT OF THE SARACENS DURING THE SIEGE OF THE TOWN OF AFRICA.--THEY SEND TO DEMAND FROM THE FRENCH THE CAUSE OF THEIR MAKING WAR AGAINST THEM.

I WILL say something of the Saracens, for it is but just they should be equally spoken of as the Christians, that the truth may be more apparent. You must know that these infidels had, for a long time, been menaced by the Genoese, and were expecting the town of Africa to be besieged, in which they were not disappointed. They had made preparations for resistance, when they heard of the arrival of the Christian fleet, an event that had been long looked for by the neighboring nations; for they are not prudent nor well advised, who fear not their enemies, however small they may be. The Saracens, however, do not hold the Christians cheap: on the contrary, they consider them as men of courage and enterprise, and much fear them. The better to resist their enemies, they assembled the most experienced warriors from the kingdoms of Bugia, Morocco, and Tunis, in which last the town of Africa is situated, and encamped on the downs near the sea-shore. They took advantage of a large and thick wood in their rear, to avoid any danger from ambuscades or skirmishes on that side. The Saracens showed much ability in thus posting themselves. They amounted, according to the estimate of able men at arms, to thirty thousand archers and ten thousand horse. Others thought they were more; but their exact numbers were unknown, for the Christians supposed many were lodged in the wood. They were very numerous, for they were in their own country, and could come and go from their army at their pleasure without danger. They received continual supplies of fresh provision, which was brought on the backs of camels.

The second day after the Christians had landed, the Saracens, about dawn, came to attack the camp; Sir Henry d'Antoing having the command of the guard of two hundred men at arms and one thousand Genoese cross bows. The skirmish lasted more than two hours, and many gallant deeds were done in shooting and thrusting the lance, for there was not any engagement with the sword hand to hand. The Saracens did not foolhardily risk themselves, but fought with valor and more prudence than the Christians. When they had skirmished some time, the Saracens retreated; for the army began to be in motion, and some of the French barons had come to witness the action, and observe the manner of their enemies' fighting, that they might be prepared to meet them another time. The Saracens retired to their camp, as did the Christians to theirs; but, during the whole time of this siege of Africa, the Christians were never left quiet, for their camp was every night or morning attacked by the enemy.

Among the Saracens was a young knight, called Agadinquor Oliferne, excellently mounted on a beautiful courser, which he managed as he willed, and which, when he galloped, seemed to fly with him. From his gallantry he showed he was a good man at arms; and when he rode abroad he had with him three javelins, well feathered and pointed, which he dexterously flung, according to the custom of his country. He was completely armed in black, and had a kind of white napkin wrapped round his head. His seat on horseback was graceful; and, from the vigor and gallantry of his actions, the Christians judged he was excited thereto by his affection to a young lady of the country. True it is, he most sincerely loved the daughter of the King of Tunis, who, according to the report of some Genoese merchants who had seen her, was very handsome, and the heiress of his kingdom. This knight called Agadinquor was the son of Duke Oliferne; but I know not if he ever married this lady. I heard that during the siege he performed many handsome feats of arms, to testify his love, which the French knights saw with pleasure, and would willingly have surrounded him; but he rode so good a horse, and had him so well in hand, that all their efforts were vain. The Christian lords were very anxious to make some Saracens prisoners, to learn from them the real state of their army; but they could not succeed, and, having noticed their intent, the Saracen chiefs gave orders accordingly. The Saracens were much afraid of the Genoese crossbows: they shielded themselves as well as they could against their bolts, but they are not armed so strongly as the Christians; for they know not the art to forge armor like theirs, nor have they workmen who could make such. Iron and steel are not common among them; and they wear light targets hanging on their necks, covered with boiled leather from Cappadocia, that no spear can penetrate if the leather has not been overboiled. Their manner of fighting, according to what I heard, was to advance on the Christians, and shoot a volley of arrows at the Genoese the moment they made their appearance, and then to fall down under shelter of their shields, by which they avoided the bolts from the crossbows that went over them: they then rose, and either shot more arrows, or launched their javelins with much dexterity.

Thus, for the space of nine weeks that the siege lasted, were continual skirmishes made ; and on both sides many were killed and wounded, more especially such as ventured too rashly. The Christians imitated the Saracens by avoiding a close combat ; and the lords from France and other countries took delight in their manner of fighting, for, to say the truth, novelty is always pleasing. The young lords of these infidels were greatly struck with the glittering armor and emblazoned banners and pennons of their enemies ; and, when returned to their camp, they conversed much about them. They were, however, astonished at one thing, which I will now relate. The Saracens within the town of Africa were anxious to know on what pretence the Christians had come with so large an army to make war on them ; and to learn the reasons they resolved, as I was told, in council, to send a person that could speak Genoese, and gave him the following orders : "Go and take the road to the camp of the Christians [and manage, before thou returnest, to speak with some lords in their army], and demand in our name why they have brought so powerful a force against us, and taken possession of the lands of the King of Africa, who has not done any thing to offend them. True it is, that in former times we were at war with the Genoese, but that should no way concern them ; for they come from very distant countries, and the Genoese are our neighbors. Our custom has been, excepting in times of truce, to seize mutually all we can from each other."

Having received these instructions, the messenger departed, and rode on to the camp. The first person he met was a Genoese, to whom he said that he was sent by the Saracens to speak with some baron from France. The Genoese to whom he had addressed himself was called

Antonio Marchi, a centurion of crossbows, who took him
under his care, to his great joy, and conducted him instantly to the Duke of Bourbon and the Lord de Coucy.
They both listened very attentively, and what they did not
understand the centurion interpreted in very good French.
When he had finished all he had been ordered to say,
he asked for an answer. The French lords told him he
should have one as soon as they had considered the
purport of his message. Twelve of the greatest barons of
the army assembled in the Duke of Bourbon's tent; and,
the messenger and interpreter being called in, the last was
ordered to tell him from the lords present, " That in consequence of their ancestors having crucified and put to
death the Son of God, called Jesus Christ, a true prophet,
without any cause or just reason, they were come to retaliate on them for this infamous and unjust judgment.
Secondly, they were unbaptized, and infidels in the faith
to the holy Virgin, mother of Jesus Christ, and had no
creed of their own. For these and other causes they held
the Saracens and their whole sect as enemies, and were
come to revenge the injuries they had done to their God
and faith, and would to this effect daily exert themselves
to the utmost of their power." When the messenger had
received this answer, he departed from the army unmolested, and returned to report to his masters what you
have just read. The Saracens laughed heartily at hearing
it, and said they made assertions without proofs; for it was
the Jews who had crucified Jesus Christ, and not they.
Things remained on the former footing: the siege was
continued, and each army on its guard.

CHAPTER IV.

SOME MIRACLES ARE SHOWN TO THE SARACENS AS THEY ATTEMPT TO ATTACK THE CAMP OF THE CHRISTIANS. — SEVERAL SKIRMISHES DURING THE SIEGE. — THE CLIMATE BECOMES UNWHOLESOME, AND OTHER ACCIDENTS BEFALL THE BESIEGERS.

SHORTLY after this message, the Saracens determined in council to remain quiet for seven or eight days, and during that time neither to skirmish nor any way to annoy the Christians, but, when they should think themselves in perfect security, to fall on their camp like a deluge. This was adopted; and the ninth evening, a little before midnight, they secretly armed their men with their accustomed arms, and marched silently in a compact body toward the Christian camp. They had proposed making a severe attack on the opposite quarter to the main guard, and would have succeeded in their mischievous attempt if God had not watched over and preserved them by miracles, as I will now relate. As the Saracens approached, they saw before them a company of ladies dressed in white; one of whom, their leader, was incomparably more beautiful than the rest, and bore in front a white flag having a vermilion cross in the centre. The Saracens were so greatly terrified at this vision, that they lost all strength and inclination to proceed, and stood still, these ladies keeping steadily before them. The Genoese crossbows had brought with them a dog, as I heard, from beyond sea; but whence, no one could tell, nor did he belong to any particular person. This dog had been very useful to them; for the Saracens never came to skirmish, but by his noise he awakened the army; and as every one now knew that whenever the dog barked, the Saracens were come or on their road, they prepared themselves instantly. In consequence of this the Genoese called him the dog of Our Lady. This night the dog was not idle, but made a louder noise than usual, and ran first to the main guard, which was under the command of the Lord de Torcy, a Norman, and Sir Henry d'Antoing. As during the night all sounds are more easily heard, the whole army was in motion, and properly prepared to receive the Saracens, who they knew were approaching.

This was the fact; but the Virgin Mary and her company, having the Christians under their care, watched over them; and this night they received no harm, for the Saracens were afraid to advance, and returned the way they had come. The Christians were more attentive to their future guards. The Saracen knights and squires within the town were much cast down at the sight they had seen, more especially those who were advanced near this company of ladies; while, on the other hand, the Christians were greatly exerting themselves to win the place, which was courageously defended. At this period the weather was exceedingly hot; for it was the month of August, when the sun is in its greatest force, and that country was warmer than France, from being nearer the sun, and from the heat of the sands. The wines the besiegers were supplied with, from La Puglia and Calabria, were fiery, and hurtful to the constitutions of the French, many of whom suffered severely by fevers from the heating quality of their liquors. I know not how the Christians were enabled to bear the fatigues in such a climate, where sweet water was difficult to be had. They, however, had much resource in the wells they dug, for there were upward of two hundred sunk through the sands along the shore; but at times even this water was muddy and heated. They were frequently distressed for provision, for the supply was irregular from Sicily and the other islands : at times they had abundance, at other times they were in want. The healthy comforted the sick, and those who had provision shared it with such as had none ; for in this campaign they were all as brothers. The Lord de Coucy, in particular, was beloved by every gentleman : he was kind to all, and behaved himself by far more graciously in all respects than the Duke of Bourbon, who was proud and haughty, and never conversed with the knights and squires from foreign countries in the same agreeable manner the Lord de Coucy did.

The Duke was accustomed to sit cross-legged the greater part of the day before his pavilion ; and those who had any thing to say to him were obliged to make many reverences, and address him through the means of a third person. He was indifferent whether the poorer knights and squires were well or ill at their case : this the Lord de Coucy always inquired into, and by it gained great popularity. It was told me by some foreign knights who had been there, that, had the Lord de Coucy been commander-in-chief instead of the Duke of Bourbon, the success would have been very different ; for many attacks on the town of Africa were frustrated by the pride and fault of the Duke of Bourbon : several thought it would have been taken if it had not been for him.

This siege lasted, by an exact account, sixty-one days, during which many were the skirmishes before the town and at the barriers : they were well defended, for the flower of the infidel chivalry was in the town. The Christians said among themselves, "If we could gain this place by storm or otherwise, and strongly re-enforce and

victual it during the winter, a large body of our countrymen might then come hither in the spring, and gain a
footing in the kingdoms of Barbary and Tunis, which
would encourage the Christians to cross the sea annually,
and extend their conquests." — "Would to God it were
so!" others replied; "for the knights now here would then
be comfortably lodged, and every day if they pleased they
might have deeds of arms." The besieged were alarmed
at the obstinacy of their attacks, and redoubled their
guards. The great heat, however, did more for them
than all the rest, added to the uncertainty of being attacked; for the policy of the Saracens was to keep them
in continual alarms. They were almost burnt up when in
armor; and it was wonderful that any escaped death, for
during the month of August the air was suffocating. An
extraordinary accident happened, which, if it had lasted
any time, must have destroyed them all. During one
week, from the heat and corruption of the air, there were
such wonderful swarms of flies, the army was covered
with them. The men knew not how to rid themselves of
these troublesome guests, which multiplied daily, to their
great astonishment; but through the grace of God, and
the Virgin Mary, to whom they were devoted, a remedy
was found in a thunder and hail storm, that fell with great
violence, and destroyed all the flies. The air, by this
storm, was much cooled, and the army got to be in better
health than it had been for some time.

Knights who are on such expeditions must cheerfully
put up with what weather may happen, for they cannot
have it according to their wishes; and, when any one falls
sick, he must be nursed to his recovery or to his death.

CHAPTER V.

A CHALLENGE IS SENT BY THE SARACENS TO OFFER COMBAT OF TEN
AGAINST TEN CHRISTIANS. — THE SARACENS FAIL IN THEIR ENGAGE-
MENT. — THE TOWN OF AFRICA IS STORMED, BUT UNSUCCESSFULLY, AND
WITH THE LOSS OF MANY WORTHY MEN.

THE besiegers and their enemies studied day and
night how they could most effectually annoy each
other. Agadinquor Oliferne, Madifer de Tunis, Belins
Maldages, and Brahadin de Bugia, and some other Saracens, consulted together, and said, "Here are our enemies
the Christians encamped before us, and we cannot defeat
them. They are so few in number when compared to us,
that they must be well advised by their able captains; for
in all our skirmishes we have never been able to make
one knight prisoner. If we could capture one or two of
their leaders, we should acquire fame, and learn from them
the state of their army and what are their intentions. Let
us now consider how we may accomplish this." Agadinquor replied, "Though I am the youngest, I wish to speak
first." — "We agree to it," said the others. "By my
faith," continued he, "I am very desirous of engaging
them; and I think, if I were matched in equal combat with
one of my size, I should conquer him. If you will therefore select ten valiant men, I will challenge the Christians
to send the same number to fight with us. We have justice on our side in this war, for they have quarrelled with
us without reason; and this right, and the courage I feel,
induce me to believe that we shall have the victory." Madifer de Tunis, who was a very valiant man, said, "Agadin-

quor, what you have proposed is much to your honor. To-morrow, if you please, you shall ride as our chief toward the camp of the Christians, taking an interpreter with you, and make a signal that you have something to say. If you be well received by them, propose your combat of ten against ten. We shall then hear what answer they give; and, though I believe the offer will be accepted, we must take good counsel how we proceed against these Christians, whom we consider as more valiant than ourselves."

This being determined on, they retired to rest. On the morrow, as usual, they advanced to skirmish; but Agadinquor rode on at some distance in front with his interpreter. The day was bright and clear, and a little after sunrise the Saracens were ready for battle. Sir Guy and Sir William de la Tremouille had commanded the guard of the night, and were on the point of retiring, when the Saracens appeared in sight about three bowshots distant. Agadinquor and his interpreter advanced toward one of the wings, and made signs to give notice that he wanted to parley with some one. By accident he came near the pennon of a good squire at arms called Affrenal, who, noticing his signs, rode forward a pace, and told his men to remain as they were, "for that he would go and see what the Saracen wanted: he has an interpreter with him, and is probably come to make some proposition." His men remained steady, and he rode toward the Saracen.

When they were near each other, the interpreter said, "Christian, are you a gentleman, of name in arms, and ready to answer what shall be asked of you?" — "Yes," replied Affrenal, "I am: speak what you please, it shall be answered." — "Well," said the interpreter, "here is a noble man of our country who demands to combat with you bodily; and, if you would like to increase the number

to ten, he will bring as many of his friends to meet you.
The cause for the challenge is this : They maintain, that
their faith is more perfect than yours ; for it has continued since the beginning of the world, when it was written
down, and that your faith has been introduced by a mor-
tal, whom the Jews hung and crucified." — "Ho!" interrupted Affrenal, "be silent on these matters, for it does
not become such as thee to dispute concerning them ; but
tell the Saracen, who has ordered thee to speak, to swear
on his faith that such a combat shall take place, and he
shall be gratified within four hours. Let him bring ten
gentlemen, and of name in arms, on his side, and I will
bring as many to meet him." The interpreter related to
the Saracen the words that had passed, who seemed much
rejoiced thereat, and pledged himself for the combat.

This being done, each returned to his friends ; but the
news had already been carried to Sir Guy and to Sir William de la Tremouille, who, meeting Affrenal, demanded
how he had settled matters with the Saracen. Affrenal
related what you have heard, and that he had accepted the
challenge. The two knights were well pleased, and said,
"Affrenal, go and speak to others, for we will be of
your number ten." He replied, "God assist us! I fancy
I shall find plenty ready to fight the Saracens." Shortly
after, Affrenal met the Lord de Thim, to whom he told
what had passed, and asked if he would make one. The
Lord de Thim willingly accepted the offer ; and of all
those to whom Affrenal related it, he might, if he pleased,
have had a hundred instead of ten. Sir Boucicaut the
younger accepted it with great courage, as did Sir Helion
de Lignac, Sir John Russel, an Englishman, Sir John
Harpedone, Alain Boudet, and Bouchet. When the number of ten was completed, they retired to their lodgings,

to prepare and arm themselves. When the news of this combat was spread through the army, and the names of the ten were told, the knights and squires said, "They are lucky fellows, thus to have such a gallant feat of arms fall to their lot." — "Would to Heaven," added many, "that we were of the ten!" All the knights and squires seemed to rejoice at this event, except the Lord de Coucy. I believe the Lord de Thim was a dependent on, or of the company of, the Lord de Coucy; for, when he repaired to his tent to arm, he found him there, and acknowledged him for his lord. He related to him the challenge of the Saracen, and that he had accepted being one of the ten. All present were loud in praise of it, except the Lord de Coucy, who said, "Hold your tongues, you youngsters, who as yet know nothing of the world, and who never consider consequences, but always applaud folly in preference to good. I see no advantage in this combat, for many reasons : one is, that ten noble and distinguished gentlemen are about to fight with ten Saracens. How do we know if their opponents are gentlemen? They may, if they choose, bring to the combat ten varlets, or knaves ; and, if they are defeated, what is the gain? We shall not the sooner win the town of Africa, but by it risk very valuable lives. Perhaps they may form an ambuscade, and, while our friends are on the plain waiting for their opponents, surround them and carry them off, by which we shall be greatly weakened. I therefore say, that Affrenal has not wisely managed this matter ; and, when he first met the Saracen, he should have otherwise answered, and said, 'I am not the commander-in-chief of our army, but one of the least in it ; and you Saracen, who address yourself to me, and blame our faith, are not qualified to discuss such matters, nor have you well addressed yourself. I will conduct you to my lords, and assure you, on my life, that no harm befall you in going or in returning, for my lords will cheerfully listen to you.' He should then have led him to the Duke of Bourbon and the council of war, when his proposal would have been heard and discussed at leisure, his intentions been known, and answers made according as they should think the matter deserved. Such a combat should never be undertaken but after great deliberation, especially with enemies like to those we are engaged with. And when it had been agreed on, and the names and qualities of each combatant should be declared, we would then have selected proper persons to meet them, and proper securities would have been required from the Saracens for the uninterrupted performance of the combat, and a due observance of the articles. If matters had been thus managed, Lord of Thim, I think it would have been better. It would be well if it could be put on this footing; and I will speak to the Duke of Bourbon and the principal barons in the army, and hear what they shall say on the subject." The Lord de Coucy then departed for the tent of the Duke of Bourbon, where the barons were assembled, as they had heard of this challenge, to consider what might be the probable event of it. Although the Lord de Coucy had intended his speech to the Lord de Thim as advice for his benefit, he did not the less arm himself: when fully equipped, he went with his companions, who were completely armed, and in good array, with Sir Guy de la Tremouille at their head, to meet the Saracens.

During this there was conversation on the subject between the lords in the tent of the Duke of Bourbon: many thought the accepting such a challenge improper, and supported the opinion of the Lord de Coucy, who said it ought to have been ordered otherwise. But some, and in particular the Lord Philip d'Artois, Count d'Eu, and the Lord Philip de Bar, said, "Since the challenge has been accepted by our knights, they would be disgraced were the combat now broken off; and in the name of God and Our Lady let them accomplish it the best manner they can." This was adopted; for it was now too far advanced to be stopped. It was therefore ordered to draw out the whole army properly arrayed, that, if the Saracens had formed any bad designs, they might be prepared to meet them. Every one, therefore, made himself ready: the whole were drawn up, as if for instant combat, the Genoese cross-bows on one side, and the knights and squires on the other; each lord under his own banner or pennon embla-zoned with his arms. It was a fine sight to view the army thus displayed; and they showed great eagerness to at-tack the Saracens.

The ten knights and squires were advanced on the plain waiting for their opponents. But they came not, nor showed any appearance of so doing; for, when they saw the Christian army so handsomely drawn out in battle-array, they were afraid to advance, though they were thrice their numbers. At times they sent horsemen, well mounted, to ride near their army, observe its disposition, and then gallop back; which was solely done through malice, to annoy the Christians.

This was the hottest day they felt, and it was so ex-tremely oppressive that the most active among them were almost stifled in their armor: they had never suffered so much before; and yet they remained expecting the ten Saracens, but in vain, for they never heard a word from them. The army was ordered to attack the town of Africa, since they were prepared, and thus pass the day;

and the ten champions, in regard to their honor, were to remain on their ground to the evening.

The knights and squires advanced with great alacrity to the attack of the town. But they were sorely oppressed with the heat, and, had the Saracens known their situation, they might have done them much damage; probably they might even have raised the siege, and obtained a complete victory, for the Christians were exceedingly weakened and worn down. True it is, they gained by storm the wall of the first enclosure, but no one inhabited that part; and the enemy retired within their second line of defence, skirmishing as they retreated, and without any great loss. The Christians paid dear for an inconsiderable advantage: the heat of the sun and its reflection on the sands, added to the fatigue of fighting, which lasted until evening, caused the death of several valiant knights and squires; the more the pity.

Now consider how great was this loss; and, had the advice of the gallant Lord de Coucy been followed, it would not have happened, for the army would have remained quietly in its camp as it had hitherto done. The whole army was dismayed at it, and each bewailed the loss of his friend. They retired late to their camp, and kept a stronger guard than usual during the night, for fear of the Saracens. It passed, however, without further accident, and more prudent arrangements were made. The Saracens were ignorant of what their enemies had suffered: had they known it, they would have had a great advantage over them; but they were in dread of the Christians, and never ventured to attack them but in skirmishes, retreating after one or two charges. The person among them who had shown the most courage was Agadinquor Oliferne. He was enamoured with the daughter of the

King of .Tunis, and, in compliment to her, was eager to perform brilliant actions.

Thus was the siege of Africa continued; but the relations and friends of the knights and squires who had gone thither, from France and other countries, received no intelligence, nor knew more of them than if they were dead. They were so much alarmed at not having any news of them, that many processions were made in England, France, and Hainault, to the churches, to pray God that he would bring them back in safety to their several homes. The intention of the Christians was to remain before the town of Africa, until they should have conquered it by storm, treaty, or famine.

CHAPTER VI.

THE SIEGE OF AFRICA IS RAISED. — THE CAUSE OF IT. — THE KNIGHTS AND SQUIRES RETURN TO THEIR OWN COUNTRIES.

YOU have before heard what pains the Christians took to conquer the town of Africa; for they thought if they succeeded they should gain renown, and be able to withstand, during the winter, all the forces the infidels could bring against them, until they should be re-enforced from Europe, especially by the King of France, who was young and fond of arms; and there were still two years to run of the truce with England. The Christians had therefore laid siege to Africa, as being the most convenient entrance into Barbary. The infidels, suspicious of such being their intentions, well victualled the place, and re-enforced it with a new garrison, the better to guard it.

The siege still continued, although, after the before-mentioned loss on the part of the Christians, little advantage was gained, and the men at arms were greatly discouraged; for they could not obtain any opportunity of changing the tiresomeness of their situation, and of revenging themselves on the enemy. Many, in consequence, began to murmur, and say, "We remain here in vain, for, if we do nothing more effectual than skirmishing, we shall never gain the town : if by accident we kill one infidel by our arrows, they supply his place with ten more, as they are in their own country, and have provision and stores in abundance, while ours are brought with much difficulty and uncertainty. What will become of us if we stay longer? The cold nights of winter freeze and benumb us to death. We shall be in a most disagreeable state, for many reasons : First, at that time of the year the sea will be so tempestuous, no one will venture on it. We have now but eight days' provision ; and should the stormy weather set in, and prevent any vessels arriving, we must inevitably perish. Secondly, suppose we have provision and stores in plenty, how can the army support for so long a time the fatigue of a regular guard? The danger will be too great ; for the enemy is on his own ground, and well acquainted with the country, and may attack us in the night-season, as we have already seen, and do us infinite damage. Thirdly, should we be infected with any disorder, from want of better air and fresh provision, it may be contagious, and we shall drop off one after another, for we have not any remedies to guard against such a misfortune. Besides, should the Genoese, who are a treacherous race, wish to return without us, they might embark in the night-time ; and when once on board their vessels we could not prevent them, and they would leave us here to pay the reckoning. It will be right that we remonstrate with our lords, who are enjoying their ease, on these our suspicions; for the Genoese do not conceal their opinions of us. Some of their talkers have said to our men, 'You Frenchmen are odd men at arms: when we sailed from Genoa, we thought you would have conquered this town of Africa within a week or a fortnight after your landing; but we have been here nearly two months, and nothing has been done: by the assaults and skirmishes you make, the town need not fear you these two years; and, at the rate you go on, you will never conquer the kingdoms of Tunis or Africa.'"

The Genoese had so frequently held this language to the varlets and others of the army, that it reached the ears of their lords, and was repeated to the Lord de Coucy, who was wise and prudent, and to whom the whole army looked up. He considered a while, and then said to himself, "The conversations of these Genoese are but too well founded in truth: to put a stop to them, a full assembly of the principal knights must be held, to consider how we are to proceed, for winter is fast approaching." At this council, which was held in the Duke of Bourbon's tent, various plans were proposed; but the conclusion was, that they would, for this season, break up the siege, and every person should return home the way he had come. The chief lords secretly made preparations accordingly, and, calling to them the masters of the galleys and other vessels, acquainted them with their intentions. The captains were much surprised, and said, "My lords, do not harbor any suspicions of us; for we are pledged to you by our honor and oaths, and we will most loyally and honestly acquit ourselves. Had we pleased, we might have accepted the favorable offers that were made us by the Africans; but we refused to enter into any treaty with them, from our attachments and engage-. ments to you."

"We have no doubts of you, gentlemen," replied the Lord de Coucy, "for we look on you as loyal and valiant men. But we have considered our situation : winter is at hand, and we have a scarcity of provision. Should it be God's good pleasure that we return to France, we will inform the king, who is young and fond of war, of the state of this country. At this moment he knows not where to employ his force ; for he and the King of England are at peace. He is unhappy when idle ; and we shall advise him to undertake an expedition hither, as well to have the pleasure of meeting the King of Sicily as to conquer this country from the Saracens. Prepare and make ready your galleys, for we shall leave this coast in a very few days." The Genoese were not well pleased with the French lords for thus breaking up the siege of the town of Africa ; but, as they could not amend it, they were forced to bear with it as well as they could.

There was a rumor current in the Christian camp, that the Genoese were treating with the Saracens to betray and deliver up to them the remainder of the army. It was firmly believed by many ; and they said, "Our principal commanders, the Duke of Bourbon, the Dauphin of Auvergne, the Lord de Coucy, Sir Guy de la Tremouille, Sir Philip de Bar, and Sir John de Vienne, are well acquainted with this plot ; and for this reason they have determined suddenly to break up the siege." When it was proclaimed that every one was to embark on board the galleys or other vessels, in an orderly manner, you would have seen the varlets in the greatest bustle packing up the purveyances of their different lords, and conveying them on board the ships which lay at anchor off the shore.

When all things were embarked, the knights entered the galleys that had brought them thither.   Many had bargained with the captains to carry them to Naples, others to Sicily, Cyprus, or Rhodes, thence to perform a pilgrimage to Jerusalem.

After having remained sixty-one days before the town of Africa, they broke up the siege, and set sail from that country in sight of the Saracens from the walls.   This gave them such joy, that they sounded horns, and beat drums, and made so great a noise by their shoutings, as to be heard in the army of the Saracens.   Several young knights mounted their horses, and galloped to the place where the camp had been, to see if they could find any thing left behind.   Agadinquor d'Oliferne and Brahadin de Tunis were the first to arrive; but the Christians had so completely cleared the camp, that there was nothing for them to carry away.   The Saracens left their station to examine the camp, and remained more than two hours noticing the manner and form of it.   They praised much their subtlety in sinking wells for fresh water, and, having for some time viewed the galleys under sail, they returned to visit their friends in the town of Africa.   But they did not know the great losses the Christians had suffered until that day, and I will tell you by what accident it happened. In the camp of the Christians was found, lying on the ground, a Genoese varlet, who was too ill with a fever to be removed when the sailors sought for their men to embark on board the barges.   The Saracens were delighted on finding this man, and ordered no harm to be done him.   They carried him to the principal commanders of their army, and told them where they had found him. An interpreter was sent for, to examine him; but at first he would not make any answers, considering himself as a dead man, and desiring they would put him out of his pain. The chiefs of the army, such as Agadinquor d'Oliferne and Brahadin de Tunis, thought they should gain nothing by his death; and to induce him to answer truly, without any equivocation, what questions should be put to him, they promised to spare his life, and send him safe and well to his own country on board of the first galley that should come thither from Genoa or Marseilles, with a present of a hundred golden besants. The varlet, hearing this, was freed from his fears of death, and made easy, for he knew that these Saracens never break their words; and, as every one dies as late as he can, he said to the interpreter, "Make them all swear on their faith to keep what they have promised, and I will truly answer whatever you may ask." The interpreter repeated this to the lords, who having consented to his demand, the varlet said, "Now ask what questions you please, and I will answer them." He was first asked who he was, and his place of residence, and replied, "Portevances [that his name was Simon Mollevin, and son to a captain of a galley at Portevances "], then as to the commanders of the Christian army. He named several; for, having kept company and drank with the heralds, he had often heard their names mentioned, and remembered some of them. He was asked if he knew the reasons why they had so suddenly raised the siege, and departed. To this he made a very prudent reply, by saying he was ignorant of it, as he was not present at the council of war when it was determined on, and could only tell them what was the common report in the army. It was said that the French suspected the Genoese of a design to betray them; but the Genoese declared this was false, and wrongfully imputed to them by the French. They had left the coast because they

were afraid to winter in this country, and risk the loss of
as many knights as they had once done. "Ask him," said
the lords to the interpreter, "to explain this." He replied, "So great was the loss on the day the combat was
to have taken place between ten of your knights with ten
of ours, that upward of sixty knights and squires, men of
renown, died that day; and it was solely on this account,"
as the Genoese said, "the siege was raised." The Saracen
chiefs seemed very much pleased on hearing this, and
made no further inquiries, but punctually kept the promise
they had made him.

On his return to Portevances and Genoa, he related all
that had passed and what answers he had made, for which
he was no way blamed. The Saracens said among themselves, "We have been very negligent in not taking better
measures against this union of the French and Genoese;
for, though they have been this time unsuccessful against
Africa, we must henceforward put our coast in a better
state of defence (which we may easily do); and we must,
in particular, guard the Straits of Morocco so strongly
that neither the Genoese nor Venetians shall carry their
merchandise to Flanders through this strait, without paying so great a toll as to make all the world wonder thereat,
and even then it shall be considered as a matter of favor."

What these Africans had proposed, they executed; and
all the kingdoms to the south, west, and east, formed an
alliance, such as Africa, Tunis, Bugia, Morocco, Benmarin,
Tremeçen, and Granada, with a resolution of well guarding
their coasts, and equipping such a fleet of galleys as should
make them masters of the sea, through hatred to the
French and Genoese for their late siege of Africa. They
interrupted so much the navigation of the Venetians and
Genoese, that merchandise from Alexandria, Cairo, Da-

mascus, Venice, Naples, or Genoa, was difficult to be had
in Flanders for money; and, in particular, every sort of
spicery was enormously dear.

CHAPTER VII.*

DEATH AND BURIAL OF KING RICHARD II.

NOW consider, ye kings, lords, dukes, prelates, and
earls, how very changeable the fortunes of this world
are. This King Richard reigned twenty-two years in
great prosperity, and with much splendor; for there never
was a king of England who expended such sums, by more
than a hundred thousand florins, as King Richard did in
keeping up his state, and his household establishments.
I, John Froissart, canon and treasurer of Chimay, know it
well; for I witnessed and examined it during my residence
with him for a quarter of a year. He made me good
cheer, because in my youth I had been secretary to King
Edward his grandfather, and the Lady Philippa of Hainault, Queen of England. When I took my leave of him
at Windsor, he presented me, by one of his knights called
Sir John Golofre, a silver gilt goblet, weighing full two
marks, filled with a hundred nobles, which were then of
service to me, and will be so as long as I live. I am bound
to pray to God for him, and sorry am I to write of his
death; but, as I have dictated and augmented this history
to the utmost of my power, it became necessary to mention it, that what became of him might be known.

* Which I have selected for a concluding chapter because it is the last
but one of Froissart's book, and brings before us several persons who have
figured in the history, as *dramatis personæ* come forth at the last act of the
play. Here are King Edward, with whose coronation my abridgment begins; Queen Philippa, whom we saw him marry; and King Richard II.,
whom we last beheld in front of Wat Tyler and his rebels. — ED.

When King Richard was born, his father was in Gàlicia, which Don Pedro had given him to conquer. A curious thing happened on my first going to England, which I have much thought on since. I was in the service of Queen Philippa; and when she accompanied King Edward and the royal family, to take leave of the Prince and Princess of Wales, at Berkhampstead, on their departure for Aquitaine, I heard an ancient knight, in conversation with some ladies, say, "We have a book called Brut, that declares neither the Prince of Wales, Dukes of Clarence, York, nor Gloucester, will be kings of England, but the descendants of the Duke of Lancaster." Now I, the author of this history, say that, considering all things, these two knights, Sir Richard de Pontchardon, and Sir Bartholomew Burghersh, in what they said, were both in the right; for all the world saw Richard reign for twenty-two years in England, and saw the crown then fall to the house of Lancaster. King Henry would never have been king, on the conditions you have heard, if his cousin Richard had treated him in the friendly manner he ought to have done. The Londoners took his part for the wrongs the king had done him and his children, whom they much compassionated.

When the funeral car of King Richard had remained in Cheapside two hours, it was conducted forward, in the same order as before, out of the town. The four knights then mounted their horses, which were waiting for them, and continued their journey with the body until they came to a village, where there is a royal mansion, called Langley, thirty miles from London. There King Richard was interred. God pardon his sins, and have mercy on his soul!

A NEW BOOK BY IK. MARVEL.

About Old Story-Tellers.

OF HOW AND WHEN THEY LIVED AND WHAT STORIES THEY TOLD.

By DONALD G. MITCHELL,

Author of "The Reveries of a Bachelor," etc., etc.

WITH NUMEROUS ILLUSTRATIONS.

One volume, square 12mo, Holiday Style, cloth extra, gilt top, $2.00.

The long silence of this favorite author is at length broken, and it is the young people whom he now invites to the feast which he has prepared for them. The somewhat quaint title of the book faithfully indicates its contents.

In the Preface, which is addressed to "Grown up People," Mr. Mitchell very charmingly says: "In the matter of books, as in the world, I believe in old friends, and don't think they should be laid away upon the shelf without good cause, and age is hardly cause enough. In short, I must confess a lurking fondness for those good old-fashioned stories which were current forty years ago and some of them, may be a hundred years ago —written in good straightforward English, with good straightforward intent."

IK. MARVEL'S WORKS.

REVERIES OF A BACHELOR; or, A Book of the Heart. A new edition. One vol. 12mo, Turkey antique, $4.00; cloth, $1.75.

THE SAME. Cabinet edition, 16mo, half calf, $3.00; cloth, $1.75.

DREAM LIFE. A Fable of the Seasons. One vol. 12mo, Turkey antique, $4.00; 12mo, cloth, $1.75.

THE SAME. Cabinet edition, 16mo, half calf, $3.00; cloth, $1.75.

SEVEN STORIES, WITH BASE- ment and Attic. One vol. 12mo, cloth, $1.75.

DR. JOHNS. Being a narrative of Certain Events in the Life of an Orthodox Minister in Connecticut. Two vols. 12mo, cloth, $3.50.

MY FARM OF EDGEWOOD, A Country Book. By the author of "Reveries of a Bachelor." One vol. 12mo, cloth, $1.75.

THE SAME. New and cheaper edition. One vol. square 12mo, cloth, $1 25.

WET DAYS AT EDGEWOOD. With Old Farmers, Old Gardeners, and Old Pastorals. By the author of "My Farm of Edgewood." One vol. 12mo, $1.75.

RURAL STUDIES. With Practical Hints for Country Places. By Ik Marvel. Illustrated by the author. One vol. 12mo, cloth, $1.75.

PICTURES OF EDGEWOOD Being Photographic Views (by Rockwood), with Text and Illustrative Diagrams by the author of "My Farm of Edgewood." One vol. 4to *Only 300 copies printed.* $12.00.

*** *The above books for sale by all booksellers, or will be sent, post or express charges paid, upon receipt of the price by the publishers.*

CHARLES SCRIBNER'S SONS,

743 AND 745 BROADWAY, NEW YORK

Now in process of publication, uniform with EPOCHS OF MODERN HISTORY, *each volume in 12mo. size, and complete in itself,*

Epochs of Ancient History.

A Series of Books narrating the HISTORY OF GREECE AND ROME, and of their relations to other Countries at Successive Epochs. Edited by the Rev. G. W. COX, M.A., Author of the "Aryan Mythology," "A History of Greece," etc., and jointly by CHARLES SANKEY, M.A., late Scholar of Queen's College, Oxford.

Volumes already issued in the "Epochs of Ancient History." Each One Volume 12mo, cloth, $1.00.

The GREEKS and the PERSIANS. By the Rev. G. W. Cox, M.A., late Scholar of Trinity College, Oxford : Joint Editor of the Series. With four colored Maps.

The EARLY ROMAN EMPIRE. From the Assassination of Julius Cæsar to the Assassination of Domitian. By the Rev. W. WOLFE CAPES, M.A., Reader of Ancient History in the University of Oxford. With two colored Maps.

The ATHENIAN EMPIRE from the FLIGHT of XERXES to the FALL of ATHENS. By the Rev. G. W. Cox, M.A., late Scholar of Trinity College, Oxford : Joint Editor of the Series. With five Maps.

The ROMAN TRIUMVIRATES. By the Very Rev. CHARLES MERIVALE, D.D., Dean of Ely.

EARLY ROME, to its Capture by the Gauls. By WILHELM IHNE, Author of "History of Rome." With Map.

THE AGE OF THE ANTONINES. By Rev. W. WOLFE CAPES, M.A. With two Maps.

OPINIONS OF THE PRESS.

"Brief but comprehensive in its narrative, it is written in a plain and simple style which will attract the attention of the general reader as well as the philosophical student."—*The Providence Journal.*

"It would be hard to find a more creditable book *(Greeks and Persians).* The author's prefatory remarks upon the origin and growth of Greek civilization are alone worth the price of the volume."—*The Christian Union.*

"The volume is compact, convenient, clearly written, and well illustrated by maps. This is a very valuable series for general readers."—*The Watchman.*

* *The above books for sale by all booksellers, or will be sent, post or express charges paid, upon receipt of the price by the publishers,*

CHARLES SCRIBNER'S SONS,
743 AND 745 BROADWAY, NEW YORK

"These volumes contain the ripe results of the studies of men who are authorities in their respective fields."—THE NATION.

Epochs of Modern History.

Each 1 vol. 16mo., with Outline Maps.   Price per volume, in cloth, $1.00.

EACH VOLUME COMPLETE IN ITSELF AND SOLD SEPARATELY.

EDITED BY EDWARD E. MORRIS, M.A.

The ERA of the PROTESTANT REVOLUTION. By F. SEEBOHM, Author of "The Oxford Reformers—Colet, Erasmus, More."   *(Now ready.)*

The CRUSADES. By the Rev. G. W. Cox, M.A., Author of the "History of Greece."   *(Now ready.)*

The THIRTY YEARS' WAR, 1618—1648. By SAMUEL RAWSON GARDINER.   *(Now ready.)*

The HOUSES of LANCASTER and YORK; with the CONQUEST and LOSS of FRANCE. By JAMES GAIRDNER, of the Public Record Office.   *(Now ready.)*

The FRENCH REVOLUTION and FIRST EMPIRE; an Historical Sketch. By WM. O'CONNOR MORRIS, with an Appendix by Hon. ANDREW D. WHITE, Prest. of Cornell University.   *(Now ready.)*

The AGE OF ELIZABETH. By the Rev. M. CREIGHTON, M.A.   *(Now ready.)*

The PURITAN REVOLUTION. By J. LANGTON SANFORD.   *(Now ready.)* .

The FALL of the STUARTS; and WESTERN EUROPE from 1678 to 1697. By the Rev. EDWARD HALE, M.A., Assist. Master at Eton.   *(Now ready.)*

The EARLY PLANTAGENETS and their relation to the HISTORY of EUROPE: the foundation and growth of CONSTITUTIONAL GOVERNMENT. By the Rev. WM. STUBBS, M.A., etc., Regius Professor of Modern History in the University of Oxford.   *(Now ready.)*

The BEGINNING of the MIDDLE AGES; CHARLES the GREAT and ALFRED; the HISTORY of ENGLAND in its connection with that of EUROPE in the NINTH CENTURY. By the Very Rev R. W. CHURCH, M.A., Dean of St Paul's.   *(Now ready.)*

The above Ten Volumes in Roxburg Style, Leather Labels and Gilt Top. Put up in a handsome Box. Sold only in Sets. Price per Set, $10.00.

The AGE of ANNE. By EDWARD E. MORRIS, M.A , Editor of the Series.   *(Now ready.)*

The NORMAN KINGS and the FEUDAL SYSTEM. By the Rev. A. H JOHNSON, M.A. EDWARD III. By the Rev. W. WARBURTON, M.A., late He? Majesty's Senior Inspector of Schools.

FREDERICK the GREAT and the SEVEN YEARS' WAR. By F. W. LONGMAN, of Ballic College, Oxford.

. *The above book for sale by all booksellers, or will be sent, post or express charges paid, upon receipt of the price by the publishers,*

CHARLES SCRIBNER'S SONS,
743 AND 745 BROADWAY, NEW YORK.

Now Complete.

THE SECOND SERIES OF

The Illustrated Library of Wonders,

ENLARGED IN SIZE, IN A NEW STYLE OF BINDING, AND EDITED BY PROMINENT AMERICAN AUTHORS.

The extraordinary success of the ILLUSTRATED LIBRARY OF WONDERS has encouraged the publishers to still further efforts to increase the attractions and value of these admirable books. In the new series, which has just been finished, the size of the volumes is increased, the style of binding changed, and the successive volumes are edited by distinguished American authors and scientists. Each 1 vol. 12mo. Price, $1.50.

THE SECOND SERIES.

FIRST SECTION.

METEORS: Aerolites, Storms and Atmospheric Phenomena. With twenty-three illustrations by LEBRETON.

WONDERS OF VEGETATION. Edited, with additions by Prof. SCHELE DE VERE. Profusely illustrated.

WONDERS OF ELECTRICITY. Edited, with additions, by Dr. J. W. ARMSTRONG, President of Normal Institute at Fredonia, N. Y. With over fifty woodcuts.

WONDERS OF WATER. Edited, with additions, by Prof. SCHELE DE VERE, of the University of Virginia. Illustrated with over seventy engravings and charts.

WONDERS OF THE MOON. Edited, with additions, by MARIA MITCHELL, of Vassar College, Poughkeepsie. One vol. 12mo, fifty illustrations.

Price of above 5 volumes in a box..$7.50

SECOND SECTION.

THE WONDERS OF ENGRAVING. By GEORGES DUPLESSIS. With thirty-four illustrations.

THE WONDERS OF SCULPTURE. With chapter on American Sculpture by CLARENCE COOK. With over sixty illustrations.

ARMS AND ARMOUR, in Antiquity and the Middle Ages, also a descriptive notice of Modern Weapons. And an additional chapter on Arms and Armour in England. By CHARLES BOUTELL, M.A.

MOUNTAIN ADVENTURES. Compiled from the Note-Books of Distinguished Travelers, including Whymper and Tyndall. Edited, with additions, by Hon. J. T. HEADLEY. With forty-one illustrations.

DIAMONDS AND PRECIOUS STONES. A Popular Account of Gems. Translated from the French of LOUIS DIEULAFAIT, by FANCHON SANFORD. 126 illustrations.

Price of above 5 volumes in a box..$7.50

Second Series Complete, 10 volumes, in a box, $15.00.

THE FIRST SERIES.

ILLUSTRATED LIBRARY OF WONDERS,

The First Series comprises:

	Illus.		*Illus.*		*Illus.*
Wonderful Escapes	26	Optical Wonders	71	Bottom of the Sea	68
Bodily Strength and Skill	70	Wonders of Acoustics	110	Italian Art	28
Balloon Ascents	30	The Heavens	48	European Art	11
Great Hunts	22	The Human Body	43	Architecture	60
Egypt 3,300 Years Ago	40	The Sublime in Nature	44	Glass-making	63
The Sun. By Guillemin	58	Intelligence of Animals	54	Wonders of Pompeii	22
Wonders of Heat	93	Thunder and Lightning	39		

Price per single volume, cloth.....................$1.25
The Same in sets of 20 volumes, cloth, with a rack.......25.00
The 20 volumes in half roan, gilt top, with a rack.......30.00

☞ Any or all the volumes of the ILLUSTRATED LIBRARY OF WONDERS sent to any address, post or express charges paid, on receipt of the price.

CHARLES SCRIBNER'S SONS,

743 AND 745 BROADWAY, NEW YORK.

How a wonderful Apparition terrified the Saracens.

("THAT PRINCE OF STORY-TELLERS."—*London Times.*)

JULES VERNE'S LATEST STORY.

HECTOR SERVADAC;

OR, THE CAREER OF A COMET.

WITH OVER ONE HUNDRED FULL-PAGE ILLUSTRATIONS.

One vol., 8vo, cloth extra (*uniform with "Michael Strogoff"*), $3.00.

Readers of the marvellous in literature will eagerly welcome Jules Verne's new story, "Hector Servadac," which fully sustains the reputation of its popular author. The heroes of this story were carried away through space on the Comet "Gallia," and their adventures are recorded with all Jules Verne's characteristic spirit. This volume contains upward of one hundred full-page illustrations of the most thrilling character.

WORKS OF JULES VERNE.

PUBLISHED BY

CHARLES SCRIBNER'S SONS.

The Complete and Authorized Editions.

MICHAEL STROGOFF; or, The Courier of the Czar. Profusely illustrated after designs by RIOU. One vol. 8vo, crown, $3.00.

The New Robinson Crusoe.

JULES VERNE'S "MYSTERIOUS ISLAND." Three parts, complete in one volume. I. Dropped from the Clouds. II. Abandoned. III. The Secret of the Island. One vol. crown 8vo, cloth, with profuse illustrations, $3.00.

FROM THE EARTH TO THE MOON in 97 Hours and 20 Minutes, and a Trip Around It. Twenty-four full-page illustrations, cloth, black and gilt. One vol. 12mo. Price, $1.50.

A JOURNEY TO THE CENTRE OF THE EARTH. With fifty-two illustrations by RIOU. Complete edition, fifty-three illustrations, on super-calendered paper, handsomely bound in cloth, black and gilt, beveled boards. One vol. crown 8vo., $3.00.

STORIES OF ADVENTURE. Comprising "Meridiana," "The Adventures of Three Englishmen and Three Russians in South Africa," and "A Journey to the Centre of the Earth." One vol. 12mo, sixty-eight full-page illustrations. Cloth, $1.50.

A FLOATING CITY, and THE BLOCKADE RUNNERS. One vol. 12mo, profusely illustrated. Cloth. One vol., crown 8vo, $3.00.

*** *The above books for sale by all booksellers, or will be sent, post or express charges paid, upon receipt of the price by the publishers,*

CHARLES SCRIBNER'S SONS,
743 AND 745 BROADWAY, NEW YORK.

"Mrs. Dodge's humor is delightful."—ATLANTIC MONTHLY.

A Summer Book for Grown Folks, by the author of "Hans Brinker."

THEOPHILUS AND OTHERS.

By MARY MAPES DODGE,

Author of "Hans Brinker," "Rhymes and Jingles;" Editor of "St. Nicholas," &c

1 vol. 12mo.   Price $1.50.

OPINIONS OF THE PRESS.

"A most amusing book, and full of humor."—*Nation.*

"Mrs. Dodge's style is bright, spirited and entertaining."—*Sat. Eve. Gazette.*

"There have been few pleasanter books than Mrs. Dodge's."—*Phila. Ev. Bulletin*

"The whole series is very clever, and makes a volume of most amusing reading."—*British Quarterly Review.*

"It will delight many a reader by its varied and brilliant expression of fancies."—*Providence Journal.*

"There is a breeziness about this book which makes it precisely the book for summer reading."—*Christian at Work.*

A CHARMING NEW VOLUME FOR GIRLS AND BOYS.

RHYMES AND JINGLES.

Profusely Illustrated.   One Vol., small 4to.   Cloth, gilt side and edges, $3.00.

MRS. MARY MAPES DODGE is not only one of the best editors of young people's literature, but one of the best of living writers for children.   Her "Hans Brinker" in prose, and her many songs and brief-rhymed stories have been among the most popular writings of their kind ever published in America.

In the present volume the child-poems by her, which have had the free range of the newspaper press for many years, are now brought together for the first time.   Thousands of children who have learned not a few of these verses by heart will now, for the first time, discover the name of their author.   "Rhymes and Jingles" are not written *about* children but *for* them, and some of them have been pronounced "without rivals in our language."   Every child should have a copy of these witty and beautiful verses.

A New and Elegantly Illustrated Edition of

HANS BRINKER; OR, THE SILVER SKATES.

A Story of Life in Holland.   With 60 Illustrations, after designs by the best French Artists.   One vol. 12mo, cloth, beveled edges, $3.00.

"We some time ago expressed our opinion that Mrs. Mary Mapes Dodge's delightful children's story called *Hans Brinker; or, The Silver Skates,* deserved an entirely new dress, with illustrations made in Holland instead of America.   The publishers have issued an edition in accordance with this suggestion.   The pictures are admirable, and the whole volume, in appearance and contents, need not fear comparison with any juvenile publication of the year, or of many years."—*Nation.*

Cheaper Edition, 1 vol., 12mo, . . Price $1.50.

⁎ *The above books for sale by all booksellers, or will be sent, post or express charges paid, upon receipt of the price by the publishers,*

CHARLES SCRIBNER'S SONS,

743 AND 745 BROADWAY, NEW YORK

www.ingramcontent.com/pod-product-compliance
Lightning Source LLC
Chambersburg PA
CBHW052337110726
47901CB00005B/1257

* 9 7 8 3 3 3 7 2 3 9 7 1 8 *